KEYGUIDE

BRITTANY

52

CONTENTS

KEY TO SYMBOLS

- Map reference
- Address
- Telephone number
- Opening times
- Admission prices
- Underground station
- Bus number
- Train station
- Ferry/boat
- Driving directions
- Tourist office
- Tours
- Guidebook
- Restaurant
- Café
- Bar
- Shop
- Number of rooms
- Air conditioning
- Swimming pool
- Gym
- Other useful information
- ▷ Cross reference
- ★ Walk/drive start point

103

132

165

UNDERSTANDING BRITTANY

UNDERSTANDING BRITTANY

Superb coastal scenery, splendid seafood and an enviable heritage of castles, churches and *villes d'histoires* or *petites cités de caractère* (historic towns and villages) make excellent reasons to visit Brittany. All these things can be found in other parts of France. What the English-speaking world finds, perhaps subconsciously, in Brittany's distinctive 'otherness' are deep cultural and geographical bonds stretching back way beyond the Conquest. Its very name means 'Little Britain', signifying a microcosm of *Grande Bretagne* across the waters of the Channel. In these ragged coastal extremities, Celtic exiles from the British Isles sought asylum and brought their faith during the Dark Ages, supplanted from their homeland by Norse and Anglo-Saxon invaders. Today, thousands of us return on well-traversed migration routes for timely top-ups of Brittany's restorative charms.

LANDSCAPE AND ENVIRONMENT

Brittany is the most westerly point in Europe, its Finistèrian capes stretching far into the Atlantic. The ancient Gauls divided Brittany into two parts, Armor (the sea country, meaning 'the coast'), and Argoat (the forest country, meaning 'the interior'). Modern Brittany, shorn since 1973 of its southeastern *département* of Loire-Atlantique, now contains only about 5 per cent of France's mainland territory. Yet it has over a third of the entire French seaboard, frayed and fretted all around its edges into a jagged fringe of bays, headlands, reefs and islands. Sinuous coastal inlets and estuaries, drowned after the last Ice Age, strike deep into its low-lying interior, much of which consists of an undulating plateau of nondescript granite-strewn moorland chequerboarded by sunken rivers and drystone walls or banks. But the great forests that once covered large parts of the Argoat have now dwindled to odd remaining patches of woodland, mainly around Paimpont, Huelgoat and Quimperlé. Elsewhere the countryside is taken up by carefully managed farmland, where artichokes or brassicas grow in serried perfection.

Brittany's diverse habitats include dunes, saltmarshes, sea cliffs, reed beds, mudflats and heath, making it a haven for many species of animals, birds, plants and seaweeds. The seas around the coast are rich in marine life, especially around the Ouessant–Molène archipelago, which forms part of the Armorique Regional Nature Park. Dolphins, seals and sea-otters can be seen in the Mer d'Iroise, while the Atlantic salmon finds its way across vast ocean tracts to spawn in Brittany's estuarial rivers.

Threats to the Breton coast and countryside arise mainly from pollution caused by periodic oil-spillages from passing tankers (*Amoco Cadiz* still strikes a note of doom into Breton hearts), and by nitrate run-off from artificial fertilizers and animal slurry entering waterways and washing into the sea. This sometimes causes abnormal growths of seaweed or plankton in summer, turning areas of some beaches into foul-smelling compost heaps and producing toxins in shellfish.

ECONOMY

Fishing, farming and tourism are Brittany's most important industries, though newer pursuits such as high-tech telecommunications are replacing traditional livelihoods such as ship-building and shoe manufacturing in some areas.

Brittany is France's most productive fishing region, still a significant source of income in many coastal communities. As everywhere in Europe, pressures to conserve declining fish stocks are affecting the catch. Several of Finistère's ports still dispatch seine-netting ships with refrigerated holds in search of tuna off the West African coast, or hunt for cod around Iceland or the Bay of Biscay, but increasingly, inshore crustacean fishing and fish-farming have replaced the great ocean-going trawler fleets of old. Oyster- and mussel-raising have become big business in several coastal areas, while lobster and crayfish are captured offshore and placed in holding tanks or viviers to reach maturity. Fish-canning is still an important industry in southern Brittany, while seaweed is harvested and processed for a great variety of uses on Brittany's north coast.

Roughly two-thirds of the Breton countryside is cultivated. Brittany accounts for a large proportion of France's total agricultural output, specializing in early vegetables (particularly cauliflowers and artichokes), cereals and fodder crops. One of the most productive market-gardening areas is known as the Ceinture d'Orée (Golden Belt) around St-Pol-de-Léon. Dairying and pig-rearing are also major sources of revenue. The climate doesn't suit vines, but cider orchards still paint the lush valleys of the Rance and the Odet with springtime blossom. Brittany's cattle and pigs account for about 20 per cent of France's dairy products, and about half its pork. Roughly one-third of the Breton workforce is involved in food production in some way: The vote of the small farmer is highly influential in this part of France.

CULTURE AND SOCIETY

Modern Brittany consists of four *départements*: Morbihan, Finistère, Côtes d'Armor and Ille-et-Vilaine. After an administrative reshuffle, Loire-Atlantique (the area around Nantes), historically part of the old Duchy of Brittany, was reassigned to the neighbouring region of Pays de la Loire. Historically and culturally, however, it still feels like part of Brittany, and many of its inhabitants retain a strong emotional attachment to the old Duchy, which persisted as a separate entity until 1532.

Brittany (Breizh in Breton) has its own language, a Celtic variant closely allied to Welsh or Cornish. Despite valiant efforts to keep the Breton language alive through educational and media projects, less than half of today's inhabitants can speak it, and very few use it as an everyday language.

Breton music, however, is thriving, encouraged by a revival of interest in folk traditions, and a lively round of festivals, concerts and summer events. All through the holiday season, the strains of woodwind instruments like the *bombarde* and the *biniou* can be heard, played by community pipe-bands. At these festivals, traditional costumes are often worn, with brightly embroidered aprons and elaborate headdresses *(coiffes)* of picot lace and starched linen. The Breton flag flies everywhere to reinforce regionalism. Known as *Gwenn ha du* (white and black), its stripes represent the ancient bishoprics of Upper and Lower Brittany, while the ermine symbol evokes the historic Duchy of Brittany.

Folklore and traditions play a great role in Breton life even today, and the tourist authorities make much of the legends of the Round Table around the Forest of Brocéliande (Paimpont), where King Arthur's court set out to search for the Holy Grail. The region of Cornouaille is associated with the Tristan and Isolde legend, and with the story of the lost city of Ys, drowned by Dahut, the wicked daughter of King Gradlon. In rural churches, *memento mori* or *danse macabre* frescoes, and representations of Ankou, the Breton incarnation of death, reminded many generations of God-fearing peasants of their mortality.

Brittany is still a fervently Catholic part of France, its shrines and parish closes cared for and its churches well attended, especially on the many saints' days and *pardons* commemorated in every community. Many Breton saints were Celtic evangelists who arrived from British shores in the fifth and sixth centuries.

Clockwise from below *Seafood from Quiberon; gardens at île de Bréhat; boats moored at low tide, Baie du Stiff*

BRITTANY'S *DÉPARTEMENTS*

MORBIHAN

The shallow, enclosed Golfe du Morbihan ('little sea') gives its name to this *département*, gnawing a huge cavity in Brittany's sheltered Atlantic seaboard. The beach resorts of Carnac and Quiberon attract many holidaymakers to these sunny southeastern shores. Hundreds of scattered islets in the gulf provide scope for boat excursions, while farther offshore, the larger islands of Belle-Île-en-Mer, Groix, Houat and Hoëdic suggest more detailed exploration. Inland, picturesque towns such as Rochefort-en-Terre, Malestroit, Questembert, La Roche-Bernard and Josselin make rewarding destinations, with their massive fortifications and carefully restored old quarters of quaint period housing. The historic walled city of Vannes is the most interesting of Morbihan's larger cities, dating back to Roman times. War-torn Lorient is mostly a modern, industrialized rebuild, where visitors' interest focuses mainly on the maritime attractions at the port of Kéroman, or on its crowd-pulling annual Celtic festival. Stretching far back into the mists of time, the tantalizing megaliths at Carnac and Locmariaquer constitute the most extensive assembly of Neolithic monuments in Europe.

FINISTÈRE

Brittany's 'Land's End' is a large and varied area with north-, west- and south-facing shores, and an unspoiled rural hinterland dominated by the Armorique regional park. This ever-changing swathe of reef-strewn seaboard fringing wild moorland and wooded hills couldn't seem more different from the orderly patchwork of early vegetables raised on the fertile Ceinture d'Orée (Golden Belt). The surf-pummelled extremities of Crozon and the Pointe du Raz contrast with mirror-calm estuaries and sheltered holiday beaches. Finistère is distinguished by its rich cultural heritage and idiosyncratic parish closes; local festivals showcase the region's traditional costumes, music and language. Largest cities are the reconstructed naval port of Brest presiding over a magnificent natural harbour, and the historic departmental capital of Quimper at the head of the lovely Odet estuary. Both have enough attractions to justify at least a day trip, and preferably an overnight stay. Smaller gems include artistic Pont-Aven and well-preserved Locronan, not forgetting the feisty harbour towns of Roscoff, Morlaix, Douarnenez and Concarneau. Offshore, strewn across busy shipping lanes and guarded by a network of winking lighthouses, crouch the windswept islands of Ouessant, Sein and Molène.

CÔTES D'ARMOR

The medieval gem of Dinan is one of Brittany's star attractions, as are splendid stretches of coast around Cap Fréhel (The Emerald Coast) and Ploumanac'h (the Pink Granite Coast). Several superb marinas attract keen sailors, and the sandy beaches of Le Val-André and Sables-d'Or-les-Pins are hard to match. Unsurprisingly, this glorious coastline is studded with well-equipped holiday resorts such as Perros-Guirec and St-Quay-Portrieux, as well as busy fishing ports like Paimpol.

Offshore, the island of Bréhat makes an idyllic excursion break. Inland, Côtes d'Armor's sparsely populated countryside reveals unexpected surprises, including the quaint linen towns of Quintin and Moncontour and the watersports haven of the Lac de Guerlédan along the Nantes–Brest canal. The largest town and administrative capital of St-Brieuc compensates for its lack of chocolate-box charm with good shops and museums.

ILLE-ET-VILAINE

Most visitors pass through this northeastern frontier zone at some point, many via the handsome ferry port of St-Malo, or through the lively regional capital of Rennes. Haute Bretagne (Upper Brittany) is the Gallo or French-speaking part of the region, its distinctive qualities guarded since medieval times by the mighty fortresses of Combourg, Vitré and Fougères, and the ethereal island abbey of Mont-St-Michel on the Normandy borders. The coast offers as much variety as a *plâteau de fruits de mer*: oysters and mussels in Cancale and Le Vivier, Hollywood glamour at Dinard, and luminous Impressionist seascapes in St-Briac. Inland, cruise tranquil waterways through staircase locks to the frontier port of Redon, chase Arthurian legends in the magical forest of Paimpont, or track down the mysterious megalithic dolmen of La Roche aux Fées.

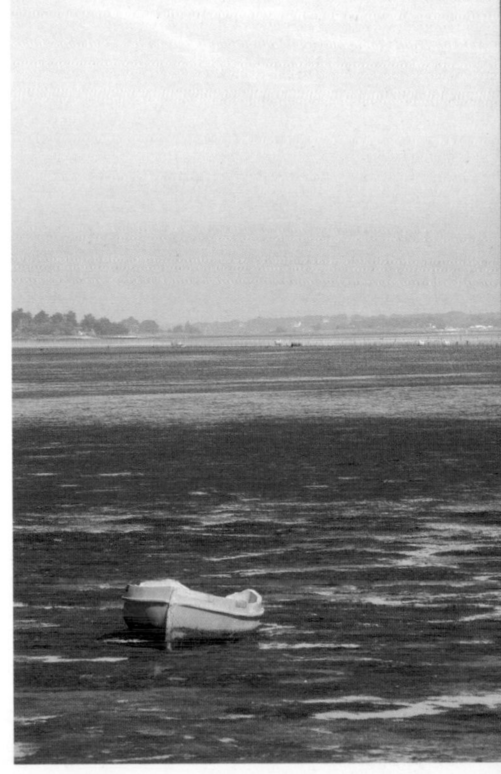

Opposite *Rennes has some interesting Breton architecture*
Right*Brillac, Golfe du Morbihan*

THE BEST OF BRITTANY

MORBIHAN

Belle-Île-en-Mer (▷ 45): Don't miss pretty Sauzon and the needle rocks of Port-Coton on Brittany's biggest island.

Carnac (▷ 46–47): The purpose of Carnac's strange lines of standing stones is still a baffling mystery.

Domaine de Kerguéhennec (▷ 52): This classic 18th-century château is now used as a modern sculpture park.

Festival Interceltique (▷ 54): Make a date with Lorient in August for France's biggest traditional music festival.

Golfe du Morbihan (▷ 50–51): This landlocked lagoon is a paradise for boat trips and birdlife.

Josselin (▷ 53): See Josselin's mighty castle floodlit at night from the Hôtel du Château.

Port-Louis (▷ 56): Find out about Brittany's colonial trading past at the citadel museums.

Quiberon (▷ 56): Try some wind-and-water sports on the west-facing Plage de Penthièvre.

La Roche-Bernard (▷ 56): For the meal of a lifetime, try the Auberge Bretonne in this pretty town.

Rochefort-en-Terre (▷ 57): Step back in time to the 16th and 17th centuries in this delightful *petite cité de caractère*.

St-Fiacre (▷ 56): Spot the Seven Deadly Sins on the intricate rood screen of this tiny chapel near Le Faouët.

Vannes (▷ 58–59): Morbihan's capital has one of the best-preserved walled 'old towns' anywhere in Brittany.

FINISTÈRE

Armorique Regional Nature Park (▷ 90, 94, 95, 98): This conservation zone encompasses a huge variety of wildlife.

Bélon (▷ 81, 121): Sample fresh seafood at Chez Jacky's waterfront brasserie overlooking this beautiful estuary.

Carantec (▷ 86): Visit the recently restored Château du Taureau, an island fortress built to keep the Morlaix estuary safe from English privateers.

Château de Kerjean (▷ 88): This grand Renaissance manor gives a vivid picture of life through the ages in the Léon region of Finistère.

Concarneau (▷ 89): Climb the ramparts of the Ville Close, visit the Musée de Pêche and the *criée* (fish auction), and take a boat trip to the Îles de Glénan.

Le Conquet (▷ 90): Follow the lighthouse trail along North Finistère's Côte des Abers.

Douarnenez (▷ 92): Visit Port-Rhu and the boat museum on Douarnenez harbour.

Guimiliau (▷ 93): Admire one of Brittany's most striking parish closes—a *tour-de-force* of Renaissance sculpture, both inside and outside the church.

Île d'Ouessant (▷ 95): Blow the cobwebs away on an excursion to Finistère's largest island, repository of a bygone Breton lifestyle.

Locronan (▷ 697): Visit the craft studios of this beautiful historic village.

Morlaix (▷ 99): Walk across the viaduct for a fantastic overview of the town.
Océanopolis (▷ 83–84): Peer through this window on the waterfront at one of Europe's largest and liveliest aquariums.
Pointe du Raz (▷ 101): Walk out to this dramatic coastal promontory to watch the tides race past the mysterious Île de Sein.
Pont-Aven (▷ 102): Wander through the Bois d'Amour to find the inspirational crucifix of Gauguin's *Christ Jaune* in the Chapelle de Trémalo.
Quimper (▷ 104–105): Buy some pottery in Cornouaille's historic capital.
Rade de Brest (▷ 84): Take a boat trip around Brest's magnificent harbour from the port.
Roscoff (▷ 107): Visit the subtropical gardens in Roscoff and the Île de Batz.
St-Pol-de-Léon (▷ 108): Try local artichokes grown locally in Brittany's Golden Belt.

CÔTES D'ARMOR

Cap Fréhel (▷ 129): This rugged headland marks the climax of the dramatically beautiful Emerald Coast.
Côte de Granit Rose (▷ 130–131): Walk the customs officers' watchpath through this rocky coastal wonderland.
Dinan (▷ 133–135): The cobbled streets and timbered buildings of this medieval gem are unforgettable.
Île de Bréhat (▷ 136): This reef-ringed island full of flowers makes the perfect away-day near Paimpol.
Lamballe (▷ 137): Join in some equine activities in this attractive old town, home to the national stud (carriage rides and horse shows on summer Thursdays).

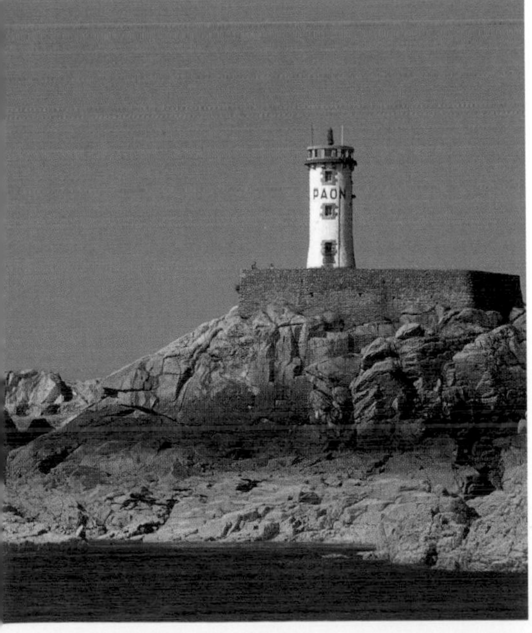

Mûr-de-Bretagne (▷ 138): Try out some watersports on the Lac de Guerlédan, and visit the Abbaye de Bon Repos during its August son-et-lumière season.
Paimpol (▷ 140): Discover the seafaring traditions of this lively old fishing port.
Le Radôme (▷ 139): The Cité des Télécoms charts the history of long- distance message-relay, in a setting both historic and futuristic.
Les Sept-Iles (▷ 131, 139, 149): Take a trip at nesting time to this seabird sanctuary off the scenic Pink Granite Coast.
Trébeurden (▷ 157): Enjoy a relaxing and hedonistic stay at Ti Al Lannec, a luxurious but friendly spa hotel in a lovely seaside setting.
Tréguier (▷ 144): Head for this handsome old river port on summer Wednesdays for its lively market day in the square dominated by one of Brittany's finest cathedrals.
Le Val-André (▷ 145): Sand doesn't get much better than the glistening beaches in this resort.
Le Vapeur de Trieux (▷ 145, 151): A steam-train excursion between two charming historic towns is a great way to explore the scenic Trieux Valley.

ILLE-ET-VILAINE

Cancale (▷ 161): Try some fresh oysters from the market at the old fishing port of La Houle.
Dinard (▷ 163): Walk the Promenade du Claire de Lune for magnificent estuary views.
Fougères (▷ 165): The intact walls of Fougères' medieval fortress make a fine sight reflected in the River Nançon.
Hédé (▷ 167): Take a towpath walk along the Ille-et-Rance Canal to watch boats sail through the lock staircase at La Madeleine.
Redon (▷ 170): Explore the Breton waterways by canal boat from this appealing inland port.
Rennes (▷ 170–173): Visit the Champs Libres museum complex south of the city centre, containing the Musée de Bretagne and the Espace des Sciences.
La Roche-aux-Fées (▷ 176): Head deep into the countryside southeast of Rennes to track down the mysterious Fairies' Rock, a megalithic monument suffused in legends.
St-Malo (▷ 174–175): Climb the ramparts and circumnavigate the corsairs' home port; best at sunset.
Usine Marémotrice de la Rance (▷ 167): Walk across the barrage and be mesmerized by the water surging through the sluice-gates; then visit the Espace Découverte to see how this innovative tidal power station operates.
Vitré (▷ 177): Explore the handsome medieval quarter of this splendidly preserved fortified town.
Le Vivier-sur-Mer (▷ 176): Find out all about mussels at the Maison de la Baie, and take a tractor tour around the *bouchots*.

Left *The stunning Brittany coastline at Belle-Île-en-Mer*
Opposite *Île de Bréhat lighthouse*

TOP EXPERIENCES

Attend a festival or *pardon* Folk events in traditional Breton costume are especially memorable. You may also hear Breton spoken.

Build some sandcastles Brittany's beaches are wonderful playgrounds for children of all ages. Explore rockpools, or join the locals in *pêche-à-pied* (beachcombing for shellfish with shrimping nets and buckets and spades—check regulations first).

Buy from the market France's lively produce markets are always photogenic and sociable occasions. Choosing picnic or self-catering provisions is a good way to practise your French—and you'll probably get a few recipe tips.

Check out the chandleries All the major harbour towns have a Cooperative Maritime or Comptoir de la Mer selling fashionable knitwear, outdoor gear and nautical souvenirs.

Commune with nature Brittany's diverse habitats suit a huge range of wildlife, especially seabirds. Visit its wild places and nature reserves, where interpretative visitor centres decode local ecosystems and identify species.

Drink some local cider Traditionally served in big breakfast cups, Brittany's customary tipple can be surprisingly potent.

Eat some pancakes Brittany's speciality fast-food comes in many guises.

Find what makes Brittany's economy tick Modern industrial sites like fish-farms, power-stations, dockyards and food factories sometimes welcome visitors for guided tours. Ask at the tourist office.

Go sailing Brittany's well-equipped marinas are thronged all summer. *Stations Voile* (sailing resorts) run courses at all levels, and hold races and regattas throughout the season, some with tall ships.

Hear Breton spoken In parts of Finistère, and at festivals, you can hear the native language. Alternatively, tune in to TV Breizh.

Investigate the interior Inland Brittany is worth exploring as well as the coastline. Walk the canal towpaths, the hills of the Armorique regional park, or the forest trails of Paimpont, Huelgoat, or Carnoët.

Pamper yourself at one of Brittany's thalassotherapy spas, and experience the healing powers of seawater.

Sample the cities The coast and countryside have most to offer, but Brittany's urban scene (Rennes, Vannes, Quimper, Brest) has its attractions too, with galleries, museums, shopping and nightlife.

See the parish closes These idiosyncratic expressions of religious art are among the most distinctive treasures of the region.

Take a boat trip Experiences vary from a motor launch excursion to an ocean voyage on a fully rigged, 18th-century-style sailing ship.

Track down some *ecomusées* These little folk museums make an entertaining way to learn more about many aspects of Breton life and culture, past and present.

Try some seafood Visit a *criée* (fish auction), then sample an *assiette de fruits de mer* in a local restaurant.

Visit an island Brittany's coastline has hundreds of varied islands, many of which make rewarding excursion destinations.

Walk the coastal footpaths If you have enough time and energy, you can walk from Mont-St-Michel to the Golfe du Morbihan in exhilarating scenery.

Watch watersports Sand-yachting, kite-surfing or body-boarding make exciting spectator sports to liven up a day at the beach. If you're feeling adventurous, try them yourself.

LIVING BRITTANY

THE SEA

The era of corsairs and privateers may be past, but modern Brittany still looks towards its distinctive coast for its identity. Beaches, coves and harbours have evolved to the needs of tourism. Their charm is the fact they are no mere historical curiosities, since fishing continues to be the principal maritime trade. Offshore fish-farming is the 21st century's newest approach to meeting market demand, with salmon-farming from platforms out at sea, such as Salmor off the coast of Morlaix. The second half of the 20th century saw renewed interest in the sport of sailing, with sailing clubs, training facilities and competitions thriving across Brittany. The Glénan archipelago gave its name to Les Glénans, an association founded in 1947 by former resistance fighters and sailors, which is now France's biggest sailing school. Modern Brittany is a major manufacturing and research base for the boating industry, with yacht-building and sail-making key to the local economy. Not surprisingly it has developed as an important stage in many international sporting events, with the Route de Rhum race departing from St-Malo every four years, and the same port gaining further fame as the finishing post of the Québec–St-Malo transatlantic race.

Above *The beach at Belle-Île-en Mer*
Opposite top *A seagull in flight*
Opposite bottom *Fish at the market in Douarnez*
Right *Dame Ellen MacArthur*

A NOBLE ADVENTURER

Brittany respects strong women and adventurous sailors, and in Dame Ellen MacArthur the region found a 21st-century heroine. The English yachtswoman regularly sets sail from Breton ports, and thousands turn out to welcome her when she returns. Her 44,012km (27,354-mile) solo circumnavigation of the globe in 71 days and just under 15 hours was declared a world record as her 22.5m (75ft) trimaran *B&Q* passed the island of Ouessant in February 2005. Four months later, MacArthur and *B&Q's* next record came when she crossed a 160km (100-mile) stretch of the English Channel between Plymouth and Roscoff in just over 6 hours and 20 minutes. In 2008, MacArthur was awarded France's highest civilian accolade, the Légion d'Honneur.

THE BLACK TIDES

Not everything that the sea has brought to the Brittany coast has been welcomed. At the end of the 20th century a succession of shipwrecked tankers smeared beaches and wildlife with oil as the region faced its toughest ever environmental crises. The first oil spills to contaminate the area spread across the Channel when the *Torrey Canyon* oil tanker was wrecked in English waters in 1967. A decade later the *Amoco Cadiz* produced black tides closer to home. Then, at the turn of the millennium, the wreck of the *Erika* created further damaging oil slicks. After each of these disasters huge international clean-up operations worked to save bird and marine life and clean up the beaches. After extensive lobbying from France and other countries, the EU finally banned single-hull oil tankers from European ports in 2003.

LUNAR POWER

Brittany has adopted an eco-friendly approach to electricity generation, by installing an innovative tidal power scheme on the Rance estuary. Medieval Bretons first exploited the enormous tides shifting up and down the Rance twice a day. Tidal mills were constructed in the 12th century to use the latent energy of the ebb tide. But since 1967, EDF (the French Electricity Board) has successfully harnessed both ebb and flow tides at the Usine Marémotrice de la Rance, a colossal structure spanning the river between Dinard and St-Malo. A long dam, which also serves as a road bridge and shipping lock, forms a reservoir controlled by six sluice gates. Turbines within a huge tunnel at the centre of the dam generate a combined capacity of some 600 million kilowatt hours per year—enough electricity to power an entire city the size of Rennes.

WEEDING THE FUTURE

The alchemy of the 21st century is *algologic*—turning seaweed into money. Once considered a poor man's harvest, the humble seaweed may hold the key to beauty, long life and even the economic future of Brittany. In the 1990s a research establishment was created in Pleubian, on the Côtes d'Armor, where scientists research more than 600 species of pure unpolluted weed found in local waters. Researchers have found different properties in marine plants found close to the shore and those growing further away in deep water. The CEVA Technical Research Centre on the Pen Lan peninsula looks at the cosmetic applications of nutrients from the weeds. Although thalassotherapy (treatments using seawater) was first offered in Roscoff in 1899 by Dr Roger Bagot, it's taken another century for fashion to catch up.

THE LAST HEROES

In the era of automated navigation, Brittany's manned lighthouses remained an almost forgotten aspect of France's maritime heritage until the great storms that hit the Breton coast during 1989. As tempests raged over the seas, Breton photographer and experienced sailor Jean Guichard took his now world-famous series of pictures focusing on last offshore lighthouse keepers of Brittany. His *Phares dans la Tempête* photographs have been reproduced around the world in magazines, calendars and posters. In one particular prize-winning shot captured at the height of the storm, as waves battered the top of the Jument lighthouse, Guichard snapped keeper Théodore Malgorne opening the door to watch his home completely engulfed by spray. None of Brittany's offshore lighthouses remain inhabited today.

BRETON TRADITION

As befits a region with a passion for its own cultural identity, Bretons guard their traditions ardently. Sea shanties are sung in festivals along the Finistère coast with an almost religious fervour; legends of magic and mysticism are kept fresh with constant retelling; and even agricultural customs are adhered to with an almost obsessive fervour. On the island of Ouessant, the distinctive local sheep—tiny creatures with brownish wool—are allowed to roam freely, grazing on whatever salty grass they can find. Each February, sheep-marking ceremonies see them allocated to named farmers. Integration with the rest of France is regarded with suspicion. A fiery spirit of cultural independence burns strongly. At the turn of the 21st century, the movement to raise the profile of the Breton language was boosted with TV and radio broadcasts in the indigenous tongue and classes in schools in a region that had been losing a worrying proportion of native speakers each year. Much of this backlash was reaction to an attempt by the state to eradicate the language and downgrade its status to a patois in the post-war years. Right-wing Breton nationalism and anti-French feeling had been associated by politicians with the sympathies of some Breton political groups to the German occupation, and Breton was banned in schools in 1947.

CELTIC INVASION

Anyone who believes that the last Celtic invasion of the Brittany coast took place in the fifth century has had their eyes tightly shut during the month of August. The annual Interceltic Festival in the port of Lorient is the biggest gathering of Celtic peoples in the world, with some 4,000 musicians and representatives of national associations in the official parade of the Celtic Nations and more than half a million revellers taking part in some 200 events over 10 days. The festival is famous for uniting Scots, Irish, Welsh and Cornish celebrants from the British Isles, Galicians from Buenos Aires, Scottish settlers from Canada and Australia and plenty of Boston Irish.

Above *The blue and white Breton flag*
Opposite left *A Breton Cross*
Opposite right *Traditional Breton costume is worn at a parade in Pont l'Abbé*

THE PRICE OF INTEGRATION

In 2005, newspapers warned of an anti-British backlash as Bretons revolted against English newcomers buying homes in Brittany. The protests in Bourbriac drew much attention, with media estimates that as many as a third of local residents were Brits. The truth was more modest: 50 full-time ex-pats and 50 holidayhome owners had sparked the reaction from A-Stroll (Breton for 'together'), a local political group. In reality, the anger was directed more at the property market. The incoming foreigners were inflating house prices, and A-Stroll was more concerned at the cultural effects of the break up of local families, priced out of their home towns, than the dangers of Anglo-Saxon influences.

JOHNNY KNOWS HIS ONIONS

If you overhear elderly men slipping occasional fluent English into Breton conversation in a Roscoff bar, don't be surprised. For generations, Roscovites knew more about England they did about France. Since the 1820s, local lads crossed the Channel to sell *troches*—tresses of onions. Battalions of 'Johnnies', as they were called, set up warehouses and sold onions door to door, bicycling along British country lanes and bringing back to Brittany elements of the English language and British customs to a region that had so far managed to avoid many French influences. Today, a few Roscoff Johnnies still board the ferries to serve their loyal customers (⊳ 107).

FROM LINENS TO YARNS

Brittany is a region of storytellers. Anywhere with Merlin, Tristan and Isolde as local gossip fodder is bound to develop a talent for spinning a yarn. In 1989, oral tradition gave way to the printed word. Bécherel, north of Rennes, became France's first 'Book Town'. Established by the Savenn Douar association, the concept evolved through the 1990s into bibliophile heaven. Bécherel now has more than a dozen bookshops, bookbinders and professional calligraphers, and a vast book market on the first Sunday each month. Having gently slumped into near obscurity since its heyday as a 17th century linen and textile market, the revival of fortunes is credited to modern capitalizing on the Breton love of a good yarn. Twice yearly, the pleasure of reading gains carnival proportions with book festivals over Easter and the second Saturday in August.

BLACK AND WHITE

Brittany's distinctive flag, one of very few which uses no colour, was designed in 1923 by Morvan Marchal. Known as *Gwenn ha du* in Breton (white and black), it has heightened regional identity and raised nationalist hopes ever since, though under French law it is an act of sedition to fly it on any public building. The five horizontal black stripes represent the five ancient bishoprics of Haute Bretagne (Rennes, Nantes, Dol, St-Malo and St-Brieuc); the four white horizontal stripes represent the four bishoprics of Basse Bretagne (Léon, Cornouaille, Vannes and Tréguier). The black ermine symbols in the top left-hand corner (looking like furled umbrellas or miniature Christmas trees) represent the power and authority of the Duchy of Brittany. Ermine fur was a precious commodity worn only by the wealthy, and hence most powerful, in medieval times.

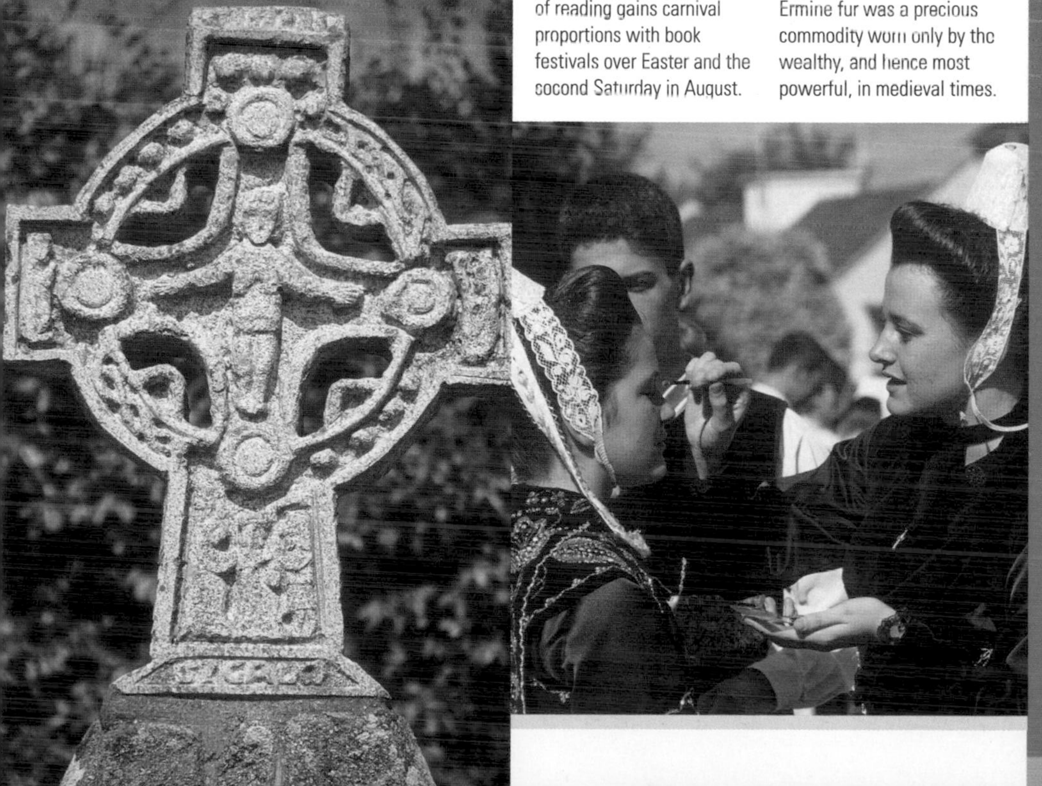

RELIGION AND MYSTICISM

Brittany's calendar is dotted with *pardons*, days of splendid procession and devotion celebrating patron saints. Thousands of people may take to the streets or the quaysides for the biggest traditional *pardons* of St. Yves at Treguier and St. Jacques in Locquirec. While steeped in Catholic tradition, the custom of the *pardon* also reflects secular life and modern issues. Since the 1950s, July has seen an annual joint Islamic-Christian *pardon* at Vieux Marché to celebrate understanding between faiths. Nothing illustrates the influence of the church on daily life in Brittany more than the parish close. Around the village cemetery evolved a distinctive cluster of buildings, including the charnel house. Calvaries, monuments depicting stories from the Passion, once illustrated outdoor sermons.

Above *Parish Close at Guimiliau*
Opposite top *The blessing of motorbikes at Porcaro*
Opposite bottom *Ankou wields his scythe*

FROM LACE TO LEATHERS

While lace headdresses, and starched collars may be traditional costume at most *pardons* in Brittany, since 1979 the dress code at Porcaro, in Morbihan, has tended towards leather with metallic accessories. Some 6,000 gleaming chrome motorbikes hit the town each 15 August for the unique *pardon* of La Madone des Motards, Our Lady of the Bikers. The blessing ceremony sees a statue of the Virgin carried through Porcaro by celebrants whose denims and T-shirts reflect the blue-and-white vestments worn by the parish priest.

THE PAGAN OPTION

Bretons are known for taking their Celtic origins very seriously, but perhaps the most passionate Celts would be the two or three dozen souls who meet each summer in a meadow in Brasparts, Finistère, to celebrate the ancient feast of Lugnasad. These are members of Brittany's contemporary Druid community. To pay homage to the god Lug, they gather in a circle of stones on the third Sunday in July for a ceremony led by Gwenc'hlan Le Scouezec, the fifth Great-Druid of La Gourzes de Bretagne. No strangers to criticism, La Gourzes' Druids nonetheless hold their ceremonies in public and are happy to welcome new members, Christians and pagans alike. Gwenc'hlan Le Scouezec, author of a dictionary of Celtic traditions, makes only one stipulation—would-be members must be able to speak Breton.

THE SEVEN SLEEPERS

Brittany has a wealth of saints. The Seven Founding Saints set up the dioceses of Brittany, and the Seven Healing Saints have protective powers. The Sept Saints are commemorated in a chapel at Vieux Marché near Lannion. In the third century a group of Christians, the Seven Sleepers of Ephesus, were walled up in a cave by the Emperor Decius for refusing to renounce their faith. They awoke miraculously 200 years later and were released unharmed. Muslims also venerate the Seven Sleepers, who are mentioned in the Koran. During the 1950s, at the start of the Franco–Algerian war, the Islamist scholar Louis Massignon established an annual pilgrimage at Vieux Marché to promote peace between Muslims and Christians. Today, marked by thousands of pilgrims, the symbolism of this ceremony seems especially relevant.

FOUNT OF DEVOTION

Breton inclination towards romance and magic has affected its approach to religion over the centuries. When Christianity finally reached the region it too was obliged to pay attention to the local penchant for the mystic. Bretons had long worshipped 'miraculous' springs, which gushed mineral waters to cure all ills. Despite a condemnation by the Christian Church in AD658 of the worship of fountains, the healing qualities of water are still regarded with awe and reverence. Thus, over the years, the Church appropriated natural springs and built chapels dedicated to Christian patron saints at the sites. So St. Mériadec is credited with the deafness cure at Pontivy (▷ 53) and St. Clair's water is said to restore sight at Réguigny, both in Morbihan.

THE BRETON WAY OF DEATH

In Brittany, the grim reaper is known as Ankou. Skeletal figures can be seen in a number of churches and parish closes throughout the region, especially in Finistère. A famous example at the parish church of Ploumilliau (illustrated below) carries both the traditional scythe and a spade to bury his victims. The story goes that the local blacksmith spent all night sharpening Ankou's scythe instead of attending mass, only to find himself the reaper's next client. You'll find Ankou at La Roche-Maurice too. In the vivid *danse macabre* frescoes at Kermaria-an-Iskuit, near Plouha south of Paimpol, three noblemen out hunting encounter three dead men in a cemetery who warn them that they too will join the dance of death one day.

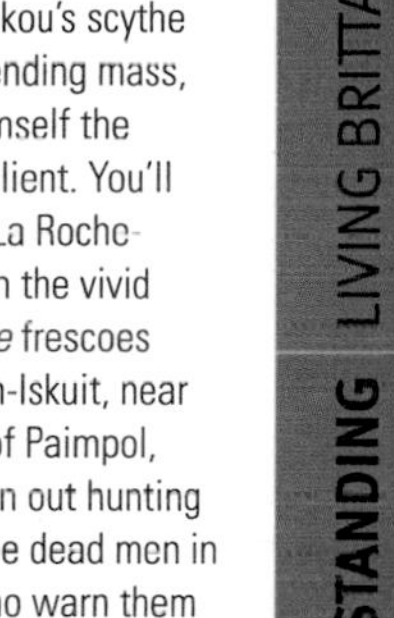

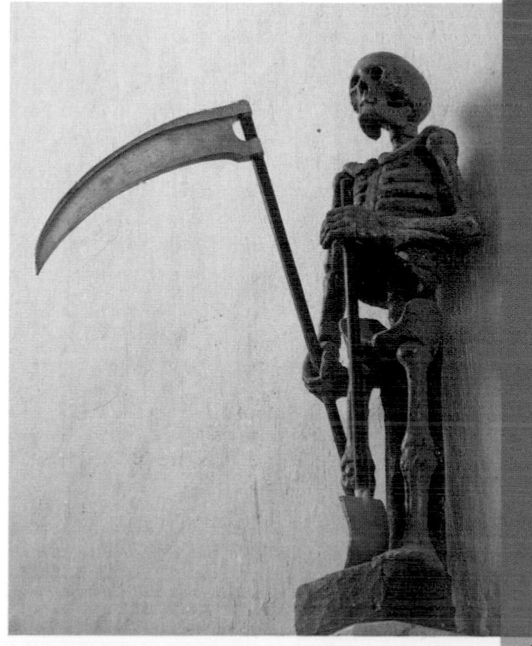

THE STORY OF BRITTANY

PREHISTORY TO THE TREATY OF VANNES

Brittany is renowned for its standing stones, or menhirs, which mostly date to the Neolithic period (*c*3000BC), yet little is known about the people who erected them. During the Bronze Age new settlers appeared; these early Celts called their land Armor—the land of the sea. In AD55, Julius Caesar invaded, marking the beginning of four centuries of Roman rule. In AD460 a fresh wave of Celtic immigration began as Angles and Saxons forced the Romans out of Britain. Thus Little Britain, or Brittany, was born. Brittany fell easy prey to the Franks in AD799, when Charlemagne seized control, and installed his own governor, Nominoë. He, however, expelled the Franks and united the diverse Breton communities under his rule. Under his son, Erispoë, the duchy was upgraded to the status of kingdom. The first half of the 10th century saw violent Viking invasions, eventually quelled in AD939 by the last Breton king, Alain Barbe-Torte. The house of Montfort inherited the title in 1365 and a period of stability saw close association with France. On the death of François II, the duchy passed to his daughter, Duchess Anne of Brittany, whose daughter, Claude, gave Brittany to France with the Treaty of Vannes in 1532.

Above *The coronation of Charles the Bald*
Opposite left *The recumbent figure of St. Yves at the cathedral of St. Tugdual at Tréguier (top); Romans fighting Gauls (bottom)*
Opposite right *The fairy Melusine, in the form of a dragon, flying over the Château de Lusignan*

FROM A VASSAL TO A KING

Even kings are not too important to learn lessons in humility. Louis I of France nominated Nominoë, Count of Vannes, as first Duke of Brittany in AD826. The newly created duchy came with strings attached, however, as the first duke was obliged to swear allegiance to Louis, and ruled Brittany as a vassal of the French Crown. In AD841 Louis died, to be succeeded by his son, Charles the Bald, and relations between the duke and the new ruler of France lacked the respect that had marked the previous reign. Nominoë refused to bow before the new king and proclaimed Brittany an independent state. When Charles attempted to bring him to heel, France was routed in the Battle of Ballon and, in AD846, it was Charles who was forced to recognize Brittany as an independent kingdom.

THE MIRACLE OF THE HONEST LAWYER

History books are filled with accounts of lawyers and saints, but there is little evidence of sainted lawyers. St. Yves, still fondly remembered in Brittany today, was a man of the law with the common touch. He died in 1303 and among his epitaphs were the lines '*Erat Brito, advocatus, et non latro. Res miranda populo!*' ('He was a Breton and a lawyer, but not dishonest—astonishing!') After serving as a judge in Rennes, he returned to his homeland, the Côtes d'Armor, and worked alongside Alan de Bruc, Bishop of Tréguier. As a judge he was known as the pauper's advocate and even took up cases representing the downtrodden in courts other than his own. The famous epitaph came from his skill as persuading litigants to settle out of court and not spend money on lawyers.

BEWARE THE SCREAMING BLONDE

Among the religious icons in Fougères' 15th-century church of St. Sulpice are reminders of secular heroines. An image etched into the stained-glass windows is a declaration of the town's founding fathers' fairy ancestry. A blonde woman with the tail of a serpent can be seen, reflecting the legend of Melusine, who killed her father and was cursed to turn into a snake every Saturday. She married Raymond of Poitiers on condition that he would never see her on a Saturday and brought him great wealth and power, building castles overnight and giving him many children. One Saturday Raymond peeked, Melusine turned into a serpent and disappeared—henceforth to be heard shrieking whenever death awaits one of her descendents.

WIVES BEHAVING BADLY

After centuries of warring, violence and Viking pillaging, it was no wonder that good behaviour was not among the key traits of medieval life. Thankfully, Brittany created one of the first self-help manuals to keep decent people on the straight and narrow. Thanks to Etienne de Fougères, Bishop of Rennes, after 1175 Bretons had the benefit of his *Livre des Manières*, an invaluable handbook of contemporary etiquette. As well as pointing out the correct way to behave, Etienne's writing gives a fascinating glimpse into the tricks of wives behaving badly. According to the bishop, wayward wives who had an urge to stray from their marriage vows would feign illness in order to persuade their husbands to recommend a pilgrimage to Santiago de Compostela—promising plenty of opportunity to dally with lapsed celibates en route.

SERIAL CHILD BRIDE

By the age of 14, Anne of Brittany was already into her second marriage. What turned the daughter of a duke into a serial child bride? Answer: inheriting a duchy at the age of 11. Before her father François II died in 1488, he had promised that his daughter would not marry without the approval of the French Crown. Of course, Brittany was an attractive dowry and many European rulers realized the advantages of wedding the 11-year-old Anne. Austria, England and Aragon sent forces to protect the young duchess. Eventually, in 1490, Archduke Maximilian of Austria married the 13-year-old duchess by proxy. The growth of French military power led Anne to annul the marriage, and wed Charles VIII of France instead in 1491. When Charles died after a childless marriage, Anne, veteran wife at 22, married his successor, Louis XII.

THE RENAISSANCE TO WORLD WAR II

The 16th century saw Brittany looking to the wider world, with explorers, privateers and merchant fleets setting out from St-Malo. Most famously Jacques Cartier discovered Canada. In 1610 Cardinal Richelieu became governor of Brittany under Louis XIII, and upgraded the region's naval defences. He was followed in the mid-17th century by Louis XIV's governor Colbert, whose efforts to raise funds for his extravagant monarch led to the imposition of taxes, culminating in the Stamped Paper Revolt in 1675 against Colbert's decree that all legal transactions should use stamped paper (on which duty was payable). Although the revolt was crushed the seething resentment remained. Any hopes that the French Revolution would improve Brittany's situation were dashed—the Breton language was banned and Brittany split into five new *départements*. Under these conditions a loyalist counter-Revolutionary group known as the Chouans attracted local support. The Chouannerie were quashed in 1804. The remainder of the 19th century was a time of cultural endeavour: Pont-Aven became an artists' haven and writers Chateaubriand and Jules Verne put Brittany on the literary map. After World War I, the economy was in the doldrums, and separatist organizations sprang up. Yet when the Nazis arrived in 1940 Brittany put up a spirited resistance, despite some politicians being openly supportive of Hitler's regime.

CARTIER'S DIAMONDS NOT A BOY'S BEST FRIEND

Jacques Cartier may have found Canada while hunting for the Northwest Passage to Asia, but the St-Malo-born sailor did not have the same good fortune when it came to discovering new sources of precious metals and diamonds. In the 1530s he explored Newfoundland, and heard many native stories about the fabulous treasures which were to be found north of the settlement. He returned in 1541 to seek an incredible fortune in a land known as Saguenay. Alas the 'diamonds' and 'gold' he discovered were merely quartz and iron pyrites, better known as fool's gold.

THE PIRATE PRIEST

When a shipbuilder's son fails as a priest, what better career to take up than becoming a respectable pirate? After centuries of long wars with its neighbours, France discovered a profitable alternative to the navy—self-employed pirates. Rather than declare outright war, France commissioned merchant sailors to seize with impunity cargoes from merchant ships of rival nations. The king issued Letters of Marque to a number of privateers, or corsairs, who sailed from St-Malo to take on the English, Spanish and Dutch. Before the legendary 19th-century adventurer Surcouf, Brittany's hero was Duquay Trouin (1673–1736), whose debauched lifestyle abruptly ended his training for the priesthood. Instead, at 16, he put to sea and by the age of 36 he had been ennobled for his exploits.

BRIDGE TO THE SOUTH SEAS

The estuary of the river Aven may seem an unlikely gateway to the South Seas, but for artist Paul Gauguin, Pont-Aven was the first step to Polynesia. In the late 1880s, the extraordinary light of this town of watermills and cheery taverns attracted a group of artists keen to explore new possibilities beyond the recent Impressionist movement. Most famous of the Pont-Aven school was Gauguin, who seized upon the potential for vivid colours in his two-dimensional portrayal of local figures bathed in the clear light of Finistère. From Pont-Aven, Gauguin moved to Le Pouldu in 1889, and six years later took the decision to follow the light to the Marquess Islands, where his famous Polynesian canvasses owed so much to his earlier paintings of the women of Brittany.

THE OWL AND THE PIMPERNEL

Ironically for a region that had spent so many years fighting against the kingdom of France, Brittany nurtured a strong royalist resistance to the Revolution. After the execution of Louis XVI in 1793, the Chouannerie monarchist guerrilla movement had a strong base in the region. The movement found its name in the fighters' practice of signalling with the call of an owl *(chouette)*. The Chouan rebellion lasted 11 years, but became enshrined in literary legend. Balzac had a huge success with his novel *Les Chouans* (1829). The movement was further glamorized by the ultimate royalist romancer of popular fiction. In 1919 Baroness Orczy followed her bestselling yarns about the Scarlet Pimpernel with The Man in Grey, billed as episodes of the Chouan conspiracies.

A WAR OF INDEPENDENCE

The surge in Breton nationalism in the 20th century dates to the trench warfare of World War I. Around one million Bretons went to the fronts at Verdun and the Marne and a quarter were killed, more than twice as many as from any other region of France. Since this was the first time that many of them had actually mixed with the French, the language and cultural differences were drawn into sharp focus, leading some commentators to conclude that the soldiers from Brittany were considered to be merely peasant canon fodder. This attitude helped to foster the political attitudes prevalent in the years that followed. The Partie National Breton (PNB) was founded in 1919, boosted by both the reaction to the losses of World War I and the success of nationalists in Ireland.

De Balzac

Above *The statue of explorer Robert Surcouf, St Malo*
Right *Novelist Honore de Balzac*
Opposite *Photographic displays at the Pont-Aven Museum*

A NEW ERA

The elements have determined much of Brittany's recent history, with winds and water wreaking havoc: Argoat woodlands devastated by hurricanes in 1987, maritime disasters and oil spills (▷ 15). Breton cultural identity is in the political foreground. The Comité d'Études et de Liaison des Intérêts Bretons was founded in 1951 to protect the economy, and bilingual French and Breton road signs were introduced in 1985. Businesses began relocating to Rennes from 1962, when President de Gaulle commissioned a giant Citroën factory, and business parks have flourished since the 1980s. Major construction projects include the Rance tidal barrage and Monts d'Arrée nuclear power station in 1966, and the Iroise and La Roche-Bernard bridges in the 1990s.

THE BRETON WHO WOULD BE FRANCE'S LEADER

For a region virtually defined by its fierce spirit of independence, 2002's presidential elections brought a double irony. Not only was there a serious chance of a Breton-born candidate—Jean-Marie le Pen—becoming president of the Republic, but the candidate himself was the most vociferous French nationalist of his generation. National voter apathy and disillusionment with the candidates for the mainstream parties meant that the usually fringe far-right Front National party was runner-up in the first round of the election. In order to ensure that the Front's highly controversial leader, le Pen, did not win the final poll, liberals, socialists and even communists found themselves voting for the less unpopular conservative Jacques Chirac.

OOPS, THERE GOES THE CAPITAL

Many visitors believe Nantes to be capital of Brittany, being, as it was, the original home to the Breton Parliament and Henri IV's Edict of Nantes. Yet not only is the city of Rennes the actual capital, but in 1971 Nantes left the political region of Brittany altogether to became the new capital of the Pays de la Loire region. Since the Revolution, Nantes had its differences with the rest of Brittany, fervently anti-Royalist and drowning monarchist rebels in the Loire. The city was first declared to be non-Breton in 1941 by the Vichy government, and in 1971 Nantes joined the newly created *département* of Loire-Atlantique. However, if you ask supporters of football club FC Nantes Atlantique where their loyalties lie and they will tell you they are proud to be Breton.

Above left *Jean-Marie Le Pen at a political rally, Paris*
Above right *La Roche-Bernard bridge*

ON THE MOVE

On the Move gives you detailed advice and information about the various options for travelling to Brittany before explaining the best ways to get around once you are there. Handy tips help you with everything from buying tickets to renting a car.

BY AIR

Patterns of air travel to northwestern France have fluctuated over recent years. After a period of rapid expansion, when low-cost operators began using several small regional airports, the network suddenly contracted. This hit the short-break market and left many holiday-home owners stranded with no direct local flights. New operators have stepped in to fill the gaps.

There are a few smallish airports in Brittany, but at present they handle few direct international flights. To get there by air from long-haul destinations such as North America or Australasia you generally have to route your journey via Paris, France's main air-gate, and take a connecting domestic flight. Lyon, Marseille, Nice and Nantes also have internal air-links with Brittany. However, it may be cheaper to fly to London and continue your journey from there.

» From the UK, there are a few direct scheduled flights to Brittany. Low-cost airline Flybe currently operates to Brest and Rennes from Southampton and several other UK airports. Ryanair operates from London to Dinard. Channel Island operator Aurigny also flies to Dinard from various UK locations via Jersey and Guernsey. British Airways and Air France both fly directly from London to Nantes, an easy distance from southern Brittany with good rail connections. Aer Arann flights to Lorient connect with Luton, Cardiff and several Irish destinations. Charter flights also use these and various other smaller airports in northwestern France.

» Paris has three airports. Busiest and most widely used for international traffic is Roissy–Charles de Gaulle, 23km (14 miles) from the heart of the city. It has three terminals, all efficiently connected with each other and with central Paris and its main railway stations by bus or train (RER Line B). The smaller Orly airport, 14km (8.5 miles) south of central Paris, takes mainly domestic but also some international flights. Its two terminals are linked by bus and train with central Paris, and also Gare Montparnasse, from which trains depart for Brittany. Beauvais Tillé airport is a much smaller and more remote airport 90km (56 miles) north of Paris. It is used by a few low-cost airlines, including Ryanair.

» From Paris, internal flights with Brit Air (Air France's domestic subsidiary) serve the Breton airports

of Brest, Lannion, Lorient, Quimper and Rennes.

» It is generally more convenient, just as quick, and almost certainly cheaper to continue your onward journey to Brittany by train or rental car from a Parisian airport. Brittany is about a 3-hour drive from Paris; the quickest route is via the A11 to Le Mans (Autoroute de l'Ouest), then the A81 and N157 to Rennes.

» Exceptionally low fares generally imply some degree of inconvenience in terms of flight times, baggage allowances or airport location. Check whether prices quoted include departure tax, fuel surcharges, and what penalties are involved if you have to change your booking.

BY RAIL

EUROSTAR

» From London (St. Pancras), up to 16 Eurostar trains per day pass through the Channel Tunnel into France. Journey time to Paris (Gare du Nord) is less than 2 hours 30 minutes.

» Some trains stop en route at Ebbsfleet, Ashford (UK), Calais Fréthun (France) and Lille, where the line splits, one branch heading for Brussels, the other for Paris.

Eurostar contact details
08705 186 186; www.eurostar.com

ONWARD TRAVEL

» To travel to Britanny, leave the Eurostar at Lille and catch a high-speed TGV Atlantique Ouest connection directly to Rennes (3 hours 50 minutes) or Quimper (6 hours 50 minutes). This will save you the bother and expense of crossing Paris.

» If you are travelling through Paris, trains to Brittany depart from Paris's Gare Montparnasse. From Gare du Nord, take Métro Line 4 (Porte d'Orléans) to Montparnasse-Bienvenue.

Right *The world-renowned TGV*
Opposite *Most flights from long-haul destinations are routed via Paris*

AIRPORT CONTACTS

General airport information	www.worldairportguide.com	
Information on all French airports	www.aeroport.fr or www.frenchairports.com	
Paris		
Roissy–Charles de Gaulle	01 48 62 22 80	www.adp.fr
Paris Orly	01 49 75 15 15	www.adp.fr
Beauvais Tillé	0892 682 066	www.aeroportbeauvais.com
Orlybus	01 40 02 32 94	
Paris Métro and RER information	0892 687 714	www.ratp.fr
Air France bus to Paris	0892 350 820	www.airfrance.com
Brittany		
Taxi fares are approximations, and vary greatly between midweek and weekend, and day and evening.		
Brest–Guipavas	02 98 32 01 00	(9km/5.6 miles NE; Bibus No. 24–place de la Liberté; taxi about €19)
Dinard–Pleurtuit	02 99 46 18 46	(5km/3 miles SW on D168; TIV bus links from Dinard and St-Malo railway station; taxi fare about €17 to Dinard, or €27 to St-Malo)
Lannion–Trégor	02 96 05 82 22	(4km/2.5 miles N on Trégastel road; CAT bus No. 15; taxi fare about €12)
Lorient–Lann-Bihoué	02 97 87 21 50	(10km/6 miles NW; CTRL bus; taxi fare €17–€22)
Quimper–Cornouaille	02 98 94 30 30	(7km/4 miles SW; QUB bus No. 25 towards Ti Lipig; taxi fare €20)
Rennes–St-Jacques-de-la-Lande	02 99 29 60 00	(6km/4 miles SW on D777; bus No. 57–place de la République; taxi fare €17)
Pays de la Loire		
Nantes–Atlantique	02 40 84 80 00	(12km/7 miles SW; TAN AIR bus service connects with main flights from railway station/place du Commerce; taxi fare €27)

ON THE MOVE ARRIVING

BY CAR

If you are taking your car from the UK to France you can either catch a ferry to a choice of ports on France's northwestern coast or take the Eurotunnel shuttle train through the Channel Tunnel. Driving to France from neighbouring countries on mainland Europe is straightforward on a comprehensive system of *autoroutes* (motorways).

FERRY CONTACT DETAILS		
Brittany Ferries	08709 076 103	www.brittany-ferries.com
Condor Ferries	0845 609 1024	www.condorferries.co.uk
Irish Ferries	0870 517 1717	www.irishferries.com
Norfolkline	0870 870 1020	www.norfolkline.com
P&O Ferries	08716 645 645	www.poferries.com
Seafrance	0871 222 0711	www.seafrance.com
SpeedFerries	0871 222 7456	www.speedferries.com
Transmanche Ferries	0800 917 1201	www.transmancheferries.com

FERRIES

Numerous cross-Channel ferries link France with the UK. To reach Brittany by sea, you must first decide whether you prefer a short crossing to Dunkirk, Calais or Boulogne, followed by a lengthy road journey through France, or a longer ferry route across the western Channel directly to a Breton port.

» It is generally a little cheaper to take a short crossing and drive down. For obvious reasons the longer sea crossings are more expensive, but don't forget you save time and energy, as well as the cost of fuel, motorway tolls, meals en route and possibly an overnight stop. From Dunkirk, Calais or Boulogne, allow 5–6 hours to reach the Brittany border, using motorways where possible.

» The cost of crossings varies widely depending on time, day and month of travel, but fares are generally lower if you book well in advance. You may get an additional discount by booking online. You must pay in full by the booking deadline to qualify for any cheap fares.

» Look out for special offers, and good-value minibreak deals for stays of limited duration (for example five- or nine-night stays). Expect to pay somewhere between £60–£120 standard return for a car plus up to five passengers on a short crossing and anywhere between £160–£380 on a longer crossing. Inexpensive ferry deals are sometimes advertised in British newspapers.

» Ferry Savers 0870 990 8492; www.ferrysavers.com can book crossings with all the principal operators.

» Before setting off, telephone or check websites to confirm any last-minute change of sailing time, as printed ferry brochures may not always be up to date. Most companies require you to check in at least 45 minutes before departure, although extra security checks may mean you have to arrive earlier. In any case, allow plenty of time. Don't fill your fuel tank to the brim just before boarding. Have your tickets or reservation number and passport handy when you reach the check-in barrier.

» Modern ferries are efficiently stabilized for a smooth ride; many have been upgraded or refurbished and are usually bright and comfortable. All have on-board shops, bars, cafés or restaurants, exchange facilities, telephones, recreational areas and lounges. You can pay for anything you need in either sterling or euros (check exchange rates), or by credit card. All carry vehicles as well as passengers, but LPG vehicles may be excluded for safety reasons.

» Access to the car decks is restricted during the crossing, so make sure you take everything you need during the voyage (including some warm clothing if you want a breath of air on the outer decks). Don't leave valuables in your car. Lock up with the car in gear and the handbrake on, but don't engage the alarm system if you have one fitted. Before you leave your vehicle, take note of the car deck number, and which door or stairway is your nearest access point.

» It is worth reserving a cabin to ensure a good rest if you are taking a lengthy overnight crossing to St-Malo or Roscoff. A basic two-berth cabin costs around £50 extra. All are well designed with comfortable bunk beds, private bathroom and clothes hanging space.

TAKING YOUR PET

UK visitors are allowed to take cats and dogs to France, subject to

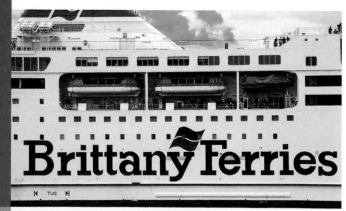

Left *Arrivals at one of Brittany's many ferry ports*

compliance with the DEFRA PETS scheme. You need the following documentation:

» Before setting off—a valid DEFRA-approved pet passport or veterinary certificate showing that your pet has been microchipped, vaccinated and blood-tested for rabies antibodies (allow at least seven months before travel to arrange all this).

» On your return—a valid DEFRA-approved pet passport or certificate showing that your animal has been treated against ticks and fox tapeworm not less than 24 hours and not more than 48 hours before returning to the UK. The timing of your return journey is therefore critical.

» Animals are not allowed on ferry passenger decks and must remain in your vehicle. Allow good ventilation and plenty of bedding. Escorted visits to the car deck may be made at specified times during the voyage.

» If documentation is not in order, your pet could be refused re-entry to the UK and placed in quarantine at your expense.

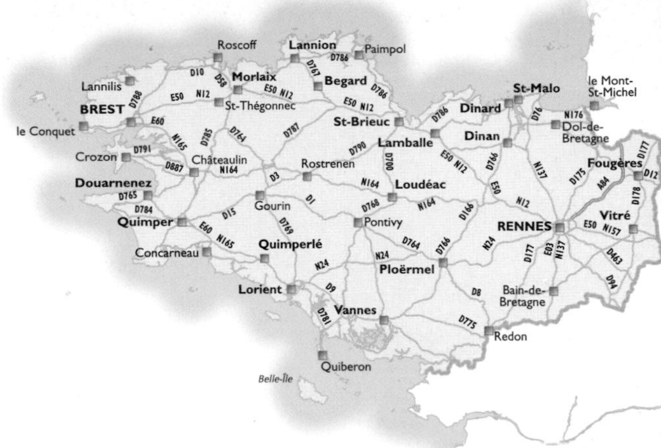

SAILING ROUTES

All sailing times are approximate and may take longer in bad weather.

» Norfolkline operates from Dover to Dunkirk (journey time 2 hours). If you don't mind the extra driving time and distance, this no-frills service is very good value, but don't forget the cost of additional motorway tolls.

» P&O Ferries and SeaFrance sail from Dover to Calais (journey time 70 to 90 minutes). Fastcraft catamarans cut the journey to about 50 minutes, although they are more prone to cancellations owing to bad weather.

» SpeedFerries operates a new fastcraft service between Dover and Boulogne (journey time 50 minutes), with startlingly competitive fares. An extra ferry on this route should reduce delays and cancellations due to technical problems.

» Transmanche Ferries operates a year-round conventional ferry service (journey time 4 hours) between Newhaven and Dieppe.

» Brittany Ferries sails from Portsmouth to Caen (journey time 6 hours); from Poole to Cherbourg (journey time 4 hours 15 minutes; Fastcraft 2 hours 15 minutes, summer only); from Portsmouth to St-Malo (journey time 8 hours 45 minutes); and from Plymouth to Roscoff (journey time 6 hours).

» Condor Ferries operates seasonal sailings between Weymouth/Poole and St-Malo via Jersey and Guernsey (journey time 4 hours 30 minutes).

» Irish Ferries sails from Cork/Rosslare to Roscoff (journey time around 12 hours).

EUROTUNNEL

Eurotunnel is a shuttle train transporting vehicles and passengers from one end of the Channel Tunnel to the other.

» The UK terminal of the Channel Tunnel lies between Dover and Folkestone. Leave the M20 at junction 11A and follow the signs.

» Drive your vehicle on to the shuttle train as directed, and you will be whisked under the Channel in just 35 minutes to the French terminal at Coquelles, near Calais.

» Eurotunnel shuttle trains depart up to five times per hour, 24 hours a day, 365 days a year; the price is charged per vehicle (reserve ahead). LPG and CNG vehicles are not currently allowed on Eurotunnel services.

» French border controls take place on the UK side, saving time when you arrive in Calais.

» You are advised to stay with your vehicle during the journey, although you can go to the toilet or walk about within the air-conditioned carriage. During the journey you can listen to the on-board radio station. Staff are available if you need any help. If you want to sit inside your vehicle, open the windows to minimize the effects of pressure changes within the carriage.

Onward Travel

» The quickest way to reach Brittany from Calais is to take the A29 towards Le Havre, avoiding Rouen. South of the Seine, the A13 takes you to Caen, and from here the A84 (known as the Autoroute des Estuaires) leads on to Rennes.

» You will have to pay autoroute charges (a *Péage* sign will warn that you're approaching a toll road). There is a hefty toll to cross the massive Pont de Normandie suspension bridge near Le Havre (have your euros ready; cards are not accepted). You can, of course, avoid motorway charges altogether by sticking to alternative and possibly more scenic routes, for example along the coast. Roads in Brittany are all toll-free.

Eurotunnel contact details 08705 35 35 35 (UK).

GETTING AROUND

DRIVING IN NORTHWEST FRANCE

Driving is the best way, indeed the only practical way, to tour rural areas of Brittany in any reasonable time-span. It is less enjoyable in larger cities such as Brest, where the traffic is heavy, the one-way systems confusing and parking sometimes difficult and expensive. Coastal resorts can also present driving headaches in high season. The roads in France are always dreadfully busy at the beginning of the summer school holidays (mid-July), and again when the holidays end at the beginning of September *(la grande rentrée)*. Try to avoid travelling during these periods.

BRINGING YOUR OWN CAR

Legal Requirements

» Private vehicles registered in another country can be taken into France for up to six months without customs formalities.

» You must always carry the following documentation: a current passport or national ID card, a full (not provisional), valid national driver's licence (even if you have an International Driving Permit), a certificate of motor insurance, and the vehicle's registration document (as well as a letter of authorization from the owner if the vehicle is not registered in your name).

» Check your motor insurance is valid for driving in France, and against damage in transit, for example on the train or ferry when your car is not being driven. Third-party motor insurance is the minimum requirement in France but fully comprehensive cover is strongly advised.

» Spot checks take place and you may be asked to produce your documents at any time. To avoid a police fine and/or confiscation of your car, be sure that your papers are in order.

» If your car does not have an EU registration plate displaying the Euro symbol, fix an international sticker or sign-plate by the rear number plate. If you don't, you risk paying an on-the-spot fine.

» To avoid dazzling oncoming drivers you should adjust the headlights of left-hand-drive vehicles for driving on the right. On older cars, you can use simple headlamp beam converters that stick onto the glass. But don't try to use these on cars with halogen headlamps—check in your car handbook or with your dealer. If your vehicle has Xenon or High Intensity Discharge (HID) headlamps, check with your dealer, who may need to make the adjustment.

» Don't forget to remove the beam converters (a good time to do this is while you're waiting in the homebound ferry queue) or have your headlamps reset as soon as you return home.

Breakdown Cover

If you are taking your own car, make sure you have adequate breakdown cover for your trip to France. For information on AA breakdown cover, call 0800 444 500 or visit www.theAA.com.

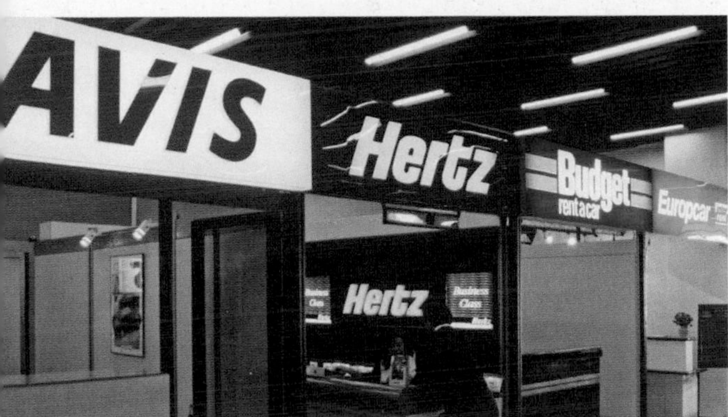

Left *Brittany has an excellent road system*
Opposite *Many visitors prefer the freedom of driving in Brittany*

RENTING A CAR

» Most major car rental agencies have offices at airports, main railway stations and in large towns and cities throughout France.

» Renting a car in France can be expensive due to high taxes. Arranging a fly-drive package through a tour operator or airline from home is generally a less expensive option. SNCF, the national railway company, has inclusive train and car-rental deals from mainline stations.

» To be able to rent a car in France you must be at least 20 years old and have held a full driver's licence for at least a year. However, some companies either do not rent to, or else add a surcharge for, drivers under the age of 25. The maximum age limit varies, but the average is 70.

» You will have to show your licence and passport or national ID card.

» Your rental agreement should include the following: unlimited mileage, comprehensive insurance cover, theft protection, 24-hour emergency roadside assistance, a replacement vehicle if the one you have rented becomes unusable.

» Some agencies include mileage in the cost but others may charge you extra above a certain distance, so check before you rent.

» Most international rental companies will let you return your car to other French cities, and even other countries, but there may be an extra charge for this. Always agree the drop-off point with the company when you reserve the vehicle.

» Make sure you have adequate insurance and that you are aware of what you are covered for in the event of an accident.

» Bear in mind that low-cost operators may have an extremely high excess charge for damage to the vehicle.

» If your car breaks down on an *autoroute*, look for emergency telephones on the roadside. You can contact the breakdown services from here.

GENERAL DRIVING

Roads

» The *autoroute* is the French counterpart of the British motorway or American expressway and is marked by an 'A' on maps and road signs. A few sections around key cities or ports may be free of charge, but tolls are charged on the rest *(autoroutes à péage)*. Tolls are expensive but may well be worth the saving in time and energy. Always have some cash available as foreign credit cards may not be accepted at toll-booths.

» Brittany has hardly any official motorways except for a short stretch of the A84, which has now extended as far as Rennes from Caen in Normandy. Brittany has not yet introduced any road-charging schemes.

» Other roads in Brittany may be almost as fast and efficient as motorways, though major routes all tend to run east–west. The next level in France's road hierarchy is occupied by trunk roads or *routes nationales* (code-marked N). The fastest of these key routes are dual carriageways (divided highways) called *voies express*, notably Brittany's N12 (Rennes–Brest) and N165 (Brest–Nantes). The next grade of road is the *route départementale* (D), often surprisingly wide and fast. Minor rural lanes are labelled as C roads, ideal for leisurely jaunts in search of picturesque scenery or a picnic spot.

» Beware of traffic-calming measures, particularly as you approach built-up areas along a fast road. Road humps or ramps (signed *passage surélevé)* are much-used ways of making you slow down in Brittany.

The Law

» In France you drive on the right *(serrez à droite)*.

» The minimum age to drive is 18, although to rent a car you must be at least 20.

» In built-up areas vehicles should give way to traffic coming from the right *(Priorité à droite)*, unless signs advise otherwise. At roundabouts (traffic circles) with signs saying *Cédez le passage* or *Vous n'avez pas la priorité*, traffic already on

CAR RENTAL COMPANIES

Company	Telephone number	Website
Avis	0820 050 505	www.avis.com
Budget	0825 003 564	www.budget.com
Europcar	0825 352 352	www.europcar.com
Hertz	01 41 91 95 25	www.hertz.com
Sixt	0820 007 498	www.sixt.com

the roundabout has priority. On roundabouts without signs, traffic entering has priority. A priority road can also be shown by a white diamond-shaped sign with a yellow diamond within it. A black line through the diamond indicates the end of priority. A red-bordered triangle with a black cross on a white background, with the words *passage protégé*, also shows priority.

» Holders of EU driver's licences who exceed the speed limit by more than 25kph (16mph) may have their licences confiscated by the police on the spot.

» You must wear a seatbelt. Children under 10 must travel in the back, with a booster seat, except for babies under nine months with a specially adapted rear-facing front seat (but not in cars with airbags).

» Do not overtake where there is a solid single central line on the road.

» There are harsh penalties if the level of alcohol in the blood is 0.05 per cent or more. If you drink, don't drive.

» You must always stop completely at STOP signs, or you may be fined.

Road signs

» Road signs are split into three categories. Triangular signs with a red border are warnings, circular signs are mandatory (such as speed limits or No Entry) and square signs display text information. In rural Brittany, you may still find a few old-fashioned signs hewn from granite.

» Common signs include: *déviation* (diversion), *attention travaux* (roadworks), *sortie* (exit), *gravillons* (loose chippings), *chaussée déformée* (uneven road and temporary surface) and *nids de poules* (potholes).

» Before you take to the road, familiarize yourself with the French highway code on www.legifrance.gouv.fr

» For more information on road signs see www.permisenligne.com.

Equipment

» Carry a red warning triangle in case you break down. Don't rely simply on hazard warning lights.

» Keep a spare-bulb kit in the car, as it is illegal to drive with faulty lights.

» It's worth stowing a parking 'clock' in your glove box; in certain areas you are allowed to park free of charge for a limited period, so you have to show what time you arrived.

» Take plenty of cloths or tissues (paper napkins or towels from cafés or service stations come in handy) to mop insects or mud off your lights and windscreen.

Fuel

» Fuel *(essence)* comes as unleaded (95 and 98 octane), lead replacement petrol *(LRP* or *supercarburant)*, diesel *(gasoil* or *gazole)* and LPG.

» Many filling stations close on Sundays and at 6pm the rest of the week. You may find it difficult to locate a 24-hour station and some automatic dispensing machines may not accept foreign credit cards.

» Prices are highest at filling stations on *autoroutes*, and lowest at large chain supermarkets such as Leclerc or Intermarché. Fuel charges are very similar to those in the UK, so there is no great advantage in filling up on one side of the Channel rather than the other.

Above *The flat, reclaimed polders around Dol de Bretagne*
Below *A town parking meter*

Parking

» Authorized parking spaces are indicated by road markings (white dotted lines). Blue markings, or those marked *Payant*, indicate a charge is due. Watch out for any signs indicating parking restrictions. Some parking attendants are lenient with foreign vehicles in tourist areas, but don't push your luck!

» Charges usually apply from about 9am to 6.30pm, Monday to Saturday. Sometimes there's a free period at lunchtime (12.30–2). Sundays and holidays are generally

ROAD SIGNS

No entry except for buses and taxis

Road-toll pay station

A sign with the road number above

Speed limits for various road types, in kph

Give way to traffic

Parking 150m to the left

Parking only for those with disabilities

No left turn

A local directional sign

free, but always check before parking your car. In certain popular holiday areas or tourist attractions, parking charges are imposed only in high season.

» To pay for parking, buy a timed ticket from a meter *(horodateur)* at the side of the road and display it in your car. Some towns operate on an honesty system and allow you some free time, but you must display a 'clock' showing when you arrived. You can get these in local shops or *tabacs*—or at the tourist office.

Car Breakdown

» If your car breaks down on an *autoroute*, look for an emergency telephone at the roadside to connect you with the breakdown services.

» If you break down on the Paris *périphérique* or an *autoroute*, you must call the police or the official breakdown service operating in that area, rather than your own breakdown/insurance company.

Road Conditions

» To find out about traffic conditions, for example on the congested coastal routes in high season, visit www.bison-fute.equipement.gouv.fr (in French only). Queues can build up, particularly at weekends or towards the end of the day when people leave the beaches.

» For the National Road Information Centre (voice service in French) call 0836 682 000.

» For information on *autoroute* conditions throughout France call 01 47 05 90 01 or Audiotel 0892 681 077; www.autoroutes.fr.

» For information on regional road conditions, call 0826 022 022.

» Autoroute FM provides useful and up-to-date traffic bulletins on the radio.

Maps

Good quality regional maps are invaluable in planning a trip. The AA (UK) publishes four France atlases as well as a series of France sheet maps. The AA website, www.theAA.com, has a helpful route planner. Most tourist offices can provide a local map free of charge.

OTHER WAYS TO GET AROUND

Driving may be the most convenient way to tour Brittany, but if you are without a car there are other reliable ways to see at least the region's larger towns. Even if you have a car, you may sometimes wish to leave it at home and make a trip by train, bus or boat.

TRAINS

In general, France has excellent trains—fast, comfortable and usually on time. France's state railway, the Société Nationale des Chemins de Fer (SNCF), runs the services. These include Grandes Lignes (mainline routes) such as the ultra-modern, high-speed TGV (Train à Grande Vitesse) which can operate at speeds of up to 300kph/186mph, and Corail (fast intercity trains). TER trains (Trains Express Régionaux) operate on regional journeys.

That said, the rail network in Brittany is not especially extensive, and while you can reach the main towns easily by train, many smaller places are served infrequently, if at all.

Tickets

» Fares are split into two categories: white (normal) and blue (off-peak). Reduced-rate fares are generally available for normal travel on mainline routes, excluding TGV and *couchette* services.

» Ticket prices vary according to the level of comfort (first or second class) and departure time. First class fares are roughly 50 per cent more expensive than second class.

» You can buy tickets in the stations, at SNCF offices or *boutiques*, which you'll find in major cities like Rennes or Brest, and through some travel agents. Tickets for TGV trains must be reserved. You can do this up to a few minutes before departure, although in peak season it is best to book well in advance. *Couchettes* must be booked at least 75 minutes before the train leaves its first station.

» Make sure you stamp your ticket *(composter)* in the orange machines on the platforms before you start your journey. You risk a fine if you forget.

» If you are under 26, you can get a 25 per cent discount (called Découverte 12–25) on train travel. Seniors also receive discounts (Découverte Senior).

» When you travel second class, there are lower rates for booking more than eight days in advance (ask for Découverte J8) and more than 30 days in advance (ask for Découverte J30).

» Ticket machines, with instructions in English, accept notes, coins and credit cards. They can also be used to collect tickets you have ordered on the internet, by telephone or Minitel.

» Once you are in France it may be difficult to change reservations made abroad.

Station Assistance

» If you need assistance or a porter, look for a member of the station staff, identifiable by their red waistcoats.

» You need a €1 coin deposit to use the luggage trolleys (carts).

» Some stations have a left- luggage office or coin-operated lockers, but security measures may mean this facility is not available. Electronic locks issue a printed ticket with a code number. You'll need to keep this ticket for when you return to collect your items.

Understanding Railway Timetables

» You can pick up free timetables *(horaires)* at stations, tourist offices, or at SNCF offices or agencies.

» There are two styles of timetable: One for the Grandes Lignes, covering high-speed TGV and other mainline services, and another for the regional TER trains.

» Be prepared to decipher French railway terminology. On Grandes Lignes timetables, two rows of boxed numbers at the top refer to the *numéro de train* (train number) and to the *notes à consulter* (footnotes). In TER timetables, the train number is not listed.

» Footnotes at the bottom explain when a particular train runs *(circule)*. *Tous les jours* means it runs every day; *sauf dimanche et fêtes* means it doesn't run on Sundays and holidays. *Jusqu'au*, followed by a date, indicates the service runs only up until that date.

Other Information

» Timetable, fare and service information is available from SNCF train stations, ticket outlets and travel agencies, by telephone (tel 08 91 67 68 69; 24 hours; (premium-rate line; €0.34 per minute) per minute), the internet or Minitel.

» A booklet called *Le Guide du Voyageur* gives you the A–Z (in French) of just about all you need to know on French railway travel (available at tourist offices, station ticket offices).

BUSES

» Buses in Brittany cover a much wider network of destinations than the trains, but most individual routes are quite short. Buses are slightly less expensive than trains, and journey times are sometimes just as quick, but in rural parts of Brittany services may be infrequent, erratic or very seasonal.

» Réseau Penn-ar-Bed, which organizes all long-distance bus (coach) travel throughout Finistère, has a flat-fare system of just €2 for any distance, with the exception of the Quimper–Brest route.

» Leaflets, available free from any tourist office, summarize local public transport systems throughout Brittany (road, rail and sea) with colour-coded maps indicating the main routes.

» Bus or coach stations *(gares routières)* are often located close to railway stations, and some attempt is made to co-ordinate train and bus services. Smaller towns without train stations are often linked by bus to the nearest railway station. These buses are sometimes operated by SNCF as a replacement for uneconomic rail services. Rail passes are valid on most SNCF buses, but check before you travel. For information on SNCF-run buses, telephone 0891 676 869 (24-hour service).

» Bus transport within cities is generally excellent and inexpensive (▷ 38–39), whereas rural areas are much less well served. Many routes operate largely for the benefit of schoolchildren or commuters rather than visitors, with long gaps during the day or complete breaks in holiday periods.

» You can generally buy tickets for short distances on board, but for longer journeys, buy tickets in advance at the bus station to reserve a seat.

TAXIS

» Taking a taxi is not the most cost-effective way of getting about but it may be the only convenient (or perhaps the only) option.

» The fare consists of an initial pick-up charge plus a charge per kilometre, (0.6 miles), and any extra charges for luggage and journeys during the evening or on Sundays. All taxis use a meter *(compteur)*.

» The best way to find a taxi is to head to a taxi stand, marked by a blue Taxis sign (often near railway stations, ferry terminals or main squares).

» Some taxis accept bank cards, but it is best to have cash available. It is usual to leave a tip of around 10 per cent.

» If you want a receipt, ask for *un reçu*.

BOATS

Boat travel is an important way of getting around in Brittany. Some island ferry links are maintained all year round, but pleasure excursions are mostly seasonal, between Easter and October.

BOAT COMPANIES

Armor Excursions 02 98 61 79 66
www.vedettes.amor.ile.de.batz.fr
trips from Roscoff around Morlaix bay and to Île de Batz.

Batobus 02 97 21 28 29; www.ctrl.fr
Rade de Lorient to Port-Louis, Gâvres, Lorient, Locmiquélic and Larmor-Plage.

Vedettes de l'Odet 0825 800 801
www.vedettes-odet.com
Excursions on the Odet from Bénodet, Concarneau, Loctudy, La Forêt-Fouesnant, Fouesnant, Quimper. Glass-bottomed boat trips to the Îles de Glénan.

Compagnie Finistérienne de Transports Maritimes (CFTM)
02 98 61 78 87
www.vedettes-ile-de-batz.com
Île de Batz, and Morlaix bay from Morlaix and Roscoff.

Compagnie Corsaire 08 25 13 80 35
www.compagniecorsaire.com
Ferry link between St-Malo and Dinard. Excursions around the bay of St-Malo and the Îles Chausey.

Compagnie Penn Ar Bed 02 98 80 80 80
www.pennarbed.com
The islands of Ouessant, Molène and Sein from Brest, Le Conquet and Audierne.

Navix 0825 132 100
www.navix.fr
Golfe du Morbihan (Île aux Moines, Île d'Arz), Belle-Île, Houat from Vannes (Conleau), Port-Navalo, La Trinité-sur-Mer, Locmariaquer, Auray, Bono.

Compagnie Océane
0820 056 156
www.compagnie-oceane.fr
Belle-Île and the islands of Groix, Houat and Hoëdic from Quiberon.

BY BICYCLE

France is an exceptionally attractive destination for keen cyclists, and nowhere more so than Brittany, with plenty of glorious, diverse countryside, not too many mountains, and good facilities. Tourist offices supply maps and touring guides specifically for bicyclists, and there are lots of places to rent or repair a bicycle. Bicycles can be taken on most trains, generally free of charge (check the SNCF website for details: www.sncf.com).

GETTING AROUND IN BRITTANY'S CITIES

Even Brittany's largest cities are modest in size compared with, say, Paris or Lyon, but they can still be confusing and harassing for motorists. However, most have excellent bus and train links to other bases in the region, along with exemplary networks of internal public transport. The areas most visitors want to see are generally quite compact, and manageable mainly on foot.

RENNES

A 20-minute stroll through the old town will take you to virtually all the city sights, largely on traffic-free streets. The main museums, however, lie on the noisier and more modern south bank, while the bus and railway stations are a lengthy trudge south. The tourist office just off quai Duguay can provide maps of the town and local transport, or you can pick one up at a Métro station. The modern buses and Métro (subway) system are both managed by the same company, called STAR. Tickets are valid on either system.

Métro Rennes is the only Breton town with a Métro system, known locally as Le VAL. Introduced in March 2002, it consists of just one line and 15 stations. Of these only three or so are likely to interest many visitors. These are Ste-Anne (at the north end of the old town, handy for place des Lices), Place de la République (at the heart of the modern city) and Gares (near the bus and railway stations). Each station is designed by a different architect and reflects some aspect of local character. Tickets cost €1.10, and are valid for one hour on local STAR buses as well as Métro trains. You must validate your ticket in a machine at the start of your journey. A day ticket costs €3.20; a carnet of 10 tickets €10.20. The Rennes Métro is entirely non-smoking, and allegedly wheelchair-friendly (although the lifts were out of action on inspection). No pets are allowed.

Buses Buses operate every day on about 40 routes until late at night. You can buy tickets on board, or in one of the Métro stations. The STAR office is at 12 rue du Pré Botté (just south of the main post office on place de la République; tel InfoSTAR 0811 555 535; www.star.fr). Bus No. 17 takes you to the railway and out-of-town bus stations from place de la République; bus 57 goes to the airport from here. One sight you may want to reach by public transport is the Ecomusée du Pays de Rennes, some distance south of the city. Take the Métro (direction Poterie) as far as Triangle, then bus No. 61 to the stop called Le Hil Bintinais.

Taxis Taxi ranks can be found at the railway station, on place de la République and by the town hall; tel 02 99 30 79 79 (Taxis Rennais).

Bicycles Rennes obligingly lets you borrow a bicycle free of charge for the day (though you have to leave a refundable deposit). Contact Clear Channel, Pont de Nemours (a kiosk opposite Galeries Lafayette, parking de la Vilaine); tel 0820 808 808; open 9–7. Or you can rent one at Cycle Guédard, 13 boulevard Beaumont; tel 02 99 30 43 78.

BREST

This sprawling city has many industrial suburbs, but the bits most people want to see in Brest are mainly around the old port and the castle, easily reachable on foot. The commercial and naval docks spread a long way in both directions from the castle, and the waterfront is not easy to follow on foot because of access restrictions and juggernaut container lorries. Brest's splendid aquarium, Océanopolis, is best reached by bus. A tram network is under construction.

Buses Brest has an excellent local bus network called Bibus. Tickets cost €1.20, a carnet costs €8.90 and a day-pass €3.20. You can buy tickets on the buses. A ticket lasts an hour after you stamp it in the machine on the bus. Most bus routes stop at place de la Liberté. To reach Océanopolis and the pleasure port, some way east of the city, take bus Nos. 3 or 15. The nearby Botanic Gardens (Conservatoire Botanique) can be reached by Nos. 25 or 27 (to Route de Quimper). Buses run from 6am until 10.40 pm (just after midnight on Friday and Saturday).

Bibus has an information kiosk at 33 avenue Georges-Clemenceau (Place de la Liberté); 02 98 80 30 30; www.bibus.fr.

Taxis You'll find taxi ranks at various points around the city, such as at the station or on rue de Siam; call 02 98 80 43 43 (Radio Taxi Brestois) or 02 98 42 11 11 (Allo Taxi).

Bicycles Torch'VTT offers bicycle rental at 93 boulevard Montaigne; tel 02 98 46 06 07.

Above *A no-entry sign*

QUIMPER

Old Quimper is a pleasantly walkable place, though the riverbank thoroughfares take a lot of traffic, and there are some gradients. The historic old town lies just north of the River Odet. It's a 10-minute waterfront stroll on level ground past flower-decked bridges to Locmaria, where the ceramics museum and *faïence* factories are located.

Buses The local network is operated by QUB (Quimper Bus), which has an office at 2 quai de l'Odet; tel: 02 98 95 26 27. Route 5 goes near Locmaria, though you still have a walk at the far end. All QUB's inner-city routes converge at place de la Résistance near the tourist office, radiating out into the hilly suburbs on both sides of the river, which are not of great interest to most visitors. Buses 9 (direction Ty Bos) and 11 (direction Kerveguen) serve out-of-town bus and railway stations.

Taxis Taxis generally congregate around the main bus terminal and parking area on the riverside, place de la Résistance. To call one, tel 02 98 90 21 21 (Radio Taxi Quimperois), 02 98 90 54 93 (Allo Taxis), or 02 98 53 42 42 (Abassides).

Bicycles You can rent a bicycle from Torch'VTT at 58 rue de la Providence; tel 02 98 53 84 41 (from about €15 per day).

VANNES

The old town of Vannes is only negotiable on foot, and it's unlikely you will make much use of public transport here. Other parts of the city you may wish to reach include Séné, Conleau and Port-Anna, on the Golfe du Morbihan, where boats take over from buses as the preferred mode of transport.

Buses Buses in and around Vannes are organized by TPV (Transports du Pays de Vannes), which has eight separate bus lines. Line 2 heads for Conleau via the port; Line 3 for the railway station to the north of the old town; Line 4 goes to Séné; Line 8 goes to the pleasant old village of Theix to the east. All buses terminate on place de la République, just west of the walled town, and there are bus stops by the marina on place Gambetta.

A more extensive network of TPV bus routes *(lignes périurbaines)* serves the greater Vannes area.

Tickets lasting one hour cost €1.20, a mini-carnet of 4 tickets costs €4.20, and a carnet of 10 costs €9.40 (children under 4 travel free). You can buy them from the driver, or in advance from local *tabacs*. A comprehensive timetable is available free at the tourist office, or from the bus information point Infobus TPV, on place de la République; tel 02 97 01 22 23 (Monday–Friday 8.30–12.30, 1.30–6.30; Sat 8.30–12.30, 2–5); www.tpv.fr.

Boats Several companies operate from the Golfe du Parc or the Presqui'île de Conleau to various points around the Golfe du Morbihan, including the islands. (For a summary of routes, ⊳ 37.)

Taxis There are taxi ranks on Place Gambetta, place de la République, and at place de la Gare; tel 02 97 54 34 34 (GIE Radio Taxis Vannetais).

Bicycles Available from Cycles Le Mellec, 51 ter rue Jean Gougaud; tel 02 97 63 00 51 (about €14 per day).

LORIENT

If you are based here for any length of time, ask about the Passe-Partout inclusive tourist pass which gives you three days unlimited transport and a trip to the island of Groix. The area of most interest to visitors is by the pleasure port and submarine base of Kéroman. The best way to get about is by Batobus, a ferry system linking various points on either side of the Rade de Lorient (estuary). Service summary: ⊳ 37.

Buses, boats and bicycles
Compagnie des Transports de la Région Lorientaise (CTRL) operates some 30 or so bus and boat routes in the Lorient area, including the Batobus network. A bus/boat timetable, tickets and information are available by the port at the Boutique Transports, Gare d'Echanges, Cours de Chazelles; tel 02 97 21 28 29; www.ctrl.fr. The ticketing system is co-ordinated; tickets cost €1.25 and last an hour; a 10-ticket carnet costs €10.80 and a day pass €3.70. Buses run until 8pm; boats run every 30 minutes or so Monday to Saturday 6.45–8, Sunday and holidays 10–7. CTRL routes cover the whole of the Blavet estuary area, including Port Louis and Hennebont/Izinzac, Larmor-Plage and Pont-Scorff.

CTRL also arranges bicycle rental at the same office at very cheap rates (about €7 per day, plus a refundable deposit). The office is open Monday–Friday 8–6.30, Saturday 8.30–12.30, 1.30–6).

Taxis Available at the port; tel 02 97 21 29 29 (Radio Taxi Lorientais, 27 boulevard de Normandie).

ST-BRIEUC

This city is not much of a tourist attraction and it is unlikely you will base yourself here. Its historic heart is manageable on foot. St-Brieuc does, however, have an efficient bus service organized by TUB (Transport Urbains Briochins), so if you need to get about locally (for example to the port or local beaches), obtain a full timetable from the office on place Duguesclin; tel 02 96 33 47 42, or ask at the tourist office.

Taxis Tel 02 96 94 70 70 (Armor Griffons); 02 96 78 39 24 (Daniel Houée).

VISITORS WITH A DISABILITY

Getting around France is gradually becoming easier, thanks to the improved design of buses and trains. Any recently constructed public building, including airports and stations, will have facilities for people with disabilities and mobility problems. But you'll still find challenges when travelling around Brittany, especially in historic towns with narrow, cobbled streets.

Before you travel, check what facilities are available, for example, at your arrival airport (www.aeroport.fr) and your hotel; many older buildings do not have an elevator. If you have mobility problems and may require help during a flight, tell your airline when you reserve your ticket. You may also find some useful information on individual airline websites.

The easiest way for visitors with disabilities to reach France from Britain is by using Eurotunnel, where you can remain in a vehicle for the whole journey. If you are taking a ferry, make sure you arrive well in advance so that you can have help with boarding.

AIRPORTS

In Paris, both Roissy–Charles de Gaulle and Orly airports are well equipped for people with reduced mobility. Shuttle buses between terminals have ramps for wheelchairs, as well as voice announcements for people with visual impairments. The terminals have adapted toilets, low-level telephones and reserved parking spaces. The Guide des Aeroports Français pour les Passagers à Mobilité Réduite (available at airports or online) provides more information. Various organizations offer specialist services from the airports into Paris, which you'll need to reserve in advance, such as Airhop (tel 01 41 29 01 29).

For information on facilities at airports in Brittany, contact Aeroguides (tel 01 46 55 93 43; www.aeroguide.fr).

TRAINS

Eurostar trains and terminals are wheelchair-friendly and wheelchair-users can also benefit from discounted tickets. France's long-distance trains are equipped for people with reduced mobility. On TGV and Corail trains, spaces for wheelchair-users are reserved in first class, although only a second-class fare is payable. Reserve at least 24 hours in advance. There are also adapted toilets. Most large stations have elevators or ramps to the platform. If you need assistance, request it when you reserve your ticket.

Facilities on regional trains tend to be more varied—check before you travel. For more information, call 0800 154 753, look up SNCF's website (www.sncf.com), or see the pamphlet Mémento du Voyageur à Mobilité Réduite.

Further information

See the website of the French tourist office for useful information on facilities for disabled visitors: www.franceguide.com. The French volume of a series called *Smooth Ride Guides* is available free of charge in English from the Maison de la France. This travel-planning handbook has been compiled with the co-operation of many disability organizations and tourist boards throughout France. Various venues, including airports, ferries, railways, museums and accommodation, are assessed for their user-friendliness for disabled visitors.

USEFUL ORGANIZATIONS

Association des Paralysés de France	01 40 78 69 00 (Paris)	www.apf.asso.fr
This French organization for the disabled is represented in each *département*. See the website for more information on local facilities.		
Holiday Care Service	08451 249 971 (UK)	www.holidaycare.org.uk
Travel and holiday information for people with disabilities.		
Mobile en Ville		www.mobile-en-ville.asso.fr
A website packed with information on disability access and related issues.		
Mobility International USA		www.miusa.org
Promotes international travel and exchange schemes for people with disabilities.		
RADAR (Royal Association for Disability and Rehabilitation)	020 7250 3222	www.radar.org.uk
Literature on travelling with disabilities.		
Society for Accessible Travel and Hospitality (SATH)	212 447 7284 (from US)	www.sath.org
A US-based organization offering advice for visitors with disabilities and promoting awareness of their travel requirements.		
Tripscope	08457 585641 (UK)	www.tripscope.org.uk
Travel and transport information.		

REGIONS

This chapter is divided ino the four *départements* of Brittany (▷ 8–9). Places of interest are listed alphabetically in each region.

Brittany's Regions 42–187

MORBIHAN

Brittany's most southerly *département* is its warmest and most sheltered. Holidaymakers flock to its beach resorts and sailing centres. Figs and grapes flourish in the sunny microclimate of the Rhuys peninsula, where vegetation takes on an almost Mediterranean look. Morbihan's natural scenery is rarely as spectacular as the Emerald or Pink Granite coasts or the wilder capes of Finistère, but it is never short of variety and interest. Belle-Île and Groix are two of Brittany's most enticing offshore islands, while the strange inland sea called the Golfe du Morbihan tempts waterbirds and pleasure boats to explore its maze of creeks and islets. Morbihan's charms extend inland too. Across its northern boundaries, the Nantes–Brest Canal traverses an idyllic rural tapestry of hedgerows and copses, while stately rivers—the Etel, the Blavet, the Oust and the Vilaine—carve their way gracefully towards the Atlantic in glassy estuaries.

Few of France's *départements* can claim such a fascinating and comprehensive legacy of the past, ranging through several millennia from the world-renowned megalithic monuments of Carnac to Lorient's World War II submarine pens. Morbihan's impressive heritage includes medieval castles (Josselin, Rochefort-en-Terre), 15th-century religious art (St-Fiacre, Kernescléden), Vauban fortresses (Belle-Île)—even an entire Napoleonic townscape (Pontivy). Ploërmel was the site of a famous chivalric tournament in the Hundred Years War (1351), Port-Louis recalls France's 17th-century colonial adventures in the Orient, Quiberon witnessed a royalist rebellion against the French Revolution, and St-Marcel staged a daring Resistance operation in 1944.

You don't have to be mad on history to appreciate the timeless appeal of picturesque towns like Malestroit and La Roche-Bernard, or the walled city of Vannes. Morbihan has lots of attractions and activities for the least antiquated visitor. There's nothing superannuated about Lorient's Festival Interceltique, a thalassotherapy session at Quiberon or Carnac, Kerguéhennec's wacky outdoor sculpture park, or the yachts in La Trinité-sur-Mer's sleek marina.

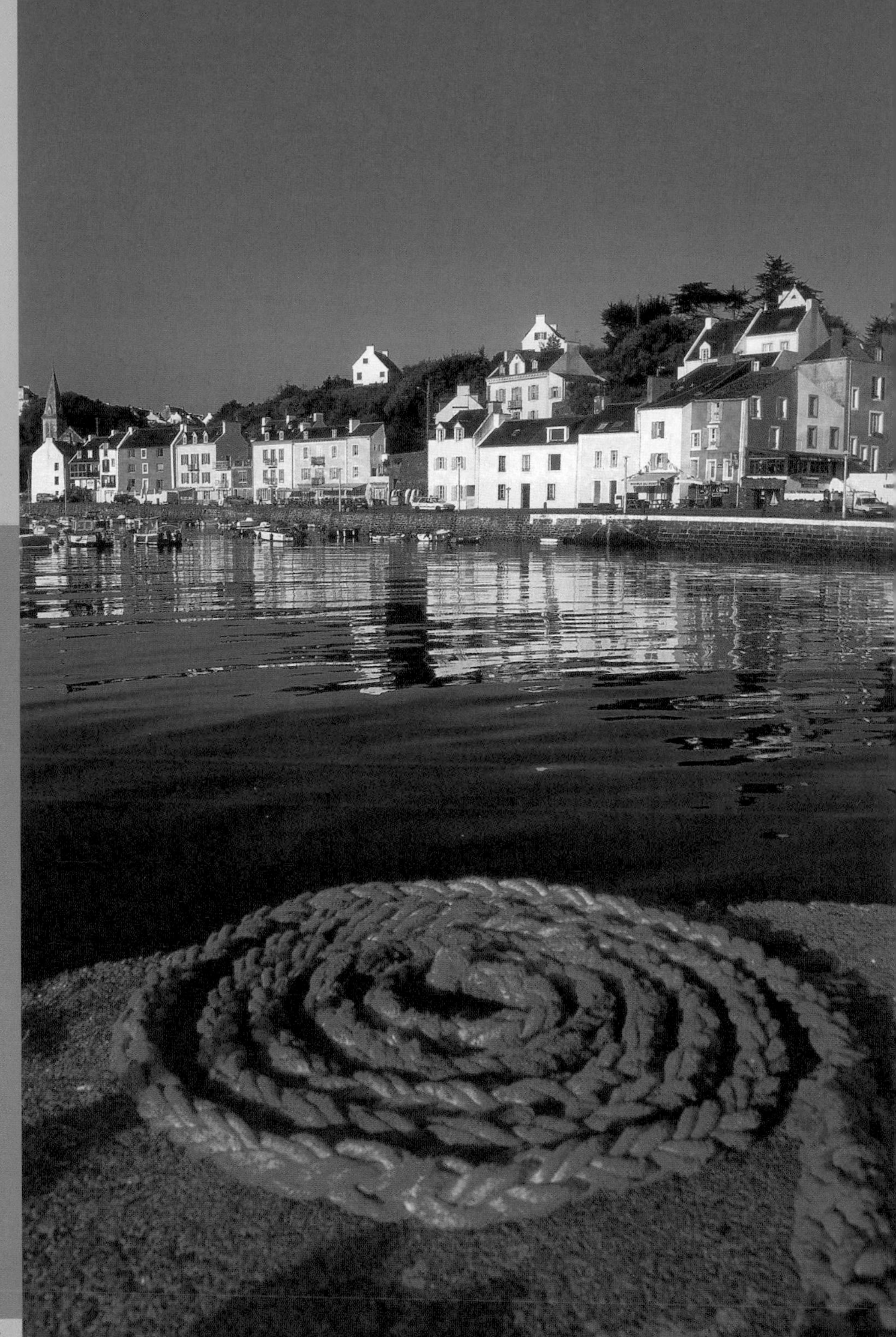

BELLE-ÎLE-EN-MER

The largest of Brittany's islands lives up to its name, with glorious, varied scenery and many historic associations. Belle-Île makes a perfect excursion from Quiberon, a 40-minute boat ride away (some 15km/9 miles due south). Its population rises to more than 35,000 in summer, but the island never seems overcrowded. The western Côte Sauvage faces the full force of the Atlantic Ocean, and breakers pound its rugged cliffs. At one point Belle-Île was captured by British forces, but was exchanged for the island of Menorca in 1763. Towards the end of the 18th century a number of French Canadian families, reluctant to accept British rule, were resettled on Belle-Île. Many famous visitors, including actress Sarah Bernhardt, have since developed a lasting affection for this Breton outpost.

PORTS AND BEACHES

The island's capital and main port, Le Palais, lies on the more sheltered eastern side. Excursion boats approach the harbour from the mainland beneath the ramparts of its star-shaped citadel, reinforced by Louis XIV's military strategist Vauban in 1682. The fortress, now privately owned and undergoing a lengthy restoration, contains the Musée Historique (tel 02 97 31 84 17; Jul, Aug daily 9–7; Apr–end Jun, Sep, Oct daily 9.30–6; Nov–end Mar daily 9.30–12, 2–5; adult €6.10, child 7–18 €3.05), tracing the island's past. Sauzon, Belle-Île's second port, is smaller but even prettier, a postcard scene of cottages painted in ice-cream hues, a toytown lighthouse and a harbour lined with fishing nets and crates of shellfish.

The coastline is pocked with caves and ringed with reef-strewn sandy beaches, some wild and exposed, others calm and sheltered. The 2km (1-mile) Plage des Grands Sables is one of the best for families. Port de Donnant on the west coast is popular with surfers, but is not for novice swimmers. The view of Les Aiguilles de Port-Coton, a series of sharp rocks off the western cliffs, was painted by Monet.

MENHIRS

Interior landscapes range from treeless moorland to lush farmland, crossed by footpaths and bicycle tracks. Here and there are prehistoric menhirs (standing stones); two in the northwest are known as Jean and Jeanne, lovers turned to stone as punishment for a pre-wedding night of passion.

INFORMATION

www.belle-ile.com
www.iles-du-ponant.com
234 G14 Quai Bonnelle, BP30, 56360 02 97 31 81 93 Jul, Aug daily 9–7.30; rest of year Mon–Sat 9–12.30, 2–6 Local buses run by Taol Mor (02 97 31 32 32; Apr–end Sep, school holidays); excursion coaches by Les Cars Bleus: 02 97 31 56 64 or Les Cars Verts: 02 97 31 81 88 Year-round ferry from Quiberon (0820 056 156). Seasonal services from Lorient, Port-Navalo and La Turballe. Excursions from Belle-Île to the smaller islands of Houat and Hoëdic (Jul, Aug)

TIPS

» You can get round Belle-Île very cheaply by local bus operated by Taol Mor (see bus information above), or rent a car, motor scooter or bicycle from Le Palais.
» Belle-Île's 100km (62 miles) of coastal footpaths are especially scenic, but some sections are risky (unstable cliffs and sea caves and paths are very slippery after rain). Escorted walks can be arranged with an experienced local guide. No bicycling is allowed on the coastal paths.
» Belle-Île has several riding stables, giving another way to explore the island.

Opposite *The harbour in the busy fishing port of Sauzon*
Below *The huge rock stacks of Aiguilles viewed from Port-Coton*

CARNAC

INFORMATION

www.carnac.fr

www.ot-carnac.fr

234 G13 The main office is in Carnac-Plage, 74 avenue des Druides, 56342 02 97 52 13 52 Jul, Aug Mon–Sat 9–1, 2–7, Sun 2–7; Sep–end Jun Mon–Sat 9–12, 2–6. There's a seasonal office in Carnac-Ville, place de l'Église; Apr–end Sep Mon–Sat 9–1, 2–7, Sun 2–7 Line 1 runs from Vannes via Auray to Quiberon; Line 18 goes to Lorient. A local bus connects Carnac-Plage and Carnac town with the main *alignements* several times a day, Jun–end Sep A petit train links Carnac-Plage with the alignements and La Trinité-sur-Mer in summer

Above*La Trinité-sur-Mer, Carnac*

INTRODUCTION

Carnac is a town of several parts. Its original core is an old village-like community known as Carnac-Ville. To the south, beyond a belt of saltmarsh lagoons, is Carnac-Plage, a modern seaside resort with five sandy beaches along the Baie de Quiberon. Facilities are excellent for families with children, and the resort is very busy in high season. But what most visitors want to see in Carnac are the *alignements* (long lines of standing stones), arrayed in three main groups just north of the town.

The scale of Carnac's fields of standing stones is impressive. More than 3,000 menhirs and other megalithic structures stand within a 4.5km (3-mile) radius. No one knows exactly who put them there or why. Theories abound, and estimates of the age and even the precise number of the stones vary widely. What most experts agree on is that the monuments—mostly long lines *(alignements)* of standing stones (menhirs) less than 2m (6ft) high—were erected sometime between 4500 and 1800BC and were used for some sort of religious or ritual activity. Some archaeologists believe the *alignements* are even older, far predating Stonehenge or the Pyramids.

WHAT TO SEE

MUSÉE DE PRÉHISTOIRE

www.museedecarnac.com

A preliminary visit to this museum near the town church helps put Carnac's wealth of antiquities in context. Founded by a Scottish archaeologist, James Miln, in 1881, this two-floor building houses more than 6,000 prehistoric items (jewellery, tools, ceramics and human bones). Contents span many millennia, from the Paleolithic era (some 450,000 years ago) to the early Middle Ages, but most of the exhibits date from Neolithic times (4000–1000BC). An explanatory booklet is available in English.

✉ 10 place de la Chapelle, 56340 Carnac-Ville ☎ 02 97 52 22 04 ⌚ Jul, Aug daily 10–6; Apr–end Jun, Sep Wed–Mon 10–12.30, 2–6; rest of year Wed–Mon 10–12.30, 2–5 (closed Jan and Tue except in school holidays) Adult €5, child 6–18 €2.50 Guided tours throughout the year; adult €7.50, child €4.20

LES ALIGNEMENTS

Largest of the menhir complexes is the Alignements du Ménec, containing 1,099 stones. A short way east are the Alignements de Kermario (1,029 stones in 10 lines), and farther on are the Alignements de Kerlescan, a smaller group of around 240 menhirs. Many of the stones have been removed or displaced over the years, and it is impossible to know exactly what the original formations looked like. Most can clearly be seen from the fenced roadside along the rue des Alignements, but conservation measures restrict visitors from wandering at will among the stones. To get closer to the *alignements* you must join an hour-long guided tour (adult €4, child (12–25) €3); available in English Jul, Aug; reserve in advance (see below).

MAISON DES MEGALITHES

www.monum.fr

This information point near the Alignements de Ménec has a video presentation, topographic models and a selection of books about the sites. Sign up here for a guided tour around the megaliths. A terrace above the building provides a grandstand view of the *alignements*, enabling you to see the patterns more clearly than at ground level.

✉ Route des Alignements ☎ 02 97 52 88 99 ⌚ Jul, Aug daily 9–8; May, Jun daily 9–7; Sep–end Apr 10–5 Free

TUMULUS ST-MICHEL

Some 300m (328 yards) east of the town, the tumulus of St-Michel is a prehistoric burial mound looking much like a natural hill. The mound, 12m (40ft) high, 125m (400ft) long and 60m (200ft) wide, is thought to date from around 4500BC. A low passage inside (no longer accessible for safety reasons) leads to two funerary chambers and stone compartments originally used for storing precious offerings. There's a fine view over the Baie de Quiberon from the top.

✉ Rue du Tumulus ☎ 02 97 52 29 81 ⌚ Freely accessible, but currently undergoing restoration

TIPS

» The official English-language publication, *The Carnac Alignments*, gives a clear summary of the antiquities (€7; available in local bookshops and information points).

» Large expanses of brackish water near Carnac-Plage encourage mosquitoes, so bring some insect repellent.

» Combination tickets are available for the megaliths at Carnac and Locmariaquer; adult €7.

Below left *A statue of Saint Cornely, Carnac*

Below *Standing Stones, Carnac*

Left *Half-timbered buildings around the port at Auray*
Opposite *The calvary, dating from 1550, at the parish close in Guéhenno*

AURAY

www.auray-tourisme.com
www.sainte-anne-auray.com

A striking valley setting at the tidal limit of the River Auray makes the historic port of St-Goustan the most memorable part of Auray. Here, forced ashore by a storm, Benjamin Franklin spent a night in 1776. The object of his visit was to enlist Louis XVI's support in the American War of Independence. Quaint timbered inns and restaurants cluster around the cobbled quayside, and an old tuna-fishing schooner (now used as a souvenir shop) is permanently moored on the waterfront. The Promenade du Loc'h on the western bank gives views over the port. Auray's upper town focuses on place de la République, with its 18th-century Hôtel de Ville. In a nearby square, the church of St-Gildas has a Renaissance porch and marble altarpiece. An even more famous church lies a short distance northeast of Auray. The basilica at Sainte-Anne-d'Auray hosts one of Brittany's most important *pardons*, on 25–26 July, when thousands converge to celebrate the feast day of the Virgin's mother, and a miraculous vision experienced by a local ploughman. Other shrines near Auray commemorate the unsuccessful counter-Revolutionary uprising by the Chouans, led by Georges Cadoudal (▷ 25).

Near the basilica of Sainte-Anne-d'Auray stands a war memorial in the form of a huge wall enclosing a formal garden. The Monument aux Morts lists by name the quarter million or so Bretons killed in World War I (freely accessible).

234 H12 20 rue du Lait, 56400 Auray 02 97 24 09 75 Jul, Aug Mon–Sat 9–7, Sun 9–12; Sep–end Jun Mon–Fri 9–12, 2–6; Sat am only except in school holidays. In Sainte-Anne-d'Auray, 26 rue de Vannes 02 97 57 69 16; Jun–end Sep Mon–Sat 9.30–12.30, 1.30–6; Oct–end May Mon–Fri 9–12, 2–5 Local buses operated by Auray-Bus (02 97 47 29 64); Line 1 to Vannes, Carnac, Quiberon; Line 16 to Ploërmel, Hennebont, Lorient; Line 6 to Bono, Larmor Baden, Port-Blanc Auray TGV services to Quimper, Vannes, Lorient and Paris; 'Tire Bouchon' service to Quiberon (Jul, Aug only) Pleasure cruises on River Auray and Golfe du Morbihan from St-Goustan Guided tours of the town available from tourist office in summer (Jul, Aug Thu 10.30; adult €4, child over 10 €2.50). A petit train operates to St-Goustan in summer (30-min ride)

LE FAOUËT

www.paysroimorvan.com

The main feature of this appealing little backwater in the Montagnes Noires is its handsome covered market, which dominates the main square. The slate roof, topped with a clock tower, sweeps down almost to ground level; inside a forest of timbers propped on granite pillars shores it up. The market has been in use continuously since the 16th century. The nearby art museum, housed in a former Ursuline convent, contains a collection of works by Breton artists who settled here in the early 20th century (tel 02 97 23 15 27; mid Jun–end Sep daily 10–12, 2–6).

The best-known local chapel is Sainte-Barbe, about 3km (2 miles) north of the town. This 15th-century building in Flamboyant Gothic style has a striking setting in a rocky gully overlooking the wooded Ellé valley. Legend has it that the chapel was built by a grateful knight caught in a terrible storm, which caused a rockslide. He prayed to Sainte Barbe, patron saint of lightning and artillery fire, and escaped unscathed. Visitors clamber down a steep flight of steps to see the chapel, which contains statues and stained-glass windows depicting the saint's life (Jul, Aug daily 9.30–12.30, 2–7; Apr–end Jun, Sep, Oct 10–12, 2–6; rest of year Sat–Sun 2–7, Mon 2–4.15). Toll the bell at the top of the chapel steps to invoke Sainte Barbe's protection against thunderbolts—or attract the custodian's attention.

229 F10 3 rue des Cendres, 56320 Le Faouët 02 97 23 23 23 Jul, Aug Mon–Sat 10–12.30, 2–6, Sun 10–12.30, Sep Mon–Sat 10–12.30, 2–6; rest of year Tue–Sat 10–12.30, 2–6 Line 15 to Lorient; Line 22 to Quimperlé

GUÉHENNO

www.pays-st-jean.com/guehenno

About 10km (6 miles) southwest of Josselin along the D778, the small, drowsy village of Guéhenno is worth a detour to see the calvary which dates from the mid-16th century. It suffered severe damage in the Revolution, but the local stonemasons demanded such high fees to restore it that parish clergy did the work themselves. The amateurish results are unexpectedly delightful. The cock crows on a pillar in front of the cross to announce Peter's denial of Christ, who lies in the ossuary guarded by soldiers (all year; free; tours in summer).

231 J11 At church Jul, Aug or Le Mairie, 4 rue Nationale, 56420 Guéhenno 02 97 42 29 89 Line 11 from Vannes via St-Jean Brévalay

GOLFE DU MORBIHAN

INFORMATION
www.golfedumorbihan.com
www.tourisme-sarzeau.com
www.crouesty.fr
234 H13 Rue du Général de Gaulle BP19, 56370 Sarzeau 02 97 41 82 37 Jul, Aug Mon–Sat 9–12.30, 2–7, Sun 10–12; Sep–end Jun Mon–Sat 9–12, 2–6 Rond-point du Crouesty, 56640 Arzon 02 97 53 69 69 Jul, Aug Mon–Sat 9–12.30, 2–7, Sun 10–1; Sep–end Jun Mon–Sat 9–12, 2–6 Tour Prison, place Monseigneur Ropert, 56370 St-Gildas-de-Rhuys 02 97 45 31 45 Jul, Aug only Maison du Tourisme de Rhuys, BP 46, St-Colombier, 56370 Sarzeau 02 97 26 45 26 Jul, Aug Mon–Sat 9.30–12.30, 2–6, Sun 10–1; Sep–end Jun 9.30–12.30, 2–6, Sun 10–12.30 Lines 6 and 7 serve the gulf area; many more routes converge on Vannes Vannes, Auray Gulf tours start from Vannes (Conleau), Port-Navalo, La Trinité-sur-Mer, Auray, Locmariaquer, Bono, Port-Blanc and Larmor-Baden

INTRODUCTION

This landlocked tidal lagoon is one of the most remarkable natural features of the Breton coastline. Meaning 'Little Sea' in Breton, its mild climate and picturesque islands make it an irresistible destination for water sports enthusiasts. The island-speckled gulf is virtually enclosed by the Presqu'île de Rhuys apart from a narrow channel near Locmariaquer, through which tides race furiously. The strong currents and muddy shores make swimming inadvisable, but despite this it's a popular holiday area, well equipped with campsites, water sports and small, low-key resorts. Bono is one of the prettiest ports on the gulf, tucked away up the Auray estuary. Immediately south of the village is the megalithic site of Kernous, an impressive cluster of tumuli in a pine grove setting. The gulf has few good beaches, but the Plage des Sept-Îles is an idyllic pale, secluded sandbar accessible from the Pointe de Locmiquel on Île Berder (low-tide access on foot from Larmor-Baden).

Boating is by far the best way to see the gulf. In summer, dozens of pleasure craft scoot across the shallow waters from various points, threading a skilful course through the maze of islands. A few of the islands can be visited (foot passengers only), notably the Île aux Moines and Île de Gavrinis.

Several thousand years ago, sea levels rose to create the Little Sea (*Morbihan* in Breton) which gives its name to this part of Brittany. The waters are once again rising, drowning the myriad grassy islets that emerge at low tide. Measuring some 20km (12 miles) by 15km (9 miles), the gulf changes dramatically as the strong tides ebb and flow. A huge variety of wildlife occupies the diverse habitats (dunes, saltmarshes, heath and pinewoods).

WHAT TO SEE

ÎLE DE GAVRINIS

www.gavrinis.info

Gavrinis has one of Brittany's most impressive Neolithic monuments. An ornately decorated tomb buried beneath a grassy cairn displays a remarkable

variety of carved patterns, including snakes and spirals, sunbursts and chevrons. Reached by a 15-minute ferry ride, it makes one of the most popular excursions anywhere on the gulf. The ferry fare includes the entrance charge to the site. Visitor numbers are limited, so reserve a place on the excursion in advance in high season.

Ferries from Larmor-Baden 02 97 57 19 38 Apr–Sep daily 9.30–12.30; 1.30–6.30 (7 Jul, Aug); rest of year Thu–Tue 1.30–5; closed Dec–end Feb Adult €12, child (8–17) €5, including boat fare Guided tours; site freely accessible between 12 and 2

ÎLE AUX MOINES

Although called Monks' Isle, this, the largest and most varied of the gulf's islands, never actually accommodated a resident religious community. The monks commemorated in the island's name were absentee landlords, who merely collected taxes from the inhabitants. Apart from a couple of megalithic monuments, there isn't a great deal to see, but it's a pretty place of stone-built and thatched fishermen's cottages, attractive creeks, palm groves and stands of woodland.

At Port Blanc 02 97 26 32 45 Jul, Aug daily 10–1, 2–6; Apr, May, Jun, Sep daily 10.30–12. 2.30–5 Izenah boats from Port-Blanc all year; Navix operates cruises from the *gare maritime* in Vannes (Apr–end Sep) Bicycles can be rented

PRESQU'ÎLE DU RHUYS

The mild microclimate prevalent on this straggling peninsula encourages the growth of lush, subtropical vegetation. Brittany's only vineyards grow here, as well as figs, pomegranates and camellias. Much of the waterfront on this part of the gulf is devoted to oyster-rearing, including the old salt pans at Le Tour du Parc.

Arzon, at the far end of the peninsula, is one of the most attractive villages, while nearby Port Crouesty is home to a glitzy marina development offering a range of health spa treatments.

CHÂTEAU DU SUSCINIO

www.suscinio.info

This impressively moated 14th-century castle in the marshes southeast of Sarzeau was once used as a hunting lodge for the dukes of Brittany. Still partly roofless, but much restored over the years, the château has a medieval tiled floor in bright mosaic. Concerts are sometimes staged here during the summer months.

234 H13 56370 Sarzeau 02 97 41 91 91 Apr–end Sep daily 10–7; Oct, Feb, Mar daily 10–12, 2–6; Nov–end Jan daily 10–12, 2–5 Adult €7, child (8–17) €2, family €15

TIP

» For a more romantic way to appreciate the gulf, take a ride on an old-fashioned *sinagot*, a traditional oyster-fishing boat from Séné/Port Anna or Arradon (▷ 66).

Above left *The small sand… Navalo on the Rhuys Peni…*
Above right *Pomegranate… here*
Opposite *Lobster creels o… harbourside at Port Naval…*

HENNEBONT

www.hennebont.net

Doughty fortifications indicate this town has quite a history, but Hennebont's metalworking industry and its unfortunate location just upstream from the submarine pens of Lorient were the cause of wholescale destruction in World War II.

The massive towered gateway of Porte Broërec survives, and a wander round the ramparts gives fine views over the River Blavet. Most of the old walled city succumbed to incendiary bombs, but a few elegant old houses can be spotted here and there (as at 1 rue de la Paix), dwarfed by the huge basilica of Notre-Dame-du-Paradis at the top of the main street. Vivid modern stained glass by Max Ingrand replaces the damage caused to the basilica in World War II.

The Parc de Kerbihan in the heart of the city contains some 400 species of trees and shrubs. Hennebont springs to life on Thursdays with one of the largest markets in Morbihan (no parking on main street).

North of town at Inzinzac-Lochrist, ghosts of a once-great industrial scene linger on the waterfront. The Ecomusée Industriel traces the history of Hennebont's defunct iron-and-steel trade, and the Blavet canal that was its lifeline (tel 02 97 36 98 21; Jul, Aug Mon–Fri 10–6.30, Sat, Sun 2–6; Sep–end Jun Mon–Fri 10–12, 2–6, Sun 2–6; Sat 2–6 in Jun).

230 G12 9 place Maréchal 56700 Hennebont 02 97 36 24 52 Jul, Aug daily 9–7; Sep–end Jun Mon–Sat 9–12.30, 2–6 Line 17 (Lorient–Pontivy); Line 16 (Lorient–Auray) River trips on the Blavet to Port-Louis and Lorient, or to Île de Groix

ÎLE DE GROIX

This island, a 50-minute ferry ride from Lorient, is a raised plateau fringed by steep cliffs. Most of the island's 3,000 residents live in the capital, Groix, just inland from Port-Tudy. The sheltered eastern coast has the best beaches, including the convex, almost tropical-looking Plage des Grands Sables, with fine, pale sand. The clear seas make it a popular spot for scuba-diving. The force of the Atlantic has left its mark on the western Côte Sauvage (wild coast), and the Trou d'Enfer blowhole on the southern coast is a memorable sight in rough weather.

The island, 8km (5 miles) by 2km (1 mile), has little in the way of visitor facilities, but offers a welcome break from mainland bustle, with 25km (15 miles) of footpaths to explore. Rare minerals are found here, and there is a geological reserve near Locmaria (free access all year).

During the 1930s Groix had the largest tuna-fishing fleet in France. You can learn more about the history of the fleet at Port-Tudy's well-presented Écomusée, in a former canning factory (tel 02 97 86 84 60; Jul, Aug Tue–Sun 9.30–12.30, 3–7; Apr–end Jun, Sep–end Nov Tue–Sun 10–12.30, 2–5; Dec–end Mar Wed, Sat, Sun 10–12.30, 2–5). The tuna-fish weather vane on Groix church indicates the importance of the local industry.

229 F12 Quai de Port-Tudy, 56590 Port-Tudy 02 97 86 53 08 Jul, Aug daily 9–1, 2–7; Sep–end Jun Mon–Fri 9–12, 2–5 From Lorient (all year), Larmor-Plage or Port-Louis (summer only) You can rent bicycles, motor scooters or cars on quai de Port-Tudy, or take a taxi tour of the island

KERGUÉHENNEC

www.art-kerguehennec.com

The classical parkland of an 18th-century château conceals a bizarre collection of surprises—a broken skiff dangling in the branches of a tree, a railway sleeper from which a sapling sprouts, a glasshouse filled with empty red plant pots. The Domaine de Kerguéhennec is an imaginative modern sculpture park (one of Europe's largest), administered by Morbihan's departmental authorities.

New pieces are constantly being installed, and the château's outbuildings are used as *ateliers* by visiting artists, or to stage exhibitions. There are tours of the interior in summer. A plan is available in English indicating the locations of the exhibits.

231 J11 56500 Bignan 02 97 60 44 44 Sculpture park and grounds daily 11–dusk; château interior mid-Jun to mid-Sep (guided tours) Light refreshments at the Café du Parc, served on the terrace in summer

JOSSELIN

Mirrored in the sparkling waters of the Oust, Josselin's turreted medieval castle is just as impressive inside as from the outside, and full of history from many periods. You can learn more about Brittany's medieval history in this inland town than almost anywhere else. The town supposedly dates back to AD1000, when a ruling nobleman named it after his eldest son. Throughout the complex struggles of the Hundred Years War, the War of Succession and the Wars of Religion, Josselin stood in the thick of the fighting. The castle was built during the 14th century by Olivier de Clisson, one of the leading warlords of the Middle Ages, who succeeded Bertrand du Guesclin as Constable of France. He married into the powerful Rohan family, who at that time owned about a third of Brittany.

CHÂTEAU DE JOSSELIN

The castle (tel 02 97 22 36 45; www.chateaujosselin.com; mid-Jul to end Aug daily 10–6; Apr to mid-Jul, Sep daily 2–6; Oct Sat, Sun and holidays 2–6) was constructed on a bulwark of solid rock above the river. It was heavily restored in the 19th century after being dismantled on Cardinal Richelieu's orders in 1629, and damaged during the Revolution. A sober wall of stone guards the waterfront, with three circular towers topped by witch-hat turrets. A Renaissance screen was added between 1490 and 1510, its courtyard façade decorated with a riot of exquisitely carved detail. The interior is decorated in 17th- and 18th-century style. Remarkably, the castle is still inhabited by descendants of the Rohan family. In the converted stable block, the Musée des Poupées displays an absorbing collection of around 600 dolls, some dating from 1880.

OUR LADY OF THE BRAMBLES

A maze of cobbled alleyways links the courtyard to Josselin's main town square, where you'll find the 15th-century Notre-Dame-du Roncier (Our Lady of the Brambles), allegedly built on the spot where a miraculous statue of the Virgin was found in a blackberry bush. Most of the church is in Flamboyant style, all gargoyles and lofty spires (guided tours in summer). Inside are the marble tombs of Olivier de Clisson and his second wife, Marguerite de Rohan. The belltower and the steeple date from the early 20th century.

INFORMATION

www.paysdejosselin-tourisme.com
231 J11 Place de la Congrégation, 56120 Josselin 02 97 22 36 43 Mid-Jul to Aug daily 10–6.30; rest of year Mon–Sat 9.30–12, 2–5.30 Line 19 (Rennes–Pontivy via Ploërmel)

TIPS

» An important *pardon* is held each year on 8 September, in honour of the town's patron, Notre-Dame du Roncier.
» You'll get superb views of the castle from across the river in the Quartier Sainte-Croix.
» A joint ticket for the castle and the doll museum (adult €11.90, child 7–14 €8.20) is the best value, though each can be visited separately (castle €7.30, child €5; museum €6.40, child €4 60).
» A pleasant walk along the banks of the Oust leads to the Île de Beaufort, an idyllic spot for a picnic, watching boats pass through the lock.

Opposite left *Modern sculpture by Keith Sonnier at Kerguéhennec*
Opposite right *Boats moored in the clear waters at Port-Tudy on the Île de Groix*
Below *The magnificent château at Josselin*

KERNASCLÉDEN

www.kernascleden.com

This village's claim on the visitor's attention is its 15th-century chapel built by the influential Rohan family, who ruled the roost around Josselin and Pontivy in medieval times. The elaborately carved exterior has many interesting features, but it is the bright frescoes inside that really catch the eye. Most startling are the scenes in the south transept depicting hell, where hideous demons kebab the damned on sharp spikes, then stew them in cauldrons or roast them in barrels. Above the vaulted choir, the Virgin's life and the Passion are depicted. Christ rises from his tomb, and angelic musicians tune up for an everlasting concert in the north transept.

230 G11 Information at the Mairie, 56540 Kernascléden 02 97 51 61 16

LOCMARIAQUER

www.monum.fr

Megaliths are the chief attraction of this oyster port. The largest dwarf anything in nearby Carnac (▷ 46–47). The main monuments, in a fenced enclosure near the village entrance, are the Table des Marchands (a 30m/100ft dolmen), and the Grand Menhir Brise, shattered and recumbent, but still impressive at more than 20m (66ft) long. Others include the Dolmen des Pierres Plates beside the sea, its 24m (80ft) chamber decorated with mysterious carvings (freely accessible; take a torch). Some tours are available in English—reserve well in advance.

Locmariaquer is on the narrow straits at the entrance to the Golfe du Morbihan (▷ 50–51), where tides fizz in and out with all the force of agitated champagne. Sandy beaches line the seaward coast west of the Pointe de Kerpenhir.

234 H13 1 rue de la Victoire, 56740 Locmariaquer 02 97 57 33 05 Jul, Aug Mon–Sat 9–1, 2–6, Sun 10–1; rest of year Mon–Fri 9–12, 2–5.30, Wed, Sat 9.30–12.30 Golfe du Morbihan excursions (including visits to Île aux Moines/Île d'Arz); ferry to Port-Navalo on the east side of the straits (Jul, Aug; foot passengers/bicyclists only) The *Fête de l'Huître* (oyster festival) celebrates the local *creuse de Locmariaquer* with tastings and exhibitions (third Sun in Aug)

Site Mégalithique de Locmariaquer

Route de Kerlogonan 02 97 57 37 59 Jul, Aug daily 10–7; May–end Jun daily 10–6; Sep–end Apr daily 10–12.30, 2–5.15 (last entry 30 min before closing time) Adult €5, under 18 free

LORIENT

www.lorient-tourisme.com

The name gives a clue to its colonial past. For Lorient, read Port de l'Orient, former HQ of the Compagnie des Indes, France's 17th-century trading company. An immense natural harbour was the source of Lorient's success as a commercial, naval and fishing port. But it was also the cause of its downfall in World War II, when Allied bombers pulverized the city in a frantic bid to destroy the German U-boat installations that presented such a threat to transatlantic shipping. Ironically, the concrete submarine pens in the port of Keroman mostly survived the raids, while the civilian quarters were smashed into rubble. Post-war reconstruction was rapid but mostly unimaginative.

Today little attracts visitors to Lorient except its August *Festival Interceltique*, the biggest musical event anywhere in France (▷ 71). Otherwise, Brittany's fourth-largest city is a lively commercial and university centre. The modern church of Notre-Dame-de-Victoire is vividly lit by jagged stained-glass windows. *La Thalassa* is an oceanographic research vessel, now turned into a museum and maritime exhibition permanently moored at the Port de Plaisance (tel 02 97 35 13 00; Jul, Aug daily 9–7; Sep–Jun Mon–Fri 9–12.30, 2–6, Sat, Sun 2–6; closed Mon outside school holidays).

230 F12 Maison de la Mer, quai de Rohan, 56100 Lorient 02 97 21 07 84 Jul, Aug Mon–Sat 9–1, 2–7, Sun 10–1; rest of year Mon–Fri 10–12, 2–6, Sat 10–12, 2–5 (closed Sat in winter) Lorient (trains to Quimper, Auray, Vannes and Rennes, plus TGV to Paris Gare Montparnasse) Batobus links across the estuary (Port-Louis/Sainte-Catherine/Larmor-Plage); Île de Groix excursions; river trips up the Blavet and around the harbour, including the submarine base Tours of the submarine base at Keroman arranged by the tourist office; mid-Jun to mid-Sep daily; adult €6, child €4 (under 12 free)

Below left *The Dolmen des Pierres Plates stands sentinel at Locmariaquer*
Below *Detail of a church ceiling painting in the village of Kernascléden*

MALESTROIT

www.malestroit.com

This quaint little baronial town on the river Oust (part of the Nantes-Brest Canal) has a long history, as the ancient buildings in its historic area suggest. In the now-ruinous Chapelle de la Madeleine, the kings of France and England signed a truce during the Hundred Years War. Slate-hung Gothic and Renaissance houses decked with turrets and droll carvings surround place du Bouffay and the church of St-Gilles. Here a hare plays the bagpipes, there a man in a nightshirt beats his wife.

At St-Marcel, 3km (2 miles) west of town, the Musée de la Résistance Bretonne (tel 02 97 75 16 90; mid-Jun to mid-Sep daily 10–7; mid-Sep to mid-Jun Wed–Mon 10–12, 2–6) recounts the contribution of the Morbihan Maquis (French Resistance) to the Allied effort in World War II. Ration cards, propaganda posters and the buckled engines of an American bomber are on display; an English translation of the guidebook is available. Local memorials commemorate the bloody battle fought here in 1944, when Maquis and Free French forces successfully diverted German troops from the Normandy landing beaches before D-Day.

231 K12 17 place du Bouffay, 56140 Malestroit 02 97 75 14 57 Jul, Aug Mon–Sat 9–7, Sun 10–4; Sep–end Jun Mon–Sat 9.30–12.30, 2.30–6.30 A *voie verte* bicycle trail begins at Malestroit; the tourist office supplies many suggested itineraries for walks and tours, some along the canal

PLOËRMEL

www.ploermel.com

Located at a strategic junction of major roads, Ploërmel is now a thriving regional hub with a busy agricultural market. Visitors are reminded of its distinguished past in the patchy historic quarters that survived wartime damage. Curious carved figures adorn the 15th-century Maison des Marmousets at 7 rue Beaumanoir and the 16th-century church of St-Armel. A famous chivalric tournament, The Battle of the Thirty, was fought near Ploërmel in 1351. This gentlemanly attempt to determine the outcome of the War of Succession failed to prevent the debilitating struggle lasting a further 13 years.

Northeast of Ploërmel, the forest of Paimpont (▷ 167) extends over the boundaries of Ille-et-Vilaine, offering many legend-packed excursions. The local tourist office promotes attractions on the Morbihan side of the border under the Franco-Arthurian label of Brocéliande.

A large lake called the Lac au Duc, about 2km (1 mile) northwest of Ploërmel, is a great venue for outdoor pursuits such as fishing, canoeing, waterskiing and windsurfing. Paths lead around the shore, parts using a disused railway line. The lovely 3km (2 mile) lakeside Circuit des Hortensias leads through a magnificent collection of hydrangeas, which grow exceptionally well in Brittany (tel 02 97 74 02 70; open all year but best May–end Sep; free access).

231 K11 5 rue du Val, BP 106, 56804 Ploërmel 02 97 74 02 70 Jul, Aug Mon–Sat 9.30–7, Sun, holidays 10–12.30; Sep–end Jun Mon–Sat 10–12.30, 2–6.30

PONTIVY

www.pays-pontivy.com

A former fiefdom of the Rohan family of Josselin (▷ 53), Pontivy's riverside château dates from around 1485 (tel 02 97 25 12 93; Jul, Aug daily 10.30–7; Apr–end Jun, Sep 10–12, 2–6; closed Mon, Tue off-season, and Dec, Jan), its twin turrets looming over a deep, dry moat. Events and exhibitions are sometimes held here in summer. A tangle of twisting streets, contemporary with the castle and now mostly pedestrianized, extends around the place du Martray, where an animated market is held on Tuesdays. Much of the town's present appearance owes more to Napoleon than to the Rohans. His ambitious plan to link Nantes and Brest by a canal route safe from seaborne attack resulted in a neoclassical makeover of Pontivy's southwestern sector in a neat grid of stately boulevards and landscaped plazas. For a while, the town was known as Napoléonville.

Above *The riverside château at Pontivy*

The Blavet splits from the Nantes–Brest Canal at Pontivy, but both waterways are canalized, and the choice of routes makes it a major canal-boating hub. Downstream along the Blavet, about 12km (7 miles) southwest, many pleasure boats reach St-Nicholas-des-Eaux, many of whose thatched cottages are used as holiday homes. The Site de Castennac just outside St-Nicholas gives a dramatic view over a bend in the river.

230 H10 61 rue Général de Gaulle (by the castle), 56306 Pontivy 02 97 25 04 10 Jul, Aug Mon–Sat 9.30–6.30, Sun 9.30–12.30; rest of year Mon–Sat 9.30–12.30, 2–6

Above *Yachts moored in the Vilaine, at the old port of La Roche-Bernard*

PORT-LOUIS

www.ville-portlouis.fr

Port-Louis was the original headquarters of the Compagnie des Indes, a trading company set up by Cardinal Richelieu during Louis XIII's reign. After its initial failure it was relocated to the burgeoning port of Lorient (▷ 54), on the opposite side of the Blavet estuary. Despite this commercial setback, Port-Louis has retained a charm of scale and atmosphere conspicuously lacking in its upstart offspring across the roadstead. Its cobbled streets contain a number of elegant shipowners' houses dating from the 18th century. The imposing citadel overlooking the Rade de Lorient houses two excellent museums. One recounts France's 17th- and 18th-century colonial adventures, and the bitter rivalry with British and Dutch entrepreneurs; the other is the Musée National de la Marine. Both have the same entrance ticket and opening hours (tel 02 97 82 19 13 or 02 97 82 56 72; mid-May to end Aug daily 10–6.30; Sep to mid-Dec, Feb, Mar Wed–Mon 2–6).

230 F12 1 rue de la Citadelle, 56290 Port-Louis 02 97 82 52 93 Jul, Aug Mon–Sat 10–1, 2.30–6.30; Apr, May Sep Mon 1.30–5.30, Tue–Fri 9.30–12.30, 1.30–5.30, Sat 9.30–12.30 Lorient Batobus ferry services connect Port-Louis with Lorient, Larmor-Plage and Gâvres, linking with local bus services

PRESQU'ÎLE DE QUIBERON

www.quiberon.com

Quiberon is one of Brittany's most popular holiday resorts, a long, slim peninsula in places scarcely wider than the single access road, fringed by sublime sandy beaches, and guarded by a 19th-century fort. The main town (also called Quiberon) lies at the southern tip of the peninsula, and from the *gare maritime* at Port-Maria ferries ply to and fro all year to Belle-Île (▷ 45). In high season the main road can be clogged with traffic as day-trippers head for the seaside. Grande Plage is the most popular family beach. Tourism has now replaced Quiberon's former dependence on sardine fishing, but the local fleet still lands its varied catch for the early morning *criée* (fish market). A well-known Breton fish-processing enterprise continues to thrive in Quiberon, and welcomes visitors for factory tours (▷ 68).

234 G13 14 rue de Verdun, 56174 Quiberon 0825 135 600 (€0.15/min) Jun–Aug daily 9–7.30; Sep–end May Mon–Sat 9–12.30, 2–6 Line 1 to Vannes via Carnac and Auray Quiberon. In Jul and Aug the Tire-Bouchon (corkscrew) shuttle train operates between Quiberon and Auray, replaced by SNCF buses off-season Year-round connections to Belle-Île, and the smaller islands of Houat and Hoëdic Tourist office organizes walking tours in high season The Sémaphore park-and-ride on the main road, 1.5km (1 mile) north of town (free shuttle bus into town; Jul, Aug only) saves sitting in traffic jams Bathing is forbidden on the westerly Côte Sauvage (dangerous currents and sharp rocks), but the coastal footpath is a spectacular walk

LA ROCHE-BERNARD

www.cc-pays-la-roche-bernard.fr

This petite *cité de charactère* makes a most appealing touring base, its narrow streets clinging to a steep rocky bluff overlooking the Vilaine. An elegant modern suspension bridge carries the N165 *autoroute* across the river gorge, replacing one destroyed in World War II. The charming historic quarter has a fine selection of hotels and restaurants.

The fortunes of this inland port once flourished on riverine trade and boat-building. Barges laden with grain, salt, timber and wine sailed past to its quaysides on the River Vilaine. The Musée de la Vilaine Maritime (tel 02 99 90 83 47; mid-Jun to mid-Sep daily 10.30–12.30, 2.30–6.30; early Jun, late Sep 2.30–6.30; Apr, May, Oct Sat, Sun 2.30–6.30) shows how busy this waterway was in its heydey, when La Roche-Bernard served as the port for the towns of Rennes and Redon. The museum is housed in an elegant 16th-century building constructed into the cliffside. Since the construction of the Barrage d'Arzal 10km (6 miles) downstream, the river is no longer navigable to the sea. You can visit the dam by boat, and watch fish migrating up or downstream through a glass-walled observation room.

There's a lovely beach at Pénestin, near the estuary mouth, called La Mine d'Or (gold mine). At sunset in fine weather you can see how it got its name.

235 K13 14 rue du Docteur-Cornudet, 56130 La Roche-Bernard 02 99 90 67 98 Mid-Jul to mid-Sep daily 10–7; early to mid-Jul daily 10–12.30, 2–6.30; Apr–end Jun Mon–Sat 10–12.30, 2–6 and Sun in school holidays; mid-Sep to end Mar Tue–Sat 10–12.30, 2–5.30 River trips to the Arzal dam in Jul and Aug

ST-FIACRE

This little place, 2km (just over a mile) south of La Faouët, has one of Morbihan's most memorable churches. The unusual gable belfry, with its graceful spires, sets it apart, but the interior is even more remarkable. The brightly tinted rood screen dating from 1480 features a mass of delicate woodcarvings on biblical themes from both Old and New Testaments. Angels pirouette gracefully above a series of scenes representing the seven deadly sins in human form. Avarice is a peasant stealing apples; sloth a man playing the bagpipes; gluttony a man bizarrely vomiting a fox. Early 16th-century glass depicts the life of St. Fiacre.

206 F10 See La Faouët (▷ 48) The pardon of St-Fiacre takes place third Sun in Aug

ROCHEFORT-EN-TERRE

This enchanting place wins award after award in 'most beautiful village' competitions for its spectacular setting and historic charm. Perched on a high schist spur overlooking the Arz valley, Rochefort-en-Terre is a showpiece village surrounded by oak and chestnut woods.

The Grande Rue (several streets linked by small squares) is lined with patrician-looking mansions sporting quirky details in every nook and cranny. Their individuality enhances rather than detracts from the essential harmony of Rochefort's architecture. Many of the sturdy granite buildings now house souvenir shops, art galleries, restaurants and *crêperies*. Flowers billow from dozens of tubs and window-boxes, making the village a photographer's delight with cameras snapping at every turn.

THE CASTLE

The castle at the top of the village, a true 'rock fort'—the origin of the town's name—was originally built in the Middle Ages but destroyed during the Revolution. Subsequently it was rebuilt piecemeal by two American brothers, Alfred and Trafford Klots, in the early 20th century. The building is furnished in 16th- and 17th-century style. The grounds contain a folklore museum (tel 02 97 43 31 56; Jul, Aug daily 10–7; Jun, Sep daily 2–7; Apr, May, Oct Sat–Sun, holidays 2–6.30).

RELIGIOUS RELIC

The church of Notre-Dame-de-la-Tronchaye houses one of the most important religious relics in Brittany—a revered statue of Our Lady of Tronchaye. The statue was discovered in a tree in the 12th century.

INFORMATION

www.rochefort-en-terre.com
235 K12 Place du Puits, 56220 Rochefort-en-Terre 02 97 43 33 57
Jul, Aug Mon–Fri 10–12.30, 2–6.30; Sat–Sun 2–6 (rest of year reduced hours)

TIP

» Circular waymarked walks lead round the town (blue signs; 6km/4 miles), and beyond into the scenic shale hills of the Grées plateau and the Malansac slate quarries to the east (yellow signs; 10km/6 miles).

Below *16th- and 17th-century houses in Rochefort-en-Terre*

VANNES

INFORMATION

www.tourisme-vannes.com
234 H13 1 rue Thiers, 56039 Vannes 0825 135 610 Jul, Aug daily 9–7; Sep–end Jun Mon–Sat 9.30–12.30, 1.30–6 Local city services are run by TPV 02 97 01 22 23. Vannes is a major hub for many routes to Carnac, Auray, Quiberon (Line 1), Questembert, Rochefort-en-Terre (Line 9), La Roche-Bernard (Line 8) and the Golfe du Morbihan. SNCF/TER bus service to St-Brieuc via Pontivy Vannes is a major rail junction, with links to Auray, Quimper, Lorient, Brest, Redon, Rennes, Nantes, Paris Boat trips around the Golfe du Morbihan and to Belle-Île from the port of Conleau The Animation du Patrimoine department runs several guided walks throughout the summer (02 97 01 64 00)

INTRODUCTION

This good-looking town has a livelier, more cosmopolitan feel than many Breton towns, and its well-preserved historic quarter is perfect for strolling. At the northwestern end of the Golfe du Morbihan, Vannes is the most important tourist town in southern Brittany. The modern city is extensive and constantly busy with traffic, but its splendid walled old town is compact and mostly pedestrianized. The best starting point is the Porte St-Vincent in place Gambetta. A web of narrow cobbled alleys full of timber-framed 15th- to 17th-century architecture surrounds the cathedral. Place des Lices is a focal point, once the setting for medieval tournaments, while place Henri-IV has another eye-catching assembly of overhanging, gabled houses. A produce market is held in the streets around the cathedral on Wednesdays and Saturdays, supplementing the covered market and the daily fish market on place de la Poissonnerie. Today, the administrative heart of Vannes has shifted to place de la République, outside the city walls. Beyond Porte St-Vincent, the Port de Plaisance bristles with yacht masts. The tree-lined Promenade de la Rabine runs along the waterfront to the *gare maritime* (commercial port) at Conleau, set on a trailing peninsula 4km (2.5 miles) to the south of town. Excursion boats bustle back and forth around the Golfe du Morbihan (▷ 50–51) all summer.

With access to the sea from the perfectly sheltered waters of the Golfe du Morbihan, Vannes made an obvious power-base for the Veneti, the seafaring Gaulish tribe defeated by Caesar in 56BC. In the ninth century it became the focus of Breton unity under Nominoë, first Duke of Brittany, and shared the honour of being the Breton capital with Nantes before Brittany was formally signed over to the French crown in 1532. Its superbly protected port played an important trading role, but today it caters only for pleasure traffic from the peninsula of Conleau, south of the city, and the canalized harbour that links the old town with the Golfe du Morbihan.

WHAT TO SEE

CATHÉDRALE ST-PIERRE

The much-restored Cathédrale St-Pierre is a mixture of architectural styles from the 13th to the 20th centuries. The main entrance on rue des Chanoines takes you through a fine Flamboyant Gothic doorway flanked by niches containing Renaissance statues of the Apostles. Modern stained glass admits some variegated light to the cathedral's sombre but airy interior. The Rotunda Chapel contains the remains of the city's patron, St. Vincent-Ferrier, a Spanish Dominican monk who achieved fame as a preacher and allegedly performed miraculous cures. When he died in Vannes in 1419, the townsfolk refused to return his body to Spain, and here it still lies in a black sarcophagus.

☎ 02 97 47 10 88 🕓 Mon–Sat 8–7, Sun 9–7 (except during services) ☛ Jul, Aug

LA COHUE

Almost opposite the cathedral, this medieval covered market dates from the 16th century and is worth a visit in itself. Over the centuries it has served as a market building, a hall of justice and a general meeting place, but now houses the Musée des Beaux-Arts, containing permanent collections of paintings, silverware and engravings. There are a number of star exhibits, including the Crucifixion by Eugène Delacroix, and many works by Breton artists. Temporary exhibitions are held on the ground floor, and guided tours are available.

✉ Place St-Pierre ☎ 02 97 01 63 00 🕓 Mid-Jun to end Sep daily 10–6; Oct to mid-Jun daily 1.30–6 ✋ Adult €4.20, child €2.60, under 12 free ❓ A combined Pass'Musées ticket covers both municipal museums in La Cohue and Le Château Gaillard; adult €6, child €4

RAMPARTS

Whatever else you do in Vannes, don't miss the chance to walk past the fortifications along the Promenade de la Garenne, a raised walk along a stream past the most photogenic bits of the old city walls, carpeted with immaculate formal gardens. The Porte Prison is the oldest surviving gate, dating from the 13th century. It once served as the main entrance to the city, and as the name implies, was also used as a jail. Near the Porte Poterne, look out for the well-preserved 19th-century *lavoirs* (washhouses), which remained in use until the middle of the 20th century. The distinctively turreted Tour de Connetable was built in the 16th century. Highest of Vannes' defensive towers, it has been carefully restored by the city authorities. Just south of the Porte Poterne, the handsome Château de l'Hermine stands on a site formerly occupied by the ducal palace (▷ 60–63, town walk.)

TIPS

» La Huche à Pains, at 23 place des Lices, is a superb bakery selling mouth-watering Breton cakes, pastries and savoury snacks.

» Rusty-sailed sloops ply the waters of the Golfe du Morbihan from Port Anna. These are *sinagots* (traditional shellfish-gathering craft), now restored for use as summer excursion vessels. Contact Les Amis du Sinagot, 6 rue de la Tannerie, tel 06 14 93 04 69.; wwwamis-du-sinagot.net

Opposite *Yachts and pleasure boats in the marina area*

Below left *A stained-glass window, Vannes*

Below *Vannes has many pretty timbered houses*

THE OLD TOWN OF VANNES

Vannes now extends far beyond its original walls, a thoroughly modern city with varied commercial and industrial interests. But the historic quarter is miraculously well preserved inside its fortifications. Most motorized traffic is banned from its confines, so exploring Old Vannes on foot is a positive pleasure—a great relief from its noisy and confusing outlying road systems.

THE WALK
Length: 2km (1.25 miles)
Allow: 2 hours
Start/end at: Place Gambetta

HOW TO GET THERE
Follow signs to the Port de Plaisance, where plenty of parking is available along the waterfront.

★ Crescent-shaped place Gambetta, laid out in the 19th century, presides at the head of the pleasure port, its lively bars and brasseries within sight and earshot of bristling masts and clanking halyards. The marina occupies the canalized, partly culverted River Marle, a mere trickle as it flows past the ramparts, but a vital link between the old city and the Golfe du Morbihan, Vannes' gateway to the Atlantic.

Follow signs to the tourist office immediately west of place Gambetta, in a fine 17th-century building on rue Thiers. Pick up a plan of the old town, then return to place Gambetta and enter the old town via Porte St-Vincent.

❶ Porte St-Vincent is the city's finest surviving gateway. It was first built in 1624, but underwent a neoclassical makeover in the mid-18th century, when its defensive machicolations were replaced with ornamental shell niches, columns and capitals.

Walk up rue St-Vincent Ferrier, lined by imposing 17th-century mansions. Some of these buildings housed distinguished residents, including Breton parliamentarians. One, known as the Hôtel Dondel, served as General Hoche's headquarters during his campaign against Chouan rebels in 1795 (⊳ 25). Glance down an alley to your left, where the daily fish-market *(poissonnerie)* is held. Continue as far as the place des Lices.

❷ Place des Lices, a large, sloping space of several interlinked squares, was used as a tilt-yard in the 16th century, but these days it's a marketplace. On it stand the bright, airy premises of Les Halles (covered food market). A produce market is held in the square on Wednesdays and Saturdays. Don't miss a wonderful *pâtisserie* called La Huche à Pains, opposite Les Halles (▷ 70). Also on the square is a turreted house containing a statue of the Spanish mystic and city patron St. Vincent-Ferrier in a niche. The saint preached here in 1418.

Take rue Rogue, leading off the square to the left, and walk just a few paces to the first junction (rue Noé). On this corner, you'll see a quaint red-timbered building that is now an Italian restaurant. From its upper floor lean the carved granite figures of a jolly 16th-century couple known as Vannes and his Wife, as if greeting passers-by. On the other side of rue Noé stands the Château Gaillard, a 15th-century mansion now housing the archaeology museum.

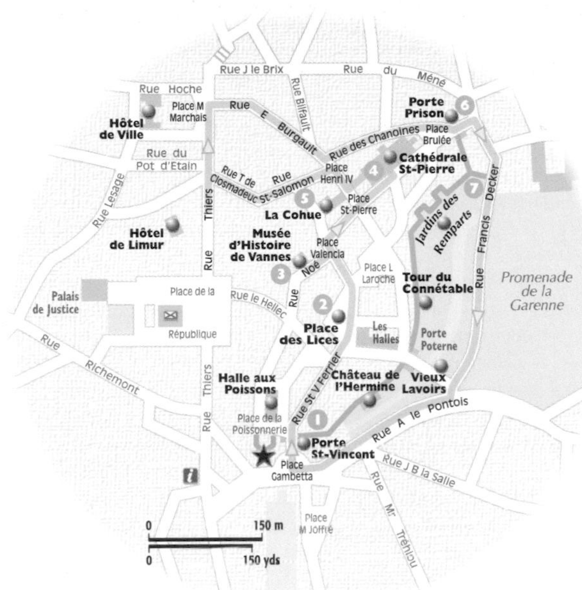

Clockwise from right *13th-century ramparts; relaxing on shady Promenade de la Garemme; 16th-century mansions, Vannes*

❸ The Musée d'Histoire et d'Archéologie contains finds from various sites in Morbihan, ranging from Neolithic axe-heads of smooth, polished jadeite to coins and scraps of glass and pottery. The building itself is worth seeing; it was formerly used as an assembly hall for Brittany's parliament.

Crossing place Valencia, you will pass the stone and timber-framed house (No. 17) where the Spanish mystic and city patron St. Vincent-Ferrier died in 1419. It was substantially redesigned in the 16th century. Wind through the narrow, shop-filled lane called rue des

Orfèvres into hilly place St-Pierre, where the huge cathedral dwarfs the buildings around it.

❹ The Cathédrale St-Pierre displays elements from many different periods, in parts austerely sombre, elsewhere riotously ornate. The oldest section is the north tower, dating from the 13th century, although the steeple is a more recent addition. On the north side of the cathedral is the 16th-century cloister in a garden. The main entrance door is finely carved in Flamboyant Gothic style. Inside the cathedral, 17th- and 18th-century memorials and altarpieces line the various chapels surrounding the nave. The nave was altered during the 18th century, when cumbersome vaulting was added. The elegant rotunda chapel, built in Italian Renaissance style, contains the tomb of St. Vincent-Ferrier. A painting depicting the saint's death scene hangs by the transept door.

Leave by the main west door, and walk across place St-Pierre to La Cohue.

❺ This handsome old market hall is now used as Vannes' fine arts museum. Its permanent collections date back to the mid-19th century, and include many works by Breton artists. The spacious lower floor, which would have been crowded with traders' stalls in the 13th century, is now used to host regular temporary exhibitions and cultural events.
Turn left into place Henri-IV, a postcard scene of ancient gabled buildings, and left again down rue St-Salomon, glancing down sidestreets for captivating reminders of the medieval city. Rue des Halles, again to your left, is a typically atmospheric street with several good restaurants. Head along rue Closmadeuc until you reach busy rue Thiers, outside the original walls. Turn briefly left to admire the Hôtel de Limur, a grand late 17th-century town house in formal gardens. Retrace your steps and walk up rue Thiers to the imposing place M. Marchais with its equestrian statue, flanked by the 19th-century Hôtel de Ville in Renaissance style. Take rue Burgault on your right back into the old town, bearing left past the cathedral on rue des Chanoines towards the Porte Prison.

❻ The Porte Prison, a machicolated gateway, dates from the 15th century, and is the oldest one left in Vannes. It was restored in the mid-1970s. You get the best view of it from beyond the walls.

Turn right outside the gateway and walk along rue Francis Decker. From here climb to the raised Promenade de la Garenne, above the road to your left. This walkway and the surrounding public gardens once belonged to the ducal castle, and both give splendid views of the city ramparts.

❼ This is the most complete and picturesque stretch of the walls, which have been repeatedly remodelled since Roman times. Velvet lawns and jewel-like flowerbeds soften these stern fortifications, and stone benches sheltered from the wind are ideal places from which to admire them. Notable landmarks include the turreted Tour du Connetable (Constable's Tower), and the symmetrical façade of the Château de l'Hermine. Near the Porte Poterne (Postern Gate) stand some early 19th-century *lavoirs* (wash-houses), topped with picturesque slate roofs.

Continue past the Porte Poterne along rue Le Pontois, which brings you back to place Gambetta and the Port de Plaisance, where an old langoustine boat called the *Corbeau des Mers* is permanently moored. This was part of the little fleet that carried the spirited men of the Île de Sein to the UK to join General de Gaulle's Resistance movement in June 1940. Virtually the entire adult male population of the island immediately volunteered for action.

WHERE TO EAT

Rue des Halles, off place des Lices, has three recommendable restaurants to suit all budgets in adjacent buildings. Alternatively, buy some picnic supplies in the market or from La Huche à Pains (⊳ 70), and enjoy them in the rampart gardens.

LE ROSCANVEC

✉ 17 rue des Halles, Vannes ☎ 02 97 47 15 96 🕒 Jul, Aug Mon–Sat 12.15–1.30, 7.15–9.30; Sep–end Jun Tue–Sat 12.15–1.30, 7.15–9.30

BREIZH CAFFÉ

✉ 13 rue des Halles, Vannes ☎ 02 97 54 37 41 🕒 Summer daily 12–2, 7–10; reduced hours off-season

BRASSERIE DES HALLES

✉ 9 rue des Halles, Vannes ☎ 02 97 54 08 34 🕒 Jul, Aug daily 12–midnight; Sep–end Jun 12–2.30, 7–12

Above *A window-box decorates a timber-framed house in the enclosed old town*
Opposite *Old wash-houses on the River Marle*
Below *The Hôtel de Ville in place Maurice-Marchais*

VANNES TO THE LANDES DE LANVAUX

Morbihan is the most southerly *département* in Brittany, an area full of interesting towns, pretty villages and fine countryside. The region's most popular attraction is the Golfe du Morbihan, and you can take a boat trip from Vannes to the small islands in the gulf. This drive heads inland, away from the gulf, to explore lesser-known places, slightly off the beaten track but well worth visiting.

THE DRIVE
Length: 97km (60 miles)
Allow: 1 day
Start/end at: Vannes

★ The historic city of Vannes stands at the head of the Golfe du Morbihan, its medieval kernel still intact within a shell of protective ramparts (▷ 59). From the Port de Plaisance on place Gambetta just beyond the city walls, the tree-lined Promenade de la Rabine follows the waterfront to the Parc du Golfe, 2km (1 mile) south of the town. This is one of the main departure points for ferries and excursion boats exploring the gulf and its islands.

From place Gambetta, head eastwards out of the city following signs for Nantes and the N165. After approximately 2km (1 mile), take a brief detour to the right (signed Sené), then bear to the left to the Réserve Naturelle de Sené at Brouel-Kerbihan.

❶ The Réserve Naturelle de Sené is an expanse of marshes and mudflats, where fresh and salt water mingle. It is one of the best places in Brittany for bird-watching. The reserve has a visitor centre and several observation hides, where you may spot a number of resident and migratory species including spoonbills, egrets and herons.

Return to the main road and continue eastwards on the D779/N165, following signs to the village of Theix on your right.

❷ The pretty village of Theix has some interesting sights, including La Chapelle-de-la-Dame-Blanche, built in 1239 and one of the oldest chapels in the province. It has been restored several times. Nearby is the Château du Plessis-Josso, which dates from the 14th to the 18th centuries.

Pick up the D7, signed for le Gorvello and Questembert, and follow it to the market town of Questembert.

❸ Questembert's great covered market hall dates from the mid-16th century and is surrounded by a square with medieval houses.

From the middle of Questembert, follow the Toutes Directions signs onto the ring road, and then take the D777 for 10km (6 miles) to Rochefort-en-Terre.

❹ Pretty Rochefort-en-Terre (▷ 57) is the capital of the moorlands of the Landes de Lanvaux. The town is on a ridge above the river Arz and most of it is medieval or dates from the 16th or 17th centuries. Aristocratic stone mansions line the cobbled streets, and some have been turned into shops and restaurants catering for the village's many visitors.

From Rochefort-en-Terre stay on the D777 to St-Gravé, turning left 1km (0.6 miles) before the village of St-Gravé and head north to Malestroit.

❺ The small town of Malestroit (▷ 55) stands between the winding river Oust and the moors of the Landes de Lanvaux. Its historic core is around place du Bouffay and the church of St-Gilles. Look for the bizarre carvings on the houses here, such as a hare playing the bagpipes. A little to the west, in the village of St-Marcel, the Musée de la Résistance Bretonne tells the story of the Morbihan Maquis (French Resistance).

The road out of Malestroit, the D10, follows the river Oust for a short distance before veering off west towards Sérent.

❻ Sérent, a village on the northern edge of the Landes de Lanvaux, has a number of fine houses and a church in flamboyant Gothic style.

From Sérent take the D766 south to Elven.

❼ Elven has a church with a 16th-century choir, but the main attractions lie outside the town. To the north is the Château de Kerfily, in a park beside the Arz, while to the south is the Forteresse de Largoët.

After another 3km (2 miles), turn right to the Forteresse de Largoët.

❽ The Forteresse de Largoët, also called Tours d'Elven, is an impressive feudal ruin in extensive wooded parkland. In 1488 the castle was burned down by Charles XIII of France, and now the ruins make an atmospheric setting for sound-and-light shows. With a height of 44m (145ft), the main tower, or *donjon*, of Largoët is the tallest medieval tower in France, with supporting walls 6–9m (20–30ft) thick.

Return to the D766 for 3km (2 miles), join the N166, and continue back into Vannes.

WHERE TO EAT

LE CANOTIER

✉ 11 bis place du Docteur Queinnec, 56140 Malestroit ☎ 02 97 75 08 69 🕐 Tue–Sat 12–2.30, 7.15–9.15, Sun 12–2

PLACES TO VISIT

RÉSERVE NATURELLE DE SÉNÉ

☎ 02 97 66 92 76 🕐 Jul, Aug daily 10–1, 2–7; Feb–end Jun Sun and holidays, afternoons only

CHÂTEAU DU PLESSIS-JOSSO

☎ 02 97 43 16 16 🕐 Jul, Aug 2–6.30

MUSÉE DE LA RÉSISTANCE BRETONNE

☎ 02 97 75 16 90 🕐 Mid-Jun to mid-Sep daily 10–7; mid-Sep to mid Jun Wed–Mon 10–12, 2–6

FORTERESSE DE LARGOËT

☎ 02 97 53 35 96 🕐 Jul, Aug daily 10.30–12.10, 2.20–6.30; Jun, Sep Wed–Mon 10.30–12.10, 2.20–6.30; May Sat–Sun only

Above *An unusual carving on a building in Malestroit*

Opposite *The feudal ruins of the Forteresse de Largoët*

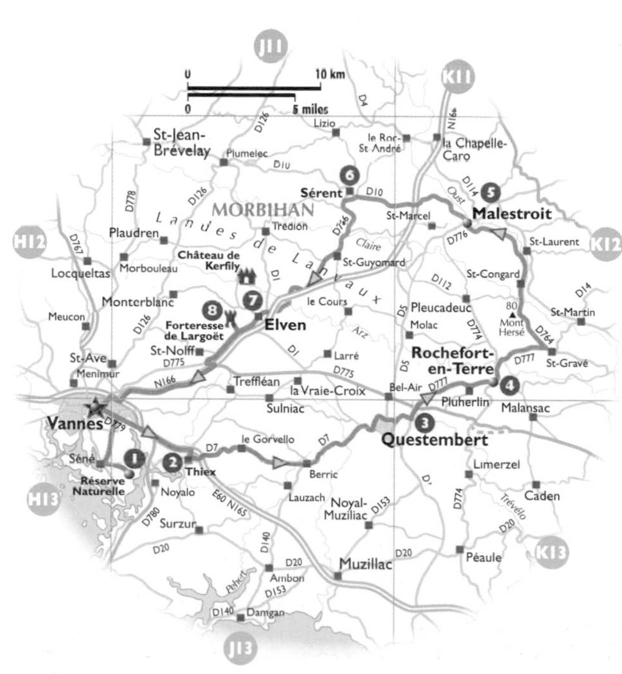

ARRADON

BELLE PLAISANCE

www.belleplaisance.com

On the Golfe du Morbihan you can rent traditional, beautifully restored sailing boats with a sailor to navigate and instruct. Decide where you want to go and for how long, or leave it to the experts. Reserve at least one week in advance; credit cards are not accepted. You can also rent kayaks and motor boats.

✉ Nicolas Bourdy, 24 chemin de Gravellic, 56610 Arradon ☎ 02 97 44 80 91 🕐 Easter–end Oct, by appointment 🖐 Prices on request for skippered or bareboat trips; Kayak hire from €10 per hour, motorboats from €120 (half day) or €170 (full day)

ARZAL

BARRAGE D'ARZAL

www.lavilaine.com

This huge dam near the mouth of the Vilaine estuary is always lively with boats, but an additional attraction is a fish pass *(passe à poissons),* which allows migrating fish to find their way upstream. An observation room contains display boards and a video. A guide tells you which species you might spot.

✉ 56190 Arzal, southeast of Vannes on D139 ☎ 02 99 90 88 44 🕐 May Sat–Sun 2–6; Jun to mid-Sep Mon–Fri, late Sep Wed–Fri 🖐 Adult €3, under 18 free

LES VEDETTES JAUNES

www.vedettesjaunes.com

Book an excursion upstream on the Vilaine from the Arzal dam (departures also from Redon and La Roche-Bernard in summer). Easily identifiable in vivid sunshine yellow, these sleek, double-decker motor-launches give excellent visibility. Lunch and candlelit dinner cruises are available. Boats have sun-decks, air-conditioning and commentary.

✉ Barrage d'Arzal, 56190 Arzal ☎ 02 97 45 02 81 🕐 Year-round, but most choice in Jul and Aug 🖐 From adult €10, child (4–11) €6 for a basic cruise, or from €39–€53 (adult), including an on-board meal (reduced prices and special menus for children under 8); drinks extra

BELLE-ÎLE

LES CALÈCHES DE LOCMARIA

www.lescaleches.com

Horse-drawn carriage rides lasting one hour, half a day or a whole day (with a picnic if you like) can be arranged every day of the year at this village on the southeastern side of the island. Carriages hold up to five passengers each; parties of 10 can be catered for on a single tour.

Above *Dark-red sails set, a traditional gaff-rigged sailing boat approaches the coast*

✉ Chemin du Petit-Houx, 56360 Locmaria ☎ 02 97 31 76 67

LES CARS BLEUS

www.lescarsbleus.com

Smooth modern coaches await new arrivals near the boat jetty on Belle-Île, offering various itineraries geared to the ferry timetables. Take a comfortable ride around the island, with commentary, stopping for lunch on the Côte Sauvage (café or picnic), and visiting Port Goulphar, the Pointe des Poulains and Sauzon. Tailor-made tours and hotel transfers.

✉ Rue Jules Simon, 56360 Le Palais, Belle-Île-en-Mer ☎ 02 97 31 56 64 🕐 All year 🖐 Grand Tour: adult €14, child (4–12) €7, under 4 free

BILLIERS

DOMAINE DE ROCHEVILAINE

www.domainerochevilaine.com

The Aqua Phénicia spa at this gorgeously located luxury hotel (▷ 75–76) has an impressive range of health and beauty treatments, including hydromassage, seaweed masks and anti-cellulite sessions. Ladies can have their moustaches removed for as little as €10, while a five-day well-being course costs €490, excluding board and lodging. Pointe de Pen-Lan, 56190 Billiers 02 97 41 61 61

BRANDÉRION

LA TISSERIE

www.la-tisserie.fr

A well-organized *espace découverte* (discovery centre) near Lorient, this weaving discovery centre shows how the skill developed through history. You can watch weavers at work, and have a go yourself in summer workshops aimed especially at children.

1 rue Vincent Renaud 56700 Brandérion (7km/4 miles east of Hennebont; signed off N165) 02 97 32 90 27 Jul, Aug daily 10–7, May, Jun, Sep Tue–Fri 9.30–12.30, 2–6, Sun 2–6, daily in school holidays Adult €3.80, child (5–17) €3

CARNAC

CASINO BARRIÈRE DE CARNAC

www.lucienbarriere.com

Carnac's casino offers slot machines and gaming tables, with dinner-dancing, cabaret shows, discothèque evenings and other events. There is a smart dress code. Take some ID.

41 avenue des Salines, 56340 Carnac 02 97 52 64 64 Daily from 11am until the small hours; gaming tables daily from 8pm, Fri–Sat 9pm–3am Free entrance; minimum stakes €1 for boule or roulette, €3 for blackjack, €5 for poker

EXPLORASUB

www.explorasub56.com

Explorasub runs PADI-approved sub-aqua courses at all levels in the Baie de Quiberon. They also arrange themed expeditions in a semi-rigid boat. Beginners' trials are available from eight years old.

12 boulevard de la Plage (Hôtel Le Plancton), 56340 Carnac 02 97 52 62 80 All year

CARNAC/QUIBERON/ VANNES

PETITS TRAINS DU MORBIHAN

www.petittrain-morbihan.com

Suitable for children of all ages, these 'toytown' road-trains operate in three popular Morbihan locations. Take a trip through Old Vannes and the rampart gardens (30-minute tours from place Gambetta), discover the wild west coast of the Quiberon peninsula (50-minute tours from place Hoche) or trundle past the megaliths of Carnac and down to the beach (50-minute tours from Ménec car park).

02 97 24 06 29 Apr–end Oct daily every 30 min from 10am (except on market days in Vannes—Wed, Sat am) Adult €5 (Vannes) or €6 (Quiberon/Carnac), child (under 12) €3 for all locations

LE FAOUËT

L'ABEILLE VIVANTE ET LA CITÉ DES FOURMIS

www.abeilles-et-fourmis.com

Welcome to the sociable world of the bees and the ants, revealed in transparent display cases, including a glass sweet-jar and an old television set. You can try the honey and buy honey products in the shop. There's a picnic site, bar and wheelchair access.

Kercadoret, 56320 Le Faouët 02 97 23 08 05 Apr–end Sep daily 10–12.30, 1.30–6 (10–7 in Jul and Aug) Adult €6, child (4–15) €4

LA GACILLY

YVES ROCHER

www.yves-rocher.fr

www.paysdelagacilly.com

Beauty magnate Yves Rocher has turned his home village and production headquarters into a high-profile tourist attraction. Imaginative botanical gardens contain a fascinating collection of plants used for culinary, pharmaceutical, cosmetic and industrial purposes. The Végétarium is a multimedia exhibition space devoted to the plant kingdom. Guided tours of the production site show how the plants are used in Yves Rocher's eco-friendly beauty products. There are also shops offering arts and crafts.

La Croix des Archers, 56200 La Gacilly 02 99 08 35 84 Gardens open all year free of charge; Végétarium Apr to mid-Sep; closes lunchtimes; telephone for precise dates and times Guided tours of the entire complex daily mid-Jun to early Oct Adult €6.50, child €5.50, under 10 free

LE GUERNO

PARC DE BRANFÉRÉ

www.branfere.com

This entertaining, family-friendly animal park occupies the grounds of a stately château with lakes, woods and waterfalls. There are bird shows, a botanical garden and nature school offering eco-mission residential discovery courses, outdoor pursuits and mountain bikes. For a more relaxing experience you could enjoy a meal at the panoramic restaurant, or in the picnic area. No dogs.

56190 Le Guerno 02 97 42 94 66 Jul, Aug daily 10–6; May, Jun, Sep Mon–Fri 10–5, Sat–Sun 10–6; mid-Feb to end Apr, early to mid-Oct 1.30–4. Last entrance 90 minutes before closing Adult €12.50, child (13–17) €11, (4–12) €8.50, under 4 free Guided tours of château Jul and Aug (extra charge)

GUIDEL

LABYRINTHE DU CORSAIRE

www.labyrintheducorsaire.com

One of Europe's largest maize mazes, covering some 11ha (4.5 acres) with 10km (6 miles) of pathways, picnic sites, and lots of fun things to do while you're getting lost, such as strategy games, bouncy castles and puzzles. There's a similar attraction near St-Malo.

Kerdrien, 56520 Guidel 02 99 81 17 23 Mid-Jul to end Aug daily 10.30–7 €7, under 3 free (last ticket one hour before closing)

LORIENT

LE TOUR-DAVIS

www.tour-davis.com

This fascinating museum in the old German submarine base at the port of Lorient operates excellent 50-minute guided tours ('An undersea voyage through time'). Audiovisual rooms recreate the experience of life in a submarine, with vivid sound effects.

Base des Sous-Marins de Keroman, 56100 Lorient 06 07 10 69 41 Jul, Aug daily 1.30–6.30, rest of year Sun only 2–6 Adult €5, child €3

MALANSAC

PARC DE PRÉHISTOIRE

www.prehistoire-bretagne.com

Dinosaurs roam the forests of a disused slate quarry not far from Rochefort-en-Terre. This is a multi-language introduction to the evolution of man specifically in Brittany. The site is enhanced by the provision of a shop, bar, picnic site and disabled access.

✉ Croix Neuve, 56220 Malansac ☎ 02 97 43 34 17 🕓 Apr to mid-Oct daily 10–7.30 (last entry 5.30); mid-Oct to mid-Nov Sun only 1.30–6 🎫 Adult €9, child (5–11) €5

PLOËRMEL

CLUB NAUTIQUE PLOËRMEL–TAUPONT

www.clubnautiqueploermel.com

The huge reservoir lake north of Ploërmel makes a great playground for waterbabies of all ages. There are optimist dinghies suitable for four- to six-year-olds, waterskis from six years old, canoe-kayaks, rowing boats, catamarans, windsurfers, sailboats and RIBs for adults. You can also have private tuition or join a course.

✉ Base Nautique, Lac du Duc, 56800 Ploërmel ☎ 02 97 74 14 51 🕓 Jul, Aug Mon–Fri 9–7, Sat, Sun 2–7; rest of year Mon–Fri 9–12, 2–6, Sat 2–6

PONT-SCORFF

L'ODYSSAUM

www.odyssaum.fr

Follow the complex lifestyle of wild salmon as they travel up to 14,000km (8,750 miles) across the Atlantic from Greenland to their birthplace to spawn and die. This excellent interactive discovery outlet in a verdant setting on the River Scorff enables you to learn about migration research, fishing techniques and conservation measures. Afterwards, taste some of the fish in the riverside Bistrot Saumon with its panoramic terrace. Summer events, field trips.

✉ Moulin des Princes, 56620 Pont-Scorff ☎ 02 97 32 42 00 🕓 Jul, Aug daily 10–7; May–end Jun, Sep Tue–Fri 9.30–12.30, 2–6, Sat–Mon 2–6; daily in school holidays 🎫 Adult €5.50, child (5–17) €4.20

ZOO DE PONT-SCORFF

www.zoo-pont-scorff.com

In attractive 12-hectare (30-acre) grounds on the D6 north of Lorient, this zoo has plenty of family appeal, though the hilly site may be tricky for very young or for visitors with pushchairs and wheelchairs. It accommodates more than 600 animals (120 species) and is a noted breeding centre for big cats and elephants. Imaginative activities include daily shows of seabirds and unpopular creatures *(mal-aimés)* such as rats and snakes.

✉ Kernisseau, 56620 Pont-Scorff ☎ 02 97 32 60 86 🕓 Jun–end Aug daily 9–7; Apr, May, Sep 9.30–5; rest of year 9.30–5; shows from 11.30 🎫 Adult €15.50, child (3–11) €10; last tickets 1hr before closing

QUIBERON

CONSERVERIE LA BELLE-ILOISE

www.labelleiloise.fr

Many of Brittany's seaside towns (including Quiberon) have an outlet selling this well-known firm's beautifully packaged gourmet fish products (including tuna, sardines, mackerel and more). At the canning factory on an industrial estate on the edge of town, visitors are welcome to take a 45-minute guided tour to see the packing process and discover the history of the industry. There is also a film show, and free tastings are available at the end of the tour.

✉ Zone d'Activité Plein Ouest, 56170 Quiberon ☎ 02 97 50 08 77 🕓 Summer Mon–Sat 9–11.30, 2–6; spring and autumn 10–11, 3–5; winter Mon–Fri 11–4 🎫 Free 🎁

HOUAT AND HOËDIC

www.compagnie-oceane.fr

Besides serving the major islands of Belle-Île and Groix, ferries also ply from Quiberon and Lorient to the smaller, quieter islands of Houat and Hoëdic (Duck and Duckling) all year round. With a combined population of around 500, these two tiny islands derive their income from a mix of fishing and tourism. Summer ferry departures also leave from Vannes, La Trinité-sur-Mer and Port-Navalo (Navix, Compagnie des Îles). Cars are not allowed on the islands, but you can take a bicycle with you to explore farther afield.

✉ Gare Maritime, Port-Maria, 56170 Quiberon ☎ 0820 056 156 🕓 Sailings range from just one per day in winter to about six in high season; journey time around 45 minutes 🎫 Adult return €30 approx (seasonal variations)

LA MAISON D'ARMORINE

www.maison-armorine.com

Find out how the traditional Breton sweet called a *niniche* (a type of long, thin lollipop) has been made here since 1946 by visiting the factory showroom *(éspace découverte)* at Quiberon. The four branches of this sweetshop (candy store) in Carnac Plage, Quiberon, Belle-Île and Pont-Aven sell about 50 different varieties of *niniche*. Other typical sweets include *Salidou* (toffee with butter).

✉ Zone Artisanale Plein Ouest, 1 rue des Confiseurs, 56170 Quiberon ☎ 02 97 50 24 24 🕓 Guided tours (40 min) Feb–end Nov; (closed Dec and Jan) 🎫 Free

MAISON LUCAS

www.maisonlucas.net

Michel Lucas welcomes visitors to have a look around his smoke-house, where top-quality fish straight from the fishmarket just down the road are expertly filleted, oak-smoked and vacuum packed. Try smoked salmon or mackerel, tuna sausage, eel, haddock, kippers or marinated sardines. Naturally you can also buy on site, and there's even a refrigerated mail-order service within France. Check out the wet-fish *poissonnerie* down on the seafront, too, next to M. Lucas's superb fish restaurant, La Criée (▷ 74).

✉ Zone Artisanale, Plein Ouest, quai des Saveurs, 56170 Quiberon ☎ 02 97 50 59 50 🕓 Closed Jan 🎫 Free

RHUMERIE LE NELSON

This lively rum pub down near the port is not to be missed. It serves about 50 different types of rum from all over the world and plays music dating from the 1960s onwards.

Live concerts (mostly rock) are held about twice a week. Internet access is also laid on.
✉ 20 place Hoche, 56170 Quiberon ☎ 02 97 50 31 37 🕐 Mon–Sat 4pm–2am (also Sun in high season); closed Jan

VENT DE SABLE

www.char-a-voile.bretagne.com
The smooth expanses of gleaming sand at Penthièvre on the breezy northwest shores of the Quiberon peninsula are ideal to watch or learn sand-yachting *(char à voile)*. Safety helmets are supplied; eye protection and protective gloves are advised. Keep your distance if you are spectating, as the speeds attained by these craft are awesome. The minimum age for participants is 10.
✉ Isthme de Penthièvre, 1 avenue de St-Malo, 56510 St-Pierre Quiberon ☎ 02 97 52 39 90 🕐 All year, depending on tides 🎟 From about €34 for a 2-hour session

QUISTINIC

VILLAGE DE POUL-FÉTAN

www.poul-fetan.com
This 'living history' attraction re-creates a typical Breton village of the 16th century. Costumed staff show how everyday domestic tasks such as spinning, laundry and butter-making were carried out in days gone by, and there's a film show and demonstrations and events every afternoon.
✉ 56310 Quistinic ☎ 02 97 39 51 74 🕐 Jul, Aug daily 10.45–7; Jun, Sep daily 11–6.30; Apr, May Wed, Sat, Sun 2–6.30 🎟 Adult €6 (€7 Jun–end Sep), child (6–12) €4 ☛ Guided tours Jun–end Sep mornings only

RIANTEC

LA MAISON DE L'ILE KERNER

www.maison-kerner.fr
This interesting *espace découverte* (discovery centre) run by the Pays de Lorient tourist authorities is located on a small islet in the tidal lagoon of Gâvres near Port-Louis. Guided bird-watching and flower-spotting expeditions are organized all year round to introduce visitors to some of the flora and fauna of this rich conservation zone. There's also an on-site shop.
✉ 56670 Riantec ☎ 02 97 84 51 49 🕐 Jul, Aug daily 10–7; May, Jun, Sep Tue–Fri 9.30–12.30, 2–6, Sat–Mon 2–6; Apr and Oct reduced hours 🎟 Adult €4; child €3.10; family €12 (ticket sales end one hour before closing time)

Below *Locally made wicker baskets*

ROCHEFORT-EN-TERRE

LE RUCHER FLEURI

www.painsdepices.com

Wafts of warm baking and spices assail passers-by at this traditional bakery located near the main square. Its speciality is *pain d'epices* (spiced bread) produced in a variety of delicious flavours (for example nut, raisin, chocolate, orange, prune), which you can watch being carefully prepared to an ancient recipe in the adjacent kitchens. There are also home-made biscuits, jams in exotic flavours and fragrant honeys, sweets (candies) and toffees. A mail order service is available.

✉ 7 Rue du Porche, 56220 Rochefort-en-Terre ☎ 02 97 43 35 78 🕐 Tue–Fri 9–12, 2.30–6, Sat–Mon2.30–6.30

VANNERIE TY AR MAN

A quaint little shop in one of Rochefort's charming old timbered houses near the castle, crammed to the ceiling with rustic caneware—mainly baskets of all shapes and sizes, but also mats, furnishings, ornaments and similar items.

✉ 6 rue du Château, 56220 Rochefort-en-Terre ☎ 02 97 43 41 64 🕐 All year, though erratic off-season

ST-GILDAS-DE-RHUYS

GOLF DE RHUYS-KERVER

www.formule-golf.com

This standard 18-hole, par-72 golf course has a great location at the heart of a bird sanctuary on the Golfe du Morbihan. It also has 30 practice holes and a putting green.

✉ Domaine de Kerver, 56730 St-Gildas-de-Rhuys ☎ 02 97 45 30 09 🕐 Jul, Aug daily 8–8; rest of year daily 9–dusk 🎫 Apr–end Sep €50, rest of year €35

SAINT-PHILIBERT

LA TRINITAINE

www.latrinitaine.com

There are more than a dozen outlets of this huge food-processing company in Brittany, but this one on the road between Auray and Locmariaquer is one of the biggest, and, being well supplied with parking spaces; is a good place to stock up with provisions or presents. The extensive modern premises stock a vast array of Breton produce, including fresh fruit and vegetables, charcuterie and bakery goods, as well as the trademark biscuits. When you need a break from shopping, there are play and picnic areas and an on-site café. The store also has wheelchair access.

✉ Kerluesse, 56470 Saint-Philibert ☎ 02 97 55 02 04 🕐 Daily 9–12.30, 2–7

LA TRINITÉ-SUR-MER

GALÉRIE PLISSON

www.plisson.com

Brittany's foremost sailing resort makes an ideal location to showcase Philip Plisson's internationally renowned photographs of lighthouses, boats and storms at sea in many formats. Calendars, posters, limited-edition prints, and books of Plisson's works are for sale, and there is an on-site framing service.

✉ Cours des Quais, 56470 La Trinité-sur-Mer ☎ 02 97 30 15 15 🕐 Jul, Aug, school holidays daily 10–12.30, 2.30–7; rest of year Mon–Sat 10.30–12.30, 3–7

VANNES

LE COMPTOIR CELTE

www.comptoir-celte.fr

An attractive shop in the old town, this is a good place to look for typical Breton products, including woodcarvings and ceramics, kitchen utensils, boat models, gourmet fish specialities and music recordings.

✉ 8 rue Saint-Vincent, 56000 Vannes ☎ 02 97 01 05 04 🕐 Mon–Fri 10–12.30, 2–6, Sat 10–7

LA HUCHE À PAINS

A magnificent bakery and cake shop on the market place, established for more than 20 years, selling lots of delicious Breton specialities, including the house *pain d'épices*. It also does a fine range of sandwiches, quiches, pizzas, salads, home-made soup and other snacks, ideal for picnics while you're exploring the old town. Specials include *tulipe des îles* (an almond and chocolate fruit tart).

✉ 23 place des Lices, 56000 Vannes ☎ 02 97 47 23 76 🕐 Mon–Sat 7am–8pm

MONTGOLFIÈRE MORBIHAN

Floating above the Golfe du Morbihan in a hot-air balloon is an entrancing way to see this remarkable section of coast. Flights depart in the early morning and last around an hour, cruising up to about 700m (2,300 ft). The adventure includes inflating and deflating the balloon as well. Each flight takes only four to five passengers (depending on weight!). Minimum height 130cm (4ft 3in); no under-12s or pregnant women.

✉ Lescouëdec, 56890 St-Avé (3km north of Vannes on D126) 🕐 Daily all year, weather permitting 🎫 Adult €310 (€300 each for couples); child (12–16) €240

LA TAPENALGUE

A long-established grocer-deli selling local *chouchen* (mead), *pommeau* (fortified cider), Breton beers and liqueurs and speciality food products (canned sardines, soups, terrines, caramels made with salted butter).

✉ 23 rue des Halles, 56000 Vannes ☎ 02 97 42 69 65 🕐 Daily all year

THÉÂTRE ANNE DE BRETAGNE

www.mairie-vannes.fr/palaisdesarts

This large theatre with varied productions has something to please everyone, with plays, circus acts, ballet, dance, jazz, chansons, classical music and opera. Family tickets are available.

✉ Place de Bretagne, 56019 Vannes ☎ 02 97 01 62 00 🕐 Mon–Sat 8.30pm 🎫 Adult €20–€23, child (under 26) €12

VANOCÉA

www.mairie-vannes.fr

This freeform municipal swimming pool measures some 650sq m (7,000sq ft) and has a huge waterslide, geysers, bubble beds, a diving section and pools for children. The complex also includes a weights room, a fitness studio, solarium and sauna. There's wheelchair access with a submersible chair.

✉ 20 rue Emile Jourdan/Boulevard de Pontivy (N of N165), 56019 Vannes ☎ 02 97 62 68 00 🕐 Daily, but variable; late opening Tue and Fri until 10pm 🎫 Complex tariff structure with lots of special deals

JUNE–SEPTEMBER

ART DANS LES CHAPELLES
PONTIVY AREA

www.artchapelles.com

Around 15 historic chapels in and around Pontivy stage concerts and modern art exhibitions during the summer, including painting, sculpture and photography.

End Jun to mid-Sep (see website for programme and suggested touring routes)

JULY, AUGUST

FESTIVAL PLACE AUX MÔMES
CARNAC

In common with many popular Breton resorts, Carnac makes special efforts for children during the summer holidays. Free open-air entertainment involving puppets, clowns, acrobats, storytellers and singers takes place every Tuesday in high season at 6pm behind the tourist office in Carnac Plage.

Jul, Aug

FESTIVAL SAUMON
PONT-SCORFF

Music, fireworks and salmon-fishing demonstrations are dedicated to the king of the River Scorff. Instructive as well as fun.

Three days in mid-Jul

FÊTE DE LA CRÊPE
GOURIN

www.fetedelacrepe.free.fr

This town is Brittany's largest industrial producer of ready-made pancakes, but during this two-day celebration of the region's most popular fast food, *crêpes* are cooked traditionally on griddles over open fires in the grounds of a local castle, accompanied by Celtic music, dancing, crafts and traditional Breton games. Demonstrations and competitions for the biggest pancake.

Third weekend in Jul Adult €5, under 16 free

Right *Medieval festival in Moncontour*

FÊTES MÉDIÉVALES
HENNEBONT

Hennebont regresses into medieval pageantry at the end of the month with tournaments, troubadours, jugglers and a medieval market.

Last weekend in Jul

GRAND PARDON
STE-ANNE-D'AURAY

Ste-Anne-d'Auray is a major shrine and place of pilgrimage, second only to Lourdes in southwest France. Its late July *pardon* is one of Brittany's largest and most important, typically attended by around 20,000 visitors. St. Anne, mother of the Virgin Mary, is believed by followers to have visited Brittany in 1623, when she appeared to a local ploughman in a vision.

26 Jul

JAZZ À VANNES
VANNES

www.mairie-vannes.fr/jazzavannes

Jazz artists converge on Vannes for a series of open-air concerts in mid-summer.

02 97 01 62 40 Late Jul–early Aug

FESTIVAL INTERCELTIQUE
LORIENT

www.festival-interceltique.com

This is one of the biggest bashes in Brittany, indeed throughout France, attracting crowds of well over half a million people from all over the Celtic fringes of Europe. More than 4,500 performers liven up the port area in time-honoured style with traditional music, dancing, folklore, feasting and fun. Night parties *(festou-noz)* keep things humming until the small hours. Reserve well ahead for accommodation.

8 rue Nayal, 56100 Lorient 02 97 21 24 29 Early to mid-Aug

NUITS MUSICALES DU GOLFE
VANNES

A series of classical concerts arranged in the fine churches around the Golfe du Morbihan, including Elven, Arradon, Theix, Saint-Avé. Get information on bookings at Vannes tourist office.

02 97 47 24 34 2–3 weeks early to mid-Aug

SEPTEMBER

PARDON DES ABOYEUSES
JOSSELIN

The so-called 'Barking Pardon' of Our Lady of the Brambles (Notre-Dame-du-Roncier) in Josselin refers to the curious tale of a beggar woman who came to ask for a drink of water at the well. The village women drove her away with dogs and curses, but immediately their cries turned to dog-like howls as a punishment, for the beggar woman was the Virgin in disguise. Each year at the annual *pardon*, the women of Josselin ask ritual forgiveness for their lack of charity, lest the barking curse take hold.

8 Sep

Above *Al fresco lunchtime at Breizh Caffé in Vannes*

PRICES AND SYMBOLS

The restaurants are listed alphabetically within each town. The prices given for lunch (L) and dinner (D) are for three courses for one person, without drinks. The wine price is for the least expensive bottle.

For a key to the symbols, ▷ 2.

AURAY

LA CLOSERIE DE KERDRAIN

www.lacloseriedekerdrain.com

Top-flight cooking is served in a pretty, white-painted manor house surrounded by gardens. The panelled dining room is furnished in 18th-century style. Chef-patron Fernand Corfmat's signature dishes include chitterling pie with buckwheat pancakes and prawns, and lobster with artichoke and *chorizo*. A wine list features more than 400 vintages. There is a terrace for summer dining.

✉ 20 rue Louis Billet, 56400 Auray ☎ 02 97 56 61 27 ⓘ Closed Mon, Tue lunch; early Jan to mid-Feb L €28, D €65, Wine €23

L'EGLANTINE

Bric-à-brac and historic portraits adorn the snug interior of this attractive salmon-washed period building overlooking the cobbled quayside, where tables are set on sunny days. Widely regarded as the classiest restaurant along the St-Goustan waterfront, L'Eglantine specializes mainly in fish. Try a house bouillabaisse, or a salad of smoked fish à l'orange. Style and service are highly traditional, and the desserts are all home-made.

✉ 17 place St-Sauveur, Port St-Goustan, 56400 Auray ☎ 02 97 56 46 55 ⓘ Thu–Tue 12.15–2.15, 7.15–10 L €17, D €40, Wine €17

BADEN

LE GAVRINIS

www.gavrinis.com

This modern Breton hotel is no great beauty from the outside, but it has attractive gardens and a flower-decked terrace. Inside, the recently renovated dining room is restful and elegant in shades of cream and blue. Menus blend dynamic combinations of local produce and seafood, giving regional specialities a stylish update (for example, sweetbreads with langoustines). The daily *menu du marché* is good value.

✉ 1 rue de l'Ile Gavrinis, Toulbroch, 56870 Baden ☎ 02 97 57 00 82 ⓘ Mid-Jun to mid-Sep daily 12.10–1.30, 7.10–9.30; rest of year Tue–Fri 12.10–1.30, 7.10–9.30, Sat 7.10–9.30, Sun 12.10–1.30 L €23, D €55, Wine €20

BELLE-ÎLE-EN-MER

ROZ-AVEL

Just behind the church in the pretty fishing port of Sauzon, this elegant place is one of the best restaurants on the island. It offers sophisticated fare for adventurous diners (pig's trotters marinated with oysters or spiced crab claws), alongside local lamb or a *panaché de poissons*. There are terrace tables in summer.

✉ Rue du Lieutenant-Riou, 56360 Sauzon ☎ 02 97 31 61 48 ⓘ Thu–Tue 12.15–1.45, 7.15–9.15; closed Wed and mid-Nov to mid-Mar, except Christmas L €26, D €45, Wine €18

CARNAC

AUBERGE LE RATELIER

www.le-ratelier.com

A charming little place in a quiet but central enclave of Carnac Bourg, close to the church and museum. It's an old, creeper-covered house with a welcoming rustic feel. Dishes ring the changes on seafood (scorpion fish in spinach and cider butter sauce, or a terrine of sea trout and

vegetables). Meals start with a surprise *amuse-bouche,* and service couldn't be friendlier. The simple bedrooms here are very good value.
✉ 4 chemin du Douët, 56340 Carnac ☎ 02 97 52 05 04 ⊕ 12–2, 7–9.15 (10 in high season); closed most of Dec and Jan, and Tue–Wed Oct–end Apr ✋ L €27, D €36, Wine €16

LA CÔTE

Close to Carnac's megaliths, this lively, enterprising place caters for hundreds of multilingual visitors, but Pierre Michaud has built up a formidable reputation for his subtly flavoured *grande cuisine de la mer et du terroir,* blending meat and seafood flavours. Outside are large gardens with play areas.
✉ Alignements de Kermario, 56340 Carnac ☎ 02 97 52 02 80 ⊕ Tue–Sun 12.15–2.15, 7.15–9; closed Sat lunch, Sun dinner off-season and Tue lunch Jul and Aug; also Jan and several weeks between Oct and Feb ✋ L €35, D €50, Wine €25

ÎLE DE GROIX

CHEZ PAULE

This little *crêperie* in a fisherman's cottage makes a good-value stop for families, so get here early for a table in high season. Cosily furnished in local style, it has an open fireplace, wooden benches and stone floors. Prices are modest and fillings tempting, making interesting use of local fish such as sardines.
✉ 6 route de Port-Mélite, Le Bourg, 56590 Ile de Groix ☎ 02 97 86 89 72 ⊕ Wed–Mon 12–3, 7–11 (also Tue in school holidays); closed Oct–end Mar ✋ L €10, D €15, Wine €15

JOSSELIN

LA MARINE

True to its name, this waterfront *crêperie* has a blue-and-white nautical theme. Its flower-filled terrace overlooks the château and the river. *Crêpes* reflect the seasons: *L'Automne* has sweet chestnut purée and apple and pear jam; the local speciality, *La Josselinoise,* is filled with black pudding and fried apples. A lunch menu offers non-pancake alternatives.
✉ 8 rue du Canal, Josselin ☎ 02 97 22 21 98 ⊕ Jul, Aug daily 12–2.30, 7–10; Sep–end Jun 12–2, 7–9; closed Mon, Tue lunch, Wed dinner off-season ✋ L €15, D €20, Wine €14

LA TABLE D'O

www.latabledo.com

This bright new venture looks set to raise the stakes in Josselin. It has a stylish contemporary interior decked with wicker chairs and fresh flowers. Dining room and balcony views stretch over the town and river. The lunchtime *formule gourmande* is excellent value. Sample dishes include *carré d'agneau aux herbes* (best end of lamb with herbs) or beef in a foie gras sauce.
✉ 9 rue Glatinier, 56120 Josselin ☎ 02 97 70 61 39 ⊕ Mon–Sat 12–1.15, 7.30–9.15; closed Tue dinner and Wed off-season ✋ L €16, D €38, Wine €14

MALESTROIT

LE CANOTIER

This unpretentious but highly recommendable place on the main square serves a flexible and varied menu with strong leanings towards seafood—red mullet, salmon and scallops. Adventurous meat-eaters might try the foie gras fried with honey, or you can simply choose an omelette without feeling pressured. The ochre dining room with wood panels is comfortable, and in summer you can eat on the terrace.
✉ Place du Dr-Queinnec, 56140 Malestroit ☎ 02 97 75 08 69 ⊕ Tue–Sat 12–2.30, 7.15–9.15, Sun 12–2 ✋ L €15, D €30, Wine €11

PLOEMEUR

LE VIVIER

www.levivier-lomener.com

A glorious setting on a rock overlooking the sea with views towards the Île de Groix makes this family-friendly hotel-restaurant especially appealing. The seafood served here is another reason to track it down on the coastal road about 8km (5 miles) southwest of Lorient. The décor is smartly contemporary with big picture windows. If you insist, you can have a steak, or a *marmite de pigeonneau.* 'Gourmet discovery' portions and high chairs are provided on request for young children.
✉ 9 route de Beg-Er-Vir, Lomener, 56270 Ploemeur ☎ 02 97 82 99 60 ⊕ Jul, Aug daily 12–2.30, 7–10; rest of year Mon–Sat 12–2.30, 7–10, Sun 12–2.30; closed late Dec–early Jan ✋ L €26, D €50, Wine €22

PORT-NAVALO

LE GRAND LARGUE

http://grand-largue.ifrance.com

The smart upper dining room of this nautically styled restaurant is definitely club class, with spectacular waterfront views over the entrance to the Golfe du Morbihan from huge glazed windows. But you can dine steerage in the less expensive cherry-wood cabins of the brasserie and oyster-bar downstairs, where menus suit all pockets. Seafood naturally predominates in many different guises, from spicy lobster to sea bass in balsamic vinegar. One elaborate speciality is *huîtres on gelée d'eau de mer à la chlorophylle d'algue* (oysters in seawater jelly with algae chlorophyll).
✉ 1 rue du Phare, Port-Navalo, 56640 Arzon ☎ 02 97 53 71 58 ⊕ Wed–Sun 12.15–1.45, 7.30–9.45 (also Tue in Jul and Aug) ✋ L €35, D €65, Wine €25

QUESTEMBERT

LE BRETAGNE

http://perso.wanadoo.fr/bretagne

Top chef Georges Paineau and his son-in-law Claude Corlouër cook up a storm of exotic gourmet fare in this traditional little market town. The creeper-covered corner-site building may look like a classic provincial auberge from outside, but there's nothing conventional about the shocking pink dining room decked with mine host's modern artworks. Tranquil garden views aid digestion, and the on-site hotel rooms are splendidly luxurious.
✉ 13 rue St-Michel, 56230 Questembert ☎ 02 97 26 11 12 ⊕ 12.15–2.15, 7.15–9.15; closed Sun dinner, Tue lunch Oct–Apr, and Mon all year, also 3 weeks in Jan ✋ L €50, D €120, Wine €25

QUIBERON

LA CRIÉE

If you're tired of over-elaborate food, you couldn't find anything more delicious or straightforward than Michel Lucas's superb fresh seafood direct from the fish market opposite his acclaimed restaurant on Quiberon harbour. You'll be served the catch of the day (on display at the adjacent *poissonnerie),* so no menus or prices are printed. Products from the chef's highly regarded smokery just up the road are also worth trying (▷ 68).

✉ 11 quai de l'Océan, Port-Maria, 56170 Quiberon ☎ 02 97 30 53 09 🕐 12.15–2, 7.15–9.30; closed Sun eve, Mon (lunch only Jul and Aug), first half of Dec and Jan 🖐 L €16, D €16, Wine €12

LA ROCHE-BERNARD

L'AUBERGE BRETONNE

www.thorel.fr

The reputation of Solange and Jacques Thorel's exquisite Relais & Châteaux restaurant-with-rooms extends far beyond Morbihan's boundaries. It serves highly accomplished and ambitious cooking in an elegant, arty setting of sculptures, paintings and fountains. Needless to say, it isn't cheap, but the set menus at lunchtime make it worth reserving ahead for an outstanding treat. Try a *tourte de canard* (duck pie) or *baba à la mirabelle* (rum baba with plums). The hosts are kind and welcoming, and the bedrooms stunning.

✉ 2 place Duguesclin, 56130 La Roche-Bernard ☎ 02 99 90 60 28 🕐 12–1.30, 7.30–9.30; closed lunch Mon, Tue and Fri, all day Thu; mid-Nov to Christmas and 3 weeks in Jan 🖐 L €35, D €110, Wine €50

LE P'TIT MARIN

This pretty *crêperie-moulerie* is sandwiched in a row of eateries down by the waterfront. Its terrace is filled with tables in summer, but otherwise you eat upstairs in an attractive little dining room. Inventive *crêpes* place an emphasis on seafood, including oysters. A Cockpit contains scallops, and a Grande-Voile contains mussels, prawns and crab. A children's menu is available.

✉ Quai de la Douane, 56130 La Roche-Bernard ☎ 02 99 90 79 41 🕐 Daily 12–2, 7–9.30 🖐 L €15, D €15, Wine €12

LA-TRINITÉ-SUR-MER

LE BISTRO DU MARIN

www.hotel-ostrea.com

The enterprising seafood brasserie attached to a shipshape little Logis de France hotel caters mainly for the marina-users of this popular sailing resort. The bar is open all day every day from early breakfasts until late at night. Admire your yacht (or somebody else's) from the stylish glazed upper deck or terrace. Menus are sensibly priced, and there are weekday *plats du jour* and *formules,* multifarious ice creams and fresh camembert. Specialities include *carpaccio de saumon* (thinly sliced salmon) and *choucroute de la mer* (seafood sauerkraut). The style is casually smart, and the atmosphere constantly buzzing. Downstairs, under the same management, is a good pizzeria.

✉ Cours des Quais, 56470 La-Trinité-sur-Mer ☎ 02 97 55 73 23 🕐 Daily 12–2.30, 7–9.30 (later on Sat and in high season); reduced hours off-season 🖐 L €19, D €34, Wine €12

VANNES

BREIZH CAFFÉ

Hemmed in by similarly antique buildings in one of Vannes' oldest and quaintest streets, this fine brasserie is ideal for a quick lunch while sightseeing, though food is not served all day. Within the ancient stone-and-timber architecture, the interior is cool and contemporary with bold splashes of primary colour. Besides a traditional menu of regional dishes, but there's also a simple lunchtime *formule* including a main course, a cake and a hot drink, and a child menu too. À la carte selections include *moules* in lots of ways, and *assiettes composées* (cold cuts and salads). For pudding, try the house Mamich butter cake with apples, the iced nougat with raspberry sauce or a whole crottin de Chavignol goat's cheese.

✉ 13 rue des Halles, 56000 Vannes ☎ 02 97 54 37 41 🕐 Daily 12–2, 7–10 🖐 L €15, D €25, Wine €16

ROSCANVEC

A door or two away from the Breizh Caffé, this beamy old property is one of Vannes' most reputable and consistent restaurants. The talented chef-patron serves ambitious and expensive fare, reflecting whatever's best in the nearby marketplace. You might sample the boned oxtail, or turbot in honey crust. The main dining room is upstairs, though you can see what's cooking at street level. It is not too grand to provide high chairs.

✉ 17 rue des Halles, 56000 Vannes ☎ 02 97 47 15 96 🕐 Tue–Sat 12.15–1.30, 7.15–9.30 🖐 L €24, D €49, Wine €17

Left *L'Eglantine restaurant at Auray*

Above *Les Ajoncs d'Or at Carnac*

PRICES AND SYMBOLS

Prices quoted are the range for a double with private facilities. The *taxe de séjour* (▷ 214) is not included. Unless otherwise stated, breakfast is excluded from the price.

For a key to the symbols, ▷ 2.

ARRADON

LES VÉNÈTES

www.lesvenetes.com

The wonderful waterfront location is the magic factor at this stylish modern hotel. Inside the chic, glazed restaurant you could be on an ocean liner, and definitely enjoying the exclusivity at the captain's table in elegant blue-and-white surroundings furnished in teak. The panoramic views over the Golfe du Morbihan from all the stylish bedrooms are equally sublime (some rooms have the added benefit of private terraces). Luxury bathrooms with corner baths are the norm. Half-board terms are available; breakfast can be served in your room at no extra charge.

✉ La Pointe, 56610 Arradon ☎ 02 97 44 85 85 Closed 2 weeks in mid-Jan €90–€220 (breakfast €10) 10, including 2 suites

AURAY

LE MARIN

www.hotel-lemarin.com

A beguiling little bed-and-breakfast quietly placed just a few paces back from Auray's historic quayside at Saint-Goustan. Its jaunty nautical style and contemporary fittings combine well within the confines of a beamy old property. Some of its neat little bedrooms enjoy river views, and a couple have bunk beds suitable for families with children. There's no restaurant (just a convivial ground-floor bar-lounge reserved for hotel guests), but half a dozen eateries lie within a minute's walk along the waterfront.

✉ 1 place du Rolland, port de Saint-Goustan, 56400 Auray ☎ 02 97 24 14 58 Closed Jan to mid-Feb €55–€80 (breakfast €7) 12, all non-smoking

BELLE-ÎLE-EN-MER

LA DESIRADE

www.hotel-la-desirade.com

Local island architecture is evoked in this delightful, village-like complex of low-rise, shuttered buildings built around a swimming pool in flower-filled gardens. The owner-chef's seafood-based cooking is much praised. Enjoy breakfast on the pool terrace or by the fireside, depending on the weather. Reserve well ahead, as many regulars return each season. Bicycle or car rental can be arranged, along with picnic hampers for days out exploring the island. There are facilities for children, and easy access for visitors with reduced mobility.

✉ Le Petit Cosquet, 56360 Bangor, Belle-Île-en-Mer ☎ 02 97 31 70 70 Closed Nov to mid-Mar, except Christmas and New Year €122–€137 (breakfast €14.50); half-board terms only in high season 32, including 4 suites Outdoor

BILLIERS

DOMAINE DE ROCHEVILAINE

www.domainerochevilaine.com

This super-luxurious Relais & Châteaux hotel complex of converted coastguard buildings enjoys ravishing views over a rocky peninsula. A 13th-century stone gateway leads to terraced gardens surrounded by several separate buildings housing a sybaritic spa and fitness studio, a beautiful restaurant with picture windows, and a mix of individually designed but palatial bedrooms, most with private

terraces. It even has its own art gallery. Thalassotherapy and beauty treatments attract a well-heeled and glamorous clientele (there are lots of special spa breaks available throughout the year). Furnishings are a mix of Breton antiques and high-quality modern classics. In the restaurant, the food and service are formal but outstanding.
Pointe de Pen-Lan, 56190 Billiers 02 97 41 61 61 €141–€690 (breakfast €19; €12 for children under 10) 39, including 4 suites Heated outdoor seawater; indoor spa with hot tub and sauna

CARNAC

HOSTELLERIE LES AJONCS D'OR

www.lesajoncsdor.com
Watch for the signs to Kerbachique just off the Plouharnel road (D781) northwest of Carnac, and you'll soon find this charming stone-built farmhouse with country furnishings. If you have your own transport, it makes a lovely rural retreat, ideal for exploring the megaliths, or nipping off to the beaches of Quiberon and Belle-Île. The large, shady gardens add to its air of seclusion. It offers good regional cooking; half-board terms are obligatory in high season.
Kerbachique–route de Plouharnel, 56340 Carnac 02 97 52 32 02 Closed mid-Oct to late Mar €60–€83 (breakfast €8.50) 16

JOSSELIN

HÔTEL DU CHÂTEAU

www.hotel-chateau.com
A panoramic outlook towards the castle ramparts gives this efficient and welcoming Logis hotel its name—reserve ahead to make sure of a room with a view if you can, though if one is free, you may well be allocated one without asking. The spacious, highly traditional dining room shares the scene through its large picture windows. Interesting items of weaponry deck the panelled walls. Bedrooms are decorated in a mix of florals and pastels. Some cheaper rooms without full bathrooms are available. Staff speak good English and are friendly and helpful.
1 rue Général de Gaulle, 56120 Josselin 02 97 22 20 11 Closed 1 week in Nov, 1 week in Dec, 3 weeks in Feb, Sun eve and Mon in winter (restaurant also closed Fri eve off-season) €58–€75.50 (breakfast €7.50) 36

LARMOR-BADEN

AUBERGE DU PARC FÉTAN

www.hotel-parcfetan.com
This exceptionally welcoming and dynamically managed venture is on the road leading to Larmor-Baden's tiny port, with glimpses of sea from some rooms. A cluster of very attractively designed chalet-style apartments for two to five people stands around the heated pool in the hotel grounds. These have kitchenettes, and two are suitable for visitors with disabilities. Tasty, simple menus and half-board terms are available.
17 rue de Berder, 56870 Larmor-Baden 02 97 57 04 38 €45–€120 (breakfast €8) 20, plus 14 apartments Outdoor (heated Apr–end Sep)

LOCMARIAQUER

HÔTEL DES TROIS FONTAINES

www.hotel-troisfontaines.com
Situated very close to Locmariaquer's impressive prehistoric antiquities, this hotel has all the advantages of thoughtful contemporary design. The interestingly curved block is set back from the road near the entrance to the village, and stands in tidy gardens with some pretty shrubs and flower beds. The spacious interior has an airy, uncluttered feel; the soundproofed, cabin-style bedrooms are simply furnished but tasteful with plain walls, light colour schemes throughout and laminate flooring. Some of the bedrooms have fine sea views.
Route d'Auray, 56740 Locmariaquer 02 97 57 42 70 Closed Nov to early Feb (except Christmas and New Year) €72–€130 (breakfast €11) 18

PLOERMEL

LE COBH

www.hotel-lecobh.com

The colour-coded décor of this central Logis near the church evokes the Arthurian medievalism of nearby Brocéliande. Fixtures and fittings, however, are as practical and well designed as visitors could wish. The welcome is courteous and the service cheerful. Honest, unpretentious cooking is served in two relaxing dining rooms, and there's a lounge bar with an open fireplace. There is some disabled access and facilities for children.

10 rue des Forges, 56800 Ploërmel 02 97 74 00 49 All year €63–€108 (breakfast €8.50) 12, including 6 suites

PONTIVY

LE ROHAN

www.hotelpontivy.com

This smart, comfortable hotel with good facilities, occupies a late 19th century period building of some distinction in the Napoleonic quarter. Décor is upbeat and contemporary with wicker furnishings and bold, modern colours. Bedrooms are individually designed in various themes (oriental, cinema, jazz and so on), and some are geared towards honeymooners. There's a small courtyard garden set with tables, where breakfast is served in summer. The old town is within easy walking distance. Free WiFi connection is provided.

90 rue Nationale, 56300 Pontivy 02 97 25 02 01 All year €71–€98 (breakfast €10.50) 15, including 1 suite

QUIBERON

LE NEPTUNE

Close to the *criée* and the *gare maritime* in lively Port-Maria, this typical Logis hotel (owned by the same family for more than 50 years) couldn't be handier for an early-morning getaway to Belle-Île. It's very friendly and well managed, representing excellent value in an oversubscribed location. All bedrooms have both bath and shower, and are surprisingly well finished. A dozen have balconies overlooking the port, but you may prefer to trade sea views for a quieter rear room. Seafood cooking prevails in the restaurant.

4 quai de Houat, Port-Maria, 56170 Quiberon 02 97 50 09 62 Closed early Jan to mid-Feb €59–€79 (breakfast €8) 21

LA ROCHE-BERNARD

AUBERGE DES DEUX MAGOTS

www.auberge-les2magots.com

Three adjoining period houses at the heart of this historic little town create a charming picture on a quaint square, where steep steps plunge to the riverbank. In essence it's a simple, family-run restaurant-with-rooms (expect some interesting and delicious regional cooking from Joël Morice), but the bedrooms are as good value as the food. A mystery bird hidden in a covered cage may fool you with a cheery *Bonjour* at breakfast time.

1 place du Bouffay, 56130 La Roche-Bernard 02 99 90 60 75 Closed late Dec to mid-Jan; also late Jun and early Nov; Sun eve and Mon off-season (restaurant and hotel reception closed Sun eve and Mon in low season) €45–€75 (breakfast €7) 15

ROCHEFORT-EN-TERRE

CHÂTEAU DE TALHOUËT

www.chateaudetalhouet.com

At the end of a long bumpy private drive off the Malestroit road (D774), this romantic Breton manor founded by a crusader family promises a highly superior *chambre d'hôte* experience. Set in a 20ha (49-acre) park, the handsome stone building dates from the 16th century, and has been beautifully and lovingly restored by its present owner Jean-Pol Soulaine. The beautifully furnished interior is full of antiques, books, Persian rugs and plush sofas; bedrooms are on a suitably grand scale, and so too are exquisite dinners (available by prior arrangement).

56220 Rochefort-en-Terre 02 97 43 34 72 Closed most of Jan and late Nov €135–€220, including breakfast 8

SARZEAU

LE MUR DU ROY

www.lemurduroy.com

Take a sea-view room at this isolated little hotel on the quiet southern shores of the Rhuys peninsula, and watch the sun rise like Aphrodite from the waves. It's a modestly designed, sand-coloured modern building, stylish and tastefully furnished inside, with a sea-facing garden and terrace. The owners are exceptionally welcoming and obliging over any reasonable request. Cooking is dazzlingly accomplished, both at dinner and breakfast. Bedrooms are fairly small and unassuming, but assure absolute peace. Half-board terms are available.

Penvins, 56370 Sarzeau 02 97 67 34 08 Closed mid-Dec to mid-Jan €57–€86 (breakfast €10) 10

VANNES

LA VILLA KERASY

www.villakerasy.com

In a quiet corner of the city not far from the railway station, this period villa is shielded from city bustle by tranquil Japanese gardens. Decorated in flamboyant, individual styles recalling the city's former trading links with the Orient, each of the bedrooms in this quiet villa is named after a port along the spice route (Cadiz, Madras, Pondicherry). Service is personal and attentive. Sophisticated business facilities include multi-channel LCD TV and wireless internet access. The breakfasts are excellent. Expansion plans include more bedrooms and an Ayurvedic spa.

20 avenue Favrel et Lincy, 56000 Vannes 02 97 68 36 83 Closed Nov–end Mar €97–€190 (breakfast €13) 12

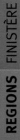

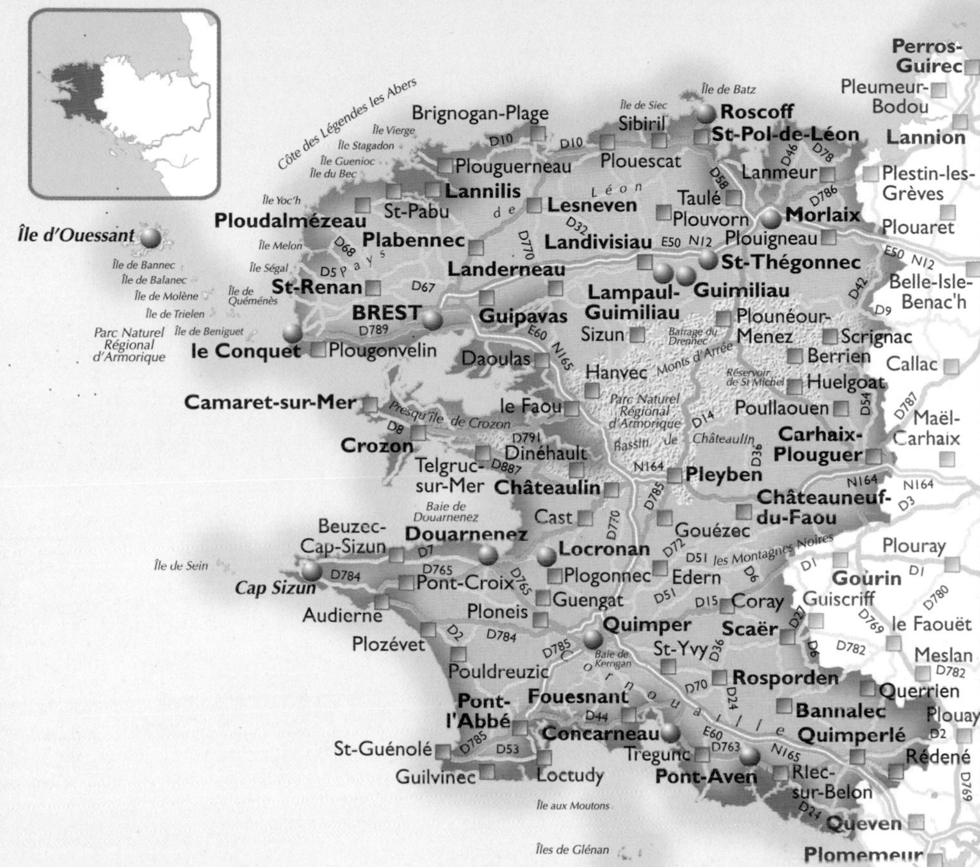

FINISTÈRE

Brittany's Land's End embodies the region's undiluted Celtic essence. This is where you are most likely to hear the Breton language spoken and traditional music played, or see *coiffes* and costumes worn at folk festivals or *pardons*. Farthest geographically from the rest of France, Finistère remained relatively isolated until only recently, looking to its Celtic cousins in Britain and Ireland for trading and cultural links. In rural areas with devoutly Catholic inhabitants, churches and parish closes still serve their original pious purposes. Yet Finistère is also a place of legend and superstition, the lost land of Lyonesse where Arthurian and Wagnerian myths swirl through the mists.

Finistère's wild Atlantic seaboard is scattered with reefs and islands; elsewhere the coastline is peppered with sandy beaches, bustling resorts, and hardworking fishing communities. The fertile parts of the interior are intensively farmed, a mosaic of carefully tended artichokes and brassicas. Linking Armor and Argoat (sea and land) is the Armorique natural park, a diverse habitat of ocean, hills, moorland and forest.

To avoid summer crowds, you could take a boat-trip to the peaceful islands of Ouessant and Batz, or even quieter Sein and Molène. Explore the rugged uplands of the Monts d'Arrée and the Montagnes Noires. Track down the remnants of Brittany's ancient woodland around Huelgoat, or drive around the shimmering tidal inlets of the remote Côte des Abers.

Finistère's largest settlements, Brest and Quimper, could hardly seem more different: one industrial, maritime and largely post-war, the other flower-decked and full of quaint Breton charm. But many smaller towns are just as distinctive and memorable: feisty Roscoff, home-port of Brittany Ferries and the Onion Johnnies; arty Pont-Aven, proud of its Gauguin associations and its local biscuits; lively Concarneau clustered round its attractive *ville close* (walled old town) and modern *criée* (fish auction); and the ancient port of Morlaix overshadowed by its viaduct and timbered buildings.

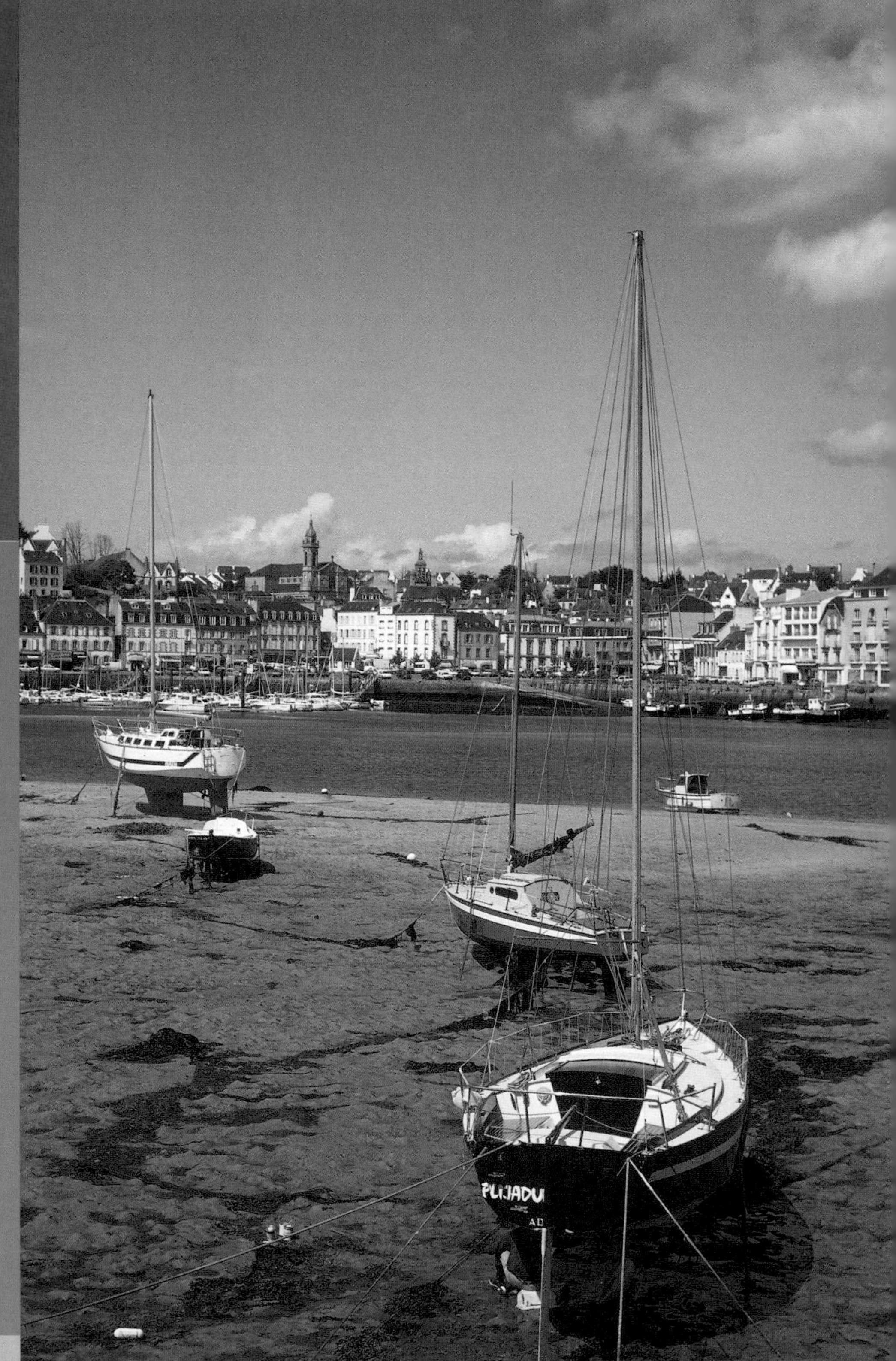

AUDIERNE

www.audierne-tourisme.com

This remote corner of Brittany is less crowded in summer than some areas, but Audierne stays active all year round. Its former prosperity is derived from tuna-fishing, and it still has a sizeable seine-netting fleet (bream, sea-bass, monkfish), but its main source of revenue comes from shellfish. Traditional Breton houses line the waterfront and rise in tiers to an upper town of narrow streets and quaint shops. The baroque belfry of 17th-century Église St-Raymond-Nonnat dominates the upper town, its exterior decorated with ship carvings. The large beach at Sainte-Evette southwest of town is one of Audierne's main assets, with a marina, water sports and the pier from which excursion boats shuttle to the Île de Sein in summer. An unexpectedly engrossing maritime attraction called Aquashow (tel 02 98 70 03 03; www.aquarium.fr; Apr–end Sep daily 10–7; Oct–end Mar, school holidays Sun–Thu 2–5; closed Jan; adult €12.80, child 4–14 €6.80) overlooks the estuary at the north end of town, showcasing the sealife of Brittany. It has an appealing café with a waterfront terrace.

228 C10 | 8 rue Victor-Hugo, 29770 Audierne | 02 98 70 12 20 | Jul, Aug Mon–Sat 9–12.30, 2–7; Sep–end Jun Mon–Sat 9–12, 3–7 | Penn-ar-Bed trips from Sainte-Evette pier to the Île de Sein take about an hour (tel 02 98 70 70 70)

BEG-MEIL

www.ot-fouesnant.fr

www.fouesnant-tourisme.com

Unspoiled pine-fringed beaches are the chief appeal of this sleepy little seaside resort: Its huge expanses of pale soft sand are ideal for families with small children. Beg-Meil's setting on a headland jutting into Concarneau bay gives it tranquil views across shimmering seas towards the Îles de Glénan and the Baie de la Forêt. Not much happens apart from fishing and a few watersports. The catch of the day is sold from a kiosk by the tourist office every evening, but you can try your luck at *pêche-à-pied* for crabs and prawns at low tide. Footpaths follow the coastline along dune-belts. Cap Coz to the north has more idyllic sheltered beaches, while the more remote south-facing beaches beyond the Pointe du Mousterlin are popular with naturists.

229 D11 | La Cale (by the port) | 02 98 94 97 47 | Mid-Jun to mid-Sep only Mon–Sat 9.30–12.30, 3–7, Sun 10.30–12.30 | Boat excursions to the Îles de Glénan, up the Odet estuary, and a summer ferry service to Concarneau

BÉLON

www.riecsurbelon.fr

www.moelan-sur-mer.fr

Bélon is all about oysters, raised here in prodigious quantities on the tidal mud-flats. This complex, estuary of labyrinthine creeks and lanes is tricky to explore by road. The best way to get an idea of these scattered villages and minuscule harbours half concealed in low-lying, wooded banks is to take a boat trip from Port de Bélon or Pont-Aven. The main communities are Riec-sur-Bélon and Moëlan-sur-Mer, both some distance from the waterfront, but most of the oyster-beds (some can be visited for guided tours and tastings) lie around the Port de Bélon, which spans both banks. A small, ruined fort guards the estuary where it meets the River Aven at the Pointe de Penquernéo. Excellent walks follow both banks of the river.

229 E11 | 2 rue des Gentilshommes, 29340 Riec-sur-Belon | 02 98 06 97 65 | Jul, Aug Mon–Sat 9.30–12.30, 2.30–7, Sun, holidays 10–12.30; Sep–end Jun, Mon, Tue, Thu, Fri 9.30–12, 2–5 (also Sat 10–12 Apr–end Jun, Sep) | Place de l'Église, 29350 Moëlan-sur-Mer | 02 98 39 67 28 | Jul, Aug Mon–Sat 9.30–12.30, 2–7, Sun 10.30–12.30; reduced hours rest of year | Vedettes Aven-Bélon river trips Jul and Aug (from east bank; summer ferry service across the river at Port de Bélon)

BÉNODET

www.benodet.fr

The Odet estuary is one of the most beautiful in Brittany, and Bénodet takes full advantage of its fine natural setting near the mouth of the sparkling river. Half-hidden châteaux peep from steep, thickly wooded banks, where herons and kingfishers search for prey. Though still small, Bénodet is one of the region's leading resorts, always packed with families and sailing enthusiasts in summer. Amenities are excellent, from water sports and seaside activities for children, to a wide choice of boat cruises (▷ 94). La Mer Blanche, a large lagoon enclosed by a long sandbar stretching west of the Pointe de Mousterlin, provides an additional water playground.

229 D11 | 29 avenue de la Mer, 29950 Bénodet | 02 98 57 00 14 | Mid-Jun to mid-Sep Mon–Sat 9–7, Sun 10–6; Apr–end Jun, mid–end Sep 9–12, 1.30–6; rest of year Mon–Sat 9.30–12, 2–5 | Boat trips up the Odet estuary to Quimper, and to Loctudy and the Îles de Glénan | Bicycle rental from Cycletty, 5 avenue de la Mer, tel 02 98 57 12 49

Right *The waters of the wooded estuary at Beg-Meil*

Opposite *Sailing boats beached on the shore at Audierne*

BR 300062

BREST

INTRODUCTION

At first sight, Brest isn't one of Brittany's most obvious tourist attractions. Its massive and costly post-war refit has left much of it tidy but unenticing in the way of many modern cities, and little beyond the waterfront repays exploration. But if you brave its relentless traffic and dispiriting industrial suburbs, you'll find some lively nightlife, good shops and worthwhile sights, notably the impressive aquarium. The port is the heart of the city, always throbbing with life. Its setting on one of the most beautiful bays in France gives views across the busy natural harbour of a constantly changing panorama of passing shipping—a harbour cruise is highly recommended. One of the liveliest central streets is the rue de Siam, named after a delegation of Siamese ambassadors bearing gifts to the court of Louis XIV in 1686. It has many shops and restaurants, and seven modern fountains in sleek black granite. The outlying St-Martin quarter to the northeast of the city survived most of the bombing and gives some idea of Brest's pre-war appearance. It is now a raffish, studenty quarter of mainly pubs and clubs.

Brest is one of France's largest cities and has been a significant settlement since Roman times. Its natural deep-water port, protected by the Presqu'île de Crozon, has long been home to a large naval base, now second in France after Toulon. As its role was primarily defensive, Brest missed out on the boom years of privateering and colonial trading that enriched many other Breton ports, and its economy remains troubled even today, especially since the decline of the shipbuilding industry. It is still a world-class marine repair base, and is gradually establishing a new wave of high-tech and service industries. Much of Brest's older architecture was destroyed during World War II, when it was an important German U-boat base. It suffered ferocious attacks both from the Allies attempting to forestall submarine assaults on transatlantic convoys, and from the retreating Germans, who blew up as many of the port installations as they could. The city was hastily rebuilt in a block, functional grid of angular boulevards and draughty plazas lined with high-rise slabs, although efforts have been made to soften the buildings with parks and gardens.

INFORMATION

www.marie-brest.fr
www.brest-metropole-tourisme.fr
228 C8 Place de la Liberté, 29200 Brest 02 98 44 24 96 Jul, Aug Mon–Sat 9.30–7, Sun, holidays 10–12; Sep–end Jun Mon–Sat 9.30–12.30, 2–6 The inner-city bus system (Bibus) is well organized with flat-fare tickets; out-of-town routes serve many west Breton destinations (Crozon, Roscoff, Le Conquet, Brignogan-Plage); regular CAT service to Quimper Brest is a major Breton rail terminal, linked to Paris by a high-speed TGV service (4hr 20min), and to many other Breton towns (Landerneau, Morlaix, Lannion, St-Brieuc, Quimper) Ferry links to the Crozon peninsula (Le Fret/Camaret); harbour trips from the Port du Commerce (near castle), or Port de Plaisance du Moulin Blanc (near Océanopolis) Brest airport, tel 02 98 32 01 00, is 11km (7 miles) east of town

Opposite *Brest's busy harbour*
Below *Inside the Océanopolis aquarium*

TIPS

» From the Port de Commerce or Moulin Blanc near Océanopolis, take a boat trip and get some idea of the scale of this magnificent natural harbour.

» EU/NATO state citizens can take a guided tour of the naval base by the castle (Jun–end Sep; you'll need some ID).

» Free shows and concerts are held at the port on Thursday evenings in July and August (Les Jeudis du Port), and the waterfront is always lively with bars and restaurants.

» A walk along the cours Dajot promenade near the castle gives an excellent overview of the dockyards and the Rade de Brest.

» Brest hosts a huge worldwide gathering of traditional sailing vessels such as tall ships every four years—the next will be in mid-July 2012.

» Brest is easy to reach by public transport if you don't want the strain of driving.

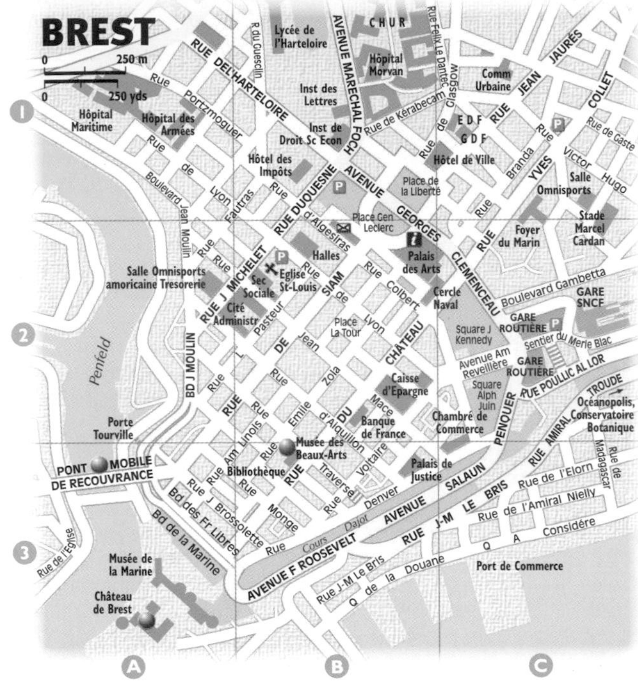

Below right *The Pont de Recouvrance*
Below *Brest Marina*

WHAT TO SEE

OCÉANOPOLIS

www.oceanopolis.com

Brest's most high-profile visitor attraction lies on the waterfront some way east of the commercial docks. Océanopolis is a vast and ambitiously presented aquarium with a serious engagement in scientific research and conservation, based on all aspects of life in the oceans. You could easily spend all day here; arrive early to beat the crowds and make the most of it. More than 10,000 marine creatures live in aquariums as large as 1 million litres (220,000 gallons). The park is divided into three sections—Polar, Tropical and Temperate—and contents cover everything from seaweeds and ocean currents to marine pollution and global warming.

84 C2 ✉ Port de Plaisance du Moulin Blanc ☎ 02 98 34 40 40 ⌚ Jul, Aug daily 9–7; Apr–end Jun daily 9–6; Sep–end Mar Tue–Sat 10–5, Sun, holidays 10–6 (also open Mon during French school holidays) Adult €15.80, child 4–17 €11, family tickets available; free access to shops and restaurant 🚌 Lines 3 or 15 from city centre

CHÂTEAU DE BREST

www.musee-marine.fr

At the mouth of the River Penfeld right by the docks, the castle miraculously escaped the bombs. Its foundations are ancient, and the 14th-century chronicler Froissart declared it one of the largest fortresses in the world. The castle houses the naval headquarters and the Musée de la Marine (Maritime Museum). One memorable exhibit is a German pocket submarine from World War II.

84 A3 Le Port (between Pont de Recouvrance and cours Dajot) 02 98 22 12 39 Apr–end Sep daily 10–6.30; Oct–end Mar daily 1.30–6.30; closed Jan Adult €5, student €3.50, under 18 free Guided tours available for groups on request

MUSÉE DES BEAUX ARTS

Brest's Fine Arts Museum is noted for its extensive collection of works from the Pont-Aven Symbolist school, including works by Paul Sérusier and Emile Bernard. One of the most eye-catching paintings is Kneipp's trompe l'oeil cow, whose real horns protrude in 3D from the canvas.

84 B3 24 rue Traverse 02 98 00 87 96 Tue–Sat and Mon 10–12, 2–6, Sun 2–6 Adult €4, under 18 free (free entrance first Sun of month)

CONSERVATOIRE BOTANIQUE

Conservation is the watchword at this fine botanical garden not far from Océanopolis. In beautifully kept grounds covering more than 20 hectares (54 acres) of a deep valley, rare and endangered species abound. A stream runs through it, feeding a chain of ponds and water features.

84 C2 52 Allée du Bot 02 98 41 88 95 Garden daily 9–6 (8 in summer), free; information point Jul to mid-Sep Sun–Thu 2–5.30; mid-Sep to end Jun Sun, Wed 2–4.30; greenhouses Jul to mid-Sep Sun–Thu 2–5.30; mid-Sep to end Jun by guided tour every Sun at 4.30 Bibus No. 3, 17, 25, 27 (Palaren stop) Head towards the airport from city centre (D712), take D233 towards Quimper at place de Strasbourg, and watch for signs on your left

MORE TO SEE

PONT DE RECOUVRANCE AND TOUR TANGUY

This huge lift-bridge is said to be the highest in Europe. The small history museum inside contains photographs, paintings and vivid dioramas showing what Brest looked like before the bombs fell.

84 A3 02 98 00 88 60 Jun–end Sep daily 10–12, 2–7; Oct–end May Wed, Thu 2–5, Sat, Sun 2–6; daily 2–6 during school holidays

Above *A view of the harbour at Brest*
Below *Océanopolis is a concrete-and-glass structure built in the form of a crab*

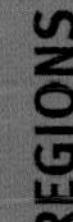

BRIGNOGAN-PLAGE

www.ot-brignogan-plage.fr

This popular resort on a horseshoe bay occupies a particularly attractive port of Brittany's northern coastline. Its eight linked coves of golden sand are scattered with eroded granite boulders, rather like those on the Côte du Granit Rose (Pink Granite Coast, ▷ 130–131) but less brilliantly tinted. The plage de Ménéham an enticing beach, 2km (1 mile) west of the village. Nearby is the Menhir Marz, an 8m (25ft) standing stone topped by a small stone cross. The church of Goulven to the southeast is a fine example of Finistère's Flamboyant Gothic architecture, dating from the 15th century. A small visitor facility called La Maison des Dunes on the Plouescat road reveals the rich flora and fauna of the Keremma shoreline, now a protected site (tel 02 98 61 69 69; www.maisondesdunes.org; Jul, Aug daily 10.30–6; Sep–end Jun Mon–Fri 2.30–5.30; escorted bird-watching and nature walks on Sun, horse-riding Jul and Aug).

223 D7 · 7 avenue Général de Gaulle, 29890 Brignogan-Plage · 02 98 83 41 08 · Jul, Aug Mon 11–1, 4–7, Tue–Sat 9.30–1.30, 4–7, Sun, holidays 10–1; Sep–end Jun Tue–Fri 10.30–12.30, Sat 10.30–12.30, 1.30–4

CAMARET-SUR-MER

www.camaret-sur-mer.com

Once a leading fishing port, Camaret has reinvented itself as a sailing and beach resort. The forlorn wrecks of abandoned fishing vessels decaying picturesquely in the harbour bear witness to the decline of its prime industry, but visitors throng its quaysides in summer. It's an attractive little place, a popular haunt of the Impressionist painter Eugène Boudin in the mid-19th century, and still something of an artists' enclave with many galleries and craft studios. The Maison du Patrimoine (tel 02 98 27 82 60; mid-Jun to mid-Sep daily 2–6; mid-Sep to mid-Jun Mon–Fri 2–5), a small maritime museum sharing premises with the tourist office, contains displays on boatbuilding and photographs of Camaret's old *sardinieres* (sardine boats). Beaches flank both sides of the harbour, which is protected by a natural shingle jetty called Le Sillon.

At the far end of Le Sillon stands the quaint 17th-century chapel of Notre-Dame-de-Rocamadour, a pilgrim site dedicated to the seafarers of Camaret. Part of the belfry was destroyed by an English cannonball in 1694. Next to the chapel is a diminutive, Vauban fort, La Tour Dorée, dating from 1689. It contains a modest museum (tel 02 98 65 00 12; mid-Jun to mid-Sep daily 10–12, 2–6; joint entrance ticket with Maison du Patrimoine) dedicated to its military architect. Summer boat trips take visitors on fishing expeditions, or to the Tas de Pois (Pile of Peas) sea stacks off the Pointe de Pen-Hir. Camaret makes a fine base from which to explore the sensational coastal scenery of the Crozon peninsula (▷ 110–113).

Just west of town beyond the striking Pointe du Toulinguet are about 40 stumpy megaliths known as the Alignements de Lagatjar (freely accessible).

222 B9 · 15 quai Kléber, 29570 Camaret-sur-Mer · 02 98 27 93 60 · Jul, Aug Mon–Sat 9–7, Sun 10–1; Jun, Sep Mon–Fri 9–12, 2–6; (5 off-season) · Seasonal ferries from Camaret to the islands of Sein and Ouessant, and to Brest

CARANTEC

www.ville-carantec.com
www.carantec-tourisme.com

This exclusive little resort stands on a headland jutting into Morlaix bay, and is best enjoyed from coastal vantage points such as the Chaise du Curé (Priest's Chair)—a clifftop rock formation. It is set amid pines and secluded coves. A tidal causeway connects Carantec with the Île Callot, reachable on foot at low water. A *pardon* and Blessing of the Sea take place in the Notre-Dame chapel here on the Sunday after 15 August. The Musée Maritime contains a modest exhibition of vintage sailing boats and displays on oyster-farming and *corsairs*, plus material on local Resistance activity during World War II (Jul, Aug Fri–Wed 10–12, 3–6; Easter holidays, late Jun, early Sep 3–6; closed Thu, Sun am). The island fortress in the bay is the Château du Taureau, built to guard Morlaix from incursions by English raiders, and used as a prison during the reign of Louis XIV (tel 02 98 62 29 73; tickets from the plage du Kelenn; adult €13, child (4–12) €6; visiting hours subject to tides; reserve ahead).

223 E7 · 4 rue Pasteur, 29660 Carantec · 02 98 67 00 43 · Jul, Aug Mon–Sat 9.30–7, Sun 9.30–12; reduced hours rest of year

CAP SIZUN

This rugged peninsula of southeastern Finistère forges due west into the Atlantic surf that crashes on its headlands. It ends in a tumble of boulders at Pointe du Raz (▷ 101), an unforgettable sight in a gale. Though this falls short of being Brittany's most westerly point by a narrow margin, it makes a fitting candidate for France's true *finis terra*—the end of the world—as indeed it was for the early Celts who inhabited the area; they believed that from here lay the route to the afterlife.

Other coastal highlights on the western cape include the Baie des Trépassés (Bay of the Dead), where currents wash up the corpses of shipwrecked mariners on its exposed beach. On a clear day, you can usually see the Île de Sein from here, just above the waterline. North of the bay lies the desolate, treeless Pointe du Van, less crowded in high season in the Pointe du Raz, and reachable only on foot across heathland. From these cliffs, magnificent views extend all around the cape.

EXPLORING THE NORTH COAST

The most impressive scenery lies to the north, and the best way to appreciate it is to walk along the coastal path west of Douarnenez. But you can get some idea of it by car, ducking off the D7 to various exhilarating viewpoints at intervals. A lighthouse warns shipping off the rocks of the Pointe du Millier. The Cap Sizun bird sanctuary (tel 02 98 70 13 53; Jul, Aug daily 10–6; Apr–end Jun 10–12, 2–6; guided tours) near Goulien is reached along a clifftop path, and best visited in the nesting season between April and mid-June. The turbines of a nearby wind-farm look ready to mince any local birdlife into pâté, but a visitor outlet called the Maison du Vent (tel 02 98 70 04 09; Jun–end Sep) explains the advantages of this renewable resource.

HEADING SOUTHWARDS

The quieter southern coastal road passes through Plogoff, scene of a fierce protest against the siting of a proposed nuclear power station during the 1970s, and Plimelin, with its charming 16th-century chapel of St-Tugen. A beautiful expanse of sandy beach graces the Anse du Cabestan near Audierne (▷ 81).

INFORMATION

www.beuzec-cap-sizun.com
www.plouhinec-tourisme.com
www.cap-sizun.com
228 B10 Pointe du Raz (▷ 101). There's a small office at 64 rue des Bruyères, 29790 Beuzec ☎ 02 98 70 55 51 Jul, Aug Mon–Sat 9–12.30, 2–6.30; Sep–end Jun Mon–Fri 9–12, 2–5 Place Jean Moulin, Plouhinec ☎ 02 98 70 74 55 Jul, Aug Mon–Sat 9.30–12.30, 2–7, Sun 9.30–12.30; Sep–end Jun Mon–Fri 9–12, 2–6, plus several small information points Lines 7 and 8 from Quimper to the Pointe du Raz via Douarnenez/Audierne

TIPS

» Wear sensible footwear if you plan any walking (the rocks can be slippery).
» Take binoculars if you're keen on bird-watching (you may be able to borrow some at the Reserve du Cap Sizun).
» The *Fête des Bruyères* (Heather Festival) takes place at Beuzec-Cap-Sizun in mid-August, celebrating Breton culture and music.

Opposite left *Dinghies sailing past the Château du Taureau at Carantec*
Opposite right *The Alignements de Lagatjar on the Crozon Peninsula*
Below *Wild flowers growing on the grassy shores of Cap Sizun*

CHÂTEAU DE KERJEAN

www.chateau-de-kerjean.com

This fortified manor was built in the 16th century, when Louis Barbier decided to commission a home that would outdo that of his rival and one-time overlord at nearby Lanhouarneau. It is one of the grandest of Brittany's Renaissance manors, and unlike some Finisterian châteaux, relatively easy to find. In summer, it hosts various exhibitions and open-air theatrical performances. The building was damaged by fire in 1710 and suffered again during the Revolution, when its last owner was guillotined. In 1911 it passed into state ownership and was restored and filled with appropriate antique furnishings from the Léon region. Though not original to the house, these authentic country pieces, such as box beds and linen presses, were once staple items in every respectable Breton household. The huge kitchen and cellars can also be visited, and so can the ornate chapel decorated with angels and dragons. The moated building sits in 20ha (50 acres) of parkland lined with stately avenues of beech trees. The grounds also contain a gallows tree where local malefactors met their end. The lovely Renaissance well in the second courtyard has a canopy supported on Corinthian columns.

223 D7 29440 St-Vougay 02 98 69 93 69 Jul, Aug daily 10–7; Jun, Sep Wed–Mon 1–6; reduced hours rest of year Adult €5, child (7–17) €1 Signposted off the D30 between Plouescat and Landivisiau

CHÂTEAULIN

www.chateaulin.fr

A tranquil setting on the meandering River Aulne, surrounded by water meadows and wooded cliffs, makes this untouristy little town a pleasant stopover. Keen fisherfolk head to Châteaulin to intercept the salmon and trout that leap upriver through its *passe à poissons* (fish ladder) in the spring (a salmon forms part of the town's coat-of-arms). Another draw is its annual grand prix cycle race, held in September. If neither of these pastimes appeals, simply enjoy a wander through the town, whose unpretentious but dignified buildings span both banks of a looping bend in the river. Thursday is the liveliest day, when the market is held in the Quartier des Halles. Downstream 2km (1 mile) on the next meander is Port-Launay, Châteaulin's former port on the tidal section of the river. The Aulne forms the western section of the Nantes–Brest Canal, and recent improvements make it navigable for leisure boats along the whole of its course.

The hillside 15th- to 16th-century Chapelle de Notre-Dame stands below the ruined château on the left bank. Outside is an early calvary bearing a carving of the Last Judgement.

223 D9 Quai Cosmao, 29150 Châteaulin 02 98 86 02 11 Jul, Aug Mon–Sat 9.30–12.30, 2–7, Jun, Sep Tue–Sat 9.30–12.30, 2–6; Apr, May Tue–Sat 9.30–12.30 Châteaulin (Brest–Quimper via Landerneau) The huge Leclerc hypermarket (the biggest in central Finistère) signed off the Crozon road is a useful stop for any essential supplies, a tank of fuel, or a decent coffee (Mon–Sat 9–7.30; closed Sun).

CHÂTEAUNEUF-DU-FAOU

www.chateauneuf-du-faou.com

www.aulnesloisirs.com

Châteauneuf is one of the main touring hubs of the Montagnes Noires (Black Mountains), a sparsely populated region of rounded escarpments along the leafy Nantes–Brest Canal, scattered with wayside chapels and quiet rural villages of dark slate. Châteauneuf is typical, set on a wooded ridge overlooking the canalized Aulne.

About 8km (5 miles) east of Châteauneuf is Spezet, right in the heart of the Montagnes Noires and the middle of a strongly Breton-speaking region. Every Whitsuntide (May/June), it holds a festival of the Breton language. If you can follow the signposts (all in Breton) it's a great area for walking, with dozens of footpaths leading through unspoiled woods, streams and moorland. On the way, you will encounter many minor curiosities—fountains, menhirs and calvaries. About a kilometre (half a mile) south of the village is the chapel of Notre-Dame-du-Crann, dating from 1535, which contains a remarkable set of stained-glass windows relating scenes from the lives of Christ, the Virgin Mary and the saints.

To the south of Châteauneuf (signed off the D36 near St-Goazec) lies the country park and château of Trévarez (tel 02 98 26 82 79; www.trevarez.com; Jul, Aug daily 11–6.30; Apr–end Jun, Sep daily 1–6; Mar, Oct, Nov Wed, Sat, Sun, holidays 2–5.30), built around the turn of the 20th century. The château grounds contain a splendid collection of roses and flowering shrubs.

The chapel containing the font in Châteauneuf's church is decorated with frescoes painted by the renowned artist Paul Sérusier, a member of the Pont-Aven school, who lived here for more than 20 years.

223 E9 Place Ar-Segal, 29520 Châteauneuf-du-Faou 02 98 81 83 90 Jul, Aug Mon–Sat 9–12, 2.30–7, Sun, holidays 10.30–12.30; Jun, Sep Tue–Sat 9–12.30, 2–6; rest of year Tue, Thu, Fri 9–12.30, 2–5.30, Wed 9–12.30, Sat 2–5.30 Canal-boat rental and excursions in summer from Aulnes Loisirs Plaisance, tel 02 98 73 28 63

Left *Frescoes in the church of Châteauneuf-du-Faou*

CONCARNEAU

The picturesque Ville-Close (walled town) is Concarneau's pride and joy, along with the fishing industry on which much of its prosperity hinges. Guarding the eastern approaches to a deep and sheltered bay, Concarneau combines the attractions of a beautifully restored historic quarter with the purposeful bustle of a working fishing port. Its dynamic fish auctions *(criées)* animate the quaysides every weekday morning. The town has excellent shops and restaurants, and is also a popular seaside resort, with good beaches and plenty of boat trips.

THE VILLE-CLOSE

Concarneau's historic walled town (Ville-Close) sits on a rocky island within the port, completely surrounded by granite ramparts. Measuring little over a kilometre (half a mile) from end to end, it can easily be explored on foot in a couple of hours. The town was first fortified in the 11th century and was at its most formidable in the 14th. It was subsequently reinforced by the military strategist Vauban during Louis XIV's reign, and has changed little since. Visitors approach the Ville-Close via a fortified bridge and gateway from place Jean Jaurès. The main street, rue Vauban, is flanked by 16th- to 18th-century buildings, now mostly occupied by flower-decked shops and cafés.

ALL ABOUT FISHING

For an illuminating overview of the fishing industry, visit the excellent Musée de la Pêche (Fishing Museum, tel 02 98 97 10 20; Jul, Aug daily 9.30–8; Apr–end Jun 10–6; rest of year 10–12, 2–6; adult €6, child €4) near the entrance to the Ville-Close (video show, live aquarium). You can go aboard one of its exhibits, the disused trawler *Hemerica*, to experience a glimpse of life at sea. Concarneau's seine-netting fleet of more than 160 deep-sea trawlers ventures well beyond home waters as far as Africa and the Indian Ocean, mainly for tropical tuna. The fish auction held at quai de la Criée (guided visits in summer with À l'Assaut des Remparts, tel 02 98 50 55 18) is the largest in Brittany; catches are offloaded throughout the night and dispatched across France.

If you prefer live fish, visit the Marinarium, on the seafront at place de la Croix (tel 02 98 50 81 64; Feb–end Dec daily), the world's oldest institute of marine biology.

INFORMATION

www.tourismeconcarneau.fr
www.concarneau.org
229 E11 Quai d'Aiguillon, 29185 Concarneau 02 98 97 01 44 Jul, Aug daily 9–7; Apr–end Jun, Sep Mon–Sat 9–12.30, 1.45–6.30, Sun 10–1; rest of year Mon–Sat 9–12, 2–6 Line 20 to the main train line at Rosporden; 21 to Port Manech; 14 to Pont-Aven/Quimperlé and Quimper via La Forêt-Fouesnant To the Îles de Glénan or along the Odet estuary Tours of the Ville-Close and the Port de Pêche; contact tourist office The Blue Nets Festival is held in late Aug (folk events)

TIPS

» Parts of the ramparts are accessible on foot, and give splendid views of the town and harbour (daily 9–5; small charge in high season).

» Good walks around Concarneau include the Boucle de Moros, following the banks of the River Moros upstream.

Above *A tranquil beach scene along the coast of Concarneau*

INFORMATION

www.leconquet.fr

222 B8 Parc de Beauséjour, 29217 Le Conquet 02 98 89 11 31 Jul, Aug Mon–Sat 9–12.30, 3–7, Sun, holidays 9–12.30; Sep–end Jun Tue–Sat 9–12 Line 31 to Brest To Molène and Ouessant

TIPS

» Ferries depart from the Sainte-Barbe *embarcadère* (landing stage) in the outer harbour.

» Choose a calm day for a boat trip to Ouessant or Molène; it is a notoriously bouncy ride.

LE CONQUET

Le Conquet is a lively fishing port, whose quaysides are always bustling with boats and full of lobsterpots and piles of netting. This ancient port is the most attractive of any of the coastal resorts in this part of Brittany. Casting a protective eye over the port entrance is La Maison des Seigneurs, part of a larger fortress dating from the 15th century and now a private home. The tiny hilltop chapel of Notre-Dame-de-Bon-Secours makes an interesting contrast to Brittany's larger, more ornate, churches.

AROUND LE CONQUET

From Le Conquet, you can tour the *abers* (fjordlike sea inlets) of northwestern Finistère, or take a ferry to Île d'Ouessant (▷ 95) and Île Molène. A glass-bottomed boat trip reveals the rich marine life in the crystal waters of the Parc Naturel Régional d'Armorique (Armorique Regional Nature Park), now classed as a Biosphere Reserve by UNESCO.

LIGHTHOUSES

Le Conquet has some excellent walks. Take a short stroll to the Kermorvan lighthouse across the estuary, or a longer 5km (3-mile) hike down the low-lying coastal watch-path *(sentier des douaniers)* to Pointe St-Mathieu, where another lighthouse guards a wild stretch of rocky coastline by the ruins of an ancient Benedictine abbey. An exhibition inside explains its history (tel 02 98 89 10 52; www.amis-st-mathieu.org; Jul, Aug daily10–12.30, 2–7; Apr–end Jun, Sep, Oct Sat–Sun 2.30–6.30; daily in school holidays; closed Nov–Feb). As dusk falls, 15 local lighthouses flash their warnings off Finistère's deadly reefs. The Pointe de Corsen, 8km (5 miles) north of Le Conquet, is the most westerly point of Finistère. Signposts say it's 5,080km (3,200 miles) to New York.

Below *Boats moored in the bay at Le Conquet*

DAOULAS

www.abbaye-daoulas.com

The old linen-weaving centre of Daoulas is famed principally for its abbey, an evocative Romanesque cloister in serene gardens. The abbey was originally founded around the year AD500, but was completely destroyed by Viking raiders and rebuilt by Augustinian monks in 1167. It stands just a short walk above the town of honey stone at the head of a creek flowing into the Rade de Brest. It was badly damaged during the Revolution, but has now been restored and is in the care of the local authority. The old abbey buildings now serve as a cultural centre, staging exhibitions all summer long. In the grounds some of the arches survive from the original 12th-century cloister. These are unique of their kind, delicately carved in local Kersanton stone with foliage and geometrical patterns. A fine Romanesque wash-basin stands nearby in a similar design. A recently planted herb garden of the type commonly found in abbeys and convents during medieval times contains an extensive collection of medicinal plants. Labels identify the different species and explain how they were used. Excavations steadily reveal more of the abbey's secrets. Also worth finding in the village are the 16th-century oratory of Notre-Dame-des-Fontaines and a curiously designed fountain with three basins adorned with masks. The waters were believed to cure infertility and also some eye diseases.

223 D8 **Abbey** 21 rue de l'Église, 29460 Daoulas 02 98 25 84 39 Jul, Aug daily 11–7; Sep–end Jun 10–5 during exhibitions only Adult €6, child €3 (10–18), park only: adult €4, child €2.50

DOMAINE DE MENEZ-MEUR

www.pnr-armorique.fr

Laid out around a renovated farm, this animal park in the heart of the Monts d'Arrée extends over some 400ha (1,000 acres) of undulating countryside, conserving many aspects of land management. Visitors may encounter a variety of endangered Breton fauna, such as rare breeds of cattle and deer. Waymarked walks, play areas, a bar-restaurant and picnic site makes this an all-purpose family day trip, enjoyable as well as educational.

223 D9 29460 Hanvec 02 98 68 81 71 Jul, Aug daily 10–7; May, Jun, Sep daily 10–6; Mar, Apr, Oct, Nov Wed, Sun, school holidays 1.30–5.30; Dec–end Feb school holidays only 1–5 Adult €3.30, child €2.10 (8–14) Various guided tours

LE FOLGOËT

www.lesneven-tourisme.com

A spectacular *pardon* takes place every September in this little village on the southwest side of Lesneven, when locals dress up in traditional Breton costumes and pilgrims converge from far and wide to pay homage to the resplendently enshrined 15th-century Black Virgin of Folgoët. Le Folgoët means 'Fool's Wood', a reference to the miraculous legend of Salaün (Solomon), a 14th-century simpleton who lived in nearby oak woods. Salaün could speak only the Breton version of 'Hail Lady Virgin Mary', which he reiterated constantly throughout his life. He begged for food and drank water from a local spring (now a fountain by the east wall of the church). When he died, a lily sprang from his grave bearing the words 'Ave Maria' in Latin, and word spread that he was a saint. The Breton nobility financed the outsized Gothic basilica of Notre-Dame which dominates the village. Restored after the Revolution, it contains a fine rood screen and altars of Kersanton granite. In late July, motorists gather in Le Folgoët to have their cars blessed at another religious ceremony, the *pardon* of St. Christophe, patron saint of travellers. Given France's appalling road accident statistics, this may not be such a crazy idea.

223 C7 14 place du Général-Le-Flo, 29260 Lesneven 02 98 83 01 47 Mid-Jun to Aug Mon–Fri 9.30–12.15, 2–6, Sat 9.30–12.15, 2–5, Sun 10.30–12.15; rest of year Mon–Fri 9.30–12, 2–5, Sat 9.30–12. Information also available at the Musée de Folgoët (€2, free under 14), near the church at Le Folgoët, tel 02 98 21 11 18; mid-Jun to mid-Sep Mon–Sat 10–12.30, 2.30–6.30, Sun 2.30–6.30 Line 38 (Brignogan–Brest)

Above *Statues at Daoulas Abbey*

DOUARNENEZ

Once a leading light of the sardine industry, this fishing port is now a guardian of Brittany's maritime heritage and its associated expertise. Douarnenez is Brittany's second fishing town after Concarneau, and was once France's largest sardine port. Its workmanlike bars and restaurants have a real salty air, cheek-by-jowl with warehouses and marine businesses of many kinds. The town has three sheltered harbours—the main reason for its long success as a fishing port. A *criée* (fish auction) takes place in the early mornings. Hilly streets zigzag down to the narrow estuary harbour of Port-Rhu, which accommodates Douarnenez's maritime museum.

Douarnenez is a good place to try the Breton cake *kouign amann*, which was invented here.

MARITIME MUSEUM

The splendid Port-Musée (tel 02 98 92 65 20; www.port-musee.org; mid-Jun to mid-Sep daily 10–7; rest of year Tue–Sun 10–12.30, 2–6 (Sun only in winter); combined entrance with Musée du Bateau adult €6.20, child 6–16 €3.80), approached from place de l'Enfer, occupies the entire harbour area of Douarnenez. Part of the maritime museum consists of an impressive assembly of traditional working vessels afloat at the quayside, the other section is the covered Musée du Bateau, containing some 40 or so smaller vessels collected from all over the world. Exhibitions focus on the lives of seafaring communities in Brittany and throughout the world. Fascinating demonstrations of traditional nautical skills such as sail-making and net-repairing take place in summer.

HISTORY AND LEGEND

The town's history pre-dates Roman times when it specialized in making *garum*, a pungent fish sauce much prized in Roman cuisine. In the 16th century, residents were plagued by the notorious pirate La Fontenelle, who ransacked houses and stole the stone to build his own château on the Île d'Tristan, just offshore.

INFORMATION

www.douarnenez-tourisme.com
228 C10 2 rue du Dr Mével, 29172 Douarnenez 02 98 92 13 35
Jul, Aug Mon–Sat 10–7, Sun 10–1, 4–7; Sep–end Jun Mon–Sat 10–12, 2–6
Lines 7A, 7B and 9 to Quimper, Pont-Croix, Audierne and the Pointe du Raz
Harbour and sea-fishing trips with Vedettes Rosmeur

TIPS

» Douarnenez is rather a disorienting place, so the first thing to do is get hold of the tourist office's excellent town map.

Above *Sunset on the bay at Douarnenez*

GUIMILIAU

Guimiliau's *enclos paroissial* (parish close) dates from 1588, and is one of the most complex and interesting anywhere in Finistère. The term 'parish close' refers to the walled enclave of consecrated ground beside a church, generally used as a graveyard. Most of the parish closes were created during the 16th and 17th centuries, when vast sums were expended on amassing the finest examples of the mason's art. Generous patrons outdid each other in their efforts to build the most impressive monuments. Parish closes typically consist of a triumphal archway through which funerary processions pass, a carved calvary depicting the passion of Christ, and an ossuary or funerary chapel in which bones were once interred (these are now sometimes used as information points, gift shops, museums). Occasional escorted summer tours can be arranged around the parish close.

THE CALVARY

More than 200 carved figures crowd the supporting plinth of this ornate granite structure, all sculpted as if clothed in contemporary 16th-century dress, and beautifully detailed (notice the braided rope on the donkey). On the cross, Christ and the Virgin are accompanied by St. Peter, St. John and local hero St. Yves. Among the busy tableau of figures below, the four evangelists stand guard at the corner buttresses, while the disciples size up the roast lamb at the Last Supper with keen anticipation.

Elsewhere is a grisly scene of a young girl being indecently assaulted and dragged into hell by sadistic demons. Catell Gollet was a careless pleasure-seeker who fell from grace when she stole consecrated wafers at Mass for her lover (the Devil in disguise).

THE CHURCH

The church, in Flamboyant Renaissance style, is just as interesting as its surrounding parish close. From the ornately carved south porch, where a cat and dog chase each other among the 12 apostles, you step into an interior encrusted with vivid carved woodwork. Highlights include a 17th-century organ loft built by Thomas Dallam and a baptismal font featuring elegant spiral columns.

INFORMATION

223 E8 Place de la Mairie, 29400 Guimiliau 02 98 68 75 06

TIPS

» There is no convenient public transport to the village, so you will need your own wheels.
» Avoid sightseeing inside the church during Mass.
» Guimiliau has no local tourist office; leaflets about the parish closes and suggested self-guided itineraries are available from other regional offices such as Landerneau or Morlaix.
» A short explanatory summary is available in English inside the church.

Below *The Calvary at Guimiliau*

FOUESNANT AND LA FORÊT-FOUESNANT

www.fouesnant-tourisme.com
www.ot-fouesnant.fr

The Fouesnant (pronounced fway-non) region incorporates scattered communities amid the fertile apple-growing country at the head of the Baie de la Forêt, where twin wooded creeks create a glassy mirror at high tide, and views extend towards the Îles de Glénan. Brittany's best cider is alleged to come from here, and the annual *Fête du Cidre* (July) involves traditional *coiffes* and Breton costumes. The smaller village of La Forêt-Fouesnant, is in a separate commune on the verdant easterly inlet of the St-Laurent estuary. Port-la-Forêt, its modern marina, bristles with the masts of some 800 pleasure-craft in high season. The tidal fishing port is a much sleepier place, though shellfish, especially oysters, are an important source of revenue; *viviers* sell live wares on the waterfront.

229 D11 Espace Kernévéleck, 29170 Fouesnant 02 98 51 18 88 Mon–Sat 9–12, 2–6 2 rue du Vieux Port, 29940 La Forêt-Fouesnant 02 98 51 42 07 Jul, Aug Mon–Sat 9–1, 2–7.30, Sun 10–1; Sep–end Jun Mon–Sat 9.30–12, 2–6 Boat trips to the Îles de Glénan and up the Odet estuary Both tourist offices are extremely efficient and a mine of useful information about the local area

HUELGOAT

www.tourismehuelgoat.fr

One of the last vestiges of Brittany's great central forest, Huelgoat (High Wood) is a prime location for a host of outdoor activities, especially walking. This waterfront site has attracted settlers since earliest times; the fortified Camp d'Artus dates from Gallo-Roman days, and canals were dug in the 19th century, when deposits of lead and silver were extracted. Now part of the Parc Naturel Régional d'Armorique, Huelgoat stands on the edge of a lake surrounded by hilly woodland where waymarked paths radiate in all directions. The 1,000ha (2,470-acre) forest extends over the southern slopes of the Monts d'Arrée, gashed by deep valleys. Much of the woodland was destroyed during the hurricane of October 1987. Replacement plantings are steadily taking over. The Jardin de l'Argoat and Arboretum du Poerup (tel 02 98 99 95 90; www.arboretum-huelgoat.com; Easter to mid-Oct daily 10–6; mid-Oct to Easter Mon–Fri by appointment) contains a fine collection of exotic trees and plants, many in danger of extinction.

The resort is a low-key cluster of slatey grey-and-white Breton houses well interspersed with vegetation. The Rivière d'Argent (Silver River) carves its tortuous, foam-flecked passage through a jumble of mossy trees and giant, strangely eroded boulders; ▷ 114–115 for a detailed walk in the Huelgoat area.

223 E9 Moulin du Chaos, 29690 Huelgoat 02 98 99 72 32 Jul, Aug daily 10–12.30, 2–6; Sep–end Jun information at the Mairie

ÎLES DE GLÉNAN

This archipelago of a couple of dozen islets and reefs just 20km (13 miles) offshore is famed for its shell-strewn white-sand beaches and calm, limpid waters, which provide perfect conditions for scuba-diving and sailing. The Les Glénans sailing school on Penfret island is world renowned for dinghy and catamaran training courses. Pleasure-boats dock only on Île de St-Nicolas, which has a scattering of houses, a scuba-diving school and a shellfish farm. Île Guiautec is a wildlife sanctuary (allegedly the smallest in the world), home to many seabirds and a unique species of narcissus, which flowers in mid-April.

229 D12 Municipal tourist office at Fouesnant; information is also available at excursion ports Boat trips from Bénodet, Concarneau, Quimper, La Forêt-Fouesnant, Loctudy, Beg-Meil (Apr–end Sep)

LANDERNEAU

www.tourisme-landerneau-daoulas.fr
www.ville-landerneau.fr

The former capital of the Léon region was once an important inland port at the tidal limit of the River Elorn, and grew rich on the cloth trade. Occasional freight vessels from Brest still unload bulk cargoes at its quaysides, then hastily depart to catch the tide. Its star asset is the Pont de Rohan, a superb, rare example of an inhabited bridge, dating from 1510. The wobbly slate-hung houses are still lived in. Other turreted buildings can be seen near the waterfront. Most date from the late 17th and early 18th centuries, when Landerneau enjoyed its commercial heyday. Landerneau is a popular angling centre (the river abounds with trout and salmon), and also good for shopping—the Comptoir des Produits Bretons on quai Cornouaille may solve present-buying requirements (▷ 117).

223 D8 Pont de Rohan, 29800 Landerneau 02 98 85 13 09 Jul, Aug daily Mon–Sat 10–7, Sun 10–1, 2–6; rest of year Tue–Sat 10–1, 2–6 (5 in winter) Landerneau (on TGV Paris-Brest route); connections to Quimper

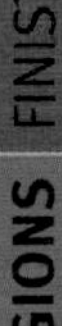

ÎLE D'OUESSANT

The largest of Finistère's westerly islands gives a fascinating insight into the bygone lifestyle of Breton seafarers. Its Breton name (anglicized as Ushant) means 'Isle of Terror', but this refers more to the notoriously hazardous shipping lanes offshore, with their razor-sharp reefs, sea fogs and powerful currents. Many shipwrecks have occurred on this coast despite the lighthouses and warning systems, most notoriously the *Amoco Cadiz*, which went aground off Portsall in 1978, spilling some 220,000 tonnes of toxic crude oil into the sea. But despite the buffetings of the Atlantic gales, the winter climate is exceptionally mild and frost-free.

AROUND THE ISLAND

Ouessant is the largest of several islands off the northwest coast of Finistère, measuring about 7km (5 miles) at its longest. Both the archipelago and its surrounding waters, which are rich in marine life, form part of the Parc Naturel Régional d'Armorique (Armorique Regional Nature Park). Large numbers of migrant birds visit the island, attracted by the lighthouse beams. Most of the islanders subsist on a traditional mix of fishing, farming and tourism. Seaweed- and mussel-farming are newer enterprises. Much of the treeless terrain consists of heathland or sparse unfenced sheep pasture.

Ferry passengers arrive at the Baie du Stiff on the east coast of Ouessant. Lampaul is the only real village; it has a few modest hotels, shops and cafés. At the ferry terminal you can rent a bicycle, or arrange a minibus, taxi or horse-drawn carriage tour around the island, or even a horse. Otherwise, best things to do on Ouessant are to explore the island and enjoy some fresh air, perhaps with a picnic. A footpath circuits the island's rocky coastline, but there are shorter walks from Lampaul, in fact 45km (28 miles) of paths altogether.

MUSEUMS

An Ecomusée at Niou Uhella (tel 02 98 48 86 37; Apr–end Sep, school holidays daily 10.30–6.30; Oct–end Mar Tue–Sun 1.30–4), set in a couple of brightly painted fisherman's cottages, reveals the traditional way of life on Ouessant and its largely matriarchal society (women ran the island economy while the men went off to sea), which persisted well into the 20th century. The Phare du Creac'h (tel 02 98 48 80 70; hours similar to Ecomusée), on the west coast, has a museum of lighthouses and coastal warning systems.

INFORMATION

www.ot-ouessant.fr
www.oessant.fr
222 A8 Place de l'Église, 29242 Lampaul 02 98 48 85 83 Jul, Aug Mon–Sat 9–1, 1.30–7, Sun, holidays 9.30–1; rest of year Mon–Sat 10–12, 2–5; Sun, holidays 10–12 There is no scheduled land transport on the island, but taxis and minibuses are on standby in the holiday season Boat trips from Le Conquet and Brest; some also call at Molène You can fly to Ouessant from Brest Airport in summer

TIPS

» The easiest beach to reach from the ferry terminal is the Plage du Corz near Lampaul, but you'll find quieter ones if you walk a bit farther.

» A bicycle is the most convenient way of getting around Ouessant if you have limited time, though you may find bicycling more strenuous than expected into a headwind. Rates from around €12 per day. Bicycling is not permitted on the coastal paths (some of the most scenic).

Above *The rugged cliffs of Île d'Ouessant*
Opposite *A mansion on the bridge at Landerneau*

INFORMATION

www.lampaul-guimiliau.com

223 D8 No tourist office, but information available from the Mairie, 6 place Villiers, 29400 Lampaul-Guimiliau 02 98 68 76 67; or at the Maison du Patrimoine (opposite the church) Jul, Aug Mon–Sat 10.30–1, 2.30–6.30, Sun 10–12.30. Church open all year daily 8.30–6 (until 8 in summer) Landivisiau The ossuary is now a souvenir shop, as at Guimiliau

TIPS

» Pick up a leaflet inside the church, available in English.

» There is no public transport to the village itself, but Landivisiau station is a short taxi-ride away, and within feasible walking distance.

Above *A terrace of creeper-covered houses in the old village*

LAMPAUL-GUIMILIAU

Lampaul-Guimiliau, near Landivisiau in the Elorn valley, vies with nearby Guimiliau (▷ 93) and St-Thégonnec (▷ 109) for the distinction of best parish close. The calvary itself, which is older than the rest of the close, is relatively plain compared with those of its rivals, but its other features are magnificent. The *porte triomphale* (triumphal arch) is surmounted by three crosses, while the adjoining *chapelle funéraire* (ossuary) has turreted buttresses and grapevine decorations.

INSIDE THE CHURCH

The church, its tower foreshortened by a lightning strike in 1809, seems modest from outside (notice the porch of Kersanton stone), but its lavish baroque interior of polychrome timbers and riotous carvings is astonishing. Wherever you look, you will spot some intriguing detail or unusual feature. Visitors are welcomed to this fine church with lights, music and interesting interpretative storyboards.

In pride of place across the nave stretches a wonderful 16th-century rood beam *(poutre de gloire)*, carved with scenes from Christ's passion and crowned with a large, brightly painted crucifix. The robbers look particularly malevolent. The six high-relief 17th-century altarpieces are especially note-worthy, all crowded with detail and decorated with vines and barley-sugar columns. One of the most accomplished recounts the life of John the Baptist; others depict the Birth of the Virgin and the Breton legend of St. Miliau, beheaded by his jealous brother. Fountaining crimson arterial blood, he calmly holds his severed head in his hands. On the north wall, the virginal Sainte Marguerite triumphs over an extremely grumpy devil (represented here as a dragon). More devils squirm in the church stoup as they come into contact with holy water.

In the southeast corner of the church, the masterly *Entombment* scene in polychrome stone was sculpted by Antoine Chavagnac, a naval artist from Brest, in 1676. The mourners stand in anguish around the dead Christ, still tense with agony. The font in the south aisle is covered with a baldaquin, or canopy.

LOCRONAN

This glamorous little town is one of the prettiest in Brittany, its patrician architectural heritage exceptionally harmonious and virtually unaltered since the 17th century.

Locronan was a sacred site for the Druids, then a place of Christian pilgrimage after the death of the Irish missionary St. Ronan in the fifth century. The town's golden age in the 17th century was based on the production of sailcloth, but when Louis XIV abolished its monopoly in hemp, Locronan's economy quickly collapsed. In the ensuing centuries, money was never available to update the buildings, leaving the architecture much as it was in the town's heyday. Today, the lovely old Renaissance houses of warm granite and silvery slate are perfectly preserved, and decked in flowers all summer long. Many have been converted into restaurants, shops or galleries, and tourist revenue has revived the town's fortunes.

EXPLORING THE OLD TOWN

At the heart is the old town square, place de l'Église, where the 15th-century church of St. Ronan (summer daily 9–12, 2–6; reduced hours rest of year) is a masterly example of a style known as Ogival Flamboyant. The pulpit is carved with scenes from the patron saint's life. The square contains an old well, and is surrounded by superbly preserved 17th- and 18th-century buildings; some are the former homes of rich cloth merchants, or administrative offices of the East India Company. It was used as a backdrop during the filming of Roman Polanski's *Tess* (1979). Rue Moal, with more humble weavers' homes, leads to the 15th- and 16th-century church of Notre-Dame-de-Bonne-Nouvelle (Our Lady of Good News; daily 9–6), with stained glass by Alfred Manessier (1911–93). The Musée d'Art et d'Histoire, in place de la Mairie, houses historic items and exhibits relating to the local area (hours similar to tourist office).

ARTS AND CRAFTS

The Surrealist painter Yves Tanguy (1900–55) had a home on rue Lann; today various potters, painters and sculptors have studio and gallery space in the town. The Tissage du Lain (tel 02 98 91 83 96), on place de l'Église, displays high-quality craft products in a splendid dormered building.

INFORMATION

www.locronan.org

228 D10 Place de la Mairie, 29180 Locronan 02 98 91 70 14 Jul, Aug Mon–Sat 10–1, 2–7; Mar–end Jun, Sep Mon–Fri 10–12, 2–6; closed Oct–end Feb except school hols Line 10 (Quimper–Camaret) runs through Locronan

TIP

» Every year in mid-July a procession called *La Petite Troménie* re-enacts St. Ronan's penitential daily climb up the hill behind the town. Every sixth year, a longer pilgrimage (*Grande Troménie*) takes place through the countryside—the next is due in 2013. These ancient rituals are major religious events and a great visitor attraction.

Below *The medieval centre of Locronan by night*

LANDÉVENNEC

www.pnr-armorique.fr

On a hook-nosed peninsula where the final bend of the Aulne estuary meets the Rade de Brest, Landévennec enjoys an exceptionally mild microclimate, as the lush, Mediterranean-style vegetation billowing all around local gardens amply testifies. It is a most picturesque spot (a *site naturel protégé)*, with views over the Rade de Brest, and upstream to the modern Térénez suspension bridge. Visitors come here to see the ruins of its ancient abbey, founded by St. Guénolé in the fifth century. King Gradlon, who ruled the legendary island city of Ys before it flooded in the sixth century, is allegedly buried here. Over the centuries, the abbey has undergone many vicissitudes, but retains some beautifully carved capitals and columns in Romanesque style. A museum presents the history of the abbey and displays archaeological finds. A modern abbey nearby still houses a Benedictine community, who welcome visitors to join in their services. There is also an on-site shop selling a number of regional products, including the monks' delicious homemade fruit preserves.

The Corniche de Térénez, following the D791 from Le Faou to the Pont de Térénez, gives marvellous views over the estuary, and the shipyard where decommissioned naval vessels are stripped down for scrap.

223D9 Abbey: 29560 Landévennec 02 98 27 35 90 Jul to mid-Sep daily 10–7; Apr–end Jun, mid–end Sep Mon–Fri 10–6, Sun 2–6; Oct–end Mar Sun 2–6 (Sun–Fri 2–6 in school holidays) Adult €4; child 8–18 €3; new abbey free of charge. A guide is available in English Abbey shop selling regional products, some made by the monks

MONTS D'ARRÉE

www.pnr-armorique.fr

This sparsely populated belt of ancient hills stretches in a long, narrow ridge across some 60,000ha (148,000 acres) of central Finistère, through a variety of landscapes, including bogland, gorse and heather moors, and granite plateaux. Once these hills towered higher than the Alps, but present altitudes rarely exceed 350m (1,148ft). The summits themselves range from saw-toothed crests to softly contoured dumplings. It's an area imbued with legends and full of wildlife, including wild boar and even some reintroduced beavers. It is now a protected zone, part of the Parc Naturel Régional d'Armorique, but certain areas are used as military training grounds. The most memorable way to experience these hills is on foot; otherwise car-touring is the only practical method. A climb up Roc'h Trévézel, the highest summit (384m/1,260ft), gives extensive views, while the eerie peat bog of Yeun Elez makes an unusual walk—stick to the waymarked paths.

223 E8 The head office for the Armorique Regional Nature Park is at 15 place aux Foires, 29590 Le Faou 02 98 81 90 08. Local tourist offices include 10 rue du Général-de-Gaulle, 29590 Le Faou, tel 02 98 81 06 85; 3 rue Argoat, 29450 Sizun, tel 02 98 68 88 40 (Apr–end Sep). You can pick up information in many local villages and ecomusées, such as at Domaine de Menez-Meur (▷ 91). See also Huelgoat, Moulins de Kerouat

MORGAT

A popular holiday spot on the Crozon peninsula, Morgat has a sheltered sandy beach in an alluring pine-backed setting. It became fashionable at the end of the 19th century, when belle-époque hotels were built by the Peugeot family. It has a large yacht marina, and various other water sports (windsurfing, kayaking, catamaran sailing) are catered for at the *centre nautique*. One popular boat tour goes to the sea caves beyond the headland of Beg-ar-Gador, noted for their strange mineral tints. A breezy clifftop walk leads around the coast to the wild Cap de la Chèvre. Large areas of coastal marshland near Morgat are a great magnet for birdlife, and are now nature reserves.

La Grotte de l'Autel (Altar Cave) is the largest and most impressive of the local caves, whose cathedral-like dimensions give it its name. It is reachable only by boat.

222 C9 Place d'Ys, 29160 Morgat 02 98 27 29 49 Jul, Aug daily 10–1, 3–7 (an all-year office is just up the road in Crozon, ▷ 111) Boat trips to the sea caves (Apr–end Sep); summer ferry to Douarnenez

Below left *Morgat's wide, sandy beach*
Below *Blooms adorn the countryside in this pretty region*

MORLAIX

A handsome old town, a striking setting and lots of attractive shops make this historic port an enjoyable visit. Morlaix sits in a ravine at the head of a large estuary, in the shadow of a monumental 58m (190ft) viaduct, built in the 1860s to carry the Paris–Brest railway. Below it, the old town rises up the steep valley sides in a series of narrow lanes, known locally as *venelles*. It's a rewarding place to explore on foot, though the best views involve some steep gradients. Despite being some 12km (7.5 miles) from the open sea, the town still serves as a significant port, though most of the present traffic in the canalized marina just north of the viaduct consists of pleasure-craft rather than cargo vessels. A handsome if shabby old cigar factory (used for exhibitions) makes an impressive waterfront landmark.

REVENGE IS SWEET

Morlaix was Brittany's third city, prospering on fishing, ship-building, linen, tobacco, paper and more than a little piracy, which made it a target for reprisals. In 1522 the English fleet attacked after Breton *corsairs* ransacked Bristol. Morlaix's citizens took their revenge when they found the English sleeping off hangovers after helping themselves to the town's wine. The town's coat of arms reflects this incident, showing an English leopard fighting a French lion, with the motto *S'ils te mordent, mords-les* (If they bite you, bite them back).

THE PAST PRESERVED

In the old town, several of Morlaix's idiosyncratic timbered *maisons à lanterne* (lantern houses) survive, characterized by a central hall and a fireplace that carries through to the top of the house. The Maison de la Reine Anne, in the rue du Mur, is where Anne of Brittany stayed in 1505 (tel 02 98 88 23 26; May–end Sep Mon–Fri 11–6, Sat 11–5). The recently restored Maison à Pondalez is at 9 Grand Rue (tel 02 98 88 68 88; Jul, Aug daily 10–12.30, 2–6.30; Apr, May, Sep Mon, Wed–Sat 10–12. 2–6, Sun 2–6; Oct–end Mar, Jun Mon, Wed–Sat 10–12. 2–5), and now forms the reception building for the reconfigured Musée de Morlaix. Léon furniture and Breton paintings are on display inside, but the building itself is the main focus of interest.

INFORMATION

www.morlaix.fr
www.morlaixtourisme.fr
223 E8 Place des Otages, 29600 Morlaix 02 98 62 14 94 Jul, Aug Mon–Sat 9–12.30, 1.30–7, Sun 10.30–12.30; Sep–end Jun Mon–Sat 9.30–12.30, 2–6 Lines 16 (Lannion); 51 (Locquirec); 52 and 61 (Huelgoat); 53 (Roscoff, St-Pol-de-Léon via Carantec); 55 (Plougasnou, le Diben) SNCF (Roscoff) Morlaix is on the main Paris–Brest route, with frequent services to St-Brieuc, Brest and Roscoff River trips from the port

TIPS

» Morlaix has lots of enticing food shops and wine-merchants, as well as an excellent market (Saturday).

» The wooded banks of the Morlaix river make fine routes for walking and bicycling, past boatyards, oyster-beds and artichoke fields.

Above *Market stalls beneath the 19th-century viaduct*

MOULINS DE KÉROUAT

www.pnr-armorique.fr

This mill complex in an abandoned Monts d'Arrée village east of Sizun has been restored, and now forms one of the Armorique Regional Nature Park's small *écomusées*, showing how this rural community would have functioned during the 19th century. Besides the two mills, you can see the mill-owner's house, and the bread-ovens, tannery, stables and barns. The earliest parts of the Moulins de Kérouat date from 1610. One of the mills is in working order, and you can watch the grinding mechanisms in action. Buckwheat flour (still used in classic Breton pancakes called *galettes*) ground at the mills is on sale in the shop. A guide leaflet is available.

223 E8 29450 Commana 02 98 68 87 76 Jul, Aug daily 11–7, Jun Mon–Fri 10–6, Sat–Sun 2–6; mid-Mar to end May, Sep, Oct Mon–Fri 10–6, Sun, holidays 2–6; in winter school holidays Mon–Fri 10–5 Adult €4.50, child (8–18) €2.10; last tickets sold one hour before closing time Guided visits and demonstrations You can buy stone-ground flour and bakery products made from it

PLEYBEN

Pleyben is famed for its parish close and unusual calvary, one of Finistère's finest and worth a detour. South of the Monts d'Arrée, Pleyben lies some way from the majority of the parish closes up in the Elorn valley. The calvary base is taller than in most parish closes, with two tiers of carvings. Scenes from Christ's life enliven the structure, which is full of quirky details (a pie ready for the Last Supper, and Christ washing the disciples' feet). The church of St-Germain d'Auxerre has a mix of styles: a Renaissance tower flanked by a Gothic spire. The interior has panelled vaulting, coloured statuary, painted beams and a stained-glass window depicting the Passion of Christ. The ossuary dates from the mid-16th century and contains a little history exhibition.

223 E9 Place Charles de Gaulle, 29190 Pleyben 02 98 26 71 05 Mid-Jun to mid-Sep Mon–Sat 10–12, 2.30–6.30 At Pont Coblant you can rent a kayak to explore the canalized River Aulne or a houseboat.

PLOUGUERNEAU

www.abers-tourisme.com

The main attraction of this low-key resort village is the lovely beaches scattered around the coast to the northwest. From Lilia summer boat trips ply to the Phare de la Vierge, tallest lighthouse in France (82.5m/274ft) set amid a chaos of low-tide rocks. Plouguerneau itself has a small museum devoted to the local trade of seaweed-gathering—the Écomusée de Plouguerneau (tel 02 98 37 13 35; mid-Jun to end Sep Wed–Mon 2–6; rest of year weekends only). The village church contains wooden statuettes of saints, placed here by parishioners who had escaped the plague.

The church of Notre-Dame du Grouanec just southeast of Plouguerneau has a restored parish close. Grouanec also has a display in the Chapelle St-Michel dedicated to the zealous 17th-century missionary Michel Le Nobletz, who used maps and paintings on wood or sheepskins to illustrate the Christian message to his often-illiterate flock (Jul–end Sep).

Plouguerneau is a useful base for exploring the scenic *abers* (fjord-like sea inlets) that characterize the far northwest coast of Finistère. These are drowned river valleys flooded after the last Ice Age. Tides alternately turn them into brimming mirrors or straggling mud-slicks. Heading southwest over the bridge at Lannilis, you reach Aber-Wrac'h, one of the most picturesque stretches of the Finistère coast, a popular sailing resort with dune-backed sandy beaches and boat trips. The island-scattered Baie des Anges (Angel Bay) is a magical scene, best viewed from the breakfast room of the hotel that bears its name (▷ 124). Sunset views are also stunning on this coast. Nearby Aber-Benoît specializes in shellfish-rearing and is a scuba-diving resort.

222 C7 Place de l'Europe, 29880 Plouguerneau 02 98 04 70 93 Jul, Aug Mon–Sat 9.30–12.30, 2.30–6.30, Sun, holidays 10.30–12.30; Easter–end Jun, Sep Mon–Sat 9.30–12, 2–5 (closed Wed pm); Oct–Easter Mon, Tue 9.30–12, Thu–Sat 9.30–12, 2–5 (the office in nearby Lannilis may be open if Plouguerneau is closed: Place de l'Église 29870 02 98 04 05 43) Visits to Île Vierge lighthouse (from Lilia; Apr–end Oct); glass-bottomed boat trips (from Perros)

PONT L'ABBÉ

www.ot-pontlabbe29.fr

The former port and self-styled capital of the Penmarc'h peninsula commands the bridgehead on a complicated estuary which forms a sheltered lagoon just south of the town. Pont-l'Abbé has a long and eventful history dating from medieval times. Attractive granite houses line its main streets. A museum of Bigouden culture rambles over three floors of its 14th-century château (tel 02 98 66 09 03; Jun–end Sep daily 10–12.30, 2–6.30 (until 7 Jul, Aug); Easter–end May Tue–Sun 2–6). Unmissable exhibits are the distinctive costumes of the Bigouden region, including the gravity-defying *coiffes* (headdresses) measuring up to 30cm (1ft) high, which were habitually worn well into the 20th century. Costumes, lace and hand-embroidered dolls are on sale in local shops, and a large regional market is held on the two main squares on Thursdays.

About 2km (1 mile) south of town, the richly furnished Manoir de Kérazan once belonged to the Astor family; the estate can be visited (tel 02 98 87 50 10; mid-Jun to mid-Sep daily 10.30–7; Apr to mid-Jun, mid–late Sep Tue–Sun 2–6; adult €6, child (7–15) €3). A passenger ferry connects Loctudy with its opposite number Île-Tudy, on a trailing sandspit virtually blocking the estuary mouth. A magnificent beach stretches to Sainte-Marine, on the nearby Odet estuary.

228 C11 · 11 place Gambetta, 29120 Pont l'Abbé · 02 98 82 37 99 · Jun–end Aug Mon–Sat 9.30–12.30, 2–7; Mar–end May Mon–Sat 9.30–12, 2–5. There's a useful regional office, Maison de Tourisme, rond-point de Kermaria (spot the beached trawler at the roundabout just north of town); tel 02 98 82 30 30; Mon–Fri 9–12, 2–6 and also a Point Accueil at Le Sémaphore, Lesconil, 29740 Plobannalec-Lesconil, tel 02 98 87 86 99; Jul, Aug Mon–Sat 9.30–12.30, 2–7; Sep–end Jun Tue–Fri 9.30–12.30 · Boat trips from Loctudy to Îles de Glénan, Bénodet, Odet estuary · The *Fête des Brodeuses* is a major folk festival in mid-July

POINTE DU RAZ

www.pointeduraz.com

Pointe du Raz is a dramatic wild headland, at the western tip of Cap Sizun (▷ 87). The views plunging to the sea through rugged chasms in the rocks and across to the Île-de-Sein are awe-inspiring. You can't drive out to the point; park inland at the reception complex where a video presentation relays the legend of the Lost City of Ys, submerged as a punishment for the evil ways of Dahut, daughter of King Gradlon, whose murdered lovers were thrown into the Gouffre de Plogoff, a pothole where the sea boils amid rocks far below. It is a walk of about 1km (0.5 miles) along a paved footpath to the lighthouse. More than a million people visit annually, hence the stringent conservation measures. You can walk out to the last rocky ridge, where there are safety ropes and cables, but the rocks can be slippery. A powerful tidal race pours through the straits between Raz and Sein at up to 7 knots, but a few adventurous line fishermen catch sea bass. The statue of Notre-Dame des Naufragés (Our Lady of the Shipwrecked) by the signal station gazes towards the reefs and rocks of the Île-de-Sein, a sentimental but poignant reminder of the perils of this coastline.

228 B10 · Maison du Site Pointe du Raz, 29770 Plogoff · 02 98 70 67 18 · Jul, Aug daily 9.30–7.30; Apr–end Jun, Sep and school holidays daily 10.30–6 · Lines 7, 8 (Quimper via Douarnenez/Audierne); free shuttle bus from parking area (Jul and Aug) · Guided nature rambles

PONT-CROIX

www.pont-croix.info

This historic hilltown at the gateway to Cap Sizun is an obvious defensive site, and was the seat of a powerful medieval family. Pont-Croix stands at the River Goyen's tidal limit and was once a significant inland port, its imposing architecture an indication of its amassed wealth. The town rises up in terraces through a maze of narrow streets flanked by houses of mellow stone. One impressive 16th-century residence on rue de la Prison contains the Musée du Marquisat, a local history exhibition of traditional Breton costumes and furnishings (tel 02 98 70 51 86; Jul, Aug daily 10.30–12.30, 3.30–6.30; Jun, Sep daily 3–6; rest of year Sun, holidays 3–6). However, the town's most interesting building is the church of Notre-Dame de Roscudon, founded in the 13th century and constructed in a distinctive English-influenced style. It has a striking Flamboyant Gothic porch with three delicate gables and a fine belfry with a tall spire. Romanesque arches prop up the nave, superseded by Gothic ones in the choir. There is a superb woodcarving of the Last Supper in the chapel behind the altar.

228 C10 · Rue Laennec, 29790 Pont-Croix · 02 98 70 40 38 · Jul–end Sep Mon–Sat 10–12.30, 2–7, Sun 10–12.30, 3–5; Oct–end Jun Mon–Sat 10–12.30, 2–5

Opposite left *Men and women in traditional Breton costume in Pont l'Abbé*
Opposite right *Notre-Dame de Roscudon in Pont-Croix*
Below *Pointe du Raz*

INFORMATION

www.pontaven.com

229 E11 5 place de l'Hôtel-de-Ville, 29930 Pont-Aven 02 98 06 04 70 Mon–Sat 10–12.30, 2–6 Line 14a (Quimper–Quimperlé via Concarneau Boat trips explore the estuary in summer

TIPS

» Pont-Aven is a good place for souvenir shopping, with more than 70 art galleries of all kinds. Food products (especially biscuits) and Quimper *faïence* are also widely available. Note that the *galettes* sold here are biscuits, not pancakes.

» A boat trip or drive down the estuary to Port-Manec'h takes you past glorious scenery and photogenic waterfront settlements such as Kerdruc and Rosbras.

Above *Pleasure-boats moored in the harbour at Pont-Aven*
Opposite *The wide sandy beach at the popular resort of Le Pouldu*

PONT-AVEN

It's hard to imagine that this little place was once a busy cargo port and a water-powered industrial base with more than a dozen racing mills. The tightly packed granite houses that line its hilly streets were built during its prosperous heyday in the 17th and 18th centuries. Today Pont-Aven's main sources of revenue are the visitors who come to discover more about its famous school of painters, supplemented by a successful line in biscuit-manufacturing.

DICOVERING THE TOWN

Many artists still live and work in Pont-Aven, but you don't have to be an art connoisseur (or a biscuit fan) to enjoy this town. Most visitors discover its charms during a quiet stroll beside the rock-strewn River Aven past old mills and waterfalls. The Promenade Xavier Grall is a landscaped garden walkway leading from the bridge that gives the town its name. Dense woods cloak the riverbanks, most famously at the painterly haunt of the Bois d'Amour to the north of the town.

The town occupies the final bridging point before the tumbling river leaves its rock-bound valley and broadens into a dazzlingly beautiful ria (drowned estuary), some 12km (7.5km) north of the open sea. On a fine day towards sunset, the quality of the light is unforgettable.

THE PONT-AVEN SCHOOL

The town's principal sight, just off the main square by the tourist office, is the Musée de Pont-Aven (tel 02 98 06 14 43, Jul, Aug daily 10–7; Apr–end Jun, Sep, Oct 10–12.30, 2–6.30; Feb, Mar, Nov, Dec 10–12.30, 2–6; closed Jan; adult €4, child 12–20 €2.50). This houses both permanent collections of the Pont-Aven school, and temporary exhibitions of past and present art. Here you'll find historic photographs of Pont-Aven, and works by leading artists such as Paul Serusier and Emile Bernard. There are even one or two minor pieces by Paul Gauguin, most renowned of all the painters associated with Pont-Aven.

PORT MANEC'H

www.nevez.com

This little resort presides over the mouth of the Aven–Belon estuary. Its chief asset is a fine sandy beach, which became popular at the turn of the 20th century; the beach huts date from this period. A hillside path links the port and the beach, with views of the pine-strewn coast. The sheltered waters provide an ideal water sports venue; good facilities for boat rental and sailing tuition are available at the prestigious Centre Nautique de Cornouaille. Nearby Raguenez-Plage, with its solitary hotel, is a gorgeous bit of coastline overlooking a tidal island. Inviting walks follow the banks and cliffs. Inland, distinctive houses built of 2m (6.5ft) standing stones and thatch are unique to this region. Signed near Port-Manec'h, the English-style Jardins de Rospico contain more than 2,000 species (tel 02 98 06 71 29; www.jardins rospico.com; mid-Jun to mid-Sep Sun–Fri 11–7; Apr to mid-Jun Sun–Fri 2–6).

229 E11 18 place de l'Église, 29920 Névez 02 98 06 87 90 Jul, Aug Mon–Sat 9.30–12, 2–6, Sun 10–1; rest of year Mon–Sat 9.30–12, 2–6 (tickets for boat excursions, guided walks, exchange facilities in summer, maps and guides)

LE POULDU

www.cloharscarnoet.com

www.cloharscarnoettourisme.com

In 1889, a group of Pont-Aven painters, led by Gauguin, broke away from their fellow artists and moved to quieter Le Pouldu at the mouth of the River Laïta farther east. Close to the Morbihan border, this resort is now much expanded with holiday homes, and the long, enticing beaches that made it fashionable in the late 19th century attract summer crowds. The mural paintings at La Maison de Marie Henry, where Gauguin lodged (now the Café de la Plage), are copies of works the artist left behind in lieu of rent (tel 02 98 39 98 51; www.maisonmariehenry.fr; guided tours Jul, Aug daily 10.30–12.30, 3–7; Jun, Sep Wed–Sun 2–6; Apr, May, Oct, Nov Thu–Sun 2–6).

229 F12 Place de l'Océan, 29360 Clohars-Carnoët 02 98 39 93 42 Jul, Aug Mon–Sat 9.30–12.30, 1.30–5.30, Sun 10–12; Sep–end Jun Mon–Sat 9.30–12.30, 1.30–5.30

PRESQU'ÎLE DE CROZON

www.pnr-armorique.fr

This spectacular peninsula forms part of the Armorique regional park, culminating in a three-pronged cape of irresistible wave-lashed drama. Scenic highlights of its cliff-lined westerly coast are the Pointe des Espagnols, the Pointe de Pen-Hir, the Château de Dinan and Cap de la Chèvre. The main resorts are Camaret-sur-Mer (▷ 112) and Morgat (▷ 98).

Other sightseeing includes the evocative abbey of Landévennec (▷ 98), plus a handful of little museums operated by the regional park authorities. The rounded heathery summit of Ménez-Hom at its eastern end gives a vast panorama of the area, while the north coast offers fine glimpses of the Rade de Brest through wooded inlets. Exquisite beaches of pale sand lapped by turquoise seas line its southern shores around Douarnenez Bay. Crozon, the largest community on the peninsula, has a fascinating altarpiece in its church of St-Pierre, whose wonderfully crowded panels relate the story of the Ten Thousand Martyrs, slaughtered for their Christian faith by the Emperor Hadrian in the second century AD. (For a drive around the Crozon peninsula, ▷ 110–113.)

229 C9 Boulevard Pralognan-la-Vanoise, 29160 Crozon 02 98 27 07 92 Mon–Sat 9.15–12, 2–5.30 (6 in school holidays) Summer ferry from Le Fret to Brest; boat trips from Camaret and Morgat

PRESQU'ÎLE DE PENMARC'H

www.penmarch.fr

Traditional culture is kept alive in this remote southwesterly peninsula, sometimes known as the Pays Bigouden. Breton costumes are still worn for *pardons* and festivals, and Celtic dancing and music can be enjoyed at local *festou-noz* (night parties) in summer. This region used to enjoy great prosperity, but pirate raids led by the brutal La Fontanelle and the vagaries of the fishing industry caused economic hardship.

Guilvinec, France's fourth fishing port, showcases the industry in an interactive discovery centre with a terrace overlooking the *criée* called Haliotika (tel 02 98 58 28 38; Apr–early Oct, school holidays Mon–Fri 10.30–12.30, 2.30–7; also Sat and Sun in summer 3–6.30). St-Guénolé, on Finistère's southwestern tip, has a fine lighthouse of Kersanton granite. The 65m (214ft) Phare d'Eckmühl beams its rays over 50km (30 miles). It is open to visitors for a small charge (tel 02 98 58 60 19; Apr–end Sep daily 10.30–6.30; Oct–end Mar weekends only).

228 C11 Place Maréchal-Davout, 29760 St-Pierre 02 98 58 81 44 Jul, Aug daily 9.30–12.30, 2–7, Sep–end Jun Mon–Fri 9.30–12.30, 2–6, Sat 2–6. Also at Lesconil, Guilvinec, St-Guénolé, Pouldreuzic, or the Maison de Tourisme on the northern outskirts of Pont-l'Abbé

QUIMPER

INFORMATION

www.quimper-tourisme.com 229 D10 Place de la Résistance, 29000 Quimper 02 98 53 04 05 Jul, Aug Mon–Sat 9–7, Sun 10–12.45, 3–5.45; Apr to end Jun, Sep Mon–Sat 9.30–12.30, 1.30–6.30 (and Sun 10–12.45 in Jun and early Sep only); Oct–end Mar Mon–Sat 9.30–12.30, 1.30–6 A major hub for west Finistère with services in all directions, including Lines 1 (Brest via Le Faou, Plougastel-Daoulas); 4 (Pont-l'Abbé, Guilvinec, Penmarc'h); 7 and 8 (Pointe du Raz via Audierne); 9 (Douarnenez); 10 (Camaret-sur-Mer via Locronan, Crozon, Le Fret); 14 (Concarneau, Pont-Aven, Quimperlé); 15 (Beg-Meil); 16 (Bénodet); 28 (Pont-l'Abbé, Île-Tudy) Quimper. Frequent TGV and other services to Brest, Lorient, Vannes, Rennes, Paris Boat trips down the Odet to Bénodet; kayak rental at Locmaria The tourist office organizes guided tours of the cathedral and the old town The Festival de Cornouaille (Jul) attracts Celts from across Europe

INTRODUCTION

The name comes from the Breton word *kemper,* meaning a confluence of rivers. The Steir meets the Odet in the middle of the city, crossed by numerous flower-lined footbridges. The *vieille ville* extends on either side of the Steir, mainly to the west of the cathedral, whose soaring spires help you keep your bearings. Narrow, cobbled alleys wind past tottering, dormered houses. Parisian-style outdoor cafés and waterfront brasseries make Quimper an inviting place to watch the world go by. It's also an excellent place to shop for classy Breton souvenirs, particularly knitwear and ceramics.

Quimper stands on ancient foundations; evidence of settlements dates back to the Iron Age. In Roman times the city was known as Aquilonia, and served as an inland port. During the Dark Ages, Quimper became associated with the legendary King Gradlon of Cornouaille, whose equestrian statue rides high on the cathedral's west façade. He appointed the saintly hermit Corentin Bishop of Quimper. Quimper was an influential city throughout Brittany's independence but lost its power after the union with France in 1532.

Although Quimper is one of Brittany's oldest cities, it has a thriving economy. Tourism is a mainstay, but it also has a number of high-tech industries, including food processing. Modern buildings near the centre blend in well with its quaint medieval heritage. The Halles St-François (covered market, open Monday to Saturday) replaced an earlier version destroyed by fire in 1979. Views of the cathedral can be seen through its imaginative boat-like roof.

WHAT TO SEE

CATHÉDRALE ST-CORENTIN

The magnificent cathedral was founded in the 13th century, but not completed until the 19th, when the twin spires were added. Its renovated interior gives an air of light and space, but the nave is oddly skewed in relation to the chancel, an architectural stratagem adopted by medieval masons to avoid surrounding buildings, and a nearby stream-bed. Stained glass depicts local Cornouaille nobility along with their patron saints—a veritable Who's Who of Breton feudal luminaries.

✉ Place St-Corentin ⌚ May–end Oct Mon–Sat 9.30–12, 1.30–6.30, Sun pm only; open from 9am in winter

MUSÉE DÉPARTEMENTAL BRETON

A splendid array of furniture, crafts and archaeology illustrates the history and culture of south Finistère. A highlight is the collection of Breton costumes. Prehistoric and medieval items are displayed on the ground floor, with embroidery and ceramics on upper floors. It is housed in the former Bishop's Palace, dating from the 16th century.

Adjoining the museum is the palace garden (Jardin de l'Évêque), used for summer concerts.

✉ 1 rue du Roi Gradlon ☎ 02 98 95 21 60 ⌚ Jun–end Sep daily 9–6; Oct–end May Tue–Sat 9–12, 2–5. Sun 2–5; closed Mon and holidays ✋ Adult €4, under 18 free

MUSÉE DES BEAUX-ARTS

www.musee-beauxarts.quimper.fr

This is one of the largest and best art galleries in Brittany, containing more than 400 French, Dutch, Flemish and Italian old masters and 19th-century Breton works. The Pont-Aven school is well represented (look out for Gauguin's goose, originally painted on the door of his lodging house). One room is devoted to the drawings and watercolours of Max Jacob, a poet and artist from Quimper.

✉ 40 place St-Corentin ☎ 02 98 95 45 20 ⌚ Jul, Aug daily 10–7; Wed–Mon 10–12, 2–6, Sun 2–6, rest of year; ✋ Adult €4.50, youth 12–26 €2.50 ? Access for people with disabilities

LOCMARIA

Quimper has been connected with the production of ceramics *(faïence)* for three centuries. The industry developed in Locmaria, on the site of the Roman settlement of Aquilonia, and the first *faïencerie* was set up in 1690, producing a tin-glazed earthenware that became immensely popular. True Quimper-ware, with its blue and yellow flower and bird pattern, is handmade, with a potter's or decorator's signature. One of Quimper's biggest and oldest ceramics producers, H. B. Henriot, is in rue Haute. It gives regular guided tours, and has a huge factory showroom (▷ 118).

TIPS

» Quimper is easily reached by public transport from many towns in Brittany, which saves you the trouble of finding somewhere to park.

» Mount Frugy, the wooded hill on the south bank of the Odet (70m/230ft), gives a wonderful view of the town—good for walks and picnics.

» Traditional Breton music sessions are held on summer Thursday evenings in the Jardin de l'Évêque.

» The modern Halles (covered market) on quai du Steir is a great place to stock up on provisions. Look for its delicatessen stalls and bakeries.

Opposite *A statue detail on a house in Quimper town*
Below left *The bridge at Quimper*
Below *A typical Breton motif, used in traditional* faïence *decoration*

ROSCOFF

This *petite cité de caractère* is arguably the most attractive of any of the French Channel ferry ports. Small, compact and unspoiled, it deserves more exploration than many of its transient visitors give it.

For a place of such modest dimensions, Roscoff certainly sings for its supper. Besides being a major ferry terminal, it is also a seaside resort specializing in thalassotherapy and seaweed products, and a busy commercial port, mainly for the export of locally reared shellfish and *primeurs* (early vegetables). In earlier centuries, Roscovite privateers took a lively interest in plundering foreign shipping (mainly British), but they also assisted in smuggling huge quantities of contraband to English shores. In 1973 the construction of the deepwater Port de Bloscon for car ferries and container shipping to the east of the town revitalized Roscoff's economy, while leaving the delightful old town behind its original fishing port undisturbed.

EXPLORING THE TOWN

Roscoff occupies a twin-pronged promontory west of Morlaix Bay. The old quarters splay behind the seafront around the Vieux Port. Many handsome granite buildings hint at its lucrative privateering past. A significant landmark is the church of Notre-Dame-de-Croaz-Batz, a Gothic church originally funded by the merchants and corsairs of the town. Near the railway station, La Maison des Johnnies tells the story of the itinerant salesmen who took their prized *onions rosés* to Britain in the early part of the 20th century (tel 02 98 61 25 48; guided visits mid-Jun to late Sep Sun–Fri; rest of year Tue, Thu; closed Jan). Near the ferry terminal is an exotic subtropical garden, with more than 3,000 species (tel 02 98 61 29 19; Mar–Nov daily).

ÎLE DE BATZ

The boat ride to this little outpost (pronounced 'Ba') of sandy beaches just offshore takes 15 minutes, but ferries depart from two different landing stages, depending on the state of the tide. The island itself is just 4km (2.5 miles) long, and easily walkable in half a day. The main sight on Batz is another exotic garden, the Jardin Georges Delaselle (tel 02 98 61 75 65; Jul, Aug daily afternoons; Apr–end Jun, Sep, Oct Wed–Mon; guided tours on Sun at 3pm).

INFORMATION

www.roscoff-tourisme.com

223 E7 46 rue Gambetta, 29681 Roscoff 02 98 61 12 13 Jul, Aug Mon–Sat 9–12.30, 1.30–7, Sun and public holidays 10–12.30, 2–7; rest of year Mon–Sat 9–12, 2–6 Lines 40 (Brest), 52B (Quimper via St-Pol-de-Léon, Morlaix, Huelgoat, Pleyben), 53 (Morlaix via Carantec) Roscoff; regular services to Morlaix for connections with Brest, Quimper, St-Brieuc Brittany Ferries to Plymouth (all year) and Cork (summer only); year-round trips to Batz

TIPS

» Roscoff has some attractive shops. It's a good place to look for presents, such as stripy Breton knitwear and unusual seaweed beauty products.

» Every August, Roscoff holds a festival dedicated to its most famous vegetable, the Fête de l'Onion Rosé (Breton dancing and music, and lots of onions).

Opposite *An exterior of a Corsaire's house in Roscoff*

Below *Low tide at Roscoff harbour*

QUIMPERLÉ

www.quimperletourisme.com

As the preponderance of religious architecture in the town suggests, Quimperlé began life as a monastic community. It was founded by Benedictines in the 11th century, and later joined by Ursuline and Capuchin houses, but despite its pious origins, Quimperlé has no shortage of convivial pubs and bars. The name of the town, like Quimper, indicates a meeting place of rivers, in this case the Ellé and the Isole, which converge here to form the Laïta estuary, once navigable by sizeable vessels as far as Quimperlé. The town is built on two levels. The old town clusters around the Église Sainte-Croix on an island where the two rivers meet, while the newer *haute ville* lies uphill, focused on the Gothic church of Notre-Dame de l'Assomption, generally known as St-Michel. Sainte-Croix is one of Brittany's most refined examples of Romanesque architecture, designed to a circular Greek Cross plan echoing the Church of the Holy Sepulchre in Jerusalem. The original belltower collapsed in 1862, causing considerable damage to the rest of the church. Its replacement stands separate from the main building. A number of quaint, half-timbered buildings are scattered around the town. The Maison des Archers on rue Dom-Morice is one of the best examples (used for temporary exhibitions); other fine houses can be seen on rue Bremond-d'Ars. South of the town, the Forêt de Carnoët extends through the Laita valley, a popular area for walks and picnics.

229 F11 Main office, open all year, is in the upper town at 45 place St-Michel, 29300 Quimperlé 02 98 96 04 32 Jul, Aug Mon–Sat 9.30–1, 2–7, Sun 10–12; Sep–end Jun Mon–Sat 9.30–12.30, 2–6. A seasonal *point d'information* can be found by the bridge in the lower town, Le Bourgneuf, same tel; Jul, Aug Mon–Sat Quimperlé (TGV Quimper–Paris line) Summer cruises and kayak rental along the Laïta Guided tours of the town, and through the national forest of Carnoët

ST-HERBOT

This Monts d'Arrée village 7km (4 miles) southwest of Huelgoat has a gem of a church in Flamboyant Gothic style. Set in a glade of trees, it seems disproportionate in size and grandeur to the modest scale of the community it serves. Its formidable 30m (97ft) tower is encrusted with delicate pinnacles and openwork arches. Outside stands a calvary dating from 1571, sculpted in Kersanton stone in a curiously modern, almost cartoon-like style. St. Herbot, patron saint of cattle, presides at one of the elegant porch entrances to the church, framed by angels. The church interior contains some fine glass and woodwork and a granite floor, but its most striking feature is the carved oak screen around the chancel. In times gone by, farmers would leave pats of butter or hair from the tails of their cattle on the stone tables by the screen as an offering to St. Herbot, for a blessing for their livestock.

223 E9 Huelgoat (▷ 94)

ST-POL-DE-LÉON

www.saintpoldeleon.fr

At the heart of a busy market-gardening region, St-Pol's primary role is that of agricultural hub. Huge container lorries and tractors laden with cauliflowers, artichokes and onions thunder through the town for most of the year, especially for its Tuesday market, which takes place in the main square. The tourist office arranges summer tours round some of the farms in the area to show how the top-quality vegetables of the *Ceinture d'Orée* (Gold Belt) are grown and packed for market.

Historically, St-Pol served as one of Lower Brittany's leading religious areas, and was the seat of its first bishop, St. Paul (Pol) the Aurelian, a Welsh monk. The town is no longer a bishopric, but the cathedral (Mon–Fri 10–12, 2–6, Sun 2–6; guided tours Jul, Aug), built between the 13th and 16th centuries, still looms over the marketplace. Unusually, it is constructed in Norman limestone rather than the ubiquitous granite of most Breton churches. The weighty Gothic towers of the cathedral are overshadowed by St-Pol's most dominant building, the soaring belltower of La Chapelle Notre-Dame-du-Kreisker (Jul, Aug daily 10–12, 2–6; reduced hours in low season). Topped by Brittany's highest spire, it rises to 78m (256ft), pierced by flower-like shapes to reduce wind resistance. You can climb the tower for magnificent views extending as far as the Monts d'Arrée (Jul and Aug only). Several historic buildings can be seen in St-Pol's older streets, particularly in rue Général-Leclerc. The 16th-century Maison Prébendale, distinguished by its emblazoned façade, was a former canon's residence (Jul, Aug Tue–Sun 3–7; rest of year Wed–Sun 2–6).

St-Pol has one or two beaches and good water sports facilities, so attracts some seaside tourism.

223 E7 Place de l'Evéché, 29250 02 98 69 05 69 Jul, Aug Mon–Sat 9–12, 2–7, Sun, holidays 10–12; Sep–end Jun Mon–Sat 9–12, 2–5.30 St-Pol-de-Léon (on Morlaix–Roscoff line)

ST-THÉGONNEC

This star parish close was one of the last to be built in Finistère, and no expense was spared. Its magnificent calvary vividly encapsulates the torment of Christ. The parish of St-Thégonnec was one of the richest in Léon by the end of the 16th century. Its wealthy merchants dug deep into their pockets to outdo all their rivals in this idiosyncratic Finistèrian art form. From the outset, this church clearly aims to impress its earthly visitors as well as God. The patron saint of this village is little known outside Brittany, but the story goes that St. Thégonnec tamed one of the wolves that had eaten his donkey, and harnessed it to his cart to carry him around. Depictions of him in his wolf-cart are clearly recognizable throughout the region.

THE CLOSE

The archway at the entrance to the parish close is suitably triumphal, constructed in 1587 in Renaissance style with niches and scrolls, surmounted by lantern turrets. The exuberantly decorated ossuary crypt contains a masterly oak Entombment sculpture dating from 1702. It was carved by the Morlaix sculptor Jacques Lespaignol.

THE CALVARY

The calvary was constructed in 1610. Scenes from the Passion on this multi-branched calvary are especially graphic. Notice the Roman soldiers, and the faces of the Christ's revilers, grimacing monstrously. The figures carved on the calvary were portrayed wearing Renaissance dress. One of these figures is alleged to have been modelled on the Protestant king Henry IV, who expediently converted to Catholicism in 1592 before signing the Edict of Nantes. St. Thégonnec puts in an appearance in his trademark wolf-cart on a low niche.

THE CHURCH

The church suffered a serious fire in 1998 and has, since then, undergone major restoration. The chapels on the north side of the church were severely damaged when the roof collapsed during the fire, but the valiant efforts of parishioners and dozens of firefighters managed to prevent the flames from destroying its most precious treasures, including its splendid carved pulpit, dating from 1683. The figures intricately depicted on the pulpit's crowded surfaces include the four Cardinal Virtues, the Evangelists, and the Angel of Judgement.

INFORMATION

223 E8 A small information point operates in summer at Park an Illis, 29410 St-Thégonnec 02 98 79 67 80 Jul, Aug Mon–Sat 10–6; Jun, Sep Mon–Fri 10–1, 2–6; otherwise contact the local Mairie 02 98 79 61 06 The calvary and close are freely accessible at all times; the church is open at conventional hours all year round (Jul, Aug daily 9–7; rest of year 9–6 except during services)

TIPS

» A Quimper-based organization called SPREV (Sauvegarde du Patrimoine Religieux en Vie) arranges free guided tours of the parish closes in July and August (ask the local tourist office for details tel 02 98 79 67 80).

» There's no convenient public transport to St-Thégonnec, but it does have a little railway station on a line from Morlaix; alternatively catch a coach from Morlaix railway station.

» Keen walkers can find their way to St-Thégonnec on the GR380 (long-distance footpath), which runs from Morlaix to Lampaul-Guimiliau (another fine parish close, ▷ 96).

Opposite *The rooftops of St-Pol-de-Léon, viewed from the Kreisker chapel*
Below *The calvary in the parish close of St Thégonnec*

THE CROZON PENINSULA

This drive takes you past some of Brittany's most exciting coastal scenery—giddy headlands, breathtaking beaches, a curvaceous estuary and one of the world's greatest natural harbours, the Rade de Brest. The entire peninsula and its inshore waters form part of the Armorique Regional Nature Park in recognition of its exceptional environmental status. This far-flung Finistèrian outpost has man-made attractions too, including boat trips and water sports, art galleries, excellent restaurants and some unusual sightseeing. But most of Crozon's appeal lies outdoors, so choose fine weather if you can. There are lots of good possibilities for walking (ask the tourist office in Crozon for suggestions) and it is excellent for bird-watching.

THE DRIVE
Length: 154km (96 miles)
Allow: 1 day
Start at: Châteaulin (▷ map 112)
End at: Le Faou

★ Several major roads converge near Châteaulin (▷ 88), an appealing little town on the serpentine River Aulne, giving speedy access from most places in western Brittany.

Fill up with fuel (about the least expensive you'll find in this area) at Châteaulin's big Leclerc hypermarket signed just off the Crozon road, then head westwards on the D887. After about 10km (6.25 miles) you will reach the tiny double-gabled chapel of Ste-Marie-du-Ménez-Hom, which is well worth a glance as you're passing. The chapel stands in a simple parish close with a Calvary of three crosses. It has a handsome galleried belfry surmounted by a domed cupola. The interior of the chapel contains some exceptional carving. Several elaborate altarpieces occupy most of the east wall, showing the life of the Virgin, with saints and apostles.

A brief detour north of Ste-Marie-du-Ménez-Hom on the D47 will take you to Trégarvan on the south bank of the Aulne, where a disused school has been converted into a little museum, the Musée de l'Ecole Rurale. This shows what classroom life was like in this part of Brittany during the early 20th century, with the old slates and inkwells once in use. All teaching was in French only—use of the Breton language in class was strictly forbidden.

Return to the D887 from Trégarvan via a minor road and turn left. After about 3.5km (2 miles) take a steep turning on your left (D83) to the summit of Ménez-Hom.

❶ Ménez-Hom marks the western limit of the Montagnes Noires, a belt of hills stretching across central Finistère. A viewing table on the summit shows it to be exactly equidistant from both Paris and London (483km/300 miles). Considering the modest height of Ménez-Hom (just 330m/1,082ft), the views from this isolated, gorse-clad hillock are surprisingly impressive, extending from Douarnenez Bay and the Sizun peninsula right across to the Rade de Brest.

On a clear day, it is easy to understand why the ancient Celts regarded this peak as a sacred place. Even in much later times, local people held Ménez-Hom in awe, believing it to be the haunt of *korrigans* (the evil elves of Armorican folk myth). These days, visitors are more likely to spot a bird of prey wheeling majestically in the thermals overhead, or perhaps be startled by the vivid canopy of a hang-glider sailing past from time to time. Ménez-Hom is a popular site for aerial adventure sports, and is occasionally used by the army for training exercises. If you happen to be in the area in mid-August, the air will ring with the lively sound of traditional Breton *bagadou* bands using bagpipes and bombards during the Festival du Ménez-Hom (▷ 119).

Drive back to the main road and continue westwards, almost immediately turning left on to the D108 (signed Pentrez-Plage).

❷ The huge Lieue de Grève beyond St-Nic is an exquisite beach by any standards, facing southwest across Dournenez Bay between unspoiled headlands. Several little chapels (St-Côme, St-Nicaise) are worth tracking down nearby.

Hug the coastline along minor roads to Telgruc-sur-Mer, past more lovely beaches, then return to the main road (D887) and proceed to Crozon, 11km (7 miles) farther on.

❸ Crozon (▷ 103) is equipped with a helpful tourist office and a first-rate hotel-restaurant (▷ 120–121). Don't miss the church of St-Pierre, whose eye-popping altarpiece of the Ten Thousand Martyrs is one of the highlights of 16th-century Breton sculpture. The complexities of this obscure tale take some fathoming, but the overall effect, clarified by the church's obliging automatic lighting system, is stunning.

Above *The altarpiece in Eglise St-Pierre at Crozon*

Below *The Crozon peninsula has a wild and rugged appearance*

Opposite *The bay at Morgat*

From Crozon, several routes radiate to outlying headlands. You can skip one or two if you are short of time, but each has distinctive scenery. Follow the D887 southwards to Morgat 3km (2 miles).

❹ Morgat (▷ 98) is an appealing little resort tucked into an east-facing bay and sheltered by pines. Its beach and harbour are popular for sailing and water sports. Sea caves eroded by wave action are the focus of summer boat trips.

Head on down the D255 towards Cap de la Chèvre.

❺ Cap de la Chèvre is one of the wildest of Crozon's rugged headlands. Along the way, the Maison des Minéraux may divert you, especially if you have any children on board. This delightful little geology museum in an old rural school contains Europe's largest collection of fluorescent rocks, including quartz and manganese. Displayed in darkened rooms under ultra-violet light, the exhibits glow mysteriously in all the colours of the rainbow.

Return to Crozon, then take signs for the Pointe de Dinan (6km/4 miles west).

❻ The spectacular heathery cliffs of the Pointe de Dinan rear to a height of 40m/132ft from the Atlantic breakers. A natural rock-arch connects the mainland with a striking formation called the Château de Dinan just offshore (accessible on foot).

Return to Crozon again, then take the D8 to Camaret-sur-Mer and follow signs to the Pointe de Pen-Hir, perhaps the grandest of all the Crozon headlands, where a scattering of offshore rocks called Les Tas de Pois (pile of peas) adds to the coastal interest. Return into Camaret and go past the Alignements de Lagatjar (a group of roadside menhirs).

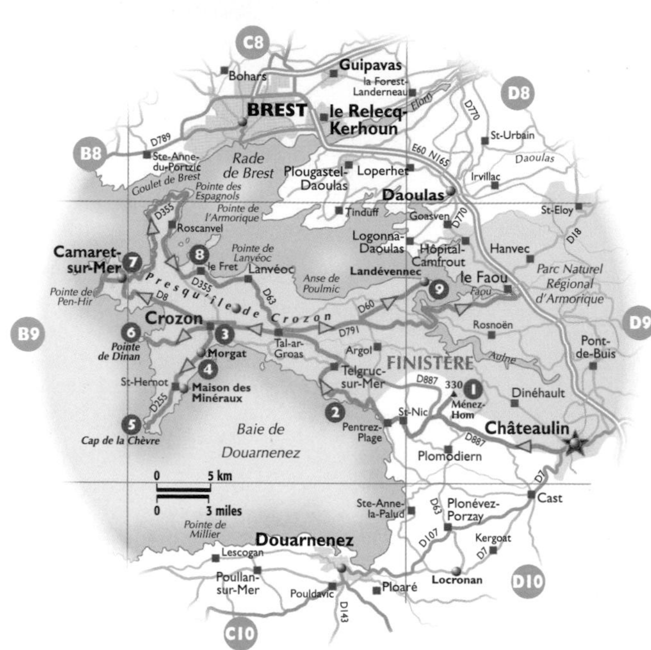

❼ Camaret-sur-Mer is a quiet seaside resort renowned for spiny lobster, listed on local menus. A chapel and a Vauban fortress of toytown dimensions perch on a long sandspit (Le Sillon) protecting the harbour.

A circular drive around the verdant Pointe des Espagnols (on the D355) gives fine views of the Rade de Brest. The point was named after a Spanish garrison occupied and fortified the headland briefly in 1594. From Roscanvel you can see the Île Longue to the east, now used as a nuclear submarine base and inaccessible to the public. Continue eastwards past the Ile Longue (a military naval base, no public access), following signs to Le Fret.

❽ This charming little port has a summer ferry service to Brest. A waterfront hotel-restaurant makes the perfect lunch spot, but book ahead to reserve a table.

Return to the main road via Lanvéoc and the D63, taking the D791 towards Le Faou. At Les Quatre Chemins, turn left on to the D60 to Landévennec (6.5km/4 miles).

❾ The main interest at Landévennec is a ruined Romanesque abbey (▷ 98) on a lonely wooded peninsula at the mouth of the Aulne. A museum traces its history. Benedictine monks welcome visitors to their modern church nearby.

Return to the main road, turn left and cross the Aulne (admiring the views near the Térénez suspension bridge). Then head along the scenic corniche road to the pleasant village of Le Faou, where you can continue your journey on the N165. Le Faou is a pretty place, especially when the tide is in. It was a sizeable port in medieval times, handling large volumes of timber. A number of picturesque 16th-century houses survive in the main street.

Opposite top *A natural archway links the rocky mass of Dinan Castle to the mainland*
Opposite *Menhirs on the Crozon Peninsula*

WHERE TO EAT

HOSTELLERIE DE LA MER

11 quai du Fret 02 98 27 61 90 Easter to mid Nov daily lunch, dinner (closed Jan and Sat lunch, Sun eve off season)

PLACES TO VISIT

MAISON DES MINÉRAUX

Route du Cap de la Chèvre, St-Hernot, 29160 Crozon 02 98 27 19 73 Jul, Aug daily 10–7; Sep–end Jun Mon–Fri 10–12, 2–5, Sun 2–5 Adult €4.50, child (8–14) €2.50

L'ANCIENNE ABBAYE DE LANDÉVENNEC

02 98 27 35 90 Museum and abbey ruins: Jul to mid-Sep daily 10–7; Apr–end Jun, mid–end Sep Sun–Fri 2–6; Oct–end Mar Sun 2–6 (Sun–Fri in school holidays) Adult €4; child (8–18) €3; new abbey free Abbey shop sells regional products, some made by the monks

AROUND HUELGOAT

At the heart of inland Brittany, within the Parc Naturel Régional d'Armorique, Huelgoat is the largest community of one of the region's last remaining natural forests. The surrounding countryside makes ideal territory for hiking and fishing, combining a lake, an unruly river and woodland scattered with chaotic rocks. This walk takes you through many different types of scenery.

THE WALK
Length: 5km (3 miles)
Allow: 2 hours
Start at: Place Aristide Briand
End at: La Roche Cintrée

HOW TO GET THERE
The village is 25km (15 miles) south of Morlaix and the N12 express road, in the northwest corner of Brittany.

Huelgoat (meaning 'high forest') stands beside a lake amid wooded hills. Its location makes it a popular summer resort and a base for activity holidays. Until the 1980s, the woods around the town formed a dense, primeval jungle of ancient trees, mysteriously tangled with lichen, moss and ferns. The devastating hurricane of October 1987 cut a swathe through it, uprooting many trees within minutes and leaving behind a chaotic scene of fallen timber. Today the forest is a patchier mix of mature broadleaved trees that survived the storm, younger saplings and recent (mostly coniferous) plantings.

★ Start from place Aristide Briand at the heart of Huelgoat. Turn left at the northern end of the square, with the lake on your left. On the other side of the street, a well-marked path leads through the rocks past an old mill beside the bridge. This serves as a seasonal information office, and contains an exhibition about the Huelgoat area.

❶ Almost immediately you will encounter the Chaos du Moulin, where huge granite boulders lie jumbled in bizarre formations. Granite is a mixture of different components: the softer parts weather quickly while harder minerals resist the elements for longer, creating strange, organic shapes. Breton legends attribute the tumbled rocks to an epic battle between giants from rival villages who used the boulders as weapons.

Continue along the waymarked path following the course of the Rivière d'Argent (Silver River).

❷ On the eastern (right) side of the river is the Grotte du Diable (Devil's Grotto), where you can climb down a ladder and watch the river foaming against the rocks. On the opposite bank is the Roche Tremblante, a single boulder weighing an estimated 100 tonnes, which is alleged to rock slightly when pushed at exactly the right point. A little farther on, a cluster of rocks called the Ménage de la Vierge (Virgin's Kitchen) is fancifully supposed to look a bit like a collection of household utensils.

Where the path forks at this point, take the right-hand route, the Allée Violette, on through the woods to the Pont Rouge, where it meets the D769A road leading to Carhaix. Turn left along the road for about 100m (110 yards), then turn right on to a looping path called the Promenade du Fer à Cheval (Horseshoe Walk), which curves along the riverside through lovely scenery before rejoining the road again. Turn right and follow the road for another 300m (330 yards).

❸ At this point of the route, a narrow staircase on your right leads down to Le Gouffre (The Abyss), a swallow-hole into which the river vanishes before reappearing about 150m (165 yards) farther on.

Carry on along the footpath past the Mare aux Fées (Fairies' Pool), until you meet an unsurfaced road. Turn right along this, following signs to La Mine.

❹ This is the site of an old lead and silver mine, known as long ago as Roman times. There isn't much to see now apart from a clearing with a stream running through it.

Cross the stream and take the footpath up the hill following the signs *'Huelgoat par le canal'*. Halfway up the hill the route splits. Keep left and continue to the top, where you'll find a small hydro-electric station at the head of the canal.

❺ The canal is little more than a channel a metre (3ft) wide, created during the 19th century when the old mine-workings were re-opened. The water was used to wash the ore and drive crushing machinery. The mines were not very productive and were eventually abandoned at the end of the 19th century.

Follow the Promenade du Canal back towards the town, about 3.5km (2 miles) away. Just before you arrive, take a road to your left signed La Roche Cintrée (Arched Rock), an excellent viewpoint of the town and surrounding countryside. If you need a meal, this charming *crêperie* in a typical old Breton house on the main square should fit the bill. It has an attractive terrace for summer dining.

WHEN TO GO

This walk is best in early summer when woodland foliage is at its prettiest, or in autumn when the leaves turn. Beware of slippery rocks and paths after rain, and falling timber in high winds. The local tourist office, restaurants and sports facilities may be closed out of season.

WHERE TO EAT

CRÊPERIE DES MYRTILLES

✉ 26 place Aristide-Briand, 29690 Huelgoat ☎ 02 98 99 72 66 🕐 Jan–end Oct; closed Mon except Jul and Aug

Opposite *The promenade alongside the lake at Huelgoat*
Below *Dappled sunlight on the river in the forest of Huelgoat*

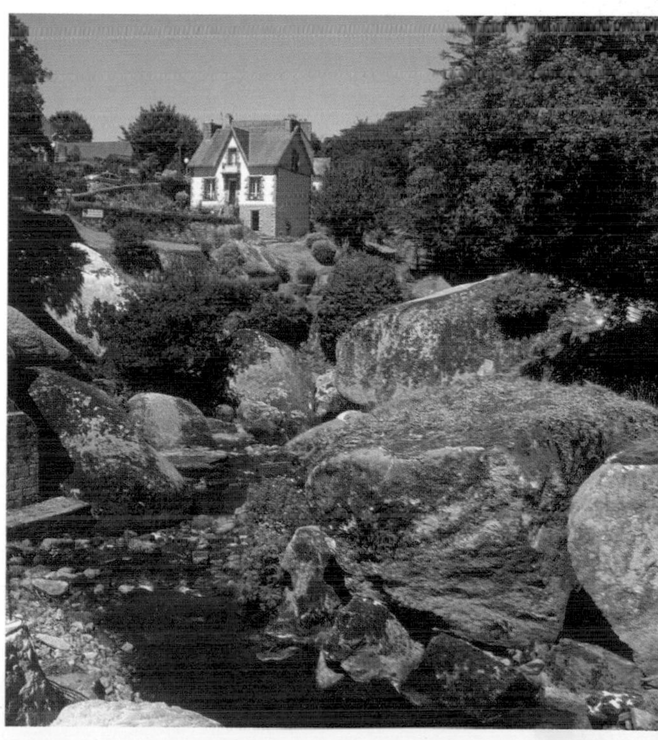

Above *A secluded beach near the tiny resort of Brignogan-Plage*

L'ABER WRAC'H

CENTRE DE VOILE DE L'ABER-WRAC'H

www.cvl-aberwrach.fr

Sailboat rental and tuition are offered in the scenic, sheltered waters of the Baie des Anges on Finistère's northwestern coast. The fully accredited sailing school supplies catamarans, sea-kayaks, sailboards and dinghies. There are events, courses and a children's club.

✉ 4 port de l'Aber Wrac'h, 29870 Landéda ☎ 02 98 04 90 64 ⏲ Jul, Aug daily 9–7, Sep 9–12, 2–6 (reception); sailing courses Jul–end Sep 9.30–12.30, 2.30–5.30 ✋ Sample prices: half-day family outings on a 6m (20ft) Blue Djinn €99 (max 5); kayak €12 (half-day), sailboard €33 (half-day)

BREST

PATINOIRE DE BREST RÏNKLA STADIUM

www.rinkla-stadium.com

This ice rink is home to the Albatross professional ice hockey team. Watch a live game or highlights on one of two huge TV screens, or go skating yourself. There is a café-bar, shop and children's play area. Take bus line 5 or 6 to Bellevue or Patinoire.

✉ Place Napoleon III, quartier Bellevue, 29210 Brest ☎ 02 98 03 01 30 ⏲ Sep–end May public skating Sun 10–12.30, 2.30–5.30 Wed, Sat, 2.30–5.30; Tue, Thu, Fri 8.30pm–11.30pm, longer hours in school holidays incl 2.30–5.30 daily ✋ Adult incl skate rental €7.50, child under 18 €6.50

LE QUARTZ

www.lequartz.com

If you are looking for culture, this major avant-garde arts venue near the tourist office off place de la Liberté has two performance halls, hosting experimental and popular theatre, ballet and dance, classical music, jazz, world music, opera, operetta and arthouse films. The Cinémathèque de Bretagne (film library) is also housed here.

✉ Square Beethoven, rue du Château, 29210 Brest ☎ 02 98 33 70 70 ⏲ Box office Tue–Sat 1–7 (until 9pm whenever there's a performance). Closed Mon, holidays, Jul and Aug ✋ Ticket prices start at around €6, averaging about €30 for a major concert or drama performance

LE CONQUET

AQUAFAUNE

www.vedette-aquafaune.fr

Take a trip on a glass-bottomed boat out to the clear waters of the Molène archipelago to watch grey seals, dolphins and a host of other sea life in this marine nature reserve, which forms part of the Armorique Regional Nature Park. Trips last two and a half hours, with commentary.

✉ Gare Martime, 26 rue Sainte-Barbe, 29217 Le Conquet ☎ 02 98 89 14 13 ⏲ Feb–end Oct (timetable tide-dependent) ✋ Adult €26, child (4–16) €16, child under 4 €2

FOUESNANT

LES BALNÉIDES

www.balneides.fr

This massive indoor waterpark is a useful family bolthole on a wet day. It claims the longest waterslide in Brittany (75m/248ft), and a range of waterjets, as well as a sauna.

✉ Allé de Loc'hilaire, 29170 Fouesnant ☎ 02 98 56 18 19 ⏲ Daily but very variable hours, 10–8 in summer (longer in school holidays) ✋ Adult €5.85, child (2–18) €4.95

GUIMAËC

DOMAINE DE KERVEGUEN

www.kerveguen.fr

Here the Cidre de l'Elysée (as served at the Elysée Palace, apparently) is carefully made by natural methods and traditionally matured in oak casks, giving a high-quality, award-winning product. The premises are ancient and mellow, with a fine dovecote among the orchards.

⊠ 29620 Guimaëc (northeast of Morlaix near Locquirec) ☎ 02 98 67 50 02 ⊙ Jul, Aug Mon–Sat 10.30–6.30; Apr–end Jun, Sep and in school holidays pm only, or by appointment ⊞ Free

LE GUILVINEC

HALIOTIKA

www.leguilvinec.com

An imaginative discovery centre at one of Brittany's leading fishing ports (▷ 103) reveals what life is like for the crew on a trawler. Watch the fleet come home, learn about fishing techniques and boats, identify species and find out how to prepare fish for cooking. Lots of activities, trips, and guided visits to the local *criée* (fish auction). Audiotours in English are available.

⊠ Le Port, 29730 Le Guilvinec ☎ 92 98 58 28 38 ⊙ Apr–early Oct Mon–Fri 10.30–12.30, 2–7 (also Sat–Sun 3–6.30 Jul and Aug) ⊞ Adult €5.50, child (4–14) €3.50 ☞ Guided tours in English Jul and Aug Thu at 3.45; €1; *criée* visits €1

ÎLE D'OUESSANT

CENTRE EQUESTRE CALECHES DU PONANT

www.cheval-cdp-29.fr

Discover France's westernmost point on horseback. Routes pass many of Ouessant's most beautiful spots. Hack for an hour or two, take a horse powered carriage tour around the island, or spend several days trekking with *gîte* accommodation and dinner included.

⊠ Le Goubars, 29242 Ouessant ☎ 02 98 48 89 29 ⊙ Daily 9–6 ⊞ Horse-and-carriage rides €51 per hour (up to three passengers), €108 for 2 hours

LANDERNEAU

COMPTOIR DES PRODUITS BRETONS

www.comptoir-produits-bretons.com

This enticing shop is one of the best places to look for presents and souvenirs. On display is a huge range of Breton crafts and regional products—foods, music recordings, maritime mementoes such as boat models or seascapes, nautical outdoor gear, Breton beers, cider and whisky, Celtic-style jewellery, Quimper *faïence* and glassware.

⊠ 3 quai de Cornouaille, 29800 Landerneau ☎ 02 98 21 35 93 ⊙ Mon–Fri 9.30–12, 2–7, Sat 9.30–12.30, 2–7, Sun 2–6.30

MORLAIX

LE LÉON À FER ET À FLOTS

www.aferaflots.org

This enjoyable circular tour by boat and train takes in St-Pol-de-Léon, Roscoff and Morlaix Bay. You visit the main sights, including Batz and the Château du Taureau. Departures from Morlaix or Roscoff. A full programme is available from either tourist office, or online.

⊠ Place des Otages, 29600 Morlaix ☎ 02 98 62 07 52 ⊙ Apr–end Oct ⊞ Adult €23, child (4–11) €12, under 4 free

LE THÉÂTRE DU PAYS DE MORLAIX

www.ville.morlaix.fr

This is a superb venue for plays, local and world music, films and ballet. There are street performances every Wednesday from mid-July to mid-August.

⊠ 27 rue de Brest, 29600 Morlaix ☎ 02 98 15 22 77 ⊙ Performances daily 8pm (ticket office open Mon 1.30–7, Tue–Fri 9–12.30, 1.30–7, Sat 10–12, 2–6) ⊞ Adult €18, child (under 12) €5

PLOMODIERN

CELTIC VOL LIBRE

www.vol-libre-menez-hom.com

The modest heights of Ménez-Hom, last of the hills in the Monts d'Arrée range, give extensive views over the Crozon peninsula, and provide sufficient elevation for hang-gliding *(parapente)*. You can take a trial flight with a qualified pilot, or hone existing skills. Check your insurance cover before take-off.

⊠ Breugnou, 29550 Plomodiern ☎ 02 98 81 50 27 ⊙ Flights depend on weather conditions ⊞ 10-minute trial flight in a two-man apparatus €70; a morning's introduction €75

PONT-AVEN

DELICES DE PONT-AVEN

www.galettes-penven.com

Pont-Aven is famed for its buttery biscuits, known locally as *galettes* (not to be confused with Brittany's classic buckwheat pancakes). Several firms in town have a long-standing reputation, including Galettes Penven and Traou Mad in adjacent premises. All sell their wares in beautifully designed tins, ideal for presents and even collectors' items. Factory tours can be arranged.

⊠ 1 quai Théodore-Botrel, 29930 Pont-Aven ☎ 02 98 06 05 87 ⊙ Mon–Thu 9.30–12.30, 2–6.30 (until 7pm on Fri, Sat), Sun 10.30–12.30, 2.30–7

VEDETTES AVEN-BÉLON

www.vedettes-aven-belon.com

Drift past manor houses, castles, tidal mills and oyster beds in a comfortable, panoramic motor-launch, accompanied by the calls of sea-birds and the occasional vivid flash of a kingfisher. Three different excursions take in the scenic wooded estuaries of the Aven and Bélon, departing from Pont Aven or Port-Bélon. The commentary is available in English.

⊠ Port du Pont-Aven, quai Théodore Botrel (Easter–end Sep) ⊠ Port du Bélon, 29340 Moëlan-sur-Mer (Jul, Aug) ☎ 02 98 71 14 59 ⊙ Daily Jul–end Sep, depending on tides ⊞ Adult €8.50–€13, child (4–12) €5.50–€8, child (1–3) €1

PONT-L'ABBE

LE MINOR

www.leminorboutique.com

This shop located near the castle is a good place to see some of the exquisite embroidery for which the town is famous. Products for sale here are made locally by hand. Go upstairs for a display of bright wall-hangings, table-mats, traycloths and household linen in cheerful traditional designs. Quimper pottery and a range of stylish knitwear are also on sale.

⊠ 5 quai Saint-Laurent, 29120 Pont-l'Abbé ☎ 02 98 87 07 22 ⊙ Mon–Sat 9–12, 2–7; closed Sun and Mon am in winter

QUIMPER

BISCUITERIE DE QUIMPER STYVELL

This venerable firm makes a traditional speciality called *crêpes dentelles* according to the *l'hermine d'or* recipe more than a century old. The name means 'lace pancakes' but these buttery confections are light, crisp biscuits, perfect with ice cream. Vanilla-flavoured batter is laid out in flat blocks, cut into thin strips and rolled up on a knife. Each pancake is made separately by hand.
✉ 8 rue du Chanoine Moreau, Locmaria, 29000 Quimper ☎ 02 98 53 10 13
🕑 Shop: Mon–Sat 9–7; crêpe making: 10.30–12, 3.30–5

LA FAÏENCERIE H. B. HENRIOT

www.hb-henriot.com
The largest and most high-profile of the pottery firms in Quimper, still uses the traditional method of hand-decoration. Each piece is personally signed by the artist. Well-advertised tours of the factory (some in English) show visitors the manufacturing process. A huge on-site showroom offers Quimper ware at a range of prices, with substantial discounts for slightly imperfect stock.
✉ Rue Haute, Locmaria, 29337 Quimper ☎ 02 98 90 09 36 or 0800 626 510 (for guided tour timetable) 🕑 35-minute tours all year, varying seasonally according to demand (Jul, Aug Mon–Sat, off-season Mon–Fri); showroom Mon–Sat 9.30–7
✋ Adult €5, child (8–14) €2.50

KELTIA MUSIQUE

Come here to browse through the wide selection of Breton and Celtic music recordings and books. There are also musical instrument manuals and similar items.
✉ 1 place au Beurre, 29000 Quimper
☎ 02 98 95 45 82 🕑 Tue–Sat 10–12, 2–7

LES MACARONS DE PHILOMÈNE

Eye-catching displays of beautifully coloured macaroons fill the windows of this quaint old shopfront in the heart of the old town. All are made on the premises by France's premier *macaronier* Rolland Padou. Sandwiched with tasty fillings like a sort of bourbon biscuit, these feather-light confections are irresistible for children, or indeed anyone with a sweet tooth. The house special is a *macaron au caramel au beurre salé*, but you might try the bright green pistachio or sugar-pink varieties.
✉ 13 rue Kéréon, 29000 Quimper ☎ 02 98 95 21 40 🕑 Tue–Sat 9–7, also Mon in Jul, Aug (same hours)

LE QUARTIER

www.le-quartier.net
Opposite the Théatre de Cornouaille, this contemporary art gallery puts on four exhibitions of modern art each year. It has disabled access and a library. Free escorted visits are held on Saturday afternoons.
✉ 10 esplanade François-Mitterand, 29107 Quimper ☎ 02 98 55 55 77 🕑 Tue–Sat 10–12, 1–6, (closed for 3 weeks between exhibitions) ✋ Adult €1.50; admission free on Sun, and for students (under 26), children (under 16), senior citizens (over 65)

THÉÂTRE DE CORNOUAILLE

www.theatrequimper.asso.fr
A mixed schedule of concerts, plays and films takes place at this leading arts venue, Quimper's regional theatre. Other shows are held in the Max-Jacob theatre, or l'Auditorium, with outposts in Le Guilvinec, Pont-l'Abbé and Châteaulin.
✉ 1 esplanade François Mitterand, 29337 Quimper ☎ 02 98 55 98 98 🕑 Performances Sep–end May
✋ Average prices about €30

QUIMPERLÉ

LA MAISON DES ARCHERS

One of the best preserved houses in the old town, dating from around 1570, is now used as a venue for

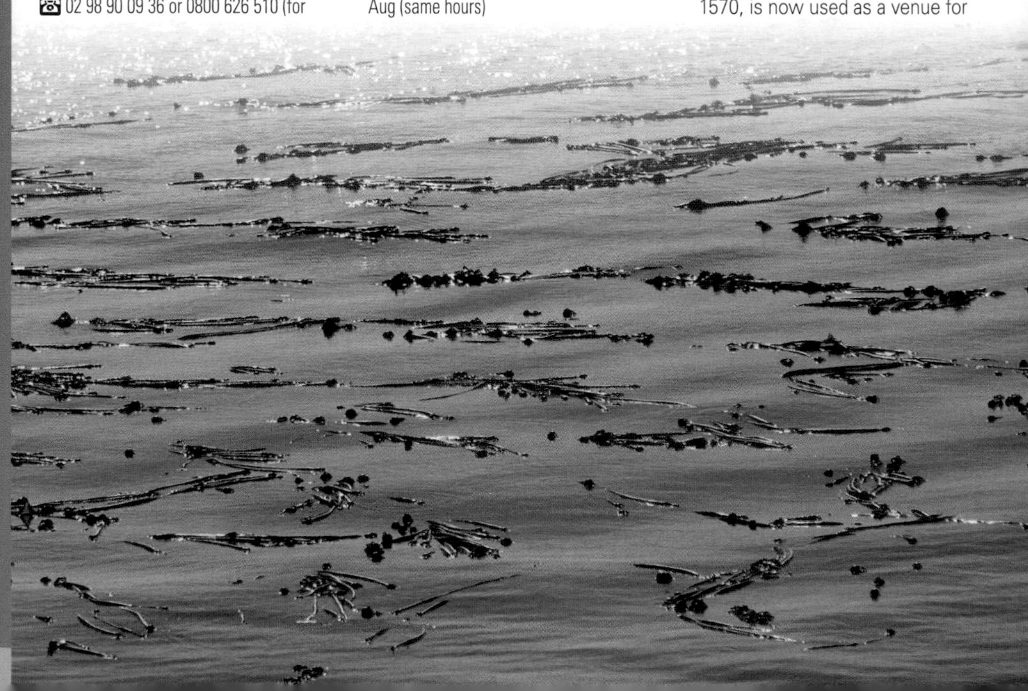

temporary summer exhibitions. It's worth going in just to see the building, but details of what's on are available at the tourist office.
✉ 7 rue Dom-Morice, 29300 Quimperlé ☎ 02 98 39 06 63 🕐 Mid-Jun to end Sep Wed–Mon 10–12, 2.30–7 ✋ Variable, but inexpensive—combined tickets are valid for two local exhibitions

ROSCOFF

LA MAISON DU KOUIGN-AMANN

This tiny shop prides itself on a Breton speciality called *kouign-amann*, a sweet cake made with best butter and wheat flour. This place serves it warm.
✉ 18 rue Armand Rousseau, 29680 Roscoff ☎ 02 98 69 71 61 🕐 Daily 8.30–12.30, 2.30–7 (8.30–7 or 8pm in summer)

THALADO

www.thalado.fr
Near the thermal spa, this discovery facility is the place to learn all about seaweed and its uses. Besides a small permanent exhibition on the history and harvesting of seaweed, it holds lectures and guided beachcombing walks. Seaweed products are on sale for culinary, pharmaceutical and cosmetic uses.
✉ 5 rue Victor-Hugo, 29680 Roscoff ☎ 02 98 69 77 05 🕐 Jun–end Sep Mon–Sat 9–12, 2–7 ✋ Free admission to centre; guided walks €5 (adult), €3.50 (child 10–16), under 10 free

SAINT-NIC-PENTREZ

CLUB DE CHAR À VOILE DE PENTREZ

www.ccvpentrez.free.fr
Try sand-yachting and kite-surfing on this superb beach north of Douarnenez, which, at low tide, is 3km (2 miles) long and 5km (3 miles) wide. The minimum age for these activities is seven, and it's a good idea to reserve in advance. Credit cards are not accepted.
✉ 5 rue du Ménez-Hom, Pentrez Plage, 29550 St-Nic ☎ 06 11 80 09 79 🕐 Jul, Aug daily 10–7; school holidays Mon–Fri 10–12, 2–6, Sat–Sun 2–6; rest of year weekends only ✋ From about €17 per hour

Left *Seaweed is sold for a variety of uses*

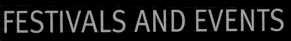

FESTIVALS AND EVENTS

JULY

FÊTE DES BRODEUSES PONT-L'ABBÉ

A popular folklore festival in honour of the local tradition of embroidery. Processions and parades with the elaborate costumes of the Bigouden region, followed by late-night parties with Breton music and dancing, and lakeside fireworks.
☎ 02 98 82 37 99 🕐 Second weekend in Jul

FESTIVAL DE CORNOUAILLE QUIMPER

www.festival-cornouaille.com
This is one of Brittany's most important cultural events, held annually for more than 80 years. Some 4,500 artists arrive from all over Europe and put on concerts, exhibitions and shows.
☎ 02 98 55 53 53 🕐 Mid to late Jul

FÊTE DES POMMIERS FOUESNANT

A traditional folk celebration of the apple orchards in this cider-producing area. Parades and fireworks, and a typical *fest-noz* with Breton music.
🕐 Third weekend in Jul

AUGUST

FESTIVAL DU MÊNEZ-HOM PLOMODIERN

A folk festival is held throughout August. On 15 August Ménez-Hom reverberates to the sound of music played on typical Breton instruments like the bagpipes and the bombard.
🕐 Aug

FESTIVAL DES FILETS BLEUS CONCARNEAU

http://filetsbleus.free.fr
The three-day Blue Nets Festival recalls the early 20th century, when the sardine shoals disappeared and Concarneau's fishing-based economy collapsed. Today it is one of Finistère's liveliest folk festivals.
☎ 02 98 97 09 09 🕐 Third week in Aug

NOVEMBER

FESTIVAL EUROPÉEN DU FILM COURT DE BREST BREST

www.filmcourt.fr
A prestigious short-film festival attracts cinema-goers and film buffs in late autumn. About 50 films compete from countries throughout Europe, all in *version originale*.
☎ 02 98 44 03 94 🕐 About 10 days in early to mid-Nov

PARDONS

Some of the most celebrated religious processions in Finistère are held at Locronan (mid-July), Sainte-Anne-la-Palud (last Sunday in August) and Le Folgoët (early September, ▷ 91). But the smaller ones encountered by chance in local villages can be just as moving.

Above *Concerts form part of the Festival de Cornouaille, Quimper*

Above *Brittany has many lovely restaurants*

PRICES AND SYMBOLS
The restaurants are listed alphabetically within each town. The prices given for lunch (L) and dinner (D) are for three courses for one person, without drinks. The wine price is for the least expensive bottle.
For a key to the symbols, ▷ 2.

BREST

AMOUR DE POMME DE TERRE

The humble *pomme de terre* assumes many varied guises at this young-at-heart, potato-themed restaurant. It's popular with hungry students, and sailors on shore leave. Ingredients are imaginatively combined, and often alcoholic, so the bill can mount higher than expected, but servings are huge, and fixed-price menus inexpensive. Specialities include chargrills, *raclettes* and deli-style salads.
✉ 23 rue des Halles, 29200 Brest ☎ 02 98 43 48 51 🕒 Daily 12–2, 7.15–10.30 (11 at weekends and in high season) ✋ L €18, D €25, Wine €13

MA PETITE FOLIE

This fine old crayfish boat permanently moored in the pleasure harbour near Océanopolis has been put to good use as a smart gourmet restaurant. As you might expect, seafood predominates on its menus (*soupe de poisson*, stuffed clams). You can dine on either deck, but be sure to book ahead in high season.
✉ Port du Moulin Blanc, 29200 Brest ☎ 02 98 42 44 42 🕒 Daily 12–2, 7.30–10 ✋ L €22, D €35, Wine €19

CARANTEC

PATRICK JEFFROY

www.hoteldecarantec.com
Views from this hotel restaurant take in a sweep of coastline, but the top-notch cooking deserves concentration, as chef-patron Patrick Jeffroy skilfully combines unexpected ingredients for innovative surf-and-turf menus (sea bass with Roscoff onion marmalade; apple tart with lavender). Service is polished but friendly. Reserve ahead.
✉ 20 rue de Kélenn, 29660 Carantec ☎ 02 98 67 00 47 🕒 Mid-Jun to mid-Sep Wed, Fri–Sun 12–2.30, 7.30–10, Mon, Tue, Thu 7.30–10; rest of year Wed–Sat lunch and dinner, Sun lunch only ✋ L €40, D €75, Wine €20

CONCARNEAU

L'AMIRAL

www.restaurant-amiral.com
A smart bar-restaurant overlooking the Ville-Close, L'Amiral is nautically decorated with handsome panelling, designer lamps and models of old sailboats. The bar is decorated with a mosaic underwater scene. The menu changes daily, but always features top-notch seafood and home-made bread. Wines come by the glass, and the lunchtime *formules* are good value. Reserve ahead in summer; both French and British visitors love the place, which was once immortalized in a story featuring Georges Simenon's most famous character, Inspector Maigret.
✉ 1 avenue Pierre Guéguin, 29900 Concarneau ☎ 02 98 60 55 23 🕒 Jul, Aug Tue–Sun 12–1.30, 7–9.30; Sep–end Jun Tue–Sat 12–1.30, 7–9.30, Sun 12–1.30; closed 2 weeks Jan–Feb and Sep–Oct ✋ L €30, D €45, Wine €15

LE PETIT CHAPERON ROUGE

This popular *crêperie* is shoehorned into a tiny square not far from the Ville-Close. As the name implies, there's a Little Red Riding Hood theme here, so miniature baskets and rustic nick-nacks dangle everywhere. Its reputation, however, stems from its top-quality *crêpes* rather than the winsome interior. La Blanchette includes goat's cheese,

spinach, ham and cream, while the house special, Petit Chaperon Rouge, contains chocolate fondue and almonds. English-speaking staff make visitors very welcome.
✉ 7 place Duguesclin, 29900 Concarneau ☎ 02 98 60 53 32 ⊙ Tue–Sat 12–2.30, 7–9.30; Sun 12–2.30; closed 2 weeks Mar, 2 weeks mid-Jun, 3 weeks Oct ✋ L €12, D €16, Wine €10

CROZON

HOSTELLERIE DE LA MER

www.hostelleriedelamer.com
You couldn't do better than arrive here at lunchtime (but reserve ahead!) for a ringside view of the Rade de Brest from the picture windows of this family-run hotel-restaurant. The dining room is spacious and light, with pink walls and carved Breton furnishings. As the lobster tank indicates, menus are mainly fishy.
✉ 11 quai du Fret 29160 Crozon ☎ 02 98 27 61 90 ⊙ Easter to mid-Nov daily lunch, dinner; closed Jan and Sat lunch, Sun dinner off-season ✋ L €18, D €25, Wine €12

LE MUTIN GOURMAND

www.chez.com/mutingourmand
An elegant place decorated to reflect sunshine and seaside with exposed stonework, contemporary watercolours and clever use of mirror-glass. Acclaimed menus echo *mer* or *terre* (yellow pollack with black wheat pancakes, egg *chaud-froid* with sea urchin corals, pigeon pie with warm foie gras). There's an eye-popping wine-list. The hotel rooms reach equally high standards.
✉ Place de l'Église, 29160 Crozon ☎ 02 98 27 06 51 ⊙ Wed–Sat 12–1.30, 7–9, Mon, Tue 7–9, Sun 12–1.30; closed Mon dinner off-season, also several weeks in winter ✋ L €30, D €50, Wine €18

GUIMILIAU

AR CHUPEN

This popular pancake restaurant occupies a renovated farmhouse by Guimiliau's famous parish close, decorated in *paysanne* style with copper pictures and antique furniture. The house special is artichokes with various accompaniments. A Fermier has ham, bacon, mushrooms and cream, while a Léonard or a Royale are based on seafood. Finish your meal with *chouchen* (mead served in a horn). When the restaurant fills up, the gregarious chef may come out of the kitchen to play his accordion.
✉ 43 rue du Calvaire, 29400 Guimiliau ☎ 02 98 68 73 63 ⊙ Jun–end Aug daily 12–9.30; Sun–Fri 12–2, Sat 12–10 rest of year ✋ L €16, D €22, Wine €11

LAMPAUL-GUIMILIAU

L'ESCAPADE

The best restaurant in the village stands by the town hall, its mellow dining space spread over two floors of an attractive yellow-painted house with green awnings. Specials include goulash soup and Finistère ostrich steaks. They also serve *crêpes* with fillings such as prunes and smoked bacon. A Lampaulaise contains salmon and leek fondue, while Le Forêt Noir is a calorific concoction of cherry, Amarena, chocolate and whipped cream.
✉ 8 place de Villers, 29400 Lampaul-Guimiliau ☎ 02 98 68 61 27 ⊙ Tue, Thu, Fri 12–1.30, 7–8.30, Wed 12–1.30, Sat, Sun 12–1.30, 7–9; closed 3 weeks in Aug ✋ L €15, D €35, Wine €13

MORLAIX

BRASSERIE DE L'EUROPE

www.brasseriedeleurope.com
This bright, elegant two-tier café-brasserie shares premises with the hotel of the same name (▷ 125), but is separately managed. Stylish and sophisticated, it specializes mainly in seafood. You can have a full meal here, or simply graze on a *tarte salée*, a platter of smoked fish or half a dozen oysters. During happy hour (6–8pm) drinks are dispensed at half price in the downstairs wine-bar, including wines by the glass.
✉ Place Emile Souvestre, 29600 Morlaix ☎ 02 98 88 81 15 ⊙ Mon–Sat 12–2, 7–10; bar open all day in season (Mon–Sat 8–1am) ✋ L €18, D €25, Wine €12

L'HERMINE

There's no shortage of eateries on this picturesque cobbled *venelle* (alley), but this charming *crêperie* is unlikely to disappoint. In a quaint stone building, its rustic interior is decked with flowers, model boats and bric-à-brac. The welcome is warm, and service courteous (good English spoken). Pancakes are always freshly cooked and *galettes* made with genuine Breton buckwheat. Try a Forestière *(lardons* in bechamel sauce), or one of the house specials made with seaweed. There's a terrace for al fresco dining.
✉ 35 rue Ange de Guernisac, 29600 Morlaix ☎ 02 98 88 10 91 ⊙ Daily 12–2.30; 7–9.30 (10 on Fri and Sat, and every day in high season) ✋ L €12, D €16, Wine €13

PONT-AVEN

MOULIN DE ROSMADEC

www.moulinderosmadec.com
With its feet in the racing waters of the River Aven, this gorgeously restored 15th-century mill is an instant hit with visitors, so reserve ahead if you want to eat or stay here. The award-winning cooking of the Sebilleau brothers is justly famous (try the house lobster or *langoustines croquantes*, followed by pancakes for pudding). Copper utensils, ceramics and Breton furnishings decorate the cosy interior; the terrace has lovely views, though the sound of water can be deafening after heavy rain.
✉ Venelle de Rosmadec, 29930 Pont-Aven (by the bridge) ☎ 02 98 06 00 22 ⊙ Closed Sun dinner Sep–end Jun and Wed ✋ L €35, D €70, Wine €22

QUIMPERLÉ

BISTRO DE LA TOUR

www.hotelvintage.com
This atmospheric restaurant and wine cellar stands on a street crammed with similar ancient timbered buildings. It has two split-level dining rooms, one on the ground floor in art-deco style, and an upstairs one decked with paintings by the Pont-Aven school. Dishes include oysters or a Breton *cassoulet* with *andouille* sausages. Allow yourself enough time to read through the wine list, which has

a staggering 700 entries. Cooked dishes are available to take away.
✉ 2 rue Dom-Morice, 29300 Quimperlé ☎ 02 98 39 29 58 ⏲ Tue–Fri 12.15–1.45, 7.30–9, Sat 7.30–9 ✋ L €24, D €38, Wine €15

RIEC-SUR-BÉLON

CHEZ JACKY

www.chez-jacky.com

This seafood-rearing enterprise has a popular on-site brasserie overlooking the Bélon waterfront. In these idyllic surroundings, you can sample home-grown oysters, lobsters and shellfish on sturdy wooden benches and tables, then take some away with you. Reserve ahead in high season. Children are welcome, but don't ask for a steak here.
✉ Port de Bélon, 29340 Riec-sur-Bélon ☎ 02 98 06 90 32 ⏲ Daily 12.15–3, 7–10 ✋ L €19, D €40, Wine €16

ROSCOFF

CHEZ JANIE

www.chezjanie.com

This informal, convivial bar-restaurant on Roscoff's old port has long been a popular watering hole for locals and visitors alike. It is now managed by the Chapalain family (Hôtel Brittany, ▷ 125), and offers an undaunting mix of drinks and snacks *(rillettes de saumon, tartare de poissons)*, salads, oysters and good-value *plats du jour*. Children's menus might include a *steak haché* (hamburger) or *jambon frites* (ham and chips). The modern bedrooms at the attached Hôtel du Centre are terrific value.
✉ Le Port, 29680 Roscoff ☎ 02 98 61 24 25 ⏲ Jul–Aug daily 12–2, 7–10; Mon, Wed–Sat 12–2, 7–9.30, Sun 12–2 rest of year; closed mid-Nov to mid-Feb ✋ L €15, D €25, Wine €16

L'ECUME DES JOURS

A 16th-century shipbuilder's house by the water's edge makes a fine setting for this highly respected restaurant. Cuisine inspired by high-quality local ingredients, especially fish and *primeurs* (early vegetables such as artichokes and pink onions) includes specialities such as *poelée de pétoncles* (a pan of scallops) or roast leg of duck with an apple and tomato chutney. With menus starting at a modest €16, it's good value. Huge fireplaces and exposed stonework add to the atmosphere.
✉ Quai d'Auxerre, 29680 Roscoff ☎ 02 98 61 22 83 ⏲ 12–2.30, 7.30–9.30; closed Tue (except Jul and Aug) and Wed, also Dec and Jan ✋ L €25, D €35, Wine €18

ST-POL-DE-LÉON

AUBERGE DE LA POMME D'API

This 16th-century building has an elegant interior with a large fireplace and exposed stone walls. The food is a treat, but you'd better brush up on your French as dishes are elaborately concocted and equally elaborately named; *dos de bar, cuit sur peau* (sea bass), *légumes oubliés* (forgotten vegetables!) and *cèpes et saucisse de Morteau* (cep mushrooms and smoked sausage). Fish dishes include wild turbot or local lobster. Vegetarian and children's options are available.
✉ 49 rue Verderel, 29250 St-Pol-de-Léon ☎ 02 98 69 04 36 ⏲ Jul, Aug daily 12–2, 7–9; closed mid–end Nov and Sun dinner, Mon off-season ✋ L €25, D €65, Wine €18

Below *Le Petit Chaperon Rouge in Concarneau*

PRICES AND SYMBOLS

Prices quoted are the range for a double with private facilities. The *taxe de séjour* (▷ 214) is not included. Unless otherwise stated, breakfast is excluded from the price.

For a key to the symbols, ▷ 2.

BÉNODET

ARMORIC

www.armoric-benodet.com

This reliable, white-painted hotel near the entrance to the resort is welcoming and well managed, with English-speaking reception staff. Its large gardens, heated pool and self-contained garden rooms have appeal for families with children. Bedrooms are stylishly refurbished with well-designed bathrooms. Half-board terms are available.

✉ 3 rue de Penfoul, 29950 Bénodet ☎ 02 98 57 04 03 ⊛ Closed late Feb–early Mar ✋ €55–€155 (breakfast €10) ⓘ 30 ≋ Outdoor heated (May–end Sep)

CONCARNEAU

AUBERGE DE JEUNESSE

www.ajconcarneau.com

This youth hostel has a lovely position right by the sea within easy walking distance of the rest of the town. It stands beside the Marinarium to the west of the Ville-Close. Accommodation is fairly basic, in bunk-bedded dormitories of varying sizes, with separate showers and toilets, but refurbishment is in progress. The management is helpful and friendly. There is no age limit, but to stay here you need an international youth hostel card (which can be purchased on arrival). Under-16s must be accompanied by an adult).

✉ Quai de la Croix, 29181 Concarneau ☎ 02 98 97 03 47 ⊛ Open all year (reception 9–12, 6–8) ✋ €14.50 per person, including breakfast. Groups of more than 10 must stay demi-pension and take the evening meal (€23.50 per person dinner, bed-and-breakfast) ⓘ Sleeps 76, in rooms for 4, 6, or 10

CROZON

JULIA

www.hoteljulia.fr

Up a quiet side street leading to the sea, this appealing Logis de France has ocean views, attractive gardens and a family atmosphere. Well kept inside and out, it offers a friendly welcome, tasteful interior and regional cooking in its pleasantly traditional restaurant. Bedrooms vary in style, some are very elegant indeed, but all reach a good standard and are well maintained—a few are suitable for visitors with reduced mobility. Half-board terms are obligatory in high season.

✉ 43 rue du Tréflez, 29160 Crozon ☎ 02 98 27 05 89 ⊛ Closed Nov–end Mar, except Christmas, New Year; reception closed Mon off season ✋ €51–€140 (breakfast €9) ⓘ 18

DOUARNENEZ

CLOS DE VALLOMBREUSE

www.closvallombreuse.com

Grandstand views over Douarnenez Bay can be seen from this belle-époque villa in large, secluded grounds. The elegant *parterres* and terraces are particularly attractive in summer. The interior has many interesting features, such as fine panelling and plasterwork, handsome fireplaces and regal furnishings. The restaurant serves ambitious and reputable fare, mostly based on fresh fish from the port a few minutes away. To find it, look for the church at the top of the hill.

✉ 7 rue d'Estienne-d'Orves, 29100 Douarnenez ☎ 02 98 92 63 64 ✋ €52–€122 (breakfast €11) ⓘ 20 ≋ Outdoor

Above *There is a variety of accommodation to suit all pockets in this region of France*

LE GUILVINEC

POISSON D'AVRIL

www.lepoissondavril.fr

This sophisticated venture lies on the remote Penmarc'h peninsula. It's a restaurant-with-rooms overlooking the *criée* of Le Guilvinec, an active fishing port. Parisian connoisseurs are already making their way here to sample Jean-Marie Le Quellec's expertly prepared seafood in its stylish dining room. Above the restaurant, a handful of imaginatively designed bedrooms are accessible via an exterior spiral staircase. These spacious refined affairs make dramatic use of colour and accessories. One or two have private terraces with stunning views over the waves. Breakfasts include delicious fresh pastries. You can borrow binoculars to watch the seabirds foraging for fish scraps. Street parking is available nearby.

✉ 19–21 rue de Men-Meur, 29730 Le Guilvinec ☎ 02 98 58 23 83 ◷ Closed Jan ✋ €85–€105 (breakfast €7) 🛏 9

LANDEDA

BAIE DES ANGES

www.baie-des-anges.com

An entrancing location on the Côte des Abers in northwestern Finistère does much for this lovely place, and the chic maritime interior of seagrass, wicker and driftwood makes it just as seductive inside. There are lovely views from the breakfast tables and the breakfast is very good. Bedrooms are an airy combination of ivory walls and crisp blue-and-white stripes or checks. The owners are charming and speak excellent English. A sauna, Jacuzzi and hydromassage are available. Annexe studios can be rented by the port. One room is suitable for visitors in wheelchairs.

✉ 350 route des Anges, Port de l'Aber-Wrac'h, 29870 Landéda ☎ 02 98 04 90 04 ◷ Closed Jan, Feb ✋ €95–€235 (breakfast €14) 🛏 25, including 2 suites

LOCQUIREC

GRAND HÔTEL DES BAINS

www.grand-hotel-des-bains.com

A ravishingly modernized belle-époque spa hotel in a glorious peaceful setting a few moments from Locquirec's pretty fishing harbour. Views encompass glimpses of sea and wooded headlands through a screen of pleached limes. The interior is imaginatively designed in a cool, contemporary style of polished floorboards and wicker seating. Bedrooms are airy and relaxing, many with private terraces. The restaurant is exceptionally appealing. The hotel also owns a brasserie by the port. Special interest and thalassotherapy breaks are available.

✉ 15 rue de l'Eglise, 29241 Locquirec ☎ 02 98 67 41 02 ◷ All year ✋ €199–€227 (includes breakfast) 🛏 36 🏋 🏊 Covered; Jacuzzi, spa

LOCRONAN

HOSTELLERIE DU BOIS DU NÉVET

www.hostellerie-bois-nevet.com

This modern hotel snakes through extensive wooded grounds about 10 minutes' walk from the historic village of Locronan (leave your car here to avoid parking charges). The comfortable rooms have no special charm, but the secluded setting is very peaceful and the reception welcoming. Accommodation includes several family apartments sleeping up to five people, and some duplex (split-level) suites. Two rooms are specially equipped to accommodate guests with disabilities. It has no restaurant.

✉ Route du Bois du Névet, 29180 Locronan ☎ 02 98 91 70 67 ◷ Closed mid-Nov to Easter €57–€65 (breakfast €7.50) 35, including 5 apartments, 6 duplex suites

MORLAIX

HÔTEL DE L'EUROPE

www.hotel-europe-com.fr

This reassuringly traditional, personally managed 200-year-old hotel is filled with antique furnishings and some fine carved woodwork, particularly on the staircase. Bedrooms are large, tastefully decorated and well soundproofed, though quite variable in style; the suites sleep up to four people. A buffet breakfast is served in the Napoleon III dining room. The adjacent restaurant (Brasserie de l'Europe) has an internal connection with the hotel but is independently run (▷ 121). Public parking is in the nearby main square.

1 rue d'Aiguillon, 29600 Morlaix 02 98 62 11 99 Closed Christmas, New Year €85–€150 (breakfast €8) 60 (10 non-smoking)

NEVEZ

AR MEN DU

www.men-du.fr

An isolated setting overlooking a tidal island and a splendid sweep of rock-and-sand coastline distinguish this attractively modernized beach hotel. It's a small, simple, white-painted building with dormer windows set into its slate roof. All the rooms have splendid sea views. The decorative theme is a jaunty nautical 'Clipper' style; neat, practical bedrooms are as shipshape as a captain's cabin complete with high-quality fittings and facilities. The brasserie-style restaurant is a popular place for lunchtime seafood—some grilled lobster, perhaps, or a *menu du terroir*.

Raguenes-Plage, Port-Manec'h, 29920 Nevez 01 98 06 84 22 Closed mid-Nov to mid-Mar, except Christmas and New Year €80–€160 (breakfast €11) 15

OUESSANT

TI JAN AR C'HAFE

A bouncy ferry-ride off the Finistère coast lies the Île d'Ouessant, Brittany's most distant island. Set near the harbour about 600m (660 yards) from Ouessant's main village, this recently opened little two-star has quickly made its way into the 'Charming Hotels' lists. Named after the owner's granny (Jan), it promises a peaceful retreat in idyllic surroundings. The interior is colourful and stylish, using red, orange and green with panache. Brolleys and loungers are set up on the wooden-decked terrace and the gardens. There's no restaurant, but plenty of bars and simple *crêperies* lie within easy walking distance.

Kernigou, 29242 Ouessant 02 98 48 82 64 Closed mid-Nov to late Dec; early Jan to mid-Feb €78–€88 (breakfast €9) 8

PONT-AVEN

HÔTEL DES MIMOSAS

www.hotels-pont-aven.com

A charming little place at the far end of the harbour, whose brightly lit bar-bistro attracts a convivial crowd of non-residents to dine on steaks or flambéd lobster amid parlour palms, bentwood chairs and polished wooden tables. It is especially popular with British visitors. There's a nautical theme, reinforced by a design of lifebelts and yachts on the fabric wall-coverings. The bedrooms are very pleasant and cosy, and all have views of the port. Staff and owners are young and informal. There's parking at the quayside.

Quai Théodore Botrel, 29930 Pont-Aven 02 98 06 00 30 Closed mid-Nov to mid-Dec €49–€80 (breakfast €8) 10

QUIMPER

DUPLEIX

www.hotel-dupleix.com

This central business hotel stands on the south bank of the Odet, an easy stroll from the old town. Its plate glass and concrete are a sharp contrast to Quimper's historic buildings, but it has some architectural merit and is pleasantly landscaped. Public rooms include a large, comfortable lounge and terrace, while the spacious bedrooms are bland but quiet with pleasant river and cathedral views. Three rooms here also have private terraces; family rooms are spacious and sleep up to six. Reception is open 24 hours. A charge is made for parking.

34 boulevard Dupleix, 29000 Quimper 02 98 90 53 35 Closed mid-Dec to early Jan €69–€79 (breakfast €9) 29

ROSCOFF

LE BRITTANY

www.hotel-brittany.com

Under the stewardship of the charming Chapalain family, this 17th-century manor is popular with ferry travellers and has strong Anglophile connections. It stands in secluded grounds with views towards the Île de Batz. The interior is stylish and spacious, furnished with Breton antiques and elegant fabrics. Imposing fireplaces and original beams give it a snug but distinguished feel. Some bedrooms have private terraces. The restaurant (Le Yachtman) serves delicious *cuisine du terroir.*

Boulevard Sainte-Barbe, 29680 Roscoff 02 98 69 70 78 Closed mid-Nov to late Mar €115–€275 (breakfast €18) 24, including 2 suites Covered; sauna, solarium

SAINTE-MARINE

SAINTE-MARINE

www.hotelsaintemarine.com

A gorgeous setting overlooking the Odet estuary is the crowning glory of this delightful little hotel-restaurant in the tiny fishing port of Sainte-Marine. Tables spill on to the quayside from the restaurant, but every one is crammed in fine weather. The hotel is decorated in blues and golds, the colours of the seaside. An understated nautical theme—a starfish here, a seagull there—will help to get you in the holiday mood. Bedrooms, all different, are equally stylish, and in excellent order. Parking can be difficult to find in high season.

19 [illegible] Sainte-Marine 02 98 56 34 79 Closed mid-Nov to mid-[illegible] €[illegible]5 (breakfast €8) 11

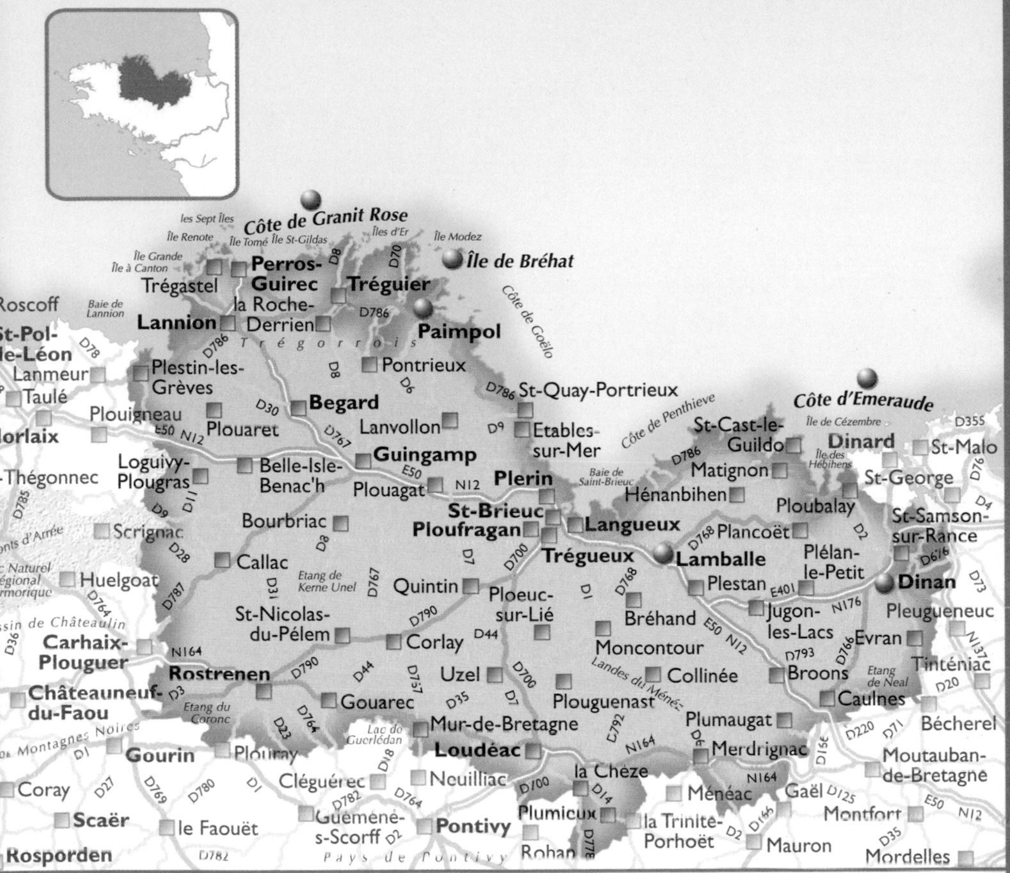

CÔTES-D'ARMOR

Laying claim to some of Brittany's most scenic stretches of coastline, Côtes d'Armor is a long-established favourite for seaside holidays, with some of the region's best-loved and most sophisticated resorts. The choicest sections of the Côte d'Emeraude (Emerald Coast), such as Cap Fréhel, fall within this *département*, along with the whole of the spectacular Côte de Granit Rose (Pink Granite Coast). These north-facing headlands meet the sea in a crescendo of coastal drama, fringed by cliffs or bizarrely colourful rock formations, and haunted by myriads of seabirds. They are best enjoyed from coastal footpaths *(sentiers des douaniers)*, or offshore from a boat. The islands of Bréhat and Les Sept-Iles make appealing excursion destinations.

Culturally, Côtes d'Armor is a transitional zone, spanning the subtle joins between French-speaking Haute Bretagne and the Celtic outposts of Finistère (Basse Bretagne). The dividing line is drawn somewhere around Plouha on the Goëlo coast, near St-Quay-Portrieux. Farther west, the Breton influences become steadily stronger, especially in local place-names beginning with Tre, Pen, Ker, Plou or Lan.

Most of the population once earned a living from the sea. Paimpol is an archetypal fishing community, former home-port for an Icelandic cod-fleet. Several other inland ports set on long, winding estuaries (Dinan, Lannion, Tréguier and Pontrieux) rank among Côtes d'Armor's most characterful historic towns. While long-range fishing has now declined, local seafood still finds its way on to innumerable menus—scallops from Erquy, or oysters from the Trieux and Jaudy estuaries. Seaweed is a more unusual crop, harvested on the wild peninsulas near Tréguier.

Inland lies some unexpectedly beautiful countryside sprinkled with châteaux and wayside chapels. Head up the river valleys from Lannion or Tréguier, or strike deep into Brittany's heart at Mur-de-Bretagne, the last navigable point of the Nantes–Brest Canal. In Côtes d'Armor's lonely interior you can avoid the coastal hubbub, and discover delectable medieval surprises like Quintin and Moncontour.

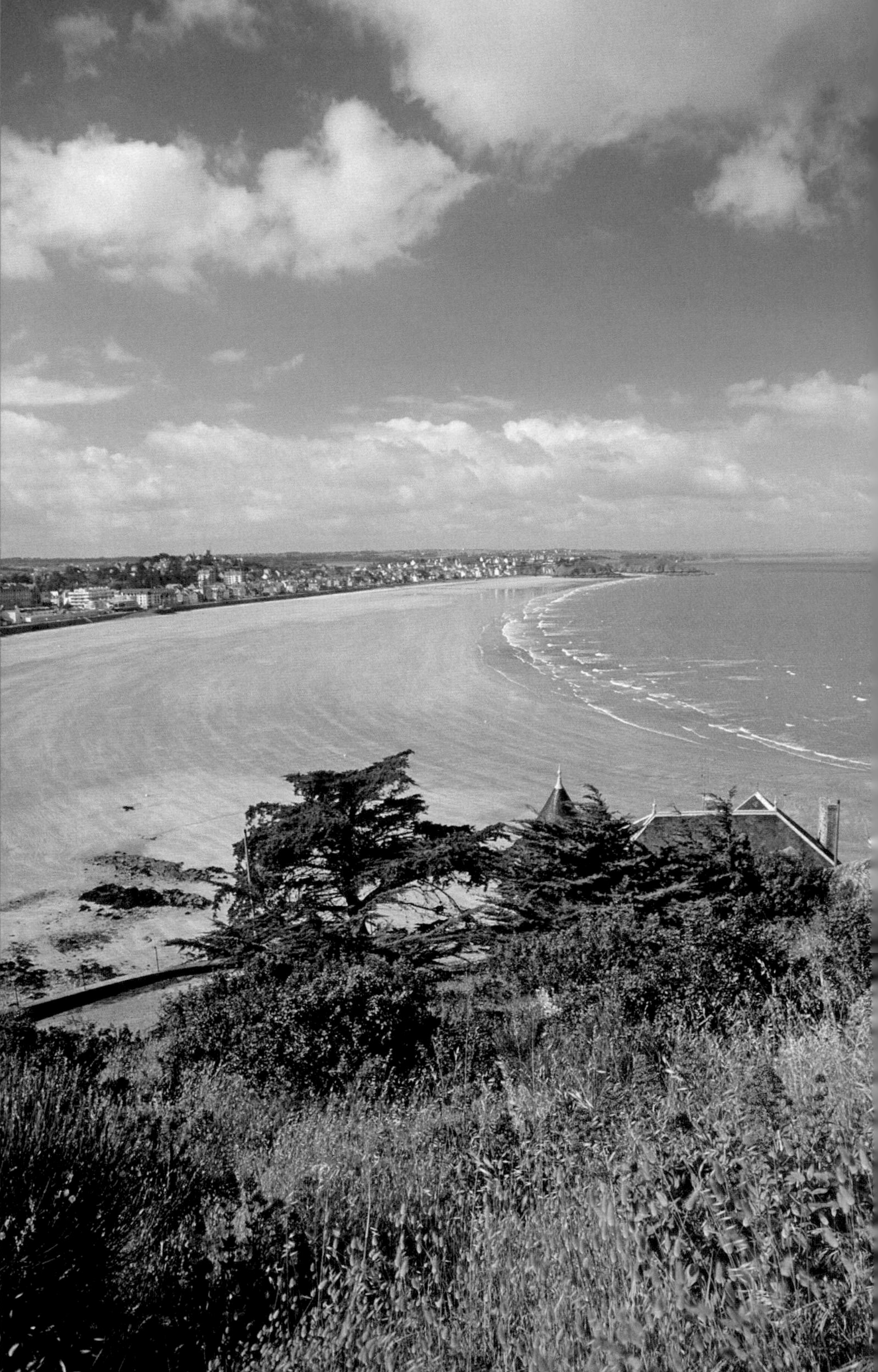

CÔTE D'EMERAUDE

Verdant cliffs and headlands give this rugged stretch of coastline its name, as well as the sparkling waters. Views are truly spectacular both from land and sea. The 19th-century artists who immortalized scenes along the Emerald Coast represent just a handful of many thousands of visitors captivated by its stunning natural beauty. The most beautiful and least built-up stretches lie immediately southwest of the Pointe de Grouin and around Cap Fréhel. Roads hug the coast closely here, making it possible to see something of this panoramic scenery by car. The best ways to experience the Emerald Coast, however, are on foot or by boat. Most of its larger resorts are described separately in this chapter; see also the driving tour ▷ 146–147.

CAP FRÉHEL

This headland, 70m (230ft) above the sea, is one of the most dramatic vantage points along the Emerald Coast. Gnarled cliffs of distinctive reddish-grey sandstone plunge to the frothing waves, providing nesting places for countless seabirds (guided nature tours Jun–end Sep daily through the Syndicat des Caps; tel 02 96 41 50 83). You can visit and climb Fréhel's square-towered lighthouse (tel 02 96 41 40 03; Apr–end Sep daily at the keeper's discretion), and on a clear day see as far as the Channel Islands. The headland east of Fréhel is memorable for the romantic, irresistibly photogenic fortress of La Latte (tel 02 96 41 40 31, guided tours Apr–end Sep daily; Oct–end Mar Sat, Sun, school holidays 2–6). West of Fréhel lie some of Brittany's most beautiful beaches, notably at Sables-d'Or-les-Pins (▷ 141) and Le Val-André (▷ 145). Between these two lies Erquy, one of France's leading scallop-fishing ports.

THE CENTRAL RESORTS

Deep inlets and estuaries gouge into the coast between Cap Fréhel and St-Malo (▷ 174–175). Most striking is the great Rance estuary, biting inland between Dinard (▷ 163) and St-Malo. A host of small, pleasantly traditional family seaside resorts capitalize on the glorious sandy beaches. Seabirds search through the oyster beds of the Baie de la Fresnaye, and hundreds of mussel-posts emerge from the inshore mudflats of the Baie d'Arguenon.

INFORMATION

www.erquy-tourisme.com
www.pays-de-frehel.com
www.valdarguenon.fr

226 L7 Main offices: Dinard, St-Malo, St-Briac-sur-Mer, St-Cast-le-Guildo and Le Val-André (see separate entries). Additional offices: Lotissement du Châtelet, 22750 St-Jacut-de-la-Mer 02 96 27 71 91 Mon 1.30–5.30, Tue–Fri 9–12, 1.30–5.30, Sat 9–12 (also Sun 10–12 in Jul and Aug) Place de Chambly, 22240 Fréhel 02 96 41 53 81 Jul, Aug Mon–Sat 10–12.30, 2–6.30; Sep–end Jun Mon–Sat 10–12.30, 2–5.30 3 rue du 19 mars 1962, 22430 Erquy 02 96 72 30 12 Jul, Aug Mon–Sat 9.30–1, 2–7, Sun 10–1, 4–6; rest of year Mon–Sat 9.30–12.30; 2–5. See also Sables-d'Or-les-Pins Line 2 (Fréhel–St-Brieuc) and Line 14 (St-Malo–St-Cast-le-Guildo) St-Malo Boat trips from all the larger resorts

TIP

» Colour-coded, numbered marker posts along the Cap Fréhel coastal footpath make things easier for emergency rescue services. Note details of the nearest one if you need to call for help.

Opposite *The beach at Le Val-André*
Below *Côte d'Emeraude's rocky coastline*

CÔTE DE GRANIT ROSE

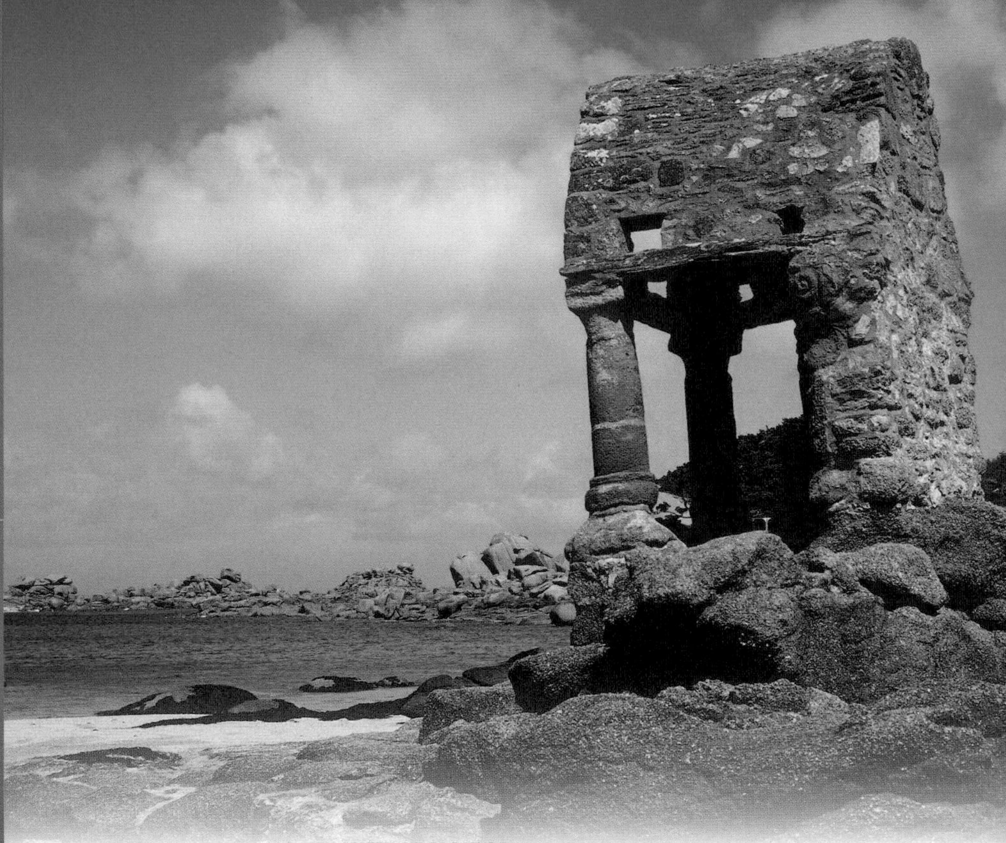

INFORMATION

224 G6

Offices at Lannion, Perros-Guirec, Tréguier and Paimpol (see separate entries); also Place de Crec'h Hery, 22560 Trébeurden 02 96 23 51 64 Jul, Aug Mon–Sat 9.30–7, Sun, holidays 10–1; Sep–end Jun Mon–Sat 9–12.30, 2–6; Maison de la Presqu'île, carrefour de Kerantour, 22740 Pleudaniel 02 96 22 16 45 Jul, Aug daily 9.30–1, 2–7; rest of year 9.30–12.30, 2–5.30; seasonal information points at Ploumanac'h, Port-Blanc, Plougrescant and Trégastel Lines 7 and 15 serve this coast, with more limited routes around Plougrescant for schools Lannion, Paimpol Trips to Les Sept Îles from Perros-Guirec, Ploumanac'h, Trégastel, and to l'Île de Bréhat from Paimpol

INTRODUCTION

The extraordinary outcrops of eroded russet granite that characterize this part of Brittany make this stretch of coastline unforgettable. The Pink Granite Coast, between Trébeurden and Paimpol, is one of the most dramatic stretches of Brittany's northern shoreline. The coastline gets its name from the local granite's startling hues: pinkish-brown in harsh sunlight, warming to a vivid coppery glow at sunset. Pink granite is a popular building material all along this coast, a sharp contrast to the grey stone or white-painted cement in other areas of Brittany. When weathered by the elements granite looks soft and smooth, almost organic, but when cut and dressed to a glittering polish it is much prized as a facing material.

WHAT TO SEE

AROUND TRÉBEURDEN

The Pink Granite Coast has no abrupt cut-off points at either end, but its most westerly resort is Trébeurden, where the granite reefs assume their characteristic form and fire. Like Perros-Guirec (▷ 139), the main centre on this popular holiday coast, Trébeurden is a major resort with lovely beaches and a large, well-equipped marina. Tidal islets add much to the charm and interest of its setting. Île Miliau and Île Molène are protected nature reserves rich in flora and fauna. Île Miliau also has a number of megaliths, including an impressive *allée couverte*, or gallery tomb. Visits can be organized with a specialist guide. Immediately behind the coastal road through Trébeurden lies a natural freshwater marsh known as the Marais de Quellen, another protected habitat for wildlife, especially wading birds and warblers. White Camargue horses roam freely here. Footpaths cross the marsh, raised on stilts where the ground is waterlogged, and there are hides from which you can observe the birds.

Farther up the coast towards Trégastel (▷ 144) is Île Grande, where the French bird conservation organization LPO (Ligue pour la Protection des Oiseaux) runs a clinic to treat and rehabilitate injured seabirds, especially those caught in oil-slicks off the Breton coast. Visitors are welcome to tour the clinic (July and August) and see a permanent wildlife exhibition. You can also join guided walks and watch the gannets nesting on nearby Île Rouzic via a web-cam.

AROUND PLOUMANAC'H

The most remarkable and easily accessible scenery lies around Ploumanac'h, just west of Perros-Guirec (▷ 148–149 for a walk along this stretch of coastline). Here the rose-coloured rocks scattered along the coastal path are at their brightest, weathered into peculiar shapes. Many of the formations have been given names: for example, Armchair, Tortoises. Pretty Ploumanac'h, much smaller but even more popular than neighbouring Perros-Guirec, offers classic seaside charms—perfect for relaxing family holidays. Resort facilities are excellent for active holidays, but this coast gets very crowded in high season. Offshore lies the bird sanctuary archipelago of Les Sept Îles, where puffins and petrels breed. The islands are easily accessible by widely advertised boat trips from Perros-Guirec, Ploumanac'h and Trégastel, but landings are permitted only on the Ile aux Moines, which has a ruined fortress.

Inland from Ploumanac'h, footpaths lead through the glorious wooded Vallées des Traouïero, weaving alongside fern-fringed streams amid chaotic piles of mossy rocks. Start from the tide-mill just outside the village (walks leaflets are available from the tourist office).

PRESQU'ÎLE DE PLOUGRESCANT

East of Perros-Guirec a maze of narrow lanes carries you through the tiny settlements of the remote Plougrescant peninsula. While the rocks are less brightly tinted here, colour is provided by vivid gorse on the heathy hinterland, earning this area the name Côte des Ajoncs—Gorse Coast. The fishing village of Port-Blanc has a quaint chapel whose eaves swoop almost to the ground. Farther north lie windblown promontories such as Pointe du Château or Le Gouffre, and a picturesque little house sandwiched between huge boulders. The church of St-Gonéry on the southern side of Plougrescant has a curious crooked lead spire set at a jaunty angle on its 10th-century tower like a feather in a hat. La Roche-Jaune, a small port on the Jaudy estuary, is renowned for its oysters. There are splendid views at the mouth of the estuary towards a maze of the scenic islands scattered in the bay.

PRESQU'ÎLE SAUVAGE

The next of these ragged coastal tatters culminates in a strange sandspit called the Sillon de Talbert, which straggles 3km (2 miles) seawards, a haunt of nesting terns. The Phare des Héaux stands some way offshore, one of the highest in France. Seaweed-gathering is an important local enterprise. You can find out more about this near the main village of Pleubian at the CEVA seaweed research centre (Centre d'Etude et de Valorisation des Algues, Pen-Lan peninsula, tel 02 96 22 89 16; guided visits mid-Jul to end Aug Mon–Fri, 2.30 and 4pm, Sun 3pm; mid-Jun to mid-Jul, first two weeks Sep Mon–Fri 2.30; less frequently off-season; adult €6; seaweed products for sale) . The Maison de l'Algue visitor centre contains an exhibition about the industry and organizes walks and activities during the summer.

TIPS

» The Sillon de Talbert makes a fine walk, but be very cautious of tidal cut-off points at the far end; access is restricted in spring when the terns are nesting.

» Take a flight from Lannion airport for an overview of this spectacular coastline; tel 02 96 46 41 00 (a 10-minute spin costs around €25 per person).

Above *The lighthouse along the coastline*
Opposite *The pink-tinged old stone oratory at St-Guirec, near Ploumanac'h*

DINAN

INTRODUCTION

Dinan clings to a steep wooded bluff high above the Rance valley, encased in sturdy walls. This gorgeous fortified town at the head of the Rance is one of Brittany's best-preserved medieval towns, with some of the region's most characterful buildings and stunning views.

The best way to see the compact old town is on foot, though the gradients are steep in places. Parts of the 600-year-old ramparts are walkable, giving magnificent views. From the old quarter, cobbled streets clamber down the hillside to an exceptionally attractive port. But the true heart of Dinan beats within its ancient walls, around picturesque lopsided buildings. The grand set pieces are the castle, the clock-tower and several churches and convents, but the humbler merchants' houses are every bit as delightful with their drunken timbering and jettied façades propped on stone pillars. Many now house hotels, restaurants, art galleries and craft shops.

Dinan dates back more than a thousand years, but it didn't achieve great prominence until it acquired a Benedictine monastery in the 10th century. It played a major role in the Hundred Years War, when it was defended by local hero Bertrand du Guesclin. Under the ownership of the Dukes of Brittany, Dinan prospered as a trading port, mainly from the proceeds of sailcloth and leather, and multifarious cargoes floated to and from its tidal quaysides. After suffering economic decline during the 14th-century Wars of Succession, Dinan flourished anew in the 17th and 18th centuries. Grand churches and convents sprang up all over the town, and wealthy merchants' houses began to line the central streets. Many of these buildings survived the Revolution, bequeathing the town an enviable legacy of superb period architecture.

INFORMATION

www.dinan-tourisme.com
226 L9 · 9 rue du Château, 22105 Dinan · 02 96 87 69 76 · Jul, Aug Mon–Sat 9–7, Sun 10–12.30, 2.30–6; Sep–end Jun Mon–Sat 9–12.30, 2–6 · Lines 10, 11, 12, 13, 17 to St-Malo, St-Cast-le-Guildo, Dinard and Rennes · Dinan; services to St-Malo via Dol-de-Bretagne · St-Malo and Dinard along the Rance · The biennial Fête des Remparts takes place in even years

WHAT TO SEE

CHÂTEAU-MUSÉE AND RAMPARTS

The museum in the ruined 14th century castle keep has displays ranging from prehistoric times to the early 20th century, including costumes, paintings and local crafts. Dinan's 3km (1.8-mile) ramparts, studded with six mighty watch-towers, are the oldest and most extensive in Brittany. From the sentry path, magnificent panoramic views extend over the town and valley. The promenade des Petits-Fossés is one of the best preserved sections. The 13th-century Tour Ste-Catherine is the oldest tower, guarding the approaches to the port. Other

Opposite *The waterfront buildings overlooking the River Rance*
Below left *An elderly lady tends flowers in a window in rue du Jerzual*
Below *The castle keep*

TIPS

» Climb the Tour de l'Horloge for wonderful views of the old town and the Rance valley (Easter–end Sep daily 10–6.30; Apr, May daily 2–6.30).

» A *petit train* will save you a steep climb up from the port if you time it right (Easter–end Oct daily 9–7; adult €6, child (3–12) €4). Dinan bus No. 4 is cheaper, but infrequent.

» On Thursdays (market day), no cars are allowed to park in place du Guesclin.

» On wet days, Dinan's cobbled streets can get very slippery. Take special care on the steep streets leading down to the port.

» Next to the tourist office is an enticing shop called Les Gavottes, selling locally made biscuits and sweets. A few free samples are usually on offer.

» If you're looking for some nightlife, head for rue de la Cordonnerie, a cobbled alley known locally as 'Thirsty Street' because of all its lively bars. A la Truye qui File (The Spinning Sow) is a typically atmospheric old inn along this street.

highlights include the 15th-century Tour de Coëtquen (the castle's old artillery tower) and the promenade de la Duchesse-Anne, which brings you into the terraced gardens of the Jardin Anglais.

Rue du Château ☎ 02 96 39 45 20 Jun–end Sep daily 10–6.30; Oct–end May daily 1.30–5.30 (closed Jan) Adult €4.35, child (12–18) €1.70, under 12 free

OLD TOWN

In the 12th century, Dinan crusader Rivallon le Roux pledged that, if he survived, he would return to his home town and pay for a church dedicated to Christ. The resulting Gothic and Romanesque St. Sauveur basilica was built between the 12th and 18th centuries. Relics include the heart of Bertrand du Guesclin, whose equestrian statue stands in the market square of place du Guesclin. The Gothic Église St-Malo has a superb English organ, dating from the Romantic period, and beautiful stained-glass windows illustrating great moments in the town's history (guided tours in both churches Jun–end Aug). Other buildings to look out for are the old monastery of the Ancien Couvent des Cordeliers with its 15th-century cloisters and pepperpot roof turrets, the quaint 16th-century Hôtel Kératry, and the 17th-century Maison du Gisant, with its recumbent statue.

Several colour-coded self-guided trails enable visitors to explore various aspects of the town. Ask for leaflets at the tourist office.

PORT

Narrow, cobbled rue du Jerzual and its continuation, rue du Petit-Fort, wind down to the river past lovely old houses galleries and studios. Many of these picturesque buildings have been converted into art galleries and craft studios.

The Maison du Gouverneur is a spectacular half-timbered house containing a display of regional furniture. Waterfront warehouses bear witness to the former success of Dinan's riverine trade, but virtually the only traffic that uses the old quaysides now are the summer excursion boats that ply up and down the Rance to St-Malo. The harbour now makes a pleasing scene of restaurants and cafés, with enticing strolls on either bank. A quaint stone bridge links the quaysides, and a 19th-century viaduct bestrides the valley just upstream from the port.

The waterfront Maison d'Artiste de la Grande Vigne is the former home of artist Yvonne Jean-Haffen (1895–1993), now a museum displaying her works (tel 02 96 87 58 72; late May–end Sep daily 2–6.30). On the opposite (Lanvallay) bank of the river, the Maison de la Rance contains an interesting exhibition about the river's history, economy and wildlife (tel 02 96 87 00 40; Jul, Aug daily 10–7; Apr–end Jun, Sep–end Nov Tue–Sun 2–6; Sun only in winter).

You can take boat trips along the Rance between St-Malo and Dinan from April to September. Tidal conditions make it tricky to go both ways within a day, but you can easily do one journey by boat and return by bus or train.

Above *Place de Guesclin, Dinan*
Opposite *Dinan has some impressive stone houses*
Below *The Pont Gothique and viaduct at Dinan*

MORE TO SEE

LÉHON

This pretty hamlet is a pleasant 2km (1-mile) walk across the river from Dinan. Visitors come principally to see the ruined 12th-century château overlooking the bridge, and the ancient priory of St-Magloire (tel 02 96 87 40 40; Jul, Aug 10–12, 2.30–6.30; guided visits; adult €3, child €2, under 12 free). The priory was originally founded in the ninth century by Nominoë, the first king of Brittany. Léhon's handsome houses indicate that it was a place of some importance in earlier times, but the settlement's influence declined after the construction of the viaduct across the Rance in the 19th century diverted passing traffic.

ÎLE DE BRÉHAT

This tiny rural idyll makes a seductive day-trip from the mainland. It has no must-see sights, but is a picturesque, traffic-free retreat for walking or bicycling. According to legend, Christopher Columbus learned of a sea route to the New World from the intrepid fishermen of Bréhat. In summer, thousands of visitors, mostly day-trippers from Pointe de l'Arcouest north of Paimpol, boost the island's resident population tenfold. It isn't hard to discover why this island paradise deserves investigation.

Just 2km (1 mile) offshore, Bréhat consists of two tiny islands like tattered butterfly wings pinned together by a 16th-century bridge called the Pont-ar-Prat. A ring of copper-coloured reefs protects its coves of pink shingle from Atlantic breakers. Each of these low-lying islands, measures less than a kilometre (half a mile) in length. Bréhat's maritime microclimate is surprisingly dry and sunny, its low-lying landmasses interrupt few Atlantic rain clouds.

ÎLE SUD

Most of Bréhat's 470 or so residents live in the south island, where the mild Gulf Stream climate has encouraged a profusion of Mediterranean plants in the gardens of prettily painted villas. Ferries dock at the tiny Port Clos, on the south coast. The hilltop fortress here houses a glass-blowing studio, the Verreries de Bréhat (tel 02 96 20 09 09; www.verreriesdebrehat.com; Easter–end Sep daily 10–6; Oct–Mar Mon–Fri). The Grève de Guerzido, the island's best beach, faces the mainland on Bréhat's southeast corner. From Port Clos it is a 500m (550yd) walk north to the main village, Le Bourg. West of here is the Chapelle St-Michel, highest point on Bréhat, whose 39 steps lead to a splendid view. Nearby, the Moulin à Marée du Birlot is a restored 17th-century tidal mill (which is occasionally open to the public, depending on the tide).

ÎLE NORD

Beyond Vauban's bridge spanning the sheltered port known as La Corderie, the northern island is quieter and more windswept than the southern island, but smothered in wild flowers and full of birds. The billowing hydrangeas, mimosa and geraniums give way to wilder, turf-covered moorland flecked with gorse, bracken and occasional pines. Two lighthouses and a semaphore signal station make focal points for walks. The pink-granite Phare du Paon, off Bréhat's northeastern tip, has marvellous coastal views. Inland, the Rosedo lighthouse dates from 1862.

INFORMATION

www.ile-de-brehat.org

225 H6 Le Bourg, 22870 02 96 20 04 15 Jul, Aug Mon–Sat 10–5.30; Apr–end Jun, Sep, school holidays Mon, Tue, Thu–Sat 10–1, 2–4.30; rest of year Mon,Thu–Sat 10–1, 2–4.30 Vedettes de Bréhat (tel 02 96 55 79 50; www.vedettesdebrehat.com) operate year-round services from Pointe de l'Arcouest, just north of Paimpol (summer crossings also run from Binic, Erquy, Perros-Guirec, Le Val-André and St-Quay-Portrieux). Round-the-island trips from Port-Clos in summer

TIPS

» No visitors' cars are allowed on the island, but you can rent bicycles at the ferry terminal to get around.

» In summer, it can be hard to find a table at local cafés or restaurants, so take a picnic and find a quiet spot well away from the main port and village.

Above *A house on Île de Bréhat*

LAMBALLE

Lamballe's *raison d'être* is its role as administrative and market hub for the prosperous Penthièvre agricultural region. Large cattle markets are held here, and related industrial enterprises such as animal feed preparation and leather-processing occupy its spreading suburbs. The area most visitors want to see is the old town, compactly knotted around place du Martray, where picturesque timbered buildings stand in an excellent state of preservation.

MUSEUMS

The eye-catching Maison du Bourreau (Hangman's House) contains a couple of worthwhile little museums. One is devoted to the folk history of Lamballe with costumes, ceramics, tools and prehistoric items (tel 02 96 34 77 63; Jul, Aug Tue–Sat 10–12, 2.30–5; variable hours rest of year). The other showcases the varied work of the local artist Mathurin Méheut, born in the town in 1882 (tel 02 96 31 19 99; Apr, Jun–end Sep Mon–Sat 10–12, 2.30–6; May, Oct–end Dec Wed, Fri, Sat 2.30–5). An early exponent of art nouveau, Méheut designed jewellery and wallpaper as well as painting Breton daily life and fishing scenes. One of his specialist interests was shipping, and after World War II he became official painter to the French Navy.

THE NATIONAL STUD

The Haras National (national stud) was originally set up in 1825. Its palatial stables house some 50 stallions, many of which are hefty Breton draught horses. Visitors are welcome to look round on guided tours (tel 02 96 50 06 98; www.haraspatrimoine.com; mid-Jul to late Aug daily 10–5.30; restricted hours rest of year).

INFORMATION

www.lamballe-tourisme.com
225 K8 Place du Champ de Foire Martray, 22402 Lamballe 02 96 31 05 38 Jul, Aug daily 10–6; Sep–end Jun Mon 1.30–5.30, Tue–Sat 10–12, 1.30–5.30 Lines 1 ,2, 3 to St-Cast, Erquy, St-Brieuc, Le Val-André Lamballe

TIPS

» Guided walking tours are organized through the tourist office on Wed and Fri in high season.

» In July and August, *Les Jeudis Lamballais* (Lamballe Thursdays) enliven the town (free concerts, carriage rides, horse shows and more).

Below *Lamballe narrow streets*

LANNION

www.ot-lannion.fr

This old port spread over the hilly banks of the Léguer is Côtes-d'Armor's second-largest town, a major route-hub and now a prosperous business centre. Despite the modern bustle, this former capital of the Trégor region has managed to retain its traditional Breton character in an old-town core of timber-framed or slate-hung buildings with overhanging façades and quaint corbels carved with strange beasts or human faces. These 16th- and 17th-century buildings are mainly concentrated around the cobbled place du Général Leclerc and the church of St-Jean-du-Baly.

Lannion's most interesting church is the Église de Brélévenez (guided tours Jul, Aug) in the upper town, reached by a long flight of steps. Founded in the 12th century by the Knights Templar, its elaborate interior is adorned with carved capitals and a Romanesque apse and crypt containing an accomplished *Entombment* sculpture. The views are well worth the 142-step climb (or you can drive to it if you prefer).

Down on the waterfront, long quaysides and wooded towpaths extend along the estuary towards the picturesque hillside hamlet of Le Yaudet. Upstream, ancient chapels and châteaux litter the sinuous Léguer valley, followed along most of its course by a long-distance footpath (GR34A).

224 G7 Quai d'Aiguillon 22300 Lannion 02 96 46 41 00 Jul, Aug Mon–Sat 9–7, Sun, holidays 10–1; Sep–end Jun Mon–Sat 9.30–12.30, 2–6 Lannion Lannion is a great base for kayaking and canoeing; the *stade d'eau vive* is an artificial white-water course near Pont Sainte-Anne where national championships and training sessions are held

MÛR-DE-BRETAGNE

Far inland on the borders of Côtes-d'Armor and Morbihan, this resort presides over the artificial Lac de Guerlédan, a serpentine reservoir that now marks the navigable limits of the Nantes–Brest Canal. The massive concrete dam across the Blavet was constructed in the 1920s and now creates the largest lake in Brittany; hydroelectric power installations and an impressive array of recreational facilities supplement its primary function of conserving a controllable water supply. All summer long, the lake is a flurry of sails as pleasure-craft and windsurfers tack in all directions. Beau Rivage has a popular shoreside leisure centre, the Ski Club de Guerlédan (tel 02 96 26 02 18 or 06 09 38 03 26), where you can rent boats and arrange waterskiing.

There's little of interest in Mûr-de-Bretagne itself, but the surrounding countryside of woodland and gorges reveals many hidden surprises: calvaries and chapels, sacred fountains and disappearing rivers. St-Aignan has a charming 12th-century church containing a carving of the Tree of Jesse. An exhibition about the Guerlédan dam can be seen in the nearby Musée de l'Electricité (tel 02 97 27 51 39; mid-Jun to mid-Sep daily 10–12, 2–6.30); guided visits of the barrage are also available.

The evocative 18th-century ruins of the Abbaye de Bon Repos, on the western side of the lake, are gradually being restored. It has a pleasant restaurant and a permanent exhibition. Various summer happenings are staged here, including exuberant sound-and-light shows in August (tel 02 96 24 82 20).

230 H10 Place de l'Église, 22530 Mûr de Bretagne 02 96 28 51 41 Jul, Aug Mon–Sat 10–12.30, 2–6, Sun 10.30–12.30; reduced hours in winter; seasonal lakeshore information points, at Bon-Repos 02 96 24 82 20; Gouarec (old station) 02 96 24 98 73; St-Aignan (Maison de Pays) 02 97 27 51 39 Lac de Guerlédan and Nantes–Brest Canal

PERROS-GUIREC

www.perros-guirec.com

Summer visitors crowd to this large resort on Brittany's Pink Granite Coast, whose fine sandy shores are littered with strangely eroded, exotically tinted outcrops of granite. The *sentier des douaniers* coastal watchpath from Perros-Guirec to Ploumanac'h leads past the best of the pink granite scenery (▷ 148–149). Many houses are built in the local stone, giving the town a mellow pink hue, especially at sunset. Just offshore lies the seabird sanctuary of Les Sept Îles, seasonal home to over a dozen nesting species, including puffins, guillemots and gannets. Several companies run boat trips in season.

With its casino (tel 02 96 49 80 80; daily 10am–3am/4am Jun–end Sep; gaming tables from 9.30pm; reduced hours in low season), smart marina and seawater spa, Perros-Guirec has an air of leisured sophistication and celebrity chic. It attracts a fashionable clientele of bright, active young things as well as families with children and retired folk, who have colonized the villas in its leafy suburbs. It is one of the biggest sailing resorts on the north Breton coast, and has some lively nightlife, good shops and lots of beach activities. Parts of the waterfront are rather spoiled by the busy coastal road, but the central beaches—Plage de Trestraou and Plage de Trestrignel—are absolutely stunning. The resort sprawls over a hilly headland circuited by serpentine roads, where elegant private villas and hotels hog magnificent views from wooded cliffs.

Apart from its spectacular natural scenery, Perros Guirec has no unmissable sights. In the heart of town, crowning the hilly promontory, the church of St-Jacques-la-Majeur has a curious spiky belfry and an elaborate trefoil porch (Mon–Sat 9.30–12, 2.30–6, Sun am outside services only).

The 15th-century Chapelle Notre-Dame de la Clarté (daily 9.30–12, 2–6), west of town, was built as a commemorative seamark by a fogbound mariner saved from imminent shipwreck by a heavenly shaft of light.

224 G6 · 21 place de l'Hôtel de Ville, 22700 Perros-Guirec · 02 96 23 21 15 · Jul, Aug Mon–Sat 9–7.30, Sun, holidays 10–12.30, 4–7; Sep–end Jun Mon–Sat 9–12.30, 2–6.30; small seasonal annexe in Ploumanac'h · Les Sept Îles from the Gare Maritime at Plage de Trestraou or Port de Ploumanac'h; also to Bréhat and along the coast · The Festival des Hortensias is a costume-packed parade in early August

PLEUMEUR-BODOU

www.pleumeur-bodou.com

Unmistakably identified by what looks like a giant golf ball, the heathland village of Pleumeur-Bodou plays host to an ambitious complex of family attractions marketed under the name of Cosmopolis. The huge Radôme (radar dome), measuring some 50m (160ft) high and more than 200m (650ft) in circumference, is made of a Dacron shell just 2mm (0.8in) thick. Raised air pressure inside protects it from high winds. Formerly the Centre National d'Etudes des Télécommunications (CNET), this hit the headlines in July 1962 when the first transatlantic signals arrived from the US satellite Telstar. It now houses the fascinating Cité des Télécoms (tel 02 96 46 63 80; www.cite-telecoms.com; Jul, Aug daily 10–7; reduced variable hours off season). These multimedia, interactive exhibits encompass more than 200 years of long-distance message-relay history, from earliest semaphore to the latest video and internet technology. Nearby is the Planétarium de Bretagne (tel 02 96 15 80 30; daily programme in summer, phone for details; closed Wed, Sat in winter, and all Jan; some shows in English). Also on the Cosmopolis site is the incongruous Village Gaulois (tel 02 96 91 83 95; Easter to Sep), a re-creation of a Gaullish village from Roman times. Proceeds go to a Third World educational charity.

224 F7 · 11 rue des Chardons, 22560 Pleumeur-Bodou · 02 96 23 91 47 · Jul, Aug Mon–Sat 9.30–12, 2.30–5, Sun 10–1; Sep–end Jun Mon–Fri 9.30–12.30, 2.30–5, Sat 10–12.30 · From nearby resorts

Above *Breton musicians on the quayside at Perros-Guirec*

Top *The church of Brélévenez, with its granite 15th-century spire*

Opposite *Lac de Guerlédan at Mûr-de-Bretagne*

INFORMATION

www.paimpol-goelo.com
www.ville-paimpol.fr
225 H7 19 rue du Général Leclerc, 22500 Paimpol 02 96 20 83 16 Jul, Aug Mon–Sat 9.30–7.30, Sun, holidays 10–1.30; Sep–end Jun Mon–Sat 9.30–12.30, 1.30–6.30 Seasonal office at Pointe de l'Arcouest Jul, Aug Mon–Sat 10–1, 2–6, Sun, public holidays 10–1 CAT Line 9 runs to Pointe de l'Arcouest (Bréhat ferry terminal) and St-Brieuc; Line 7 to Treguier and Lannion Paimpol. Trains or SNCF buses to Guingamp for connections to Brest, St-Brieuc, Rennes Ferries to Île de Bréhat from Pointe de l'Arcouest

TIP

» Combined tickets (adult €5.80, child 10–18 €2.70) allow access to the Musée de la Mer and the Musée du Costume Breton, nearby on rue Raymond-Pellier.

» A steam locomotive train follows the scenic Trieux Valley, a terrific excursion for children of all ages (▷ 151).

» Southeast of Paimpol, the graceful Gothic Abbaye de Beauport has been restored and can be visited (tel 02 96 55 18 58; www.abbaye-beauport.com; mid-Jun to mid-Sep daily 10–7; rest of year 10–12, 2–5).

PAIMPOL

Paimpol is a working port, its two crowded harbours full of activity. In centuries gone by, the town's fishermen would set sail from here to search for cod for months at a time in the perilous waters around Iceland. This deep-sea heritage is vividly recounted at the Musée de la Mer in an old cod-drying factory on rue Labenne (tel 02 96 22 02 19; www.museemerpaimpol.com; mid-Jun to end Aug daily 10.30–12.30, 2.30–6; Easter to mid-Jun, Sep daily 2.30–6). The cod-fishing industry began in the 16th century, but reached its height during the late 19th century, when over a period of 80 years more than 2,000 of Paimpol's intrepid mariners perished at sea. Today, Paimpol has replaced cod-fishing and whaling with inshore coastal fishing and oyster-farming in the Trieux estuary. It also does a brisk trade in early vegetables; *cocos de Paimpol* (haricot beans) are a local speciality—look for them in the local market, held in central streets every Tuesday.

THE PORT

Although Paimpol's port is not conventionally pretty, it has lots of character and an authentic charm. The waterfront area is always lively. The August Fête du Chant des Marins revives the seafaring traditions of Paimpol in songs and shanties, and an annual *pardon* in the church of Notre-Dame-de-Bonne-Nouvelle continues a long tradition of blessing the fishing fleet. The old centre has a solid core of period buildings. The isolated belltower in place Theodore Botrel is the last vestige of a shattered church. Some of the distinguished-looking houses spread along the quaysides were built by wealthy ship-owners. A couple have been converted into upmarket hotels.

NEARBY SIGHTS

Paimpol is an excursion base for the the Trieux estuary and the Goëlo coast. North of the town, a scenic road leads to the Pointe de l'Arcouest, departure point for the Île de Bréhat (▷ 136). A brief detour down side-roads leads to a chapel at Ploubazlanec, where the names of lost seafarers are inscribed on the cemetery walls, and the Widow's Cross in Perros-Hamon, where Paimpol's womenfolk would stand watching for returning ships.

QUINTIN

www.quintin.fr
www.pays-de-quintin.com

Renowned for its fine linen in the 17th and 18th centuries, this *petite cité de caractère* supplied materials for the elaborate headdresses *(coiffes)* and collars traditionally worn by Breton women. Today, handsome old houses rise in tiers on the hillside overlooking the River Gouët, a natural defensive site. Corbelled and timber-framed buildings dating from the 16th and 17th centuries line the streets and squares of the old quarter, particularly the Grande Rue, Place 1830, and place du Martray. The imposing neo-Gothic basilica contains the relics of St. Thuriau and a piece of the Virgin's girdle said to have been brought back from Jerusalem during the Crusades. Notre-Dame-de-Délivrance (Our Lady of Safe Delivery) is naturally venerated by expectant mothers. At the east end of the church, the Porte-Neuve is the last remaining section of the old town walls. The unfinished Château de Quintin, its earliest wing dating from 1640, houses a fine collection of porcelain (tel 02 96 74 94 79; Jul, Aug daily 10.30–12, 2–6; Jun, Sep 2–5.30; Apr, May Sun, public holidays only 2–5, temporary exhibitions). The Musée-Atelier des Toiles de Quintin, on historic rue des Degrés, recounts the local linen industry (tel 02 96 74 01 51; Jun–end Sep Tue–Sun 1.30–6.30; weaving demonstrations). The holy water stoups in the basilica of Notre-Dame-de-Délivrance are made from giant shells from Java.

225 H9 6 place 1830, 22800 Quintin 02 96 74 01 51 Jul, Aug Mon–Sat 9.30–12.30, 2–6, Sun 10.30–12.30, 2.30–4.30; mid–Jun and early Sep Mon–Sat 9.30–12, 2–5; mid-Sep to mid-Jun Tue–Sat 9.30–12, 2–5 Quintin (connections to St-Brieuc and Loudéac) Guided tours in summer

SABLES-D'OR-LES-PINS

www.plurien-tourisme.com

The long stretches of golden sand and verdant pines that give this resort its name are the main attractions. You can rent a beach buggy or take in a round of golf, but most people come here simply to enjoy an exceptionally photogenic stretch of seaside.

Sables-d'Or-les-Pins is essentially an artificial resort—even the beach is a bottle blonde created from imported sand. Work began in the early 1920s but the project was abandoned before completion after the financial crash of 1929. A wide but oddly makeshift central boulevard flanked by ornate parades of shops and cafés hints at the grand design originally envisaged, though it has the insubstantial air of a film studio backlot. Swimming on some local beaches can be dangerous because of the strong currents that swirl around the sandbanks. Just south of Sables-d'Or-les-Pins, the older village of Plurien adds some historical gravitas, with a Templar church and the remains of a Gallo-Roman villa.

226 K8 The main office is at Plurien, 2km (1 mile) inland 02 96 72 18 52 Jul, Aug Mon–Sat 9.30–12.30, 2–6.30, Sun 10–12; restricted hours off-season. Sables-d'Or-les-Pins has a small seasonal office (Jul, Aug only) Swimming in the sea can be dangerous because of strong currents

ST-BRIEUC

www.baiedesaintbrieuc.com

This sprawling town at the head of a huge bay is the administrative capital of Côtes-d'Armor. It's a thriving business hub and a rendezvous of regional transportation networks, though frankly not much of a tourist attraction. Its geography is complicated by deep river valleys, over which roads stride on stilted viaducts. Within a carapace of drab industrial suburbs, the old town occupies the fork of high ground between the converging rivers Gouédic and Gouët. The fortified cathedral of St-Etienne on place Général de Gaulle (daily 8–7) is its most prominent landmark, and the surrounding streets contain a few agreeable medieval buildings. The Musée d'Art et d'Histoire provides some well-presented background on the Côtes-d'Armor region free of charge (tel 02 96 62 55 20; Tue–Sat 9.30–11.45, 1.30–5.45, Sun 12–6).

St-Brieuc has no shortage of decent shops and restaurants (particularly around the pedestrianized rue St-Guillaume), and a lively range of performing arts and events generated by its student population. The port of Le Legué occupies an unexpectedly secluded enclave of wharves and warehouses beside the steeply wooded Gouët estuary. Yachts, fishing boats and bulk cargo vessels share this waterway, which is one of the busiest ports in Brittany, currently undergoing expansion. Several small beach resorts extend along the seafront near Plérin, enjoying fine views over the bay.

225 J8 7 rue St-Gouéno, 22044 St-Brieuc 0825 002 222 Jul, Aug Mon–Sat 9–7, Sun 10–1; Sep–end Jun Mon–Sat 9.30–12.30, 1.30–6, Sun, public holidays 10–1 Main TGV line between Paris, Rennes and Brest

Right *Weathered tree stumps and pink rocks bound the grassy dunes that line the beach at Sables-d'Or-les-Pins*
Opposite *Port Plaisance at Paimpol*

ST-CAST-LE-GUILDO

www.saintcastleguildo.fr

'Sanka' (as it's pronounced) is one of the liveliest bucket-and-spade resorts on Brittany's Emerald Coast (▷ 129), popular with families for its seven sandy beaches. It is ideally situated for excursions to Dinard, Dinan and St-Malo or for walks along the wild footpaths of Cap Fréhel. The resort became a popular watering hole in the 19th century, when prosperous villas sprang up to take advantage of Emerald Coast views. In its belle-époque heyday it had an exclusive reputation rivalling Dinard, but today it is a little too suburban to be truly chic.

The resort has several separate districts and its geography takes some fathoming. Le-Guildo is an old seaport on the Arguenon river. Its associated market town is called Notre-Dame. Here you'll find humble stone cottages set near the ocean, and the ruined château of Gilles de Bretagne overlooking the bay. St-Cast consists of L'Isle (the port), Les Mielles (the resort area, with a beautiful wide sandy beach) and Le Bourg (the administrative hub). L'Isle is a popular port of call for yachts in summer, but it is a tidal harbour and offshore islets make navigation a challenge.

The Grand Plage (Large Beach) at Les Mielles is a stunner, stretching over 2km (1 mile) south of the port. It has excellent water sports facilities, a summer fairground, and an attractive square of shops, bars and restaurants at its northern end. The southern tip of the beach is marked by the small chapel of Notre-Dame-de-la-Garde, on a headland of the same name. Between St-Cast and Le-Guildo is the tiny settlement of Pen-Guen, with its own fine beach. It is renowned in French golfing circles for its links course, one of the oldest in the country.

✚ 226 L8 ℹ Place Charles de Gaulle, BP 9, 22380 St-Cast-le-Guildo ☎ 02 96 41 81 52 🕐 Jul, Aug Mon–Sat 9–7.30, Sun, holidays 10–12.30, 3–6.30; rest of year Mon–Sat 9–12, 2–6 (5.30 in winter) 🚌 Line 1 to Lamballe (nearest rail station); 2 to St-Brieuc via Erquy and Le Val-André (Jul, Aug only); 13 to Dinan; 14 to St-Malo ? *Fête de l'Huître* (oyster festival) is at the end of Jun

ST-QUAY-PORTRIEUX

www.saintquayportrieux.com

This former cod-fishing port is now a glitzy, well-equipped beach and sailing resort besieged by Parisian families in August. Its five wide, sheltered beaches are safe and good for children. It has a seafront casino (tel 02 96 70 40 36; www.casinosaintquay.com; daily 10am–4am; musical soirées Fri, Sat from 10pm) and summer activities galore. Its older, prettier quarters have become somewhat eclipsed by amorphous modern suburbs. The massive marina of Port d'Armor bolted on to its old fishing harbour holds up to a thousand boats, and is certainly an economic asset if not a thing of beauty. Inshore fishing still continues, ranking St-Quay ninth among France's fishing ports; scallops and lobster are among the main catches.

The settlement is very old, tracing its origins back to a Celtic hermit (St. Quay or Ké), who landed here in the Dark Ages, but it was only in the 19th century that it gained popularity, as a health spa. St-Quay-Portrieux stands on the border zone between French-speaking Upper Brittany (Haute Bretagne) and the Breton-speaking Lower Brittany (Basse Bretagne), and Celtic cultural traditions and Breton place-names gradually become more prominent as you head westwards. The little fishing village of Binic 8km (5 miles) south somehow manages to retain a sense of its own identity.

✚ 225 J7 ℹ 17 bis rue Jeanne d'Arc, 22410 St-Quay-Portrieux ☎ 02 96 70 40 64 🕐 Jul, Aug Mon–Sat 9–7, Sun, hols 10.30–12.30, 3.30–6; Sep–end Jun Mon–Sat 9–12.30, 2–6.30 (6 in winter) ℹ Seasonal information point at 20 quai de la République ☎ 02 96 70 50 60 🕐 Jul, Aug Mon–Sat 10.30–12.30, 3.30–6.30, Sun, holidays 3.30–6.30 🚌 Line 9 (Paimpol–St-Brieuc, both on rail routes) ⛴ Trips to Bréhat Jun–end Sep; pleasure and fishing trips round Goëlo coast from Port d'Armor

Opposite *A view towards the castle at St-Cast-le-Guildo*

Below *The port and bay (left) and a fisherman (right) at St-Cast-le-Guildo*

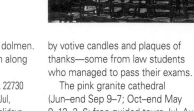

Above *An offshore islet close to Trégastel (left); inside Tréguier cathedral (right)*
Opposite *A boat passes yachts in the harbour at Pontrieux*

TRÉGASTEL

www.ville-tregastel.fr

This popular resort attracts a loyal following for its beautiful beaches of white sand amid a jumble of bizarrely rounded rocks and offshore reefs of pink granite. The coastal footpath *(sentier des douaniers)* and the Corniche Bretonne scenic road make splendid promenades from which to enjoy the scenery. One of the best vantage points is the *table d'orientation* between the beaches of Coz-Pors and Grève-Blanche. Île-Grande, farther down the coast towards Trébeurden, can be reached by a bridge from the D788. On the island, the Maison LPO (tel 02 96 91 91 40; www.lpo.fr; Apr–Sep Wed–Mon variable times) is an ornithological centre for Les Sept Îles north of Perros-Guirec (▷ 139).

The Aquarium Marin (tel 02 96 23 48 58; www.aquarium-tregastel.com; Jul, Aug daily 10–7; Apr–end Jun, Sep daily 10–6; Oct, school holidays Tue–Sun 2–5), shoehorned into crevices between startling granite boulders, showcases the sea-life around this coast, complete with a tidal model. The Forum de Trégastel houses a splendid covered swimming pool complex (tel 02 96 15 30 44; Mon 2–7.30, Tue, Thu 10.30–1.30, 3–9; Wed, Fri 10.30–1.30, 3–7.30; Sat 10.30–1.30, 3–6.30; Sun, holidays 10–6.30) with slides, flumes and fountains, accessible from the plage de Coz-Pors.

On the Trébeurden road, 2km (1 mile) south, Kerguntuil has a Neolithic passage grave and dolmen. Other megaliths can be seen along the coastal road.

224 F6 Place Sainte-Anne, 22730 Trégastel 02 96 15 38 38 Jul, Aug Mon–Sat 9.30–1, 2–7, Sun, holidays 10–12.30; Sep–end Jun Mon–Sat 9.30–12, 2–6 (5.30 in winter, closed Sat pm) Boat trips to Les Sept Îles in summer

TRÉGUIER

www.paysdetreguier.com
www.ot-cotesdesajoncs.com
www.ville-treguier.fr

On a commanding defensive site overlooking the Jaudy estuary, Tréguier's sheltered tidal port is now supplemented by an attractive yacht marina. It is a diocesan capital and an important market town for a fertile vegetable-growing area. The handsome granite and half-timbered buildings in the old town confirm its pre-Revolutionary prosperity from the flax trade, but these days it seems a sleepy place.

Tréguier was founded in the sixth century by an obscure Celtic monk (St Tugdual), but another saint has become more memorably associated with the town. Yves Helori, born near Tréguier in 1253, is the patron saint of lawyers. Famously incorruptible, St Yves became a champion of the poor, and is often depicted in Breton churches flanked by a wealthy man and a poor client in rags. His tomb (a 19th-century copy after damage caused in the Revolution) lies in Tréguier cathedral, surrounded by votive candles and plaques of thanks—some from law students who managed to pass their exams.

The pink granite cathedral (Jun–end Sep 9–7; Oct–end May 9–12, 2–6; free guided tours Jul, Aug Sun–Fri; separate access to treasury and cloisters, by chargeable tour only in summer, free off-season) is mostly Gothic with a few surviving bits of Romanesque in the Hastings tower. Most striking is its spire, pierced with geometric shapes. Immediately around the cathedral lies a spacious square and ancient streets filled with attractive old buildings. The house belonging to the writer and rationalist philosopher Ernest Renan, born here in 1823, is now a museum to his memory (tel 02 96 92 45 63; Jul, Aug daily 10–12, 2–6; Apr–end Jun, Sep Wed–Sun 10–12, 2–6); his statue presides over the main square.

On summer Wednesdays (market day), Tréguier springs into life with a series of fun-packed *Mercredis en Fête*, held in the town's main square (concerts, hog-roasts, street entertainment). A huge *pardon* (one of Brittany's largest and most celebrated) takes place in Tréguier on the anniversary of the death of St Yves (third Sunday in May).

224 G7 67 rue Ernest Renan, 22220 Tréguier 02 96 92 22 33 Jul, Aug Mon–Sat 9.30–12.30, 2–6, Sun 10–1; Sep–end Jun Tue–Sat 9.30–12.30, 2–6 Bicycles and kayaks can be rented from the Bar Les Plaisanciers down by the port; 02 96 92 49 69

TRIEUX ESTUARY

www.pontrieux.com
www.cc-lezardrieux.com

On the east bank of the river mouth, the pretty little village of Loguivy-de-la-Mer is a leading Côtes-d'Armor fishing port, though its harbour dries out at low tide. Lenin once holidayed here, relaxing from revolutionary notions. The Trieux estuary is a popular sailing playground; Lézardrieux's huge state-of-the-art yacht marina dwarfs the rest of the tiny *ville fleurie*, with its distinctive 18th-century church. A graceful suspension bridge spans the estuary at this point, carrying the busy D786 between Paimpol and Lannion, and providing grandstand river views.

More amazing vistas can be seen from the Château de la Roche-Jagu 14km (9 miles) upstream from Lézardrieux, built in the 15th century on a wooded bluff guarding a sharp meander in the river. Restored after the 1987 hurricane, it is now open to the public (tel 02 96 95 62 35; Jul, Aug daily 10–1, 2–7; Apr–end Jun, Sep, Oct 10–12, 2–6); tours include some of its ornate Renaissance-style rooms. Exhibitions and events are held here in summer, including an August jazz festival.

Straddling the head of the river between wooded banks, Pontrieux is a delightful surprise, a small, likeable town well stocked with handsome flower-strewn buildings and a strong sense of civic pride. Art galleries and craft studios fringe Pontrieux's streets, and down on the waterfront sleek yachts berth alongside homey houseboats. Many old public wash-houses, preceding the days of the laundromat, have been restored by local enthusiasts. The most striking local landmark is the Maison d'Eiffel (now the tourist office), a 16th-century timbered tower once used by the port authorities to survey river traffic.

A steam train runs along the Trieux valley between Paimpol and Pontrieux (La Vapeur du Trieux, ▷ 151). You can reserve a one-way trip from Pontrieux, but returns are available only from Paimpol.

225 H7 Main offices at Tréguier or Paimpol. Also Maison de la Presqu'île, carrefour de Kerantour, 22740 Pleudaniel 02 96 22 16 45 Jul, Aug Mon–Sat 9.30–12.45, 2–6.45; rest of year reduced hours Maison d'Eiffel, place de Trocquer, 22260 Pontrieux 02 96 95 14 03 Jul, Aug daily 10.30–6.30; rest of year reduced hours; and Place du Bourg, 22740 Lézardrieux 02 96 22 16 45 Jul, Aug Mon–Sat 10–1, 4–7, Sun 10–1; rest of year reduced hours Pontrieux Barge trips from Pontrieux (some at night); kayak rental at Loguivy or Pontrieux In August, Pontrieux holds the Fête des Lavandières, in celebration of its former washerwomen

LE VAL-ANDRÉ

www.val-andre.org

Established in the 1880s, Le Val-André still has a belle-époque feel to its elegant, bow-fronted villas set in spacious seafront plots. The resort occupies a grid-like strip of streets behind a dazzlingly beautiful beach stretching almost 2km (1 mile) between the wooded headlands of Pléneuf and La Guette. The seafront promenade provides direct, traffic-free access to the sands. Just off the Pointe de Pléneuf lies the bird sanctuary islet of Le Verdelet, which can be reached on foot at exceptionally low tides (bird-watching trips organized every Wed in Jul and Aug by Vivarmor Nature; tel 02 96 33 10 57; www.vivarmor.fr.st/). Cliff paths lead round the headland, offering marvellous views over St-Brieuc Bay, and farther beaches to the northeast. West of the resort is the picturesque old fishing port of Dahouët, squeezed behind a narrow rock-lined channel. It is now used mainly as a yacht marina, its granite quays fringed with attractive waterfront bars and restaurants.

Le Val-André is excellent for water sports; sailing dinghies, catamarans, windsurfers and kayaks can all be rented from the main beaches. The northerly beach of Plage de la Ville Berneuf is a popular destination for sand-yachting *(char à voile)*. There's a fine golf course behind the beach too; Golf Blue Green has hosted the French Open several times in recent years. The seafront Rotonde Casino with its art-deco ocean-liner architecture contains a panoramic café-restaurant, and a cinema and theatre, as well as the usual range of gaming tables and slot machines (tel 02 96 72 85 06; daily 10am–3am, 4am Fri–Sun). Beachfront bars keep things humming until the small hours. During July and August, jazz sessions are held in a park behind rue Amiral Charner.

Le Val-André is ideal for young children, with its wide expanses of soft, clean, gently shelving sand and lots of beach activities. A *petit train* plies around the seafront in summer. Pipapo is a wonderful ice-cream shop on rue Winston Churchill (near the tourist office, tel 02 96 63 18 89; summer only).

225 K8 Rue Winston Churchill (by the Casino), 22370 Pléneuf-Val-André 02 96 72 20 55 Apr–end Sep daily 9–1, 2–7; Oct–end Mar Mon–Sat 9–12.30, 2–5.30 Line 2 to St-Brieuc and Erquy/Fréhel Cruises and fishing trips around Cap Fréhel, to Île de Bréhat from Dahouët; excursions in a traditional sailing lugger *(La Pauline)*.

THE EMERALD COAST

This drive takes in the fascinating Côte d'Émeraude, with its impressive cliffs, superb sandy beaches and the unforgettable Fort la Latte on a barren promontory. Inland, the Forêt de la Hunaudaye and the surrounding area provide an interesting contrast.

THE DRIVE
Distance: 92km (57 miles)
Time: Half to a full day
Start/end at: Le-Val-André

★ The beach at Le-Val-André is one of Brittany's finest. A road running around the promontory has lovely views of the beach and of the Île du Verdelet, a bird sanctuary accessible at low tide.

Follow the D34 to Planguenoual, then take the D59 to Lamballe.

❶ Lamballe, on a hillside beside a small river, is famous for its *haras national* (national stud farm), where you can take a guided tour. The Gothic Église Notre-Dame at the top of town has a finely carved rood screen and doorways.

Leave Lamballe eastwards by the D28, then bear right onto the D52A towards Plédéliac, 11km (7 miles) away. Turn left onto the D55 and drive for another 4km (2.5 miles), following the signs to Château de la Hunaudaye.

❷ The Château de la Hunaudaye dates back to the 12th century. It was battered into its present ruins during the Revolution. The most impressive parts are the Tour de la Glacière, the Renaissance manor house and the 15th-century keep, with a remarkable spiral staircase.

Turn left and left again along the D28 and drive through the Forêt de la Hunaudaye to the hamlet of St-Aubin, 6km (4 miles). Follow the D52 and turn right. Follow the D13 and D43 for 24km (15 miles) through Hénanbihen and Pléboulle to the Baie de la Frénaye and Fort la Latte.

❸ Fort la Latte is a medieval fortress perching on a rocky promontory. It offers magnificent views of Cap Fréhel to the west and the Côte d'Émeraude to the east. Two drawbridges span the deep cracks in the rock, filled by the sea at high tide. Inside, the oven heated cannonballs to set fire to enemy ships.

Drive round the Anse des Sévignés, 4km (2.5 miles), to Cap Fréhel (▷ 129), then follow the D34a to Sables-d'Or-les-Pins, 9km (5.5 miles). The scenic coast road winds through the wild Landes de Fréhel (Fréhel moors) to Pléhérel-Plage, with its beautiful beach.

❹ Most people come to Sables-d'Or-les-Pins (▷ 141) to walk along the long golden beach. Strong currents make it unsuitable for swimming.

Continue on the D34 and turn right onto the D786 towards Erquy, 8km (5 miles).

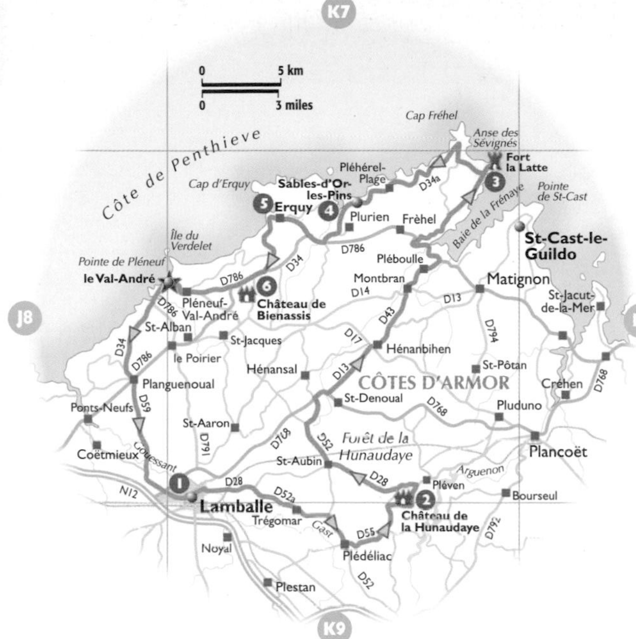

PLACES TO VISIT

CHÂTEAU DE LA HUNAUDAYE

Mid-Jun to mid-Sep daily 10.30–6
Adult €3.90, child €2.90 (6–16); reduced rates off-season

HARAS NATIONAL

02 96 50 06 98 Guided tours mid-Jul to late Aug daily 10–5.30; rest of year Tue–Sun 3pm Adult €5, child €2.50

FORT LA LATTE

02 96 41 57 11 Guided tours Jul, Aug daily 10–7; Apr–end Jun, Sep daily 10–12.30, 2–6; Oct–end Mar weekends 2–6
Adult €4.70, child (under 12) €2.60

CHÂTEAU DE BIENASSIS

02 96 72 22 03 Mid-Jun to mid-Sep Mon–Sat 10.30–12.30, 2–6.30, Sun 2–6.30
Adult €5, child €3

5 This resort and fishing port of Erquy is sheltered by the cliffs of Cap d'Erquy, 3km (2 miles) to the north, and is worth the detour. There are fine views of the wide bay of St-Brieuc as far as the Île de Bréhat.

Continue on the D786 towards Le-Val-André for 5km (3 miles), past Château de Bienassis on your left.

6 The late-medieval Château de Bienassis was rebuilt in the 17th century and furnished in Louis XIV and Breton Renaissance styles.

Continue on the D786 for 6km (4 miles) back to Le-Val-André.

WHEN TO GO

The Château de la Hunaudaye and Château de Bienassis are open in peak season only.

WHERE TO EAT

BEAUSÉJOUR

21 rue de la Corniche, Erquy 02 96 72 30 39 Lunch, dinner; closed Mon except Jul and Aug

Opposite *Fort la Latte perched on the cliffside*
Below left *The beach at Le-Val-Andre*
Below *The lighthouse at Cap Fréhel, built in 1950 to replace one destroyed in World War II*

PLOUMANAC'H WALK

The seashore between Ploumanac'h and Perros-Guirec is the most remarkable stretch of the Pink Granite Coast, where the shapes and hues of the rocks are truly mesmerizing, especially towards sunset. Whatever you do, don't forget the camera. It is best seen on foot, from an old watch-path called the Sentier des Douaniers. This is one of the most popular sections of the GR34, a long-distance footpath that runs along most of Brittany's coast.

THE WALK
Length: 8.5km (5 miles)
Allow: Half a day
Start/end at: La Chapelle de Notre-Dame de la Clarté

HOW TO GET THERE

La Clarté is signed near Ploumanac'h, off the main road (D788/boulevard du Sémaphore) between Perros-Guirec and Trégastel on the Côte de Granit Rose (Côtes d'Armor). The spire makes it easy to spot. There is parking beside the chapel.

★ Notre-Dame de la Clarté (Our Lady of Light) stands on high land surveying the sea. The chapel is built of pink granite quarried from the hillsides behind the village. It dates from 1445, a thanksgiving (so the story goes) from a local nobleman who became lost in fog while sailing around the coast. He prayed for guidance and took his bearings from a sudden shaft of sunlight that fell on this spot. The weathered granite of the chapel porch is carved into low relief. An annual *pardon* attracts many pilgrims on 15 August.

Take the rue du Tertre from the north side of the chapel. It leads to a rocky knoll from which there's a wonderful view. Follow the path to the signal station (Sémaphore), and cross the main road (boulevard du Sémaphore) on to rue des Fougères. Take a path to your left, which leads down towards the shore near a little beach (Grève St-Pierre). This connects you with the coastal footpath called the Sentier des Douaniers.

❶ The Sentier des Douaniers, a former customs officers' trail, can be crowded in summer. The route is waymarked (with yellow signs) to discourage undue erosion; stick to the marked paths. The rocks may be slippery when damp. Bicycling is strictly forbidden.

Turn left and follow the path along the shoreline. Les Sept-Îles are visible on a clear day.

❷ Les Sept-Îles, a rocky archipelago, is one of the most important seabird sanctuaries in France. Some 20,000 pairs and nearly 30 different species breed here annually, including puffins, along with a resident colony of grey seals. Motor launches take visitors around the islands from local resorts.

Carry on along the path westwards. At Pors Rolland the scenery suddenly becomes more dramatic, and you enter a conservation zone called Les Landes de Ploumanac'h.

❸ At Les Landes de Ploumanac'h the granite boulders piled on top of one another assume startling shapes. Some of the most striking rock forms can be seen around the Pointe de Squewel. Many have been given fanciful names: the Tortoise, the Skull, the Devil's Castle.

Continue westwards around the headland, following the path through the astonishing rocky wilderness, splashed with gorse and heather and occasional pines. Within a few hundred metres (half a mile) you will reach Ploumanac'h's lighthouse, and near it the lifeboat station and the Maison du Littoral.

❹ The Maison du Littoral is an information point in a typical pink granite building. It contains a permanent exhibition about the geology and ecology of this coastline, and the importance of granite to the local economy.

Walk along the path to Ploumanac'h's main beach, the Plage de St-Guirec.

❺ Though quite small, the Plage de St-Guirec is one of the most attractive resort beaches anywhere in Brittany. On one of the rocks stands a tiny stone oratory containing a statue of the Celtic monk, St Guirec, who arrived here from Wales in the sixth century. The receding tide reveals yet another dazzling rockscape, leading the eye towards a tidal islet in the bay on which a Gothic mock castle—the Château de Costaëres—stands. The castle is privately owned, and not open to the public. Several panoramic restaurants by the entrance to the beach allow you to enjoy the scene at leisure.

The final section of the Sentier des Douaniers takes you to the pretty port of Ploumanac'h, past the landing stage for trips to Les Sept-Îles, and a crowd of anchored boats in the bay. Walk along the quai de Bellevue, then take the rue de la Plaine uphill to the rue de St-Guirec, which leads out of the village. Turn right, then almost immediately left on to the rue de Ranolien, where you will see the Christian Gad sculpture park on your right.

❻ This public park contains a dozen modern sculptures in local pink granite, created for a festival in 1990. Here you'll spot L'Ankou (François Breton) and Dahud (Patrice Le Guen), inspired by Breton legends, and works by Pierre Székely.

Leave the park and cross the busy boulevard du Sémaphore. At the crossroads you will find a large shop selling biscuits and other regional products. Take rue Gabriel, passing a windmill on your right, and head back towards the spire of Notre-Dame-de-la-Clarté. A path off rue de la Vallée leads back into the car park beside the chapel.

WHEN TO GO

This walk gets very crowded during the summer school holidays, but can be enjoyed at any time of year. Choose a clear day to enjoy good views. Rocks and paths will be slippery when it's wet or frosty, and freak waves may be dangerous in stormy weather. Eating places and other facilities may not operate off-season.

WHERE TO EAT

COSTE MOR

✉ Plage St Guirec, Ploumanac'h ☎ 02 96 91 65 55 🕒 Apr–end Oct lunch and dinner

PLACES TO VISIT

MAISON DU LITTORAL

✉ Chemin du Phare, Ploumanac'h ☎ 02 96 91 62 77 🕒 Mid-Jun to mid-Sep Mon–Sat 10–1, 2–6; school holidays Mon–Fri 2–5 💳 Free

Opposite *Pink granite rocks and coastal wild flowers*
Below *Boats moored along the seafront at Ploumanac'h*

WHAT TO DO

BÉGARD

ARMORIPARK

www.armoripark.com

This popular theme park has plenty to amuse, including animals, trampolines, pedalos, bouncy castles, mini-golf, waterslides, bumper boats, heated outdoor pool and lots more. There's a picnic area inside the park, and on-site catering.

22140 Bégard (NW of Guingamp) 02 96 45 36 36 Mid-Jun to end Aug daily 11–7; Apr to mid-Jun, Sep Wed, Sat 1–6, Sun, holidays 11–6; rest of year hours vary Seasonal tariff €11 in summer €10 children, free for children under 1m (3ft 3in) tall; family tickets €36

DINAN

BOWLING LE BELEM

www.bowlinglebelem.com

For an energetic, fun-packed time, head for the ten bowling lanes of this attractively located entertainment centre just north of Dinan. Other than bowling, there are karaoke sessions and themed soirées, snooker, video games, and a snack restaurant and a bar.

8 rue de la Tramontane, ZA des Alleux, 22100 Taden 02 96 87 03 08 Jul, Aug daily 3pm–3am; rest of year Tue–Sun hours vary Prices vary depending on the time of day (the earlier you go, the cheaper, from €4 per session, including shoes)

CLUB CANOË-KAYAK DE LA RANCE

www.nautismebretagne.fr

Down by the port, just across the river, this club rents out canoes and kayaks for trips on the River Rance lasting from one hour to one day. Credit cards are not accepted. Weekend rentals and courses are available all year round.

13 rue du Four, 22100 Lanvallay 02 96 39 01 50 Jul, Aug daily 9–7; rest of year by appointment Kayak €8 per hour for single, canoe €12 per hour

COMPTOIR DE LA RANCE

An attractively stocked version of the well-known marine co-operative found in many Breton harbour towns. Here you'll find a stylish range of nautical clothing and some enticing souvenirs, including Breton linen, glass and china, bird carvings, seashell pictures and mobiles.

23 rue du Quai, 22100 Dinan 02 96 39 89 51 Summer daily 10.30–7; rest of year daily 11–1, 2–7 (6pm Sun)

DANFLEURENN NAUTIC

Rent a self-drive motor-launch from this quayside kiosk to explore the glorious River Rance at leisure. Boats hold four to eight passengers, and you don't need a licence.

Port de Dinan, 22100 Dinan 06 07 45 89 97 Easter–end Oct daily 10–7 From €26–€31 per hour; €116–€131 for a whole day (7 hours)

ITOHA

www.itoha.com

This enterprising business is based on a boat called *Donata* moored down at the port. On board, insulated fleecy clothing for sailing and other outdoor pursuits is designed and sewn up from a microfibre textile developed for use on polar expeditions. There's a rapid made-to-measure service if you want to test the quality on and around Brittany's coast.

Bateau Donata, 80 rue du Quai, 22100 Dinan 02 96 87 05 92 Mon–Sat 10–1, 2.30–7

LAMBALLE

GP KARTING

www.gp-circuit.com

This open-air karting track measures 800m (2,600ft), with 50 karts in a range of engine sizes. You can have lessons if you wish or simply rent a kart in blocks of 10 minutes. The bar, snack bar and terrace all have

Opposite *Tourist boat at Dinan port*

great views. The minimum age for participants is seven.
✉ Z1 des Noës, 22400 Lamballe ☎ 02 96 50 09 09 🕐 Mid-Jul to end Aug daily 10–dusk; rest of year Wed, Sat 2–dusk, Sun 10am–dusk; other times by appointment
✋ From €10 for 8 minutes

LANNION

STADE D'EAU VIVE

www.france-kayak.com
Lannion is famed for its white-water rafting experience on a section of the River Léguer, where Olympic teams are trained. Here you can practise kayaking or rafting all year round in the middle of town. Several supervised basins allow visitors of all ages and stages of proficiency to perfect their skills in complete safety. Rafts holding up to six people, inflatable canoes, or kayaks can be rented. Safety helmets and lifejackets are provided.
✉ 8 rue de Kermaria, 22300 Lannion
☎ 02 96 37 43 90 🕐 Jul, Aug daily 9–5.30, or by reservation

PAIMPOL

ABBAYE DE BEAUPORT

www.abbaye-beauport.com
These evocative Gothic ruins overlooking the sea just south of Paimpol have been imaginatively restored. The abbey now welcomes visitors to explore at leisure or join in a host of summer activities, including discovery walks, craft workshops, art exhibitions, concerts and cider-making. Night walks take place in July and August.
✉ Kérity, 22500 Paimpol ☎ 02 96 55 18 55 🕐 Mid-Jun to mid-Sep daily 10–7; rest of year daily 10–12, 2–5 ✋ Adult €4.50, child (11–18) €2, (5–10) €1; reduced admission off-season ☛ Guided tours in French

LE PUB

www.lepub-paimpol.fr
This piano bar and pub near the harbour puts on a varied range of music and appeals to a wide age range (Irish evening on Thursday, karaoke on Sunday). There is a bar on the ground floor (which serves meals) and a dance floor upstairs.
✉ 3 rue des Islandais, 22500 Paimpol
☎ 02 96 20 82 31 🕐 Summer Tue–Sun 9pm–5am; winter Thu–Sun 11pm–4am

LA VAPEUR DU TRIEUX

www.vapeurdutrieux.com
Take a steam train ride along the scenic Trieux estuary to Pontrieux, with a halfway stop at a manor house for music and refreshments. A grand day out for families, especially steam-train enthusiasts. The commentary is multilingual. Advance reservations are essential. at any time of year.
✉ Gare de Paimpol, avenue du Général de Gaulle, 22500 Paimpol ☎ 0892 391 427 (premium-rate line €0.34 per min) 🕐 Daily services mid-May to end Sep Tue–Sun (twice-daily in Aug) ✋ Adult return €22, child (4–16) €11; one-way and family tickets available

VOILIERS TRADITIONNELS

www.eulalie-paimpol.com
www.vieux-copain.com
Paimpol's maritime past is recalled in the elegant rigging of several traditional sailboats *(vieux gréements)*, which make a fine sight around the Bréhat archipelago and along the Goëlo coast. In summer fishing trips and pleasure cruises are advertised from Paimpol harbour. Look out for the replica sardine fishing boat called *Eulalie*, or the tuna boats *La Nébuleuse* and *Vieux Copain*.
✉ 22500 Paimpol 🕐 Jul, Aug daily cruises; Apr–end Jun, Sep to mid-Nov weekends

PERROS-GUIREC

LES GALERIES DE KER-ILIZ

www.produits-bretons-ker-iliz.com
This large mall not far from the tourist office, formerly the home of architect James Boullié, sells products made or crafted in Brittany, such as Quimper porcelain, Celtic jewellery, dolls, linen, cards, music, pottery, wooden items, biscuits and nautical clothing.
✉ 6 rue du Général de Gaulle, 22700 Perros-Guirec ☎ 02 96 91 00 96 🕐 Jul, Aug daily 10–12.30, 2.30–7.30; shorter hours off-season (closed Sun pm and Mon am)

PORT MINIATURE

Scale-model electric replicas of ferries, trawlers, tug boats, lifeboats and so on make an entertaining way to spend a quarter of an hour on an enclosed basin at the pleasure port. Learn a bit about navigation and marine signalling too.
✉ Bassin du Linkin, Port de Plaisance, 22700 Perros-Guirec ☎ 02 96 91 06 11
🕐 Jul, Aug daily 10.45–7.30; Apr–end Jun, holidays and long weekends 2.30–6 ✋ €4 per person (3–103!) for a 15-minute session (free for under 3s)

PLÉDÉLIAC

CHÂTEAU DE LA HUNAUDAYE

www.la-hunaudaye.com
Revisit the Middle Ages at this majestic moated castle dating from the 13th–15th centuries. Exhibitions, 'living history' events and family activities take place all summer, so there's lots for children to do. There are also guided tours.
✉ Le Chêne au Loup, 22270 Plédéliac
☎ 02 96 34 82 10 🕐 Mid-Jun to mid-Sep daily 10.30–6; school holidays Sun–Fri 2.30–6; Apr to mid-Jun, mid-Sep to end Oct Sun, holidays 2.30–6; closed Nov–end Mar
✋ Adult €3 (€3.90 mid Jun–mid Sep), child (6–16) €2 (€2.90)

LA FERME D'ANTAN

www.ferme-dantan22.com
This lovingly restored farm complex recreates the rural life of yesteryear. Old-fashioned crops like buckwheat and flax grow in the gardens, early agricultural machinery is on display in the barns and storehouses, and animals enliven the stables, cowshed and pigsty. A tour with costumed guides includes a film on daily life in the 1920s. Occasional summer events may include breadmaking, chestnut festival, workshops on osier-weaving or wool-spinning.
✉ St-Esprit-des-Bois, 22270 Plédeliac
☎ 02 96 34 80 77 🕐 Jun–end Aug daily 10–6.30; afternoons in school holidays
✋ Adult €4.50, child (6–16) €2.50, including guided tour

PLOUMANAC'H

LA MAISON DU LITTORAL

www.perros-guirec.com

On an amazing stretch of coastline, this visitor centre near the lighthouses organizes walks, talks and activities based on the geology and ecosystem of the Pink Granite Coast. *Les Lundis de Ploumanac'h* (Ploumanac'h Mondays) are guided walks on the coastal watchpath.

✉ Chemin du Phare, 22700 Ploumanac'h ☎ 02 96 91 62 77 🕒 Mid-Jun to mid-Sep Mon–Sat, school holidays 🖐 Exhibition: free; walks: adult €4–€5

ST-BRIEUC

LA BRIQUETERIE

www.cabri22.com

Attractions at the site of an old tile factory and brickworks on the Baie de Saint-Brieuc include the kiln where the tiles and bricks were fired in 1864, pottery workshops and a miniature railway.

✉ 22360 Langueux, Les Grèves ☎ 02 96 63 36 66 🕒 Jul, Aug Mon–Thu 10.30–6.30, Fri 11–6.30, Sat, Sun 1.30–6.30; Jun, Sep Wed, Fri–Sun 2–6.30, Oct–end May Wed, Fri–Sun 2–6; closed mid-Dec to end Jan 🖐 Adult €4, child (6–12) €2.50

MAISON DE LA BAIE

www.baiedesaintbrieuc.com

Activities and events are organized by this energetic visitor facility in the coastal nature reserve of the Baie de St-Brieuc. Find out about the effects of huge tides on the local ecosystem through talks and shoreline field trips for bird-watching (more than 200 species), beachcombing and visiting the mussel beds. Reserve outings in advance; sensible footwear and clothing are advised.

✉ Site de l'Etoile, 22120 Hillion ☎ 02 96 32 27 98 🕒 Jul, Aug Mon–Fri 10.30–6.30, Sat, Sun 1.30–6.30; Jun, Sep Wed–Fri, Sun 2–6; Oct–end May Wed, Fri, Sun 2–6 🖐 Visitor centre exhibitions adult €3, child (6–12) €2.50; outings/activities, telephone for details

ST-CAST-LE-GUILDO

LA FERME DES LANDES

www.fermedeslandes.pays-de-matignon.net

A cider lover's heaven with cider from different apple varieties, plus cider vinegar and apple juice, all home-brewed by the enthusiastic owner. Taste, buy and tour the farm. Every Friday afternoon in summer a farmers' market is held here.

✉ Notre Dame du Guildo, 22380 St-Cast-le-Guildo ☎ 02 96 41 12 48 🕒 Jun–end Aug daily 10–8; Apr, May, Sep Mon–Sat 2–7; rest of year Fri–Sat 10–12, 2–6

GOLF CLUB DE PEN-GUEN

www.golf-st-cast.com

This superbly situated 18-hole, par-68 golf course lies on the east side of town, with direct access to the lovely beach of Pen-Guen. Though quite short, the course is technically challenging and interesting for all standards. There's a driving range and putting green to keep the keenest golfer busy.

✉ Route du Golfe, 22380 St-Cast-le-Guildo ☎ 02 96 41 91 20 🕒 Apr–end Sep daily 7.30am–8pm; rest of year daily 9–5.30 🖐 Green fees €53 in summer, €42 off-season, €31 in winter (reduced rates for couples)

TRÉBEURDEN

TI AL LANNEC

www.tiallannec.com

Mini-cures and beauty treatments of many kinds are on offer at one of Côtes d'Armor's most attractive and relaxing hotels. Choose an anti-ageing seaweed facial, a synergetic massage or a reflexology session at the Espace Bleu Marine spa. The minimum age is 16.

✉ 14 allée de Mezo Guen, 22560 Trébeurden ☎ 02 96 15 01 01 🕒 Daily 9–12, 2.30–8 🖐 Entrance charge €11 (free for hotel clients); treatments start from €33

TRÉGASTEL

ÉCOLE D'ÉQUITATION FOSSEY

Go horse-riding through the Breton countryside, in a forest or along the seashore of the Côtes d'Armor region. You can also take lessons

at the school to improve your riding skills. Telephone in advance to reserve your place.

13 rue du Calvaire, 22730 Trégastel 02 96 23 86 14 Mon–Sat 9–12, 2–7; closed Sun and 3 weeks in Sep €19 per hour; €168 for 10 hours

LE VAL-ANDRÉ

ANTIQUITÉS COMPTOIRS DE L'OUEST

The old port and yacht marina of Dahouët, west of the resort, is a good place to browse for antiques. In one of the old sail-lofts down on the quayside is an Aladdin's Cave of miscellaneous bric-à-brac and Breton bygones—furniture, toys, books.

10 quai des Terres-Nuevas, port de Dahouët, 22370 Pléneuf-Val-André 02 96 63 18 84 Thu, Fri 2–5, Sat, Sun 10.30–12.30, 3–6.30 (longer hours in summer)

CASINO LA ROTONDE

This art-deco-style casino looks rather like an ocean liner berthed on the seafront esplanade. It is small and civilized but not at all snobbish. Minimum stakes are modest, so you needn't lose your shirt here. Besides slot-machines, roulette and blackjack tables, it has a restaurant, a terrace café, and a cinema and a theatre. Minimum age 18.

1 cours Winston Churchill, 22370 Pléneuf-Val-André 02 96 72 85 06 Daily 10am–3am (4am Sat) all year (4am Fri–Sun in Jul and Aug)

LES SUCETTES DU VAL-ANDRÉ

This lollipop kiosk which sets up shop in the holiday season near the tourist office and casino is not to be missed. It sells around 60 varieties of heavenly stickiness, made from natural ingredients. Flavours range from eucalyptus to pear and chocolate. Try the seaweed toffee *(craquant aux algues)* too. Tours and tastings at the factory in nearby St-Alban can be arranged.

Cours Winston Churchill, 22370 Pléneuf-Val-André 02 96 32 93 93 Summer months only

Opposite *Golf is one of many sports that Brittany has to offer*

FESTIVALS AND EVENTS

APRIL

FÊTE DE LA COQUILLE ST-JACQUES ERQUY/ST-QUAY-PORTRIEUX/ LOGUIVY-SUR-MER

Three resorts take it in turns to host this annual homage to the revered scallop, dredged in huge quantities from the seabed each year. There are exhibitions, processions and fireworks.

02 96 20 83 16 2 days in Apr

MAY

PARDON DE SAINT-YVES TRÉGUIER

This event is one of the most important and spectacular religious festivals in Brittany, marking the anniversary of the death of Yves Hélori, patron saint of lawyers, born near Tréguier in1253.

Third Sun in May

JULY, AUGUST

FESTIVAL INTERNATIONAL DE HARPE CELTIQUE DINAN

www.harpe-celtique.com

A prestigious music festival dedicated to the Celtic harp, with concerts and master-classes.

02 96 87 36 69 6 days in Jul Ticket prices from €5 (inclusive passes available)

FÊTE DES REMPARTS DINAN

This biennial festival held in even-numbered years draws large crowds for an ebullient medieval romp with jousting and jollity around the old fortifications.

Every second year, a weekend in late Jul

MERCREDIS EN FÊTE TRÉGUIER

For six consecutive Wednesdays in summer, the main streets and squares of the town bustle with life. After the weekly market held in the morning, concerts, barbecues and general entertainment go on well into the evenings.

Jul, Aug Free

JAZZ À L'AMIRAUTÉ LE VAL-ANDRÉ

On summer Tuesdays a series of jazz concerts is staged in the Parc de l'Amirauté near the seafront.

Jul, Aug Tue 9pm Free

BON-REPOS SAINT-GELVEN

www.bon-repos.com

Enterprising use is made of the evocative remains of the Abbaye de Bon-Repos, an ancient abbey near the shores of the Lac de Guerledan. In high season it hosts an elaborate son-et-lumière historical spectacle with music and special effects. Local people take part, and all profits go towards the restoration of the abbey.

02 96 24 82 20 Aug Adult €18, child (4–10) €10 (tickets are less expensive if you reserve in advance)

FESTIVAL DE LA DANSE BRETONNE ET DE LA ST-LOUP GUINGAMP

www.dansebretonne.com

Nine days of merriment involving concerts, traditional Breton dancing contests, street entertainment and exhibitions. Information from the tourist office.

02 96 43 73 89 Mid-Aug

FÊTE DU CHANT DE MARIN PAIMPOL

www.paimpol-festival.com

An immensely popular folk festival recalling the times and traditions of this seafaring community, and the songs sung by its fishermen.

02 96 55 12 77 3 days in early Aug €16 per day (adult), €32 for the whole festival; child €4–€8 (free under 6)

PRICES AND SYMBOLS
The restaurants are listed alphabetically within each town. The prices given for lunch (L) and dinner (D) are for three courses for one person, without drinks. The wine price is for the least expensive bottle.
For a key to the symbols, ▷ 2.

DINAN

CAFÉ TERRASSES
On the port beside the bridge, this bistro is popular, as much for its flexible range of well-prepared food and friendly welcome as its enticing location. A tented terrace with cane chairs caters for fine weather. Inside is a small zinc style bar with banquette seating, enlivened with typical café posters. A lunchtime *formule* might include *steak frites* followed by an ice cream. Alternatively you could choose oysters or *crevettes roses* with an aperitif, or have pasta with salad.
✉ 2–4 rue du Quai, 22100 Port de Dinan
☎ 02 96 39 09 60 ⏲ Jul, Aug daily 8am–1am; Sep–end Jun daily 9am–1am
✋ L €25, D €35, Wine €13

CHEZ LA MÈRE POURCEL
Occupying a splendid old merchant's house on one of Dinan's quaintest squares, this restaurant is a long-established temple of gastronomy. The winding staircase is a listed monument in its own right. The best tables are near the fireplace, with Louis XIII-style chairs. La Mère Pourcel specializes in *pré-salé* lamb (▷ 164) fresh from Mont-St-Michel, available from April to the end of September. Other temptations are lobster, local fish and scallops in autumn and winter. Reservations are essential in high season.
✉ 3 place des Merciers, 22100 Dinan
☎ 02 96 39 03 80 ⏲ Jul, Aug daily 12–2, 7–9.30; mid-Mar to end Jun, Sep Tue–Sat 12–2, 7–9.30, Sun 12–2; Oct to mid-Mar Wed–Sat 12–2, 7–9.30, Sun 12–2
✋ L €25, D €65, Wine €18

ERQUY

L'ESCURIAL
www.lescurial.com
Easily spotted on the seafront road next to the tourist office, this is one of the best restaurants in the area. The dining room is furnished with comfortable seating. Renowned for seasonal scallops (an Erquy special), it serves classic seafood dishes. Menus range from €22 to €56.
✉ 29 boulevard de la Mer, 22430 Erquy
☎ 02 96 72 31 56 ⏲ Jul, Aug Tue–Sun 12–2.30, 7.30–9.30; Sep–end Jun Tue, Wed, Fri, Sat 12–2.30, 7.30–9.30, Thu, Sun 12–2.30; closed Jan ✋ L €23, D €40, Wine €18

Above *Art gallery, café and bistro Art et Saveur at Le Val-André*

ÎLE DE BREHAT

L'OISEAU DES ÎLES
This popular *crêperie* is in a blue-shuttered building just 10 minutes from the port, distinguished by a large puffin sign. Inside, the bare walls of pink granite complement the blue windows and doors. In fine weather you can eat on the terrace. Besides basic *crêpes* (ham, cheese, mushroom), it serves specials such as *andouille* (Breton sausage) and salads. Reservations recommended in summer.
✉ Rue du Port, 22870 Île de Bréhat ☎ 02 96 20 00 53 ⏲ Apr–end Sep and school holidays 11.30–3.30, 7–10.30; closed Sat, Mon dinner, Tue dinner, also 2 weeks at end Jun ✋ L €12, D €15, Cider €8

MÛR-DE-BRETAGNE

AUBERGE GRAND'MAISON
This highly regarded restaurant-with-rooms near the church is about as far from the sea as you can get in Brittany, but Jacques Guillo still seems to include plenty of fish

in his inventive repertoire. House specials include Erquy lobster with wild mushrooms, and *langoustines royales*. Eating here is a serious gastronomic undertaking, so don't expect low prices. But for a treat, this is well worth tracking down. Reserve ahead.
✉ 1 rue Léon-le-Cerf, 22530 Mûr-de-Bretagne ☎ 02 96 28 51 10 🕒 Jul, Aug Tue–Sat 12.15–1.45, 7.15–8.45, Sun lunch; Sep–end Jun closed also Tue 💳 L €76, D €140, Wine €30

PAIMPOL

LA COTRIADE

www.la-cotriade-paimpol.com

A well-kept stone building with a terrace overlooking the harbour. Inside lie double-decker dining rooms (smoking permitted upstairs) with bright stripy plates. The catch of the day ends up in dishes such as *marmite Paimpolaise*. Menus are named after classic sailing ships—for example *Vieux Copain* or *Belle Poule*, try a *confit de pommes façon tatin* with *crème fraiche battue au Calvados*.
✉ 16 quai Armand Dayot, 22500 Paimpol ☎ 02 96 20 01 00 🕒 Jul, Aug Mon, Wed, Sat 7–9, Tue, Thu–Fri, Sun 12–2, 7–9; closed Mon, Wed dinner off-season and Sat lunch, and several weeks in late Nov, early Feb 💳 L €30, D €50, Wine €18

L'ECLUSE

Hidden amid the boatyards and chandleries by the harbour lock-gates, this light, airy shed-like building attracts discerning locals. Here fresh seafood is cooked before your eyes on an open hearth, and a roll of kitchen towel takes the place of a napkin. Breton sea shanties or soft jazz plays in the background, and nautical netting drapes around the ceiling fans. Chalkboard suggestions show what's just swum in; the bread is fresh and warm and puddings are reassuringly familiar *(tarte tatin, poire belle Hélène)*. A real find, so don't tell anyone.
✉ Quai Armand Dayot, 22500 Paimpol ☎ 02 96 55 03 38 🕒 Jul, Aug daily 12–3, 7–11; Sep–end Jun daily 12–2, 7–10; closed Sat off-season 💳 L €15, D €35, Wine €15

PERROS-GUIREC

LA CRÉMAILLÈRE

Dark tones, low ceilings and a rustic interior give a warm atmosphere here. The menu changes with the seasons and is based around fresh seafood and chargrilled meat. Dishes include scallop kebab with smoked duck breast, roast beef and coffee tart with a citrus marmalade. In summer it's best to reserve a table.
✉ 13 place de l'Église, 22700 Perros-Guirec ☎ 02 96 23 22 08 🕒 Mon, Sat 7–10, Tue–Fri, Sun 12–2, 7–11; closed Nov and a week in Mar 💳 L €16, D €20, Wine €14

PLANCOËT

JEAN-PIERRE CROUZIL

www.crouzil.com

Jean-Pierre's top-flight cooking is complemented by elegant glass and china, sculpted bronzes and designer flowers, but the welcome is warm and unpretentious. You may order foie gras with onion jam and grenadine, milk-fed lamb, lobster in Belgian beer, or hot oysters in a Vouvray *zabaglione*. Puddings ring the changes on chocolate, and the bread is all home-made. A virgin-pure brand of mineral water is bottled here, and some beautiful hotel rooms preclude the need to stagger any distance from the table.
✉ 20 les Quais, 22130 Plancoët ☎ 02 96 84 10 24 🕒 Daily 12.30–2.30, 7.30–9.30; closed Mon, Tue lunch in Jul and Aug; Sun dinner, Mon, Tue off-season; 2 weeks Oct and 3 weeks Jan 💳 L €50, D €90, Wine €30

PLOUMANAC'H

COSTE MOR

Despite its name, this restaurant offers remarkable value overlooking the beach at St-Guirec, surely one of Brittany's most amazing seascapes (▷ 148–149). Enjoy a glass of wine and a *plateau de fruits de mer* at the stone tables and benches on the terrace, or some hot *soupe de poissons* inside.
✉ Plage de St-Guirec, 22700 Ploumanac'h ☎ 02 96 91 65 55 🕒 Apr–end Oct daily 12–2.30, 7–9.30 (10 in high season); closed mid-Nov to end Mar 💳 L €15, D €20, Wine €13

ST-BRIEUC

AUX PESKED

www.auxpesked.com

Look for the grotesque fish on the hill leading from the heart of the city down to the port. The modern building overlooks the valley, with terrace tables outside in summer. Much use is made of seafood, but classic Breton dishes also include local specials such as *cocos de Paimpol* (haricot beans) or *andouille*. Puddings are ornate and extravagant.
✉ 59 rue du Légué, 22000 St-Brieuc ☎ 02 96 33 34 65 🕒 Tue–Fri lunch, dinner, Sat dinner, Sun lunch; closed 2 weeks early Jan and 2 weeks early Sep 💳 L €25, D €52 Wine €18

TRÉGUIER

LES TROIS RIVIÈRES

www.aiguemarine.fr

This restaurant belongs to Aigues Marine Hotel (▷ 157) down on the quayside. Seafood predominates in its light, modern dining-room, for example a double fillet of sole in a Viennese crust or some roast langoustines. Afterwards, you might toy with a crumble of William pears, or a *tarte fine aux pommes*. Prices are reasonable for a four-star hotel, and child menus are available.
✉ Port de Plaisance, 22220 Tréguier ☎ 02 96 92 97 00 🕒 Jul, Aug Mon–Sat 7.30–9, Sun 12.30–1.30; rest of year Tue–Fri 12.30–1.30, 7.30–9, Sat 7.30–9, Sun 12.30–1.30 💳 L €33, D €51, Wine €21

LE VAL-ANDRÉ

ART ET SAVEUR

In a converted sail-loft overlooking Val-André's old port of Dahouët, this is an art gallery, daytime café and wine-bar-cum-bistro, serving interesting menus with an oriental tang. Light meals *(tartines*, mixed platters, cheeses and puddings) can be ordered. Its breakfasts are popular with marina users. There are arty happenings from time to time.
✉ 28 quai des Terre-Neuvas, Port de Dahouët, 22370 Pléneuf-Val-André ☎ 02 96 63 19 17 🕒 Fri–Tue 10–7; Thu 2–9.30 (jazz evening); closed Wed 💳 L €16, D €22, Wine €18.50

PRICES AND SYMBOLS

Prices quoted are the range for a double with private facilities. The *taxe de séjour* (▷ 214) is not included. Unless otherwise stated, breakfast is excluded from the price. For a key to the symbols, ▷ 2.

BRÉLIDY

CHÂTEAU DE BRÉLIDY

www.chateau-brelidy.com

This creeper-covered, turreted manor stands inland (signed off the D8 between Tréguier and Guingamp), among woods and fields. The grounds encompass rivers with private fishing rights. Hospitality combines the comfort and grandeur of a country house hotel with the intimacy of a family home. Elegant, timbered salons are filled with antiques. A cottage in the gardens makes an ideal self-contained unit.

✉ 22140 Brélidy ☎ 02 96 95 69 38 ⊗ Closed Jan to mid-Mar ✋ €100–€168 (breakfast €13) 🛈 15, including 2 suites and a garden annexe Espace forme in the grounds; Jacuzzi Outdoor, covered

DINAN

D'AVAUGOUR

www.avaugourhotel.com

A smartly refurbished, personally managed hotel, ideally placed for exploring the old town. The entrance of this 18th-century building overlooks the main square (easy parking except on market day—Thursday). Guests make use of the idyllic rear gardens extending above parts of the castle ramparts for drinks or summer breakfasts. The interior has lots of character; each room is different and carefully designed, incorporating personal sound systems and top-range German plumbing. Some are suitable for families with inter-communicating doors, others have walk-in showers for visitors with limited mobility. There's no restaurant, but breakfast is splendid, and many eating places lie within strolling distance.

✉ 1 place du Champ, 22100 Dinan ☎ 02 96 39 07 49 ⊗ Closed Nov to mid-Feb ✋ €85–€255 (breakfast €12.50; supplement for one-night stays on Fri, Sat in high season) 🛈 21, plus 3 suites. Guests are requested not to smoke.

ERQUY

BEAUSÉJOUR

www.beausejour-erquy.com

This reliable, good-value Logis has an instantly welcoming air. The E-shaped, blue-shuttered building stands a few minutes' walk from the beach, but there are sea views from the large windows of the dining room, and from some of the well-kept bedrooms. One of the nicest is at the top of the house, with sloping ceilings tucked into the gables. The interior is attractively decorated with cane-look furnishings and bright fabrics. Appetizing, plain-looking menus highlight Erquy's famous seasonal scallops, making this place a good bet for lunch (▷ 154), and obligatory half-board terms are no hardship in high season.

✉ 21 rue de la Corniche, 22430 Erquy ☎ 02 96 72 30 39 ⊗ Closed mid-Nov to mid-Mar ✋ €55–€70 (breakfast €9) 🛈 15

ÎLE DE BRÉHAT

BELLEVUE

www.hotel-bellevue-brehat.fr

Lovely views stretch to the rocky shores from this pretty white building near Bréhat's landing stage. In summer, blue agapanthus lilies reflect the colours of the sea. Bedrooms are simple but in perfect order, some in traditional florals. Fresh seafood is served at its panoramic restaurant, decked with paintings by a local artist. Tables outside are always at a premium in this idyllic spot, so reserve ahead. Bicycles can be rented for exploring

Left *Château de Brélidy, Brélidy*

the island. Half- or full-board terms are obligatory.
Port Clos, 22870 Bréhat 02 96 20 00 05 Closed mid-Nov to mid-Dec and early Jan to mid-Feb €84–€104 per person half-board 17

PAIMPOL

LE REPAIRE DE KERROC'H

www.repaire-kerroch.com
Seafaring seems etched on the smartly dressed stonework of this superior late 18th-century corsair's residence alongside Paimpol's harbour. The refurbished interior reveals original timbers and monumental fireplaces. Most of its handsome bedrooms have port views. All are decorated in dashing, vibrant styles, and named after the islands off Brittany's coast. The well-regarded restaurant and less formal bistro serve freshly caught seafood and regional produce.
29 quai Morand, 22500 Paimpol 02 96 20 50 13 Closed mid-Nov to end Feb €50–€130 (breakfast €10) 13, plus a suite and an apartment (1 non-smoking)

PLOUËR-SUR-RANCE

MANOIR DE RIGOURDAINE

www.hotel-rigourdaine.fr
Unspoiled views stretch to the serene blue ribbon of the Rance estuary from this rambling stone property. It's an old manor farm, with a reception block in an airy converted barn, and bedrooms in double-decker outbuildings around the courtyard. Guests may come and go as they please. The interior is simple but elegant—rugs and period furnishings enhancing the natural qualities of oak and granite. Bedrooms have private terraces, and several are suitable for families. There is no restaurant; the nearest are in Plouer or Pleslin. Follow signs to Plouer and Langrolay from N176 (Dinan–Dol-de-Bretagne road).
Route de Langrolay, 22490 Plouër-sur-Rance 02 96 86 89 96 Closed mid-Nov to Easter €62–€82 (breakfast €7.50) 19

PLOUGRESCANT

MANOIR DE KERGREC'H

www.manoirdekergrech.com
Originally this impressive creeper-clad château was a bishop's palace, but since the Revolution it has been the ancestral home of the Viscounts of Roquefeuil. It stands in a huge estate near the mouth of the River Jaudy (signed near the St-Gonéry chapel with the crooked spire just south of Plougrescant). The present incumbents run a vegetable farm and ornamental plant nursery at this 17th-century granite manor as well as providing gracious *chambres d'hôtes* hospitality. The large, light bedrooms are furnished with family antiques, and have magnificent bathrooms. The tower room has medieval but operational plumbing.
Kergrec'h, 22820 Plougrescant 02 96 92 59 13 €110, including breakfast 8, including 2 family rooms and 1 suite

ST-CAST-LE-GUILDO

PORT JACQUET

www.port-jacquet.com
Set high above the bay, this stone-built hotel not far from the port has some of the best sea views in town. A warm welcome adds to the attractions of its cheerful, interior, where the Etoile des Mers restaurant dishes up seafood creations such as *moules de bouchot au cidre.* The refurbished bedrooms are bright and appealing, though not large. Pricier ones face the sea, but there are pleasant garden and courtyard views behind.
32 rue du Port, 22380 St-Cast-le-Guildo 02 96 41 97 18 €37–€58 (breakfast €7) 17

TRÉBEURDEN

TI AL LANNEC

www.tiallannec.com
Utter relaxation is promised at this long-established, family-owned Relais du Silence hotel on a small wooded hill just behind the port. Terraced gardens cascade through pine trees towards one of the most enchanting seascapes anywhere on the Pink Granite coast. Inside, the style is a French version of English country house, with rooms of all shapes and sizes furnished with care and taste, plus a generous sprinkling of antiques. Bedrooms are supremely comfortable, staff friendly. Health and beauty treatments add another dimension, but most guests just enjoy relaxing. There is also a hot tub and sauna.
14 allée de Mezo-Guen, 22560 Trébeurden 02 96 15 01 01 Closed Dec–end Feb €162–€255 (breakfast €17) 33

TRÉGUIER

AIGUE MARINE

www.aiguemarine.fr
This spacious modern construction is by the port, so is convenient for marina-users, but is only 10 minutes' walk from the main cathedral square. The light, airy reception bar-lounge overlooks a pool terrace set with palms. Bedrooms are stylish and well equipped, some with private balconies and some suitable for visitors with disabilities. One of the main attractions is the restaurant, Les Trois Rivières (▷ 155). Leisure facilities include a sauna, Jacuzzi and fitness room.
Port de Plaisance, 22220 Tréguier 02 96 92 97 00 Closed Jan–end Feb €74–€97 (breakfast €13) 48 Outdoor

LE VAL-ANDRÉ

GRAND HÔTEL DU VAL-ANDRÉ

www.grand-hotel-val-andre.fr
Easily found on the seafront road, this place has unrivalled views of Val-André's spectacular beach, with direct access through the French windows of its public rooms. The bar-lounge, restaurant and the most expensive bedrooms all enjoy glorious views of the sea. The English-speaking owner is attentive and courteous. Bedrooms are spacious and comfortable with blue-and-white decorations. Tidy gardens surround the hotel, and the sun-deck terrace is set with tables shaded by stripy parasols and mature pines.
80 rue Amiral Charner, 22370 Pléneuf-Val-André 02 96 72 20 56 Closed Jan €83–€103 (breakfast €9.50) 39

"LE MAJESTIC"
HAMBURGER
BAR
Sandwiches
LE MAJESTIC
Fish & Chips

ILLE-ET-VILAINE

Ille-et-Vilaine is Haute Bretagne, border country between France and Brittany. Its most striking natural feature is the great Baie du Mont-St-Michel, a low-slung Dutch seascape of tidal mud-flats, hinterland polders and great wide skies. Just beyond Brittany's borders on the eastern flank of the River Couesnon rises the ethereal island abbey that gives its name to the bay—essential viewing for any visitor to the area. Seafood cultivation is an important industry hereabouts. Find out how oysters are reared at Cancale, or mussels at Le Vivier-sur-Mer, then sample a local *plateau de fruits de mer*.

St-Malo is the main coastal settlement, an old corsair town combining the roles of international ferry port, commercial centre and sailing resort with pride and brio. Its opposite number on the west bank of the Rance is the *soignée* resort of Dinard, Nice of the North, famed for its glamorous casino, stripy bathing-tents and gorgeous beaches. Between the two towns, the River Rance cuts deep into Brittany's heartland, providing enough energy in its huge twice-daily tides to power a sizeable city. Partly canalized waterways run right through Ille-et-Vilaine. Redon makes a good centre for boating holidays. On either side of the Rance estuary lie short but beautiful stretches of the Emerald Coast, studded with small family resorts.

Largest centre is the regional capital of Rennes, university city and home of the Breton parliament, plus several mainstream museums. Its industries, notably the car manufacturer Citroën, propel much of Brittany's economy. The city's king-sized arts festivals of Transmusicales and Les Tombées de la Nuit attract crowds from all over Europe. Other places worth a trek from the seaside include the ancient bishopric of Dol-de-Bretagne and the three fortified towns of Fougères, Vitré and Combourg, whose castles once shielded the independent Duchy of Brittany from the unwelcome attentions of neighbouring France.

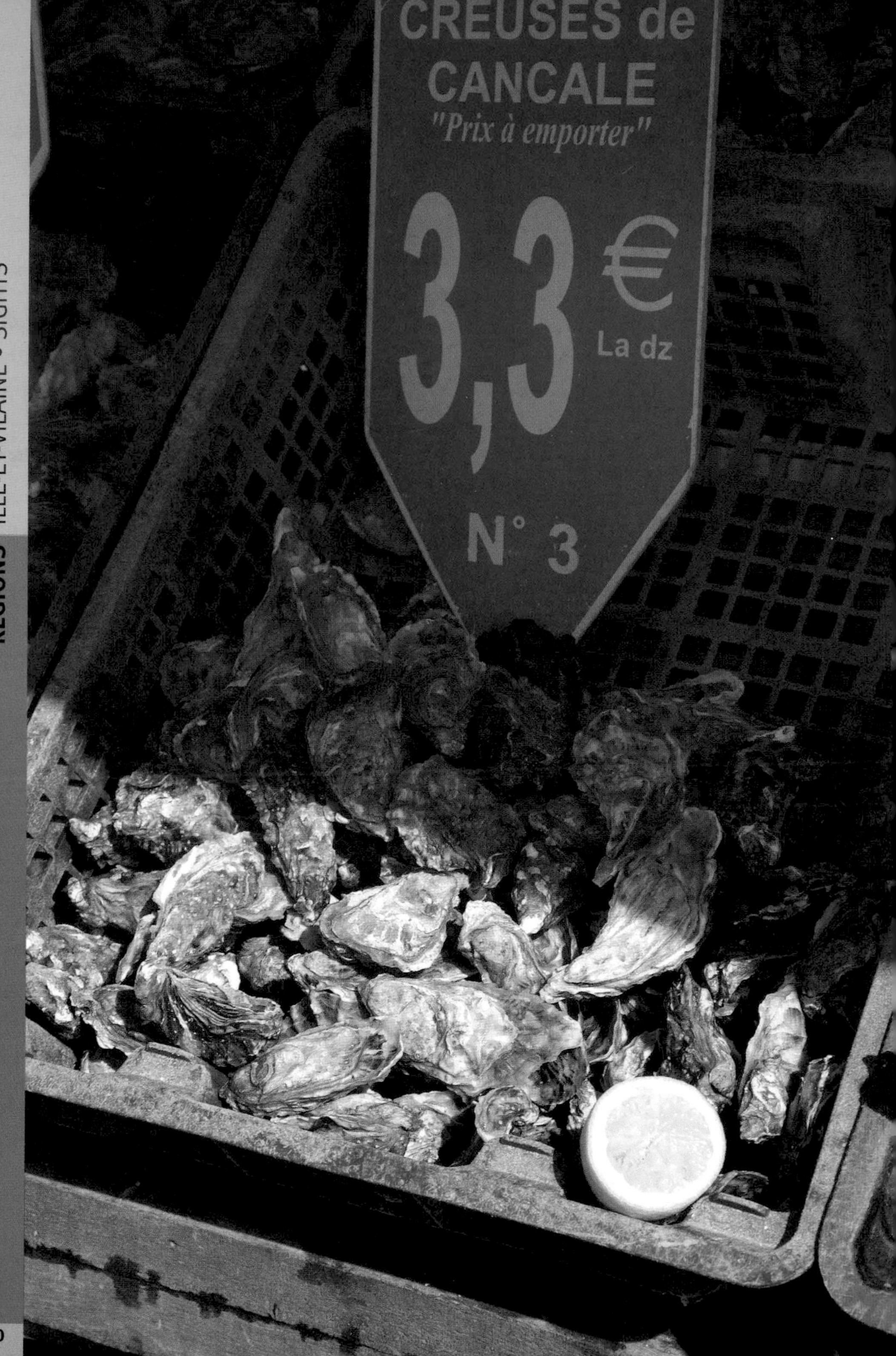
CREUSES de
CANCALE
"Prix à emporter"
3,3 €
La dz
N° 3

CANCALE

Brittany's charming oyster capital is the place to sample the perfect *plateau de fruits de mer*, or begin an exploration of the Emerald Coast. The muddy shores of Cancale may not look very inviting for a beach holiday, but they are ideal for rearing oysters.

OYSTER FARMING

Oyster-farming developed after the collapse of the cod-fishing industry, and today some 5,000 tonnes are harvested annually. It's a lengthy, labour-intensive process involving many stages—hence the high price of the finished product. First, the microscopic larvae are introduced into sheltered coastal waters and allowed to settle on piles of tiles, where the baby oysters, or spats, begin to develop. They are then moved to shallow concrete fattening beds called *parcs*. When the oysters reach maturity after several years they are sorted, cleaned and packed into seaweed-lined baskets (known as *barrels)* ready for sale. You can sample the shellfish either from the market stalls by the lighthouse (▷ 180) or at the restaurants that line the waterfront in the old fishing port of La Houle. The saucer-shaped *huîtres plats* are native to the bay; *huîtres creuses* (hollow oysters) have crinkled shells and are imported at a juvenile stage from other parts of Brittany. To find out more about oysters, visit La Ferme Marine (▷ 180), an oyster farm on the southern outskirts of the resort. After a film show, you can visit the oyster beds, and you can also taste and buy them. A small museum contains an impressive collection of seashells from all over the world.

IN AND AROUND CANCALE

In the upper town, the Musée des Arts et Traditions Populaires, in the 18th-century deconsecrated church of St-Méen, recounts the history of oyster-farming in Cancale (tel 02 99 89 71 26; Jul, Aug daily 10–12, 2.30–6.30; Jun, Sep Thu–Sun 2.30–6.30). For a small fee (keys available at the tourist office) you can climb the church tower (189 steps) for panoramic views over Mont-St-Michel bay. A fountain in the main square by the church shows local women in traditional Breton dress rinsing baskets of oysters.

Cancale is the easternmost limit of the Emerald Coast, and the first hints of this scenic drama unfold along the cliffs to the north (▷ 146–147). A fine walk starts from the rue des Parcs by the lighthouse, following the coastal footpath (GR34) about 5km (3 miles) to the Pointe de Grouin.

INFORMATION

www.ville-cancale.fr
www.cancale-tourisme.fr

226 M8 44 rue du Port, 35260 Cancale 02 99 89 63 72 Jul, Aug Mon–Sat 9–7, Sun, public holidays 9.30–1; Sep–end Jun Mon–Sat 9–12.30, 2–6. Seasonal information point at the Halle-à-Marée, port de la Houle 02 99 89 74 80 Summer holidays only TIV and Les Courriers Bretons services from St-Malo and Dol-de-Bretagne Sea-trips in *La Cancalaise*, a splendid replica of one of the elegantly rigged oyster-boats *(bisquines)* that once trawled for wild oysters in the bay (▷ 180)

TIP

» It isn't true that you can eat oysters only when there's an 'r' in the month, but seafood poisoning is generally more prevalent in the summer, when temperatures are higher. Always eat oysters on the day you buy them, and check that the shells are tightly closed, or close when tapped.

Opposite *Fresh oysters for sale at Cancale*
Below *Cancale viewed from the port of La Houle*

BÉCHEREL

www.becherel.com

Books breathe new life into this historic *petite cité de caractère* in the upper Rance valley northwest of Rennes. Once an important linen-weaving town with a reputation for producing the finest thread in Brittany, Becherel is now renowned throughout Brittany (and indeed Europe) for its wealth of antiquarian and second-hand bookstores. It ranks as Europe's third 'Book Town', attracting bibliophiles from all over the region, especially during its monthly book fairs, held on the first Sunday of the month, and its Easter book festival. Stock includes material written in the Breton language.

Bécherel has a fine assembly of well-preserved 17th- and 18th-century houses of weathered granite, which once belonged to its wealthy aristocratic and merchant élite. Some of the older streets (for example, rue de la Filanderie) evoke its textile heyday, and many of its present-day bookshops occupy dignified historic premises. The town has several pleasant literary cafés, and an exceptionally well-stocked and obliging tourist office full of regional information. Bécherel's medieval castle, dating from 1124, also deserves a visit. It played a significant role during the 14th-century War of Succession.

Just 1km (half a mile) west of Bécherel, the elegant 18th-century Château de Caradeuc features classical sculpture reminiscent of the style of Versailles (tel 02 99 66 81 10; Jul, Aug daily 12–6; Easter–end Jun, Sep, Oct Sat, Sun and holidays 2–6).

226 L10 9 place Alexandre Jehanin, 35190 Bécherel 02 99 66 75 23 Daily 10–12.30, 2–5.30

COMBOURG

www.combourg.org

The château at lakeside Combourg is where the French Romantic writer François-René de Chateaubriand (1768–1848) spent a brief but gloomy period of his youth. Neglected by his depressive, dysfunctional parents, he was left to roam the melancholy confines of his unusual family home with only his young sister for company. Chateaubriand's imagination developed against a Gothic backdrop of owls hooting in the night woods as the wind rattled the window-panes and howled through the castle corridors. A ghostly black cat apparently haunted his lonely bedroom.

Founded in the 11th century by the archbishop of Dol, the castle underwent many changes throughout the Middle Ages before coming into the hands of the Comte de Chateaubriand, father of the writer. The author's experiences here are recalled in his book *Memoires d'Outre-Tombe* (Memoirs from Beyond the Grave). In one room you can see some of his papers and furniture. The interior was completely reconfigured in 1875 in a then-fashionable style quite different from the one Chateaubriand had known.

The castle is still owned and lived in by descendants of the author's family, and open for guided tours in summer. Set on a wooded ridge, the castle's massive pepperpot towers rear through the trees, dwarfing the stone and timbered cottages of the surrounding town and giving fine views from the crenellated parapet walk. The landscaped park is a good example of the naturalistic 'English' style of garden design, with broad avenues of fine specimen trees.

The well-named Lac Tranquille mirrors the attractive little town in its glassy depths, providing residents and visitors with opportunities for angling and waterfront walks. Best views of the castle are from the far side of the lake.

227 M9 Maison de la Lanterne, 23 place Albert Parent, 35270 Combourg 02 99 73 13 93 Apr–end Sep Mon–Sat 10–1, 2.30–6.30, Sun 10–12.30; rest of year Mon–Sat 10–1, 2–6 TIV from Dinan, St-Malo Combourg; regular services from Rennes and St-Malo via Dol-de-Bretagne

Château 23 rue des Princes, 35270 Combourg 02 99 73 22 95; www.combourg.com Jul, Aug daily park 9–12, 2–6, castle 2–5.30; Apr–end Jun, Sep, Oct Sun–Fri Adult €6, child (11–18) €5, under 11 free Guided tours (45 min)

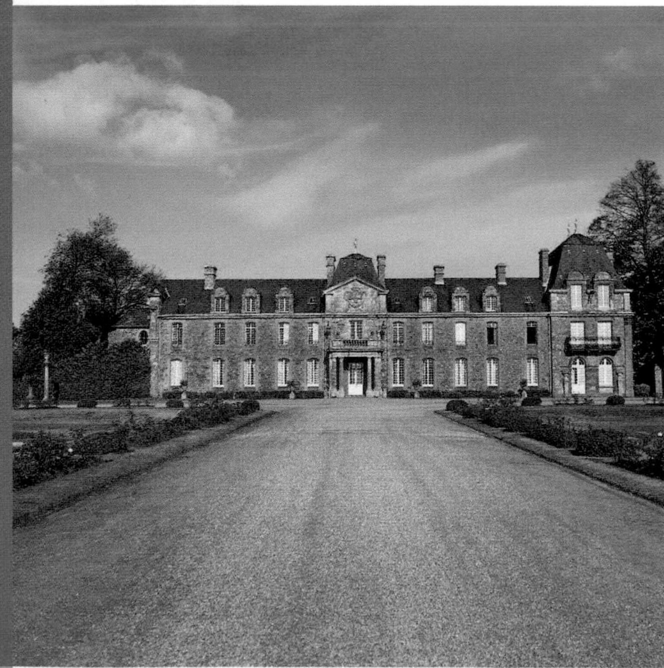

Left *18th-century Chateau de Caradeuc*

DINARD

This exclusive resort rivals the Riviera in the seaside glamour stakes. If the sea temperatures are a little cooler, the setting, cafés and beaches are no less alluring.

Dinard occupies a rocky outcrop at the mouth of the Rance estuary, just west of St-Malo (▷ 174–175). Until the mid-19th century, Dinard was just a typical Breton fishing port, but it was then discovered by the American and British moneyed classes, who colonized palatial seaside villas overlooking the glorious bay scenery. During the belle-époque years of the early 20th century, Dinard became the resort of choice for yachting, gambling and other well-heeled leisure activities. Dinard remains a chic and expensive resort, and still has strong Anglo-Saxon connections, including an air link to London.

SEAFRONT STROLLS

Dinard has several very beautiful sandy beaches. The Plage de l'Écluse (or Grande Plage) is the largest and most fashionable, while Prieuré and St-Enogat are quieter and have more of a family atmosphere. A public footpath, the Chemin de Ronde, leads along the coast past a profusion of exotic vegetation. The central section, from Plage du Prieuré in the south to the Pointe du Moulinet, is the Promenade du Clair de Lune (Moonlight Promenade)—a wonderful place for an afternoon or evening stroll, with a magical view across the estuary. Dinard's casino, bars and café terraces keep things humming until the small hours. On summer evenings the Promenade du Clair de Lune is floodlit, with concerts and son-et-lumière shows in the gardens.

HIGH ROLLERS

Mid-stage behind the main beach stands the Casino Barrière de Dinard, in boulevard Wilson (tel 02 99 16 30 30; gambling daily 9pm–4am; dining daily 12–2.30, 7.30–10.30, 11 at weekends). Nearby is an Olympic-sized, covered, heated seawater swimming pool (tel 02 99 46 22 77; daily 10–12.30, 3–7.30). Huge tides and constant sea breezes provide magnificent conditions for sailing all season. France's first tennis club was opened at Dinard in 1879, and its spectacular coastal golf links near St-Briac is one of the country's oldest and most revered courses.

A festival of British cinema attracts many celebrity visitors every October. A statue of Alfred Hitchcock balances on a giant egg near the Plage de l'Écluse, with fierce-looking birds on his shoulders.

INFORMATION

www.ville-dinard.fr
www.ot-dinard.com
226 L8 2 boulevard Féart, 35802 Dinard 02 99 46 94 12 Jul, Aug Mon–Sat 9.30–1, 2–7, Sun, holidays 10–12.15, 2.15–6.30; Apr–end Jun, Sep Mon–Sat 9.30–12.30, 2–6; Sun, holidays 10–12.15, 2.15–6; rest of year Mon–Sat 9–12.30, 2–6 Regular services to St-Malo, La Richardais, St-Lunaire, St-Briac-sur-Mer and Lancieux; to Cancale, Dol and Mont St Michel; and to Dinan and Rennes Compagnie Corsaire runs the all-year Bus-de-Mer link with St-Malo; summer cruises to Cancale bay, Cap Fréhel, and up the Rance to Dinan Dinard-Pleurtuit airport (02 99 46 18 46) is 6km (4 miles) south of the town (direct Ryanair flights from London Stansted; helicopter joyrides round the Emerald Coast)

Above *Chateau de Comborg dominates the little town of Comborg*

DOL-DE-BRETAGNE

Dol's imposing cathedral dominates the marshy hinterland of the Baie de Mont-St-Michel. Centuries ago, the sea covered the low-lying Marais de Dol, leaving the Capital of the Marshes stranded on its rocky dais above the waves. Gradually the sea retreated into the bay, and the saltmarshes or *polders* (a Dutch term) turned into fertile pasture protected by dykes. Sheep raised on this reclaimed land are much prized for their delicately flavoured meat, and are often described on local menus as *'gigot d'agneau pré-salé'* (salt-meadow lamb). The old town of Dol has some fine historic buildings along the Grande-Rue des Stuarts.

DOL CATHEDRAL

A religious community was first established in Dol by St. Samson, one of the seven founding saints, in AD548. The massive cathedral (daily 9–12, 2–6) was begun in the 12th century and constructed piecemeal over several hundred years, though it suffered repeated attacks and had to be rebuilt each time. Funds eventually ran out with the result that one of its towers was never completed. The great doorway in the south wall is one of its finest features; inside, its colossal dimensions and Gothic vaulting are impressive—the nave is almost 100m (300ft) long and 20m (65ft) high at the domed crossing. The medallion panes in the chancel window are said to be the oldest stained glass in Brittany (13th century).

The rambling premises of the adjacent bishop's palace house an ambitious exhibition called Médiévalys (tel 02 99 48 35 30; Easter–end Oct daily 10–7), devoted to documenting the history of Brittany's various medieval cathedrals and fortresses.

ANCIENT STONES

Le Mont-Dol, 2km (1 mile) to the north, is a curious outcrop of granite erupting 65m (213ft) from the surrounding *polders*. Despite its modest height, the grandstand views are remarkable. It shows signs of very early settlement and has religious associations: A supposed footprint in the rocks is alleged to belong to the Archangel Michael, left behind as he sprang across the bay to the rock of Mont-St-Michel after subduing the Devil.

About 2km (1 mile) south of Dol just off the D795 is the tallest of Brittany's standing stones, the Menhir du Champ-Dolent. It stands 9.5m (31ft) high, and is freely accessible in a small picnic site.

INFORMATION

www.pays-de-dol.com

227 M8 5 place de la Cathédrale, 35120 Dol-de-Bretagne 02 99 48 15 37 Jul, Aug Mon–Fri 9.30–7, Sat, Sun, public holidays 9.30–1, 2–7; Jun, Sep Mon–Sat 10–12.30, 2–6, Sun 2.30–6; rest of year Mon 2–6, Tue–Fri 10–12.30, 2–6, Sat 10–12.30 (also afternoons in school holidays) Routes to St-Malo, Rennes, Cancale Dol-de-Bretagne

TIPS

» The promenades des Douves, accessed from place Chateaubriand, leads along the old ramparts, giving a fine overview of the town and surrounding countryside.

» The parking area by the harbour is prone to flooding at certain high tides, so check before you leave your vehicle here for any length of time.

Above *The distinctive outline of Mont-St-Michel, viewed across misty fields from Mont-Dol*

FOUGÈRES

The picturesque fortifications guarding this border hilltown made a formidable bastion against attack from the east. A goose-necked bend in the River Nançon provided a temptingly defensible site to the great castle-builders of medieval times. When Brittany was an independent duchy, its eastern marches were always vulnerable to attack from the rapacious kings of France. Fougères' magnificent fortress (tel 02 99 99 79 59; mid-Jun to mid-Sep daily 9–7; Apr to mid-Jun, mid–end Sep 9.30–12, 2–6; Feb, Mar, Oct–end Dec daily 10–12, 2–5) is a series of concentric enclosures protected by massive curtain walls. Some of the inner structures and the high keep have vanished over the centuries, but the ramparts are virtually complete. The castle towers, bright with geraniums in summer, make a postcard scene reflected in the river, which acts as a natural moat.

The design of the fortress followed tried-and-tested medieval norms, but its location below rather than above the town it was intended to protect is unusual. The castle was captured several times during the Hundred Years War, and played a backdrop role in the Catholic anti-Republican revolt described in Balzac's novel *Les Chouans* (1821). A drawbridge over the River Nançon leads to the ramparts from the picturesque old Marchix quarter, once a place populated by the mills and tanneries for Fougères' thriving leather and shoe-making trades.

THE HAUTE VILLE

A steep climb leads to the mostly pedestrianized upper town, perched on the rocky spurs above the winding river. Exceptional views of the lower town and castle can be seen from the public gardens near the church of St-Léonard. Many of the houses in the Haute Ville date from the 18th century, but one quaint 16th-century building on the main street contains a museum dedicated to the local Impressionist artist Emmanuel de la Villéon (1858–1944; tel 02 99 99 19 98; mid-Jun to mid-Sep daily 10.30–12.30; 2–6, mid-Sep to mid-Jun Wed–Sun 10–12, 2–5). The octagonal granite belltower in a little square off rue Nationale is Brittany's oldest, dating from 1397.

A fascinating little clock museum can be visited above the shop of one of Brittany's master watchmakers at 37 rue Nationale (tel 02 99 99 40 98; mid-Jun to mid-Sep Tue–Sat 9–12, 2–7, Sun, Mon 2–6.30).

INFORMATION

www.ot-fougeres.fr

227 P9 2 rue Nationale (Haute Ville), 35300 Fougères 02 99 94 12 20 Jul, Aug Mon–Sat 9–7, Sun 10–12, 2–4; Easter–end Oct Mon–Sat 9.30–12.30, 2–6; Sun, public holidays 1.30–5.30; rest of year Tue–Sat 10.30–12.30, 2–6 Connections to Rennes; Courriers Bretons to St-Malo and Vitré (nearest station)

TIPS

» A *petit train* called the Oriental Express (May–end Sep daily 10–7) takes you up the hill from the château, with a commentated tour.

» Ask the tourist office about inclusive 'passport' tickets for the château, clock museum and a *petit train* ride.

» Fougères holds one of the largest and liveliest cattle markets in France (Thursday pm, route d'Alençon, on the Aumayllerie ring road towards Vitré).

Below *The clustered towers crowning the walls of the feudal castle at Fougères*

FORÊT DE PAIMPONT

www.broceliande-tourisme.info
www.oust-broceliande-vacances.com
www.paimpont.fr

The medieval troubadour poet Chrétien de Troyes had much to do with the transformation of this ancient forest into the mystical Brocéliande, the Breton equivalent of Camelot, land of King Arthur, Merlin and the Knights of the Round Table. Wreathed in legends, the Forest of Paimpont, or Brocéliande, is a diffuse area now extending some 7,000ha (17,500 acres) across the borders of Morbihan and Ille-et-Vilaine southwest of Rennes. It is believed to be one of the last remaining bits of the primeval forest that once covered much of Brittany's *argoat*, or interior. The countryside consists mainly of sandy heathland and scattered lakes as well as trees.

Local tourist offices arrange escorted visits to Arthurian sites, such as the sacred Fontaine de Barenton, where Merlin was enthralled by the sorceress Viviane (the Lady in the Lake). They can also provide walking maps and guides (ask for detailed directions to places of interest, which can be tricky to find). Access may be restricted in the hunting season (Nov–end Mar).

The lakeside village of Paimpont is the main touring base at the heart of the forest, an unusual settlement of purplish granite with a single main street beside a 13th-century abbey. The church has interesting wood-carving and a venerable rose window. The sacristy contains the reliquary of St. Judicaël in the form of a silver arm. At Tréhorenteuc the stained-glass windows in the church intertwine Arthurian legends with Christianity, while the mostly 19th-century Château de Comper contains the Centre de l'Imaginaire Arthurien, an exhibition of Celtic legends (tel 02 97 22 79 96; Jul, Aug Thu–Tue 10–7, Mar–end Jun, Sep, Oct Thu–Mon 10–5.30).

232 K11 By the abbey, 35380 Paimpont 02 99 07 84 23 Daily 10–12, 2–6; reduced hours in winter. Pedalos can be rented on the lake Bicycle rental from Bar Le Brécilien beside Paimpont's tourist office; rue Général de Gaulle 02 99 07 81 13 (rates from about €9 for half a day to €23 for a weekend); also from Au Pays de Merlin 02 99 07 80 23

HÉDÉ

The most noteworthy feature of this mill village on the Ille-et-Rance Canal is a staircase flight of eleven locks *(onze écluses)* in the hamlet of La Madeleine just north of Hédé. The total drop is nearly 27m (90ft). A small exhibition and film show at the Maison du Canal visitor centre (in the old lock-keeper's cottage) tell the story of this costly 19th-century project, undertaken to connect the Atlantic and Channel coasts of Brittany by canalized waterways (adult €2.50, child 8–12 €1.70). Nearby Hédé is a pretty place full of streams and ponds, with old houses of grey stone in beautifully kept gardens, and castle ruins crowning an outcrop of rock.

Tinténiac, to the northwest, is another attractive canal village with a turreted church. Its waterfront museum of rural trades, Le Musée de l'Outil et des Métiers (tel 02 99 23 09 30; Jul–end Sep Mon–Sat 10–12, 2.30–6, Sun 2.30–6), contains a collection of about 2,000 tools and equipment used by the cobblers and coopers of yesteryear.

226 M10 Maison du Canal d'Ille et Rance, by locks at La Madeleine, 35630 Bazouges-sous-Hédé 02 99 45 48 90 Jul, Aug daily 10.30–12.30, 1.30–6; May, Jun, Sep, Oct Wed–Mon 2–6; rest of year Wed, Sun 2–5

RANCE ESTUARY

Huge tides surge twice daily up the Rance, changing the river scenery almost beyond recognition. The Rance valley carvies a deep tidal trench inland as far south as Dinan, where it links with canalized waterways spanning Brittany. The best way to see the estuary is to take a boat trip upstream to Dinan, where you can visit the Maison de la Rance to find out about the river's ecosystem (▷ 132–135). The bridge near the mouth of the river between Dinard and St-Malo carries a four-lane highway. Alongside it stands the extraordinary tidal barrage known as the Usine Marémotrice de la Rance, built during the 1960s and now supplying around 3 per cent of Brittany's energy needs. This ambitious contribution to renewable energy is not without environmental costs: The expense of silt-dredging and the impact on bird and fish habitats are considerable. The visitor centre at the Dinard end of the barrage road gives background on the dam and its effects on the river (tel 02 99 16 37 14; Jul, Aug daily 10–6, mid-Feb to end Jun, Sep–end Oct Wed–Sun 10–6; free).

226 L8 See Dinard, Dinan, St-Malo St-Malo or Dinan River cruises from the *gare maritime* on the Dinard side of the barrage with Croisières Chateaubriand tel 02 99 46 44 40; also from St-Malo and Dinan

Opposite *Sailing boats line the Rance estuary*

Below *Rocks and the water source of Merlin's Fountain in Paimpont Forest*

LE MONT-ST-MICHEL

INFORMATION

www.ot-montsaintmichel.com
www.mont-saint-michel.monuments-nationeaux.fr
www.projetmontsaintmichel.fr
www.baie-mont-saint-michel.fr
227 N8 50170 Le Mont-St-Michel
02 33 60 14 30 Jul–end Aug daily 9–7; Apr–end Jun, Sep Mon–Sat 9–12.30, 2–6.30, Sun 9–12, 2–6; Oct–end Mar 9–12, 2–6, Sun 10–12, 2–5
Scheduled and excursion services from Rennes, St-Malo and Pontorson
Nearest station is Pontorson, 9km (6 miles) south (bus service to the Mount)

Above *The sunlight-bathed buildings of Mont-St-Michel*

INTRODUCTION

This fortified religious community, separated from the mainland by quicksands and tides, is a surreal sight, especially through early morning sea mists. The wavering course of the River Couesnon puts Mont-St-Michel just outside Brittany's borders in Normandy. In peak season, this UNESCO World Heritage Site is one of the most crowded visitor attractions anywhere in France, but if you are anywhere nearby, it is simply not to be missed. Don't venture onto the mudflats unless you are part of a guided walk, as tides can sweep in quickly. If you're visiting during the peak summer months, arrive at around 8am or after 5pm to miss the crowds. Never mind your aching calf muscles—continue climbing the steps of the abbey once you have reached the summit of the Mount itself. Views of the protected Baie du Mont-St-Michel from the very top of the abbey are stunning.

The Mount has drawn pilgrims since AD708, when St. Aubert, Bishop of Avranches, built a modest chapel on the 79m (260ft) granite Mont Tombe, after seeing a vision of the Archangel Michael. Benedictine monks settled here and a village soon formed around them. A Romanesque church was constructed on the site in the 11th century, and work continued on other buildings over the following years. The Mount was fortified against the English during the Hundred Years War (mid-14th to mid-15th centuries) and managed to resist attack. Work continued on the abbey from the 15th to the 17th centuries, and the site spent time as a prison after the Revolution.

The abbey opened to visitors as a national monument in 1874, and in 1897 Emmanuel Frémlet's gilded statue of St. Michael was placed on top of a new steeple, 157m (515ft) high. A monastic community returned to live and work on the site in 1969, and monks and nuns continue to provide a spiritual anchor within what might otherwise be merely a hub of tourism and history. Although 3.5 million visitors come to Mont St-Michel each year, the resident population is just 35.

An ambitious project to restore the Mount's tidal status by removing the connecting causeway will reverse a long process of silting. A footbridge will replace the causeway.

WHAT TO SEE

THE ABBEY

www.monum.fr

You can join a guided tour around the abbey and discover the huge treadmill in which prisoners once trudged to work a system of pulleys to haul building materials up the side of the Mount. The abbey is often referred to as *La Merveille* (the wonder), but this epithet actually applies to a Gothic extension commissioned by King Philippe Auguste of France in the 13th century to celebrate his conquest of Normandy. The name reflected the amazing feat of the architects and builders who created it in just 20 years. The *Merveille*, with its three floors of dining rooms for pilgrims, nobles and monks, is topped by a tranquil cloister garden, with a window looking out to sea. From the North Tower visitors watch the tides race ashore at speeds of up to 10kph (6mph).

02 33 89 80 00 May–end Aug daily 9–7 (last entry 6); Sep–end Apr daily 9.30–6 (last entry 5) Adult €8.50, under 18 free

THE MUSEUMS

Several small museums on the Mount can be visited on a combined ticket (tel 02 33 89 01 85; open daily Jul, Aug 9–6.30, Feb–end Jun, Sep to mid-Nov, Christmas holidays 9–5.30; adult €16, child 10–18 €9, under 10 free; visited separately, each costs €8 (adult), €4.50 (child). Most entertaining (and best for children) is the Archéoscope, featuring a son-et-lumière presentation of the Abbey's history guided by its archangelic patron St. Michael (www.au-mont-saint-michel.com). The Musée Maritime explains the tides and ecosystems of the bay, and the Musée Historique contains a gruesome collection of waxworks. Tiphaine's House was built by the Breton warrior Du Guesclin, a former governor of the Mount, for his scholarly wife.

MAISONS DE LA BAIE

www.maison-baie.com

Back on the mainland, you can enjoy wonderful views of the Mount from the Maison de la Baie vantage points at Le-Vivier-sur-Mer, Courtils and St-Léonard.

TIPS

» When the main street is packed with people, climb the steps to the less crowded ramparts to look down on the village and across the sea.

» Rather than pay the €8.50 admission charge to visit the abbey, you could time your visit to coincide with the midday mass, when tickets are free. You can take your time walking through the monument after the service.

» At La Mère Poulard, world-famous omelettes, beaten in age-old copper bowls, have fortified pilgrims and visitors alike for years.

Above *Purbeck marble arches in the cloisters of the abbey*
Below left *A tranquil view of the Baie du Mont-St-Michel*
Below *A typical busy street scene*

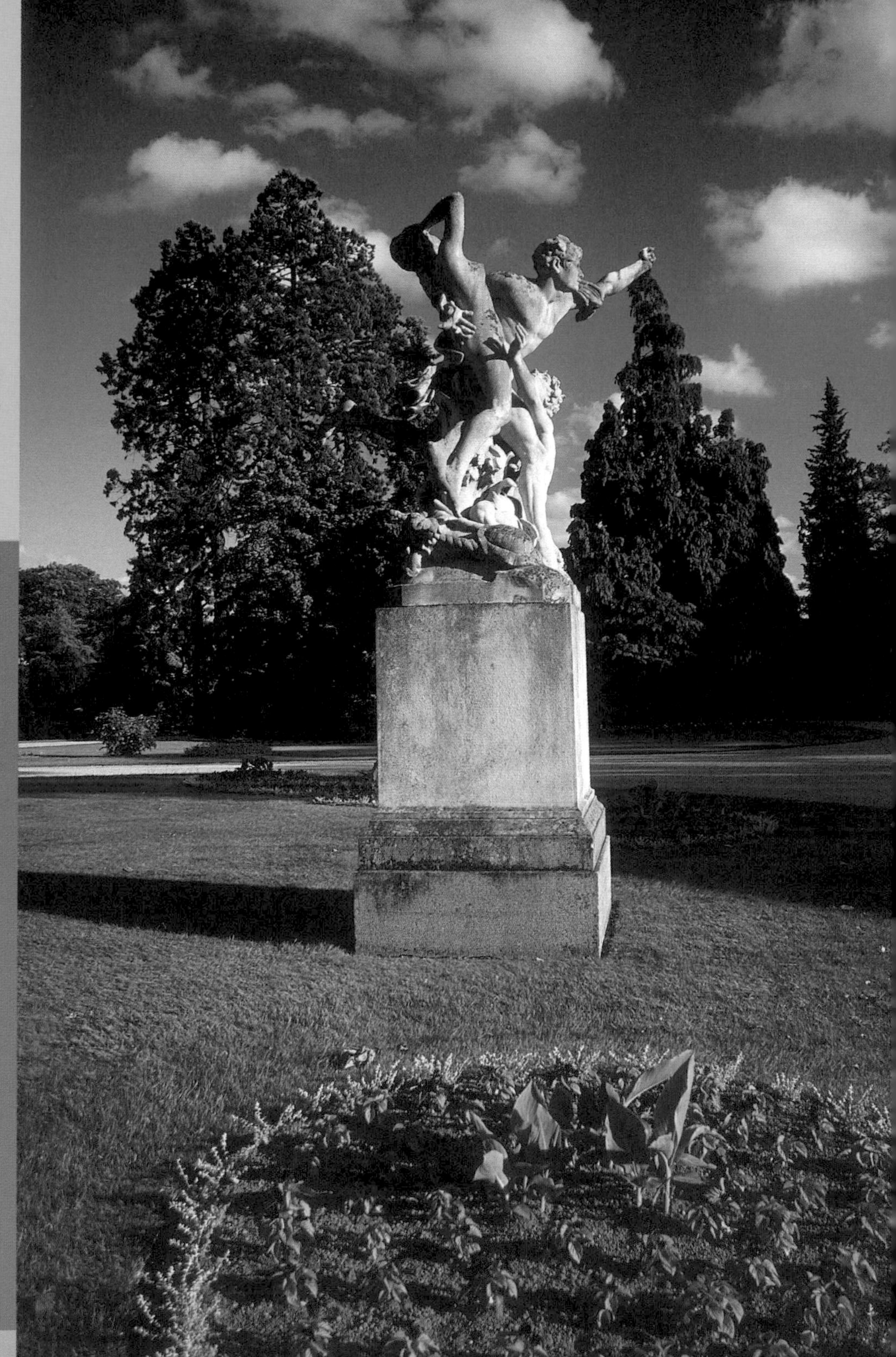

INTRODUCTION

Inside the city's modern, industrial shell is an old town of fascinating medieval streets, along with excellent museums and grand civic architecture. The rue du Champ-Jacquet has some of the city's oldest and most beautiful half-timbered buildings. The tourist office is a good place to start a visit, as you can pick up a map marked with a walking route covering the main sights (French only), and a leaflet on the city's history (English). After exploring the old town on the north bank of the Vilaine, wander through the Jardin du Thabor for a change of pace. These beautiful gardens were once the grounds of a Benedictine abbey.

Rennes hosts several major festivals. Biggest is *Les Tombées de la Nuit*, a cultural jamboree that takes over the city at the beginning of July. Organ concerts take place in the main churches in summer, and jazz concerts in October. The party spirit doesn't end with the tourist season: *Yaouank* is a *fest-noz* (night festival) held on the third Saturday in November, while the huge rock festival of *Les Transmusicales* takes place in early December.

Rennes shared parliamentary power with Nantes and Vannes during the Middle Ages, becoming the undisputed Breton capital during the time of Anne de Bretagne (1477–1514). From then on it played a key role in Brittany's political struggles, including rebellions against the taxation imposed during Louis XIV's reign, the Revolutionary Terror and the German occupation in World War II. The city was almost entirely demolished by fire in 1720; it was subsequently rebuilt in Classical style. The population has doubled since World War II to nearly 250,000, this figure boosted by students at the two universities and the prestigious medical school, who keep cultural activities and nightlife humming. Commerce and industry flourish, and the headquarters of the car manufacturer Citroën lie just outside. The city feels more French than other Breton towns.

INFORMATION

www.tourisme-rennes.com

233 M11 · 11 rue St-Yves, 35064 Rennes · 02 99 67 11 11 · Jul, Aug Mon 1–6, Tue–Sat 9–7, Sun 11–6; rest of year Tue–Sat 10–6, Sun and public holidays 11–1, 2–6 · Lots of bars surround place Sainte-Anne; most close Sat lunch · Efficient local network operated by STAR (who also operate the Métro; tickets valid on both) · Rennes; direct links to St-Malo, Dinan, Vitré, Vannes, Quimper, Brest, Nantes and many other towns · UrbaVag electric boats cruise the waterways around Rennes Apr–end Oct · Aéroport de Rennes, St-Jacques-de-la-Lande; tel 02 99 29 60 00 (Air France internal connections, and a direct Flybe service from Southampton)

WHAT TO SEE

MUSÉE DES BEAUX-ARTS

www.mbar.org

This art gallery has paintings ranging from 14th-century Primitives to Impressionists and members of the Pont-Aven school. Artists represented include Leonardo da Vinci, Rubens, Paul Gauguin and Pablo Picasso. Look for a

Opposite *Classical statuary in the Tabor Gardens, Rennes*

Below *There are many half-timbered houses in the heart of the city*

powerful canvas by the 19th-century artist Luminais, depicting the legend of Ys (▷ 7). Archaeological collections include Egyptian and classical items.

172 C2 · 20 quai Émile Zola · 02 23 62 17 45 · Tue–Sun 10–12, 2–6 · Adult €4.20, under 18 free · République

CATHÉDRALE ST-PIERRE

Rennes' cavernous cathedral dates from the 19th century, but it has a wonderful 16th-century Flemish retable in the fifth chapel on the right. Its 10 panels, depict scenes including the birth of Mary and the marriage of Mary and Joseph. The delightful rue de la Psalette, curving behind the cathedral, is a medley of beautiful half-timbered 15th-century houses. *Psalette* was the local word for the cathedral choir; the street once resounded with their singing.

172 B2 · Rue de la Monnaie · Daily 9.30–12, 3–6, except during services

PLACE DES LICES

This fine square of stone and timbered mansions once hosted jousts, although since the 17th century it has served as a market place. An animated market

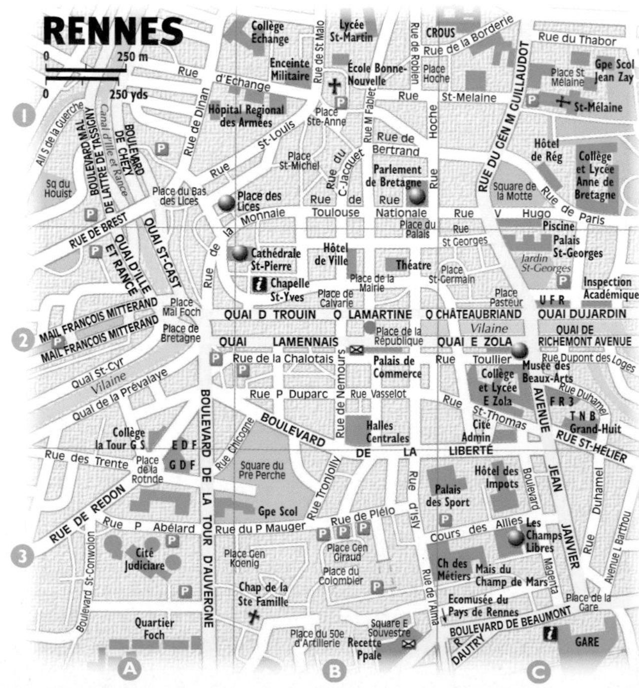

Above *A brightly coloured town house in place Ste-Anne*

Above right *The Palais St-Georges, a former Benedictine abbey*

is held here every Saturday morning. Bars and restaurants keep it lively in the evenings. Near here is Porte Mordelaise gateway with a restored drawbridge, intended as a ceremonial entrance to the city. It dates from 1440.
172 A2

LES CHAMPS LIBRES

This recently opened cultural centre houses the Musée de Bretagne (tel 02 23 40 66 70; www.musee-bretagne.fr) with displays on Breton culture and history. It also contains the city library and the futuristic Espace des Sciences, an interactive science museum and planetarium.
172 C3 Tue 12–9, Wed–Fri 12–7, Sat, Sun 2–7 Adult €7, child (8–26) €5, under 8 free; supplement for planetarium: adult €3, child €2 Gare/Charles de Gaulle

MORE TO SEE

CHAPELLE ST-YVES

The converted Chapelle St-Yves houses the tourist office, where you'll find a permanent exhibition on the history of Rennes. The building is worth seeing for its impressive beams and the restored carvings in the chapel (172 C3).

ÉCOMUSÉE DU PAYS DE RENNES

www.ecomusee-rennes-metropole.fr
On the southern outskirts of Rennes, this folk museum is set in an old cider farm. Farming equipment, reconstructed interiors, and rare livestock breeds re-create a picture of rural life from the 16th century onwards.
Off map 172 C3 Ferme de la Bintinais, route de Châtillon-sur-Seiche, 35200 Rennes 02 99 51 38 15 Tue–Fri 9–12, 2–6, Sat 2–6, Sun 2–7 Adult €4.60, child (6–14) €2.30 Triangle, then bus 61 to Hil-Bintinais Picnic site

PALAIS DU PARLEMENT DE BRETAGNE

The former seat of the Breton parliament (now housing the Court of Appeal) survived the fire of 1720 and has superb coffered ceilings.
172 B1 Place de la Mairie Guided tours can be arranged daily all year round (reservations strictly through the tourist office); adult €6.80, child (7–15) €4

TIPS

» Place Railier du Baty, a pleasant square near the cathedral, is a good place to sit and enjoy a coffee.
» Beware of traffic, even in streets or squares that appear to be pedestrian-only.
» In the spacious place de la Mairie stands the magnificent Hôtel de Ville (town hall), designed by Jacques Gabriel in the 18th century (free guided visits mid-Jul to mid-Aug Mon–Fri at 11, 2 and 5).

Above *Rennes airport terminal*
Below *Place des Lices, Rennes*

ST-MALO

INFORMATION

www.saint-malo-tourisme.com
www.saint-malo.fr
226 L8 Esplanade St-Vincent, 35400 0825 135 200 Jul, Aug Mon–Sat 9–7.30, Sun, holidays 10–6; Apr–end Jun, Sep Mon–Sat 9–12.30, 1.30–6.30, Sun, holidays 10–12.30, 2.30–6; Oct–end Mar Mon–Sat 9–12.30, 1.30–6 Urban services run by St-Malo Bus; other routes with links all over the Emerald Coast to Mont-St-Michel, Cancale (via Paramé/St-Servan), Dol-de-Bretagne, Dinan, Fougères, Rennes St-Malo Emerald Coast cruises and river trips up the Rance to Dinan with Compagnie Corsaire, Etoile Marine Croisières; Bus de Mer to Dinard; ferry connections to UK and Channel Islands with Brittany Ferries and Condor Ferries

INTRODUCTION

If possible, come to St-Malo by sea. First impressions can be disappointing for motorists, because the port has a bewildering road system and becomes very congested in high season, while the railway station is a drab and inconvenient distance from the historic quarter. But an approach from the waterfront is truly majestic, revealing the stately citadel apparently afloat on its rocky plinth, attached by slender moorings to the rest of the town. Most of the main sights and beaches lie within walking distance of the port's multiple ferry terminals and yacht marinas. The helpful tourist office just outside the city walls can quickly orientate you with an excellent range of maps and guides.

St-Malo has a long and fascinating history, dating from the sixth century, when a Welsh monk (St. Maclow) gave his name to a religious settlement on the rugged headland of Aleth (now the suburb of St-Servan). In later centuries, the inhabitants moved to the more easily defensible site of St-Malo-en-l'Isle and walled themselves in to escape Viking raiders. From then on, the isolated Malouins developed a strongly individualistic streak, and even declared their city an independent republic at one stage. Fortified by Vauban in the 17th century, St-Malo prospered as a fishing and trading port, while also growing rich on the proceeds of piracy and the slave trade. Its entrepreneurial mariners (explorers, merchants, fishermen, corsairs) built beautiful mansions *(malouinières)* all over the town. Some Malouins achieved lasting fame, notably Jacques Cartier, discoverer of Canada.

WHAT TO SEE

CITADEL

St-Malo's main attraction is its walled city, known as Intra Muros ('within the walls'), faithfully restored from Vauban's original design after large-scale devastation in 1944. The arched gateways at intervals frame inviting glimpses of cobbled shopping streets and elegant outdoor cafés. The towering ramparts (which mostly survived the bombardments) provide wonderful views of the old town and a fascinating seascape.

Offshore to the north lie the remains of the Fort National, another Vauban fortification, long used as a prison (tel 02 99 85 34 33; www.fortnational.com; Jun–end Sep, depending on the tides). Sights within the walls include the Cathédrale St-Vincent on place J. de Châtillon (daily 9.45–12, 2–6), with its modern stained glass and diamond-shaped mosaic commemorating Jacques Cartier's exploration of Canada in 1535.The 18th-century Hôtel Magon, (tel 02 99 56 09040; www.demeure-de-corsaire.com in the southeastern corner of the walled citadel is a fine example of a wealthy privateer's home (guided tours daily Jul, Aug 10–12.30, 2.30–6.30 rest of year Tue–Sun afternoons only).

MUSÉE D'HISTOIRE DE LA VILLE

The town's history museum within St-Malo's old castle recalls the port's seafaring past. Look for the carved figurehead destined for the prow of a corsair vessel, depicting a 17th-century sailor. One room describes the life of St-Malo fishermen in Newfoundland. Another floor deals with great men of St-Malo, including naval commander and privateer Robert Surcouf (1773–1827).

✉ Château de St-Malo, place Chateaubriand, Intra Muros ☎ 02 99 40 71 57 ⌚ Apr–end Sep daily 10–12.30, 2–6; Oct–end Mar Tue–Sun 10–12, 2–6 ✋ Adult €5.10, child (8–16) €2.55, under 8 free

ÎLE DU GRAND BÉ

At low tide you can cross the causeway to the rocky island of Grand Bé to see the tomb of the writer Chateaubriand (1768–1848) and splendid views of the walled city and the surrounding coastline. Children will enjoy this walk as there are rocks to clamber on and pools to explore. Don't get stranded by the tide, but if you do, there's a six-hour wait before you can walk back!

MORE TO SEE

ST-SERVAN

In this oldest part of the town, the imposing Tour Solidor houses the Musée International du Long Cours Cap-Hornier (tel 02 99 40 71 58; Apr–end Sep daily 10–12.30, 2–6; closed Mon in winter), an exhibition about the mariners who braved the perilous sea route around Cape Horn.

GRAND AQUARIUM

www.aquarium-st-malo.com

This huge modern aquarium is excellent for children and makes a good wet-weather destination.

✉ Avenue de Général Patton BP27, 35402 ☎ 02 99 21 19 00 ⌚ Daily, hours variable in high season, 10–6 in winter; closed part of Nov and Jan ✋ Adult €15.50 , child (4–14) €10.50

ROTHÉNEUF

This pleasant coastal village beyond the long beaches of Paramé was the home of Jacques Cartier, who pioneered France's colonization of eastern Canada. His family *malouinière*, the Manoir de Limoëlou, contains the Musée Jacques Cartier (tel 02 99 40 97 73; www.musee-jacques-cartier.com; Jul, Aug 10–11.30, 2.30–6; Jun, Sep Mon–Sat; Oct–end May tours Mon–Sat).

TIPS

» A rampart walk gives a splendid 360-degree panorama of the old coastline. The complete circuit is about 2km (1 mile) long. There is free access at several points, including all the main gates to the citadel (unsuitable for wheelchair users).

» Hotels and cafés within the walled city tend to be more expensive than those on the outside.

Opposite *The buildings and old city area of St-Malo*

Below *Walking along the ramparts of the citadel of St-Malo-Intra-Muros*

REDON

www.tourisme-pays-redon.com
www.redon.fr

This *ville fleurie* is a popular boating hub; you can rent canoes or barges, or take an organized boat trip along the River Vilaine or the Nantes–Brest Canal. Redon was first settled in AD832, and developed as a river port for Rennes. Don't be put off by the charmless station area; the old town (around the Grande Rue) and the quaysides of the port have fine old buildings and more character. The Musée de la Batellerie (Waterways Museum), at quai Jean-Bart, documents daily life on the canals at the height of their importance (tel 02 99 72 30 95; mid-Jun to mid-Sep daily 10–12, 3–6; mid-Sep to mid-Dec, mid-Mar to mid-Jun Sat–Mon, Wed 2–6). The Benedictine abbey of St-Sauveur in Romanesque and Gothic styles, has a separate belltower. In high season, *Les Vendredis du Port* (Port Fridays) feature *moules-frites* and sea shanties, and in autumn (chestnut time), a series of concerts called *La Bogue d'Or*, incorporate traditional Haute-Breton music.

232 L13 Place de la République, 35600 Redon 02 99 71 06 04 Jul, Aug Mon–Sat 9.30–12.30, 1.30–6.30, Sun 10–12.30, 3–5; Sep–end Jun Mon–Fri 9.30–12, 2–6, Sat 10–12.30, 3–5 Redon; connections to Vannes, Rennes and Nantes Boat trips at the port Autumn chestnut festival, Foire aux Marrons

LA ROCHE AUX FÉES

This impressive megalithic dolmen, or *allée couverte,* lies in remote countryside near Essé, some 34km (21 miles) southeast of Rennes (signed off the D41 between Janzé and Retiers). It consists of about 40 great slabs of purple schist. Experts differ on the precise purpose of the 'Fairies' Rock', but it is thought to date from the third millennium BC. According to custom, betrothed couples would walk around the monument in different directions and count the stones. If the totals differed, the prospect of a successful union was unlikely.

233 N11 A small hut with external storyboards provides some interpretative information

ST-BRIAC-SUR-MER

www.saint-briac.com
www.tourisme-saint-briac.fr

This delightful fishing resort guards the mouth of the pine-clad Frémur estuary, the boundary between Ille-et-Vilaine and Côtes-d'Armor. It has glorious coastal views, painted by many artists, including Renoir, Signac and Emile Bernard. It is now a popular sailing venue and the harbour office is in a 19th-century château on the Presqu'île du Nessey. A knot of streets around the harbour adds character to its modern holiday homes. The windows in its church show scenes from the life of St. Briac, who arrived here from Ireland in the Dark Ages. Notice the carved mackerel on the north façade.

226 L8 49 Grande Rue, 35800 St-Briac-sur-Mer 02 99 88 32 47 Jul, Aug Sun, Mon 10.30–12.30, 2.30–6.30, Tue, Fri, Sat 10–12.30,2–6.30, Wed, Thu 10–12.30, 2–5.30; rest of year Tue, Wed, Fri, Sat 10–12, 2–5; school holidays Tue–Sat 10–12.30, 2–5.30

ST-LUNAIRE

www.saint-lunaire.com

This beach resort is virtually a suburb of Dinard. It has similarly grand marine architecture: Stately belle-époque villas command fine vantage points along the Emerald Coast. Its beaches are separated by a scenic headland called the Pointe du Décollé. Best resort beach is La Grande Plage. The attractively simple 11th-century church of St-Lunaire stands in a glade of trees. It contains the tomb of the founding saint, on a Gallo-Roman sarcophagus.

226 L8 Boulevard Général de Gaulle, 35800 St-Lunaire 02 99 46 31 09 Jul, Aug 9.30–7; Apr–end Sep Mon, Tue 10–12, 2.30–5.30, Wed, Fri, Sat 2.30–5.30; rest of year Mon 10–12, 2.30–5, Wed, Thu, Fri 2.30–5

LE VIVIER-SUR-MER

www.maison-baie.com

The shallow, sheltered seas of Mont-St-Michel bay retreat far beyond mud-flats at low tide, creating ideal homes for mussels, raised here in their millions, strung on ropes attached to tall *bouchots* (posts). *Mytiliculture* (mussel farming) is serious business at Le Vivier, accounting for some 25 per cent of France's total production. Huge processing sheds can be seen by the port. A visitor centre gives an introduction to this industry and organizes tours of the mussel beds on a tractor-drawn *petit train.* The flat sand along this coast is popular for sand-yachting, especially in the resort of Cherrueix.

227 M8 Maison de la Baie, Port-Est, 35960 Le Vivier/Cherrueix 02 99 48 84 38 Jul, Aug daily 9.30–12.30, 2–6.30; Sep–end Jun Mon–Sat 10–12.30, 2–5.30

VITRÉ

King Henri IV once paid the town a famous compliment, declaring 'Were I not King of France, I would be a citizen of Vitré.' Today the handsome, compact old town remains as attractive as it was in its medieval heyday, and is easy to explore on foot. Timber-framed, slate-hung houses lurch in all directions on its hilly, cobbled streets, guarded by a turreted castle. Best seen from a belvedere by the River Vilaine called the Tertres Noires, Vitré's magnificent fortifications appear as a silhouette of bristling turrets, drum towers and ramparts.

One of its most atmospheric residential quarters of the town is called the Faubourg du Rachapt (meaning 'repurchased'), referring to a ransom paid to English forces besieging the town during the Hundred Years War.

In earlier centuries Vitré grew wealthy on the textile trade (principally dealing in hemp, wool, sailcloth and leather). Some of the most interesting and best-preserved of the merchants' houses are in rue de la Baudrairie, the street of the leather-workers.

FAMOUS RESIDENT

The 17th-century author and shrewd political observer Madame de Sévigné (famed for her letters about life at the French court) lived at 9 rue Sévigné, and also at a palatial country retreat southeast of the town, the Château des Rochers-Sévigné (tel 02 99 96 76 51; same hours as Château de Vitré).

CASTLE AND CHURCH

The medieval castle on its rocky riverside bluff played a vital role in the borderland defences between Brittany and France, and was a constant target of attack (tel 02 99 75 04 46; all museums open May–end Sep, Wed–Mon 10–12.45, 2–6, Sun 2–5.30; rest of year Wed–Sat 10–12.15, 2–5.30, Sun 2–5.30). A twin-turreted gateway leads into its triangular inner ward, where small museum displays can be visited in the Tour de l'Argenterie and the Tour St-Laurent.

The church of Notre-Dame within the ramparts dates from the 15th and 16th centuries. An unusual feature is an exterior pulpit, from which virulent Catholic sermons were preached at the Protestant Huguenot families who lived in the houses opposite. Vitré became a Huguenot stronghold during the Wars of Religion, which caused much local tension.

INFORMATION

www.ot-vitre.fr

233 P11 Place Général de Gaulle, 35500 Vitré 02 99 75 04 46 Jul, Aug Mon–Sat 9.30–12.30, 2–6.30, Sun, public holidays 10–12.30, 3–6; Sep–end Jun Mon 2.30–6, Tue–Fri 9.30–12.30, 2.30–6, Sat 10–12.30, 3–5 SNCF bus links to Fougères, and regular services to Rennes Vitré; regular services to Rennes. Vitré is on the TGV Paris–Brest route, though few express trains actually stop here Night tours of the old town are organized by the tourist office

TIPS

» Vitré can easily be visited on a day-trip by public transport from Rennes. The railway station is conveniently near the heart of the town.

» A 'passport' ticket gives access to Vitré's two châteaux and several small museums, which have standard opening hours (adult €4, child €2.50).

Above *The towers of the castle piercing the summer sky at Vitré*

Opposite left *A sandy beach in St-Briac-sur-Mer*

Opposite right *The entrance to the megalithic monument, La Roche aux Fees*

ST-MALO AND DINAN

No visitor to Brittany should miss the two north-coast towns of St-Malo and Dinan. Although very different in character—St-Malo is a busy port and Dinan a splendidly preserved medieval town—both are beautiful. The river Rance flows past Dinan and out to sea at St-Malo, and is barred on the way by a great tidal dam.

THE DRIVE
Length: 90km (56 miles)
Allow: 2 days
Start/end at: St-Malo

★ St-Malo (▷ 174–175) is a ferry port, yachting base and commercial port, with a walled citadel well worth exploring. Walk the ramparts for views of the town, the sea and nearby islands.

Follow signs for Rennes through the suburb of St-Servan-sur-Mer and, keeping the estuary of the Rance on your right, carry on past Tour Solidor.

❶ Medieval Tour Solidor, in the St-Servan district of St-Malo, was built in the late 14th century to protect shipping in the Rance from English pirates and Malouin corsairs. It was once the town jail and is now a museum with model ships and information about the mariners of Cape Horn.

Follow signs for Dinard, crossing the top of a huge dam, the Barrage de la Rance, which generates electricity by harnessing the tidal current. Turn right onto the D266 into Dinard.

❷ Dinard is a fashionable seaside town, a resort of the smart set since the turn of the 20th century, when the Prince of Wales used to holiday here. There are good views over a forest of yacht masts to the walls of St-Malo. From here you can go on a boat trip up the Rance to Dinan.

Return to the D266, following signs for Dinan and Pleurtuit. After Pleurtuit turn left onto the D766 which will take you to the N176/E401. Head south on the N176 for 6km (4 miles) and exit for Dinan. Although the town is often crowded, it's usually possible to park in place du Guesclin near to all the sights.

❸ Dinan is a place to explore on foot. Walk down to the banks of the Rance by rue du Jerzual, a steep street lined with medieval houses, including a spectacular three-floor half-timbered building, the Maison

Above *Mont St-Michel and the gardens*
Left *The tour Solidor, on the Rance estuary*

du Gouverneur. The riverside is lined with restaurants, great for lunch or dinner.

From Dinan, follow signs to the suburb of Lanvallay, east of Dinan, and pick up the D676. Fork left onto the D29 and head north past Pleudihen-sur-Rance. Continue north via the D74 and D76, following signs for Le Port as you come into Cancale.

❹ The oyster port and seaside resort of Cancale is tucked into a corner of the Baie du Mont-St-Michel. You can see the Mount itself on the far side of the bay. Oysters are bred out in the bay and are gathered from the flat-bottomed boats that you can see in the harbour. There are plenty of small restaurants along the wharf where you can sample the catch.

From Cancale harbour, follow the D201 northwards for 7km (4.5 miles) to the Pointe du Grouin (signed *St-Malo par la côte)*.

❺ Pointe du Grouin is a nature reserve and bird sanctuary, with superb views over the bay to Mont-St-Michel and, to the south, to Mont-Dol near Dol-de-Bretagne. From the parking place there is a footpath up to the tip of the Pointe and from there another footpath leads along the coast to St-Malo.

Continue westwards along the picturesque coast road (still the D201) in the direction of St-Malo past the Baie du Guesclin and through the suburb of Rothéneuf.

❻ Rothéneuf is a pleasant suburb of St-Malo, next to a wide beach. Sights here include the coastal rocks carved by the Abbé Foure in the 19th century and the manor house lived in by the 16th-century explorer and discoverer of Canada, Jacques Cartier.

Pass through Paramé, and then along the waterfront and you reach the main gateway into St-Malo.

WHERE TO EAT
LES TERRASSES
✉ 7 rue du Quai, Dinan ☎ 02 96 39 09 60 ⏲ Daily 9am–midnight (longer in Jul and Aug)

WHERE TO STAY
LE VALMARIN
www.levalmarin.com
✉ 7 rue Jean XXIII, 35400 St-Malo ☎ 02 99 81 94 76

PLACES TO VISIT
TOUR SOLIDOR
✉ St-Servan, St-Malo ☎ 02 99 40 71 58 ⏲ Apr–end Sep daily 10–12.30, 2–6; reduced hours in winter; closed Mon 🎟 Adult €5.20, child (8–23) €2.60

MANOIR DE LIMOËLOU (MUSÉE JACQUES CARTIER)
✉ Rothéneuf ☎ 02 99 40 97 73 ⏲ Jul, Aug daily 10–11.30, 2.30–6; closed Sun Sep–end Jun 🎟 Adult €4, child €3
☞ Guided tours Mon–Sat 10 and 3

Above *The historic old town of Dinan clings to the wooded slopes*

BAZOUGES-LA-PÉROUSE

LE VILLAGE

www.bazouges.com

Throughout the year, this village is the scene of an innovative artistic experiment, playing host to many artists who present visual and performing arts in several local venues. In the summer you can see open-air exhibitions, café-theatre and street entertainment.

✉ 2 place de l'Hôtel de Ville, 35560 Bazouges-la-Pérouse ☎ 02 99 97 40 94 🕓 Jul, Aug daily; rest of year mostly at weekends 🖐 Free

CANCALE

LA CANCALAISE

www.lacancalaise.org

This lovely replica of one of Cancale's traditional oyster-boats *(bisquines)*, built by a local association of enthusiasts in 1985, offers summer trips in the Baie de Mont-St-Michel. Its 350sq m (3,700sq ft) of rigging are a superb sight under full sail. Reserve places in advance.

✉ La Halle à Marée, quai Gambetta, La Houle, 35260 Cancale ☎ 02 99 89 77 87 🕓 Sailings Apr–end Oct daily 9–6; office hours 2–5 (closed Wed, Sun) 🖐 Around €42 per person per day, child (6–14) €24

LA FERME MARINE

www.ferme-marine.com

Find out all about oysters at this interesting working oyster farm. As well as a film show, there are tours of the oyster beds, tastings, and an impressive exhibition of world seashells. After the tour you will have the opportunity also to buy some oysters.

✉ L'Aurore, route de la Corniche ☎ 02 99 89 69 99 🕓 Guided visits Jul to mid-Sep daily in English at 2pm, in French at 11am, 3pm and 5pm; mid-Feb to end Jun, mid-Sep to end Oct Mon–Fri at 3pm (in French only) 🖐 Adult €6.70, child (under 15) €3.50, family €18.50 🎁 Attractive souvenir shop selling shell curios and jewellery

GRAIN DE VANILLE

www.maisons-de-bricourt.com

There's often a queue at this tiny, unobtrusive little master bakery, part of Olivier Roellinger's gastronomic empire, tucked away at the back of the old town. Here you can buy biscuits, cakes and tarts *(pomme breton, cannelle gingembre)*, herbs and spices, speciality bread, home-made ice cream and candied fruit to take away or try on the premises in the *salon de thé*.

✉ 12 place de la Victoire, 35260 Cancale ☎ 02 23 15 12 70 🕓 Jul, Aug Wed–Mon 10–12.30, 2.30–7; mid-Feb to end Jun, Sep to mid-Jan Thu–Mon 10–12.30, 2.30–6.30

MARCHÉ AUX HUÎTRES

Whether or not there's an 'r' in the month, you can buy oysters from the little stalls by the waterfront *parcs* (oysterbeds) at the old port of La Houle. Prices start at around €4 per dozen for *creuses* (hollow oysters). The flat ones *(huîtres plates)*, which can be as big as dinner-plates, are more expensive, and wild oysters trawled from farther offshore *(huîtres sauvages)* are priciest of all.

✉ Quai St-Thomas, Port de la Houle, 35260 Cancale 🕓 All day, every day, all year

CHERRUEIX

NOROIT CLUB

www.noroit-club.fr.fm

The 7km (4-mile) expanse of smooth sand exposed by the great tidal variations makes a superb playground for sand-yachting. Watch the craft hurtling along the strand, or have a go yourself. International competitions take place here.

✉ 1 rue de la Plage, 35200 Cherrueix ☎ 02 99 38 83 01 🕓 Mon–Fri 9–12, 2–6, Sat 2–6 🖐 From about €16 per hour

LE TRAIN MARIN

www.train-marin.com

Take an unforgettable two-hour tractor-drawn tour at low tide, with commentary, over the wide sands and mud-flats of Mont-St-Michel bay to visit mussel *bouchots* and spot birds. Reserve ahead.

✉ Gare St-Michel, 35120 Cherrueix ☎ 02 99 48 84 88 ◷ Apr–end Oct depending on tides 🖐 Adult €10.50, child (4–11) €7.50, family €40

DINARD

LES 2 ALIZÉS

www.emeraude-cinema.fr

Dinard is a great place for film-buffs. This cinema, just behind the main beach, puts on undubbed or *version originale* films (VO).

✉ 2 boulevard Albert 1er, 35800 Dinard ☎ 02 99 88 17 93 ◷ All year 🖐 Adult €4.50–€7.80, child (under 12) €5.50; the cheaper rate during daytime

CASINO BARRIÈRE DE DINARD

www.lucienbarriere.com

This casino is one of Brittany's more exclusive venues, overlooking the main beach of La Nice du Nord. Here you'll find roulette, blackjack, stud poker and more than 100 one armed bandits. There's a smart dress code and a minimum age limit of 18.

✉ 4 boulevard Wilson, 35802 Dinard ☎ 02 99 16 30 30 ◷ Sun–Thu 10am–3am, Fri–Sat 10am–4am; gaming tables open from 9pm; closed Mon, Tue off-season 🖐 No charge to play at the tables

PISCINE OLYMPIQUE

This large swimming pool, 50m by 25m (164ft by 82ft), is filled with heated seawater, an enticing alternative to the glamorous but often chilly waves on Dinard's lovely main beach, where there are many activities for children.

✉ 2 boulevard Wilson, 35800 Dinard ☎ 02 99 46 22 77 ◷ Jul, Aug daily 10–12.30, 3–7.30; telephone for times rest of year 🖐 Adult €4.10, child (5–18) €3.25

FOUGÈRES

LE COQUELICOT

On a hilly street a short walk from the old town, this popular bar is a well-known pub-concert offering live music (jazz, folk, rock, blues) and café-theatre. Some 70 different beers are on sale.

✉ 18 rue de Vitré, 35300 Fougères ☎ 02 99 99 82 11 ◷ Tue–Sat 4pm–3am; concerts usually Thu–Sat at 9; closed Sun, Mon and part of Jul and Aug 🖐 €5 (variable)

PARC FLORAL DE HAUTE BRETAGNE

www.parcfloralbretagne.com

This huge botanical park contains a dozen separate gardens and some 4,000 species from all over the world; there's never a day when something isn't flowering. Lots of walks, diversions and play areas for children, including mazes, a wobbly bridge and carnivorous plants. Walkways have been provided for visitors with disabilities, and there is accommodation on site.

✉ La Foltière, 35133 Le Chatellier ☎ 02 99 95 48 32 ◷ Jul, Aug daily 10.30–6.30; Apr–end Jun, Sep Mon–Sat 10–12, 2–6, Sun 10.30–6.30; Mar, Oct to mid-Nov 2–5.30; closed mid-Nov to end Feb 🖐 Adult €9.50 (€9 off-season), child (5–12) €7, family €28; guided visits €11 per person

PETIT TRAIN DE FOUGÈRES

This *petit train* (known as L'Oriental Express) gives you a good excuse to avoid climbing the steep hill to the old town. The 45-minute tour starts from the castle forecourt and finishes at the tourist office, passing through the public gardens. Your journey is enlivened by a multilingual commentary. Passport inclusive tickets include entrance to the castle and a guided tour—ask at the tourist office.

✉ 35300 Fougères ☎ 02 99 99 71 72 ◷ May–end Sep daily 10–7 🖐 Adult €5, child (under 12) €4

LANHÉLIN

COBAC PARC

www.cobac-parc.com

This theme park on a large wooded site near Combourg between Rennes and St-Malo promises lots of fun for all the family, with animals, rides, a heated boating and leisure pool, miniature railway, video games, mini-golf, magic mirrors and more.

✉ 35720 Lanhélin ☎ 02 99 73 80 16 ◷ Variable schedule Apr–end Sep (open daily Jul, Aug; closed Mon rest of year) 🖐 Adult €15, child (3–11) €3.50 with all rides included in the entry price

MESSAC

CROWN BLUE LINE

www.crownblueline.com

Houseboats and cabin cruisers sleeping from 2 to 12 can be hired from this long-established boating firm for holidays on Brittany's inland waterways. Typical destinations reachable within a week from Messac include Dinan, Josselin, Redon, La Roche-Bernard and Nantes. There's another pick-up point at Dinan (Côtes d'Armor). No licence is required.

✉ Port de Plaisance, 35480 Messac ☎ 02 99 34 60 11 ◷ Apr–end Oct; closed Sun, and weekends off-season

PLERGUER

LA CHÈVRERIE DU DÉSERT

Children will enjoy this goat farm with lots of different animals, where cheese products are on sale (you can taste the cheese first), along with other regional food products.

✉ Le Desert, 35540 Plerguer ☎ 02 99 58 92 14 ◷ Jul, Aug daily 11–6.30; Apr–end Jun, Sep Wed–Mon 2.30–6.30, Sun, holidays 11–6.30; closed Oct–end Mar 🖐 Adult €6, child €5

PLEUGUENEUC

LA BOURBANSAIS

www.labourbansais.com

You'll find this zoo, with many protected species and birds of prey, in the grounds of the impressive Château de Bourbansais (worth a visit in its own right—guided tours) just off the N137 east of Dinan. It has a playground with a bouncy castle for children, a snack bar, a tea room and a gift shop.

✉ Domaine de la Bourbansais, 35720 Pleugueneuc ☎ 02 99 69 40 07 ◷ Apr–end Sep daily 10–7; Oct–end Mar 2–6 🖐 Zoo, gardens and shows: adult €15, child (4–14) €11; supplement for château interior: adult €5, child €3

REDON

BRETAGNE CROISIÈRES

www.bretagnecroisieres.com

Cabin cruisers sleeping up to 12 can be rented from this company's two bases at Redon and Dinan for weekends or longer periods. Sail the inland waterways of Brittany in comfortable modern boats. Bicycles and baby equipment can be rented to take on board. Free parking is available at the departure point. No licence is required.

75 rue de Vannes, 35600 Redon 02 99 71 08 05 Mar–early Nov €439–€2,681, depending on rental period, time of year and size of boat; refundable deposit

CINE MANIVEL

www.cinemanivel.fr

Staffed by bright young volunteers, this sleek avant-garde cinema next to the maritime museum down on the waterfront is a breath of fresh air. It puts on independent arthouse films, some in *version originale*. There's a foyer café, open half an hour before the first screening, with modern art and occasional live music.

12 quai Jean Bart, 35600 Redon 02 99 72 28 20 Variable daily programme; phone 08 92 68 35 01 for showtimes Adult €6.70, child/student €5.60

RENNES

BERNIQUE HURLANTE

This discreet and cosy little bar/ bookshop of dark wood behind the witty blue façade is a well-known venue for an alternative clientele of artists and activists, as well as Rennes' gay community. Wines is available by the glass.

40 rue St-Malo, 35000 Rennes 02 99 38 70 09 Tue–Sat 4–12.30am, Sun 6–late

HARMONIA MUNDI

www.harmoniamundi.com

This chain of high-quality music stores has just a couple of branches in Brittany, but is one of the best places to look for recordings of all types, including classical, Celtic, jazz and modern music.

3 rue Jean-Jaurès, 35000 Rennes 02 99 78 33 64 Mon 2.30–7 (except Aug), Tue–Sat 10–7

PÉNICHE SPECTACLE

www.penichespectacle.com

Two barges—*L'Arbre d'Eau* and *La Dame Blanche*—make unusual theatre venues presenting a varied selection of world music, jazz, cabaret, workshops, readings and exhibitions, and performances for children.

30 quai St-Cyr, 35000 Rennes 02 99 59 35 38 Most shows Thu–Sat at 8.30pm Adult €13, child (under 12) €8

THÉÂTRE NATIONAL DE BRETAGNE (TNB)

www.t-n-b.fr

This theatre has three separate performance halls for drama, dance, jazz and classical music. There's also a cinema screening independent and experimental films in their original language. You can have lunch or dinner in the restaurant and bar.

1 rue St-Hélier, 35040 Rennes 02 99 31 12 31 Mon, Tue, Thu, Fri 8.30, Wed, Sat 7.30, Sun 4; Box office Tue–Fri 1–7, Sat 2–6.30; closed Sun and Mon Ticket prices from €23 Gare SNCF

LA RICHARDAIS

L'ATELIER MANOLI

www.manoli.org

More than 400 sculptures representing the innovative life work of the artist Manoli, whose creations can be seen in public places all over France, are on display in this museum and sculpture garden.

9 rue du Suet, 35780 La Richardais 02 99 88 55 53 Jul, Aug daily 10.30–12, 3–7, May–end Jun, Sep Sat, Sun holidays 3–7 Adult €3, child €2, under 12 free

ST-MALO

BAR DE L'UNIVERS

www.hotel-univers-saintmalo.com

This hugely popular old hotel bar is smothered with historic photos, and models of sailing ships dangle from the beams. In the evenings, it throbs with life, smoothly supervised by the efficient, friendly, English-speaking staff serving up lots of bottled Belgian beers, interesting cocktails, Irish whiskeys and excellent wines.

Place Chateaubriand, 35400 St-Malo 02 99 40 89 52 Daily 7am–1.30am (until 2am in summer)

LES COURRIERS BRETONS

www.lescourriersbretons.fr

Besides running a network of regular scheduled bus routes, this company organizes escorted day trips to Mont-St-Michel, Dinan, Cap Fréhel, Île de Bréhat and other destinations from St-Malo. The reservations agency is next to the main tourist office just outside the walled town.

Esplanade St-Vincent, 35400 St-Malo 02 99 19 70 80 All year

LE RENARD

www.cotre-corsaire-renard.com

A handsome recreation of privateer Robert Surcouf's last ten-cannon sailing ship, *Le Renard* is rigged as it was in 1812. In the safe hands of an experienced crew, you can take a trip around St-Malo bay or to Bréhat and the Channel Islands, and practise a few manoeuvres.

35408 St-Malo 02 99 40 53 10 Daily Apr–end Nov Adult €62 per day, child (under 12) €31; longer cruises start at €294 (2 days in St-Malo bay), including board

THÉÂTRE DE ST-MALO

www.theatresaintmalo.com

The leading theatre in the region hosts major touring productions, concerts, opera, big band shows, plays, musicals, one-man shows and children's performances. The bar is open pre-show and in the interval, and there is good access for visitors with disabilities.

6 place Bouvet, 35400 St-Malo 02 99 81 62 61 (box office) Booking office Tue–Fri 10–12, 2–6.30, Sat 10–12, 2–6 (up until 9pm on performance nights); shows start at 8.30 (4.30 on Sun); children's shows once a month on Wed at 2.30 and 4.30 Adult €26–€40, child (under 18) €10

ST-MELOIR-DES-ONDES

LES PETITS FRUITS DE LA BAIE

Pick-your-own fresh soft fruit (strawberries, raspberries and other summer fruit) at this farm. The on-site shop sells jams and preserves, and a farmers' market takes place once a week in high season.

5 rue des Clossets, 35350 St Méloir-des-Ondes 02 99 89 10 06 Jan–end May (kiwi fruit); May– end Oct (red berries) Mon–Sat 8–12.30, 3.30–7; farmers' market Jul, Aug Mon 5–8

FESTIVALS AND EVENTS

MARCH

FESTIVAL DU JAZZ VITRÉ

Artists and bands delight locals and visitors with free performances in the town's streets, bars, squares and restaurants.

A week in early Mar

JULY

PROMENADE AU CLAIR DE LUNE DINARD

This panoramic coastal walk through luxuriant vegetation is enjoyable at any time of year, but in summer the gardens are enhanced by a son-et-lumière show, and romantically illuminated with different music every evening.

Jul–end Sep

TOMBÉES DE LA NUIT RENNES

www.lestombeesdelanuit.com

A huge pan-Celtic celebration with modern rock music, dance and theatrical performances in the old streets of the city.

12 rue Jean Boucher, 35000 Rennes 02 99 32 56 56 First week in Jul

AUGUST

JUMPING INTERNATIONAL DE DINARD DINARD

This major show-jumping event attracts competitors from all over the world.

4 days in early Aug

OCTOBER

FESTIVAL DU FILM BRITANNIQUE DINARD

The British film festival is a highlight of Dinard's social calendar and a place for celebrity-spotting in autumn, originally sparked off by Alfred Hitchcock's use of Dinard as a film-set for *The Birds*.

3 days in early Oct

FOIRE TEILLOUSE REDON

www.tourisme-pays-redon.com

Each autumn, Redon marks the sweet chestnut festival with a month of celebrations culminating in a huge *fest-noz* known as the Bogue d'Or (Breton music, dancing and story-telling) and a weekend covered market (chestnuts and crafts). Meanwhile the town chefs cook up nutty treats.

Late Oct

DECEMBER

LES TRANSMUSICALES RENNES

www.lestrans.com

The bars and clubs of Rennes take on a new lease of life when this international rock-and-roll festival hits town. Some gigs are held in the Théâtre National de Bretagne.

10–12 rue Jean Guy 02 99 31 12 10 Second week in Dec

Above *Maisons de Bricourt, Cancale*

PRICES AND SYMBOLS
The restaurants are listed alphabetically within each town. The prices given for lunch (L) and dinner (D) are for three courses for one person, without drinks. The wine price is for the least expensive bottle.
For a key to the symbols, ▷ 2.

CANCALE

MAISONS DE BRICOURT

www.maisons-de-bricourt.com
Olivier Roellinger conquered the heights of France's gastronomic scene years ago, and operates several celebrated enterprises around Cancale (▷ 161). His family home, a gracious 18th-century *malouinière* in a quiet residential street, is now a theatre for the most accomplished productions of the *maître cuisinier*. Local seafood is naturally part of his stock in trade, but the subtle and aromatic mixture of flavours and spices have travelled the world (for example John Dory steamed in seaweed and coconut milk). Reserve ahead.
✉ 1 rue Duguesclin, 35260 Cancale ☎ 02 99 89 64 76 ⌚ Fri–Tue 12–1.30, 7–9; closed Mon lunch and Tue lunch off-season, and mid-Dec to mid-Mar 🖐 L €100, D €158, Wine €95

LE SURCOUF

This is not the least expensive of the restaurants lining the picturesque old port of La Houle, but definitely one of the best. The small granite building with its apron terrace, tastefully decked in blue and white, can offer you the *assiette de fruits de mer* of a lifetime, or an equally delicious roast lobster or house foie gras. Menus range from €18–€42, and much is made of local oysters. There are good wines from the Loire, and Breton cider too.
✉ 7 quai Gambetta, 35260 Cancale ☎ 02 99 89 61 75 ⌚ Jul, Aug Wed–Mon 12–2.30; 7–10.30; rest of year Thu–Mon 12–2.30; 7–10.30; closed Dec and Jan 🖐 L €25, D €50, Wine €19

COMBOURG

L'ECRIVAIN

To find this place, head for the church on the main street. One dining room is panelled and candlelit; a larger salon faces the garden. Gilles Menier's reputation has crystallized over many years, but prices are still reasonable for such inventive, tasty cooking based on fresh local ingredients. Try the home-smoked fish or a *millefeuille de canard au foie gras*. Set menus are good value, or you can just have a *plat du jour* with a glass of wine. You can buy cakes to eat in or take out. The literary theme stems from local writer Chateaubriand.
✉ Place St-Gilduin, 35270 Combourg ☎ 02 99 73 01 61 ⌚ Mid-Jul to mid-Aug Fri–Wed 12–2, 7–10; rest of year Fri–Sat 12–2, 7–9.30, Sun 12–2, Mon–Tue 7–9.30, Wed 12–2 🖐 L €18, D €35, Wine €13

DINARD

DIDIER MÉRIL

www.restaurant-didier-meril.com
The dynamic young chef who gives his name to this restaurant has made quite a hit in this exclusive Emerald Coast enclave. The modern premises are fashionably sleek and minimalist, with an elegant terrace close to the beach and casino. Service is polished but affable. Regularly changing menus include plenty of seafood. The home-made rolls (eight types) are hard to resist, but save room for a pudding *(moêlleux au chocolat, caramel à l'orange)*. There's a good-value weekday lunch *formule* (€20).
✉ 1 place du Général de Gaulle, 35800 Dinard ☎ 02 99 46 95 74 ⌚ Daily 12–2, 7–10; closed last 2 weeks Nov and first week Dec 🖐 L €45, D €60, Wine €26

FOUGÈRES

LE BUFFET

On the main street by the church of St-Léonard in the upper town, this modest little establishment is terrific value. The interior is decked with old photos and pictures, ancient coffee grinders and similar relics, and a handsome stone fireplace dispenses a warm glow on chilly days. Choose from a generous buffet of entrées, hors d'oeuvres and desserts. Simple menus all include a quarter bottle of wine, and there's a *plat du jour.*

53 bis, rue Nationale, 35300 Fougères 02 99 94 35 76 Mon–Sat 12–1.45, 7–9.15, Wed lunch only; closed 3 weeks Aug, 1 week Dec L €18, D €22, Wine €13

HEDE

LA VIEILLE AUBERGE

www.lavielleauberge35.fr

A low-slung 17th-century mill beside its own tree-lined pond gives this rustic restaurant a relaxed, informal air. But standards of cuisine are anything but sleepy; fresh produce is whistled in from the local markets to use in its classic seasonal menus. You might order beech-smoked salmon, or a risotto of scallops, mushrooms and parmesan. In fine weather you can dine al fresco on the flower-filled terrace.

La Vallée, 35630 Hédé 02 99 45 46 25 Closed Sun eve and Mon; also 2 weeks late Aug–early Sep, and several weeks Feb–early Mar L €18, D €43, Wine €19

REDON

L'AKÈNE

This little *crêperie* tucked away in a tiny alley in the old port is set in a charming stone house with red shutters. The atmosphere is welcoming and the pancakes very good value. An After Eight *crêpe* includes chocolate and *glace de menthe*. Besides pancakes, it does salads, ices and superb *raclettes* (minimum two people).

10 rue de Jeu-de-Paume, 35600 Redon 02 99 71 25 15 Jul, Aug daily 12–2, 6.45–9.30; closed Wed dinner rest of year L €12, D €18, Cider €7

LA BOGUE

In a flower-decked old stone building on the main square by the church, this welcoming place has an excellent reputation for value and traditional country cooking. You might get a *blanquette de veau à l'ancienne façon du chef* (veal in cream and mushroom sauce) or a *soufflé chaud à l'orange au Grand Marnier*. The interior is rustic and delightfully old-fashioned. Look for interesting ways with chestnuts (a local speciality) in late autumn.

3 rue des Etats, 35600 Redon 02 99 71 12 95 12–1.30, 7.15–9; closed Mon, Sun dinner, and 10 days early Jul L €21, D €35, Wine €14

RENNES

CAFÉ BRETON

Hidden away in a street near the *halles* (covered market) off place des Lices, the dark-blue frontage of this bistrot is thronged with locals most lunchtimes, so it's best to book. Bustling with life inside, the dining space is nicely broken up and full of interest with china displays in alcove shelving, and posters against sunshine-yellow walls. Chalkboard specials might include a *tagine de saumon et cabillaud* (salmon and cod), or *rillettes de thon et salade* (tuna mayonnaise). Wines are excellent. Its friendly owner-chef is very much in evidence.

14 rue Nantaise, 35000 Rennes 02 99 30 74 95 Mon 12–4, Tue–Fri 12–3, 7–11, Sat 12–4; closed 3 weeks Aug and 2 weeks Mar L €15, D €30, Wine €14 Sainte-Anne

LE BOCAL-P'TY RESTO

Jars *(bocaux)* filled with shells and glass beads give this friendly restaurant its name. Inventive dishes run to fare like seafood muffins or crumble *au moment,* and the menu changes frequently. with good value *petits plats* and *formules* at lunchtime. The well-chosen wines are all served by the glass. The staff are upbeat and young.

6 rue d'Argentré, 35000 Rennes 02 99 78 34 10 Mon–Fri 12–1.30 L €18, D €25, Wine €14 République

LE KHALIFA

An agreeable Moroccan restaurant on lively place des Lices, serving hearty platefuls of couscous, *brochettes* and delicately scented tagines at remarkable prices. Small wonder it's often full of hungry students. The levantine pastries are worth trying for dessert. North African furnishings and music, smiling staff and a complimentary glass of *sangria* will put you in a good mood. The service is prompt and friendly.

20 place des Lices, 35000 Rennes 02 99 30 87 30 Tue–Sun 12–2, 7–11.30; closed 2 weeks in Aug L €18, D €22, Wine €16 Sainte-Anne

AU MARCHÉ DES LICES

An excellent *crêperie* in the marketplace, handily placed for shopping and sightseeing. The simple, rustic dining room has an open fireplace and a display of old coffee-pots. An Argoat contains *andouille,* cream and cheese, and strong cider is served in breakfast cups. If you're fed up with pancakes, the *plat du jour* (a classic beef stew with carrots, perhaps) is excellent value at lunchtime, but there are no starters or formal menus. Friendly service is the norm.

3 place du Bas des Lices, 35000 Rennes 02 99 30 42 95 Mon–Sat 12–2.30, 7–9.30, closed 3 weeks Aug, 2 weeks Jan *Crêpe* and a pudding around €12; a pitcher of cider about €8 Sainte-Anne

ST-LUNAIRE

LE DÉCOLLÉ

Panoramic views over the Emerald Coast enhance this popular seafood establishment on a scenic rocky promontory. The nearby *crêperie* and a discotheque in a thatched cottage provide additional reasons to make your way here. In the glazed dining room or summer terraces of Le Décollé you can try roast cod or a ragout of lamb.

1 pointe du Décollé, 35800 St-Lunaire 02 99 46 01 70 Jul, Aug Tue–Sun 12.15–2, 7.15–9; closed Tue off-season and mid-Nov to Jan L €22, D €40, Wine €16

ST-MALO

LE BENETIN

www.restaurant-lebenetin.com

Huge windows take advantage of a spectacular view of the bay from this relaxed but stylish clifftop restaurant and *salon de thé*. It's beside the entrance to curious rock carvings created in the cliff-face by a local 19th-century priest, but whether or not these interest you, this place deserves a visit for its magnificent setting and sophisticated menus, which might include Cancale oysters or *pré salé* lamb (▷ 164) from the Baie de Mont-St-Michel. The wine list is extensive.

Les Rochers Sculptés, Rothéneuf, 35400 St-Malo 02 99 56 97 64 Jul, Aug Thu–Tue 12–2.30, 7.30–10; rest of year Thu–Mon 12–2.30, 7.30–10; Jun–end Aug open for tea and early evening drinks L €20, D €30, Wine €18

LA BRIGANTINE

Soothingly decorated in light colours with pictures of sailing ships on the walls, this pleasant *crêperie* has a well-established reputation. It occupies a stone building in the heart of the walled town. You can have omelettes, or warm Chavignol goat's cheese with a glass of sauvignon, if you prefer.

13 rue de Dinan, 35400 St-Malo 02 99 56 82 82 Jul, Aug daily 12–3, 6.30–11; Sep–end Jun Thu–Mon 12–3, 6.30–11; closed late Nov and most of Jan L €12, D €16, Cider €8

LES EMBRUNS

Seafood dishes are served here in a salmon-pink painted dining room close to the beach, on Paramé's hotel strip. The menu follows the seasons, but some classics are fat scampi with mayonnaise, lightly salted salmon with asparagus and lamb's kidneys with purple Brive mustard. Alternatively you can choose your meal from the lobster tank on display. The artwork on the walls is also for sale.

120 chaussée du Sillon, 35400 St-Malo 02 99 56 33 57 Tue–Sat 12–2, 7–9.15, Sun 12–2, all year L €20, D €25, Wine €16

VITRÉ

LE CHÊNE VERT

The cheerful yellow awnings of this handy brasserie near the tourist office are easy to spot. The stylish interior, split into several bar-dining zones, uses bright modern furnishings, pictures, mirrors and flowers to good effect. Menus offer a flexible range of simple but imaginative fish and meat dishes and a *vin du mois* (wine of the month). Tasty *tartines*, salads, omelettes and soups set you up for exploring the old town. The pleasant young team provides prompt, agreeable service. There's also a sunny terrace for al fresco dining.

2 place du Général de Gaulle, 35500 Vitré 02 23 55 14 62 Mon, Tue 8–8, Thu–Sun 8am–1am; closed Wed L €15, D €20, Wine €11

TAVERNE DE L'ECU

www.tavernedelecru.fr

This restaurant is in a beautiful 16th-century building with two dining rooms, each with a large fireplace and exposed beams. The menu changes with the seasons, and everything is made on the premises, even the bread. You might be tempted by the roasted rabbit leg with white beans and dried Italian tomatoes, boar fillet with salad and spicy apple chutney or the catch of the day served with preserved tomatoes. There is an extensive wine list.

12 rue de la Baudrairie, 35500 Vitré 02 99 75 11 09 Jul, Aug Thu–Mon 12.15–1.45, 7.30–9, Tue 12.15–1.45; rest of year Thu–Sat, Mon 12.15–1.45, 7.30–9, Sun, Tue 12.15–1.45 L €23, D €30, Wine €13

PRICES AND SYMBOLS

Prices quoted are the range for a double with private facilities. The *taxe de séjour* (▷ 214) is not included. Unless otherwise stated, breakfast is excluded from the price. For a key to the symbols, ▷ 2.

CANCALE

LE CONTINENTAL

www.hotel-cancale.com

Streetside dining space takes over most of the ground floor of this traditional restaurant-with-rooms overlooking Cancale's old harbour of La Houle. Inside, the panelled walls of this 'English-style' restaurant are adorned with seascape paintings. Diners on its canopied veranda get a ringside view of the fishing fleet setting off into the bay, and tractors bustling around the nearby oysterbeds. Needless to say, Cancale's prized molluscs appear on every menu. In the hotel, the front bedrooms enjoy the sweeping panoramic views, and are therefore understandably pricier, but all are extrememly comfortable and tastefully furnished.

4 quai Thomas, 35260 Cancale 02 99 89 60 16 Closed mid to end Nov and early Jan to early Feb €88–€148 (breakfast €12.50) 18

CHATEAUBOURG

PEN'ROC

www.penroc.fr

This former farm on a pilgrimage site in deep countryside has been substantially modernized and upgraded, but has kept its restful air. Excellent facilities include a sauna and hot tub. The entire house is bright, tasteful and immaculate, and the grounds are beautifully kept. Some bedrooms have private terraces and whirlpool baths. Ambitious, varied menus ring the changes on fresh market produce.

La Peinière, St-Didier, 35221 Chateaubourg 02 99 00 33 02 Closed mid Dec–mid Jan €84–€135 (breakfast €13) 29 Indoor

COMBOURG

HÔTEL DU CHÂTEAU

www.hotelduchateau.com

Easy to spot at a junction near Combourg's impressive castle, this hotel is a superior Logis de France, well known for its restaurant. Bedrooms are very varied, some stylishly modern in muted minimalism, others more traditional with William Morris wallpapers, but all are very comfortable and generously heated even on the coldest of nights. Some are in an annexe facing the attractive rear gardens; others have views of the castle or the lake across the road. The restaurant is warm and intimate, and there's a comfortable bar-lounge with a piano. A generous buffet breakfast is served.

1 place Chateaubriand, 35270 Combourg 02 99 73 00 38 Closed mid-Dec to late Jan; reception closed Sun eve €79–€200 (breakfast €11) 33

Above *Le Château Richeux at St-Meloir-des-Ondes*

DINARD

PRINTANIA

www.printaniahotel.com

This winsome place is one of the oldest (1920s) and most beautiful hotels in Dinard. It virtually paddles in the Rance, and views of the estuary from many of its windows are superb. Inside, it has distinctive character and many fine old Breton antiques, including carved linen-presses and box beds. In the restaurant, waitresses wear regional costume. Reserve ahead for lunch. Street parking is available.

5 avenue George V, 35800 Dinard 02 99 46 13 07 Late Nov–late Mar €70–€120 (breakfast €9) 57, including a suite

FOUGÈRES

BALZAC

www.balzachotel.com

A traditional, classic hotel on a main street, well placed for exploring the old town and very good value. It occupies a handsome period town house handy for shops, restaurants and the tourist office. Public space by the reception entrance includes an intimate little breakfast room from which you can watch passers-by on the cobbled street, and a sitting area with internet access. Bedrooms are variable, simple but clean and brightly furnished. Several are suitable for families, and the upper floor can be let as a complete unit. Half-board deals can be arranged using two well-regarded local restaurants. The friendly owner speaks fluent English.

✉ 15 rue Nationale, 35300 Fougères ☎ 02 99 99 42 46 From €52 (breakfast €6) 22

HÉDÉ

HOSTELLERIE DU VIEUX MOULIN

British visitors constitute some 25 per cent of the trade of this friendly, good-value Logis in a wooded valley. Set in an old granite watermill, the elongated, creeper-clad building with its mini-belltower at one end looks instantly inviting. Flower-filled gardens reach to the foot of the ramparts on which the main village stands. Inside, original timbers and stone fireplaces are still on show. The recently refurbished bedrooms are cheerful and bright, the restaurant a roomy oblong of red-and-gold seating. The Irish chef-patron might dish up oysters and foie gras, or a hearty beef casserole.

✉ La Vallée des Moulins, 35630 Hédé ☎ 02 99 45 45 70 Closed part of Oct and Jan; reception closed Sun eve, Mon From €50 (breakfast €7) 13

QUÉDILLAC

RELAIS DE LA RANCE

This classic *maison bourgeoise*, part of the Logis group, makes a useful touring base for the Forêt de Paimpont. The well-kept, attractively lit stone house is easy to find on the main street of a pleasant if undistinguished little town on the Rennes–Brest road. The very French interior is full of personality, with the focus squarely on its spacious twin dining rooms (look for the *menu du terroir)*. Three generations of the Guitton family have run the place since 1946, transforming it from a modest café into an acclaimed restaurant with a reassuring air of continuity and tradition.

✉ 6 rue de Rennes, 35290 Quédillac ☎ 02 99 06 20 20 Closed Christmas–late Jan; restaurant and hotel reception closed Fri eve and Sun eve €53–€70 (breakfast €9.50) 13

REDON

CHANDOUINEAU

The rather charmless location near the railway station gives no accurate picture of this opulently decorated restaurant-with-rooms. Chef-patron Jean-Marc Chandouineau's reputation has steadily developed over more than 30 years, and you may well find some captain of industry or local bigwig sitting on the next balloon-back at lunch- or dinnertime. The bedrooms reach the same high standards as the cooking, pleasantly decorated in soothing tones with stylish, spacious bathrooms. All are well insulated against the sound of passing trains.

✉ 1 rue Thiers, avenue de la Gare, 35600 Redon ☎ 02 99 71 02 04 Closed 2 weeks Apr–May, 2 weeks Jul and Aug, 2 weeks in Jan From €50 (breakfast €11) 7

RENNES

HOTEL DES LICES

www.hotel-des-lices.com

This modern, unobtrusive hotel overlooks a famous old-town square lined with historic buildings, many now turned into bars or restaurants. The market is held here on Saturday mornings. Nearly all rooms have their own balconies, and are practical and contemporary with blondwood fittings, trendy lighting and English-language satellite TV. Plumbing, insulation and workspace have been carefully considered. The breakfast room is calm and elegant with fresh flowers. There is public parking near the hotel (concessionary rates and spaces reserved for hotel guests).

✉ 7 place des Lices, 35000 Rennes ☎ 02 99 79 14 81 €59–€72 (breakfast €8) 45 (all non-smoking) Sainte-Anne

ST-MALO

LE BEAUFORT

www.hotel-beaufort.com

Sea views are spectacular from the breakfast room and best bedrooms of this elegant mid-19th-century hotel, and there's direct access to St-Malo's main beach. The building is a handsome town house with balustrades and dormers, smartly painted in gold and blue. The interior is cool and restrained, using a sophisticated muted palette and chic contemporary furnishings. No dinners are served, but you can relax in the piano bar in the evenings. It's about a 15-minute stroll along the beach to the old town.

✉ 25 chaussée du Sillon, 35400 St-Malo ☎ 02 99 40 99 99 €77–€207 (breakfast €12) 22

MANOIR DU CUNNINGHAM

www.st-malo-hotel-cunningham.com

Overlooking Port des Sablons and the old citadel, this flamboyant hotel in the St-Servan district is within easy striking distance of both the marina and the ferry terminal. The cream-rendered exterior of the 17th-century building sports red faux timbering and open woodwork. Bedrooms are spacious and kitted out in a dynamic combination of colonial-looking mahogany and vibrant modern shades. Many enjoy magnificent views. One room is suitable for wheelchair users.

✉ 9 place Monseigneur Duchesne, St-Servan, 35400 St-Malo ☎ 02 99 21 33 33 Closed mid-Nov to mid-Mar, except weekends €90–€190 (breakfast €10) 13, including 3 suites

QUIC EN GROIGNE

www.quic-en-groigne.com

This sweet little place in the heart of the walled city makes the perfect first or last night in Brittany if you're travelling by ferry. It is exceptionally friendly and very good value for such a delightful location. Rooms, some sleeping up to four, are prettily decorated and well finished with fitted furnishings and good bathrooms. Generous breakfasts are served in a light conservatory facing a tidy interior courtyard. Secure off-street parking is an unusual bonus in this part of town, though access is a little tricky.

✉ 8 rue d'Estrées, 35400 St-Malo ☎ 02 99 20 22 20 ⏲ Closed Christmas, 2 weeks mid-Jan ✋ €57–€69 (breakfast €8) ⓘ 15

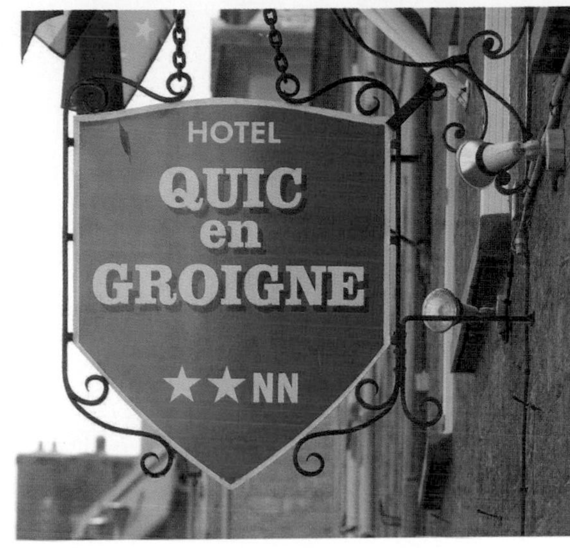

Above *St-Malo has a good choice of places to stay*

LE VALMARIN

www.levalmarin.com

An elegant 18th-century *malouinière* built by a wealthy ship-owner makes a distinguished setting for this hotel in the suburb of St-Servan. It stands in secluded, shady gardens on a hill near the church of Sainte-Croix. It's a lovely old place inside, its antique furnishings and period features suggesting a private country house rather than a hotel. The welcome is warm and the atmosphere utterly relaxing. Bedrooms are graciously individual and full of character. Breakfast can be served outside in fine weather. There's no restaurant, but plenty lie around nearby Port Solidor. Secure off-street parking is available (arrive before 10.30pm).

✉ 7 rue Jean XXIII, 35400 St-Malo ☎ 02 99 81 94 76 ✋ €95–€135 (breakfast €10) ⓘ 12

ST-MELOIR-DES-ONDES

TIREL GUÉRIN

www.tirel-guerin.com

This chic place is an unexpected find beside a tiny old-fashioned railway station on the main road south of Cancale. Now an acclaimed restaurant-with-rooms, both food and accommodation reach high standards. Immaculately kept throughout, it has beautiful gardens and superior leisure facilities, including a splendid indoor pool in an annexe wing. The classically elegant dining room is a popular venue for discerning patrons, especially at lunchtime. Bedrooms are spacious and very soignée, the suites and apartments much more expensive.

✉ Gare de la Gouesnière, 35350 St-Méloir-des-Ondes ☎ 02 99 89 10 46 ⏲ Closed late Dec–end Jan ✋ €82–€110 (breakfast €12) ⓘ 56, including 6 apartments and 12 suites 🏋 🏊 Indoor; sauna, Jacuzzi

LE CHÂTEAU RICHEUX

www.maisons-de-bricourt.com

Top chef Olivier Roellinger's family empire is based in Cancale, but this classy 1920s mansion lies about 5km (3 miles) down the coast (signed off the D155 near St-Benoît). It stands in a secluded clifftop park on the ruins of a medieval fortress, its huge windows framing wondrous vistas of the bay of Mont-St-Michel. Though grand and sophisticated, it's also very relaxing, with attentive and friendly staff. The lounge bar has stylish tan furnishings and an eye-catching boat model (guests may charter the splendid Roellinger yacht in summer). The *bistrot marin* called Le Coquillage serves predictably super seafood in an informal atmosphere. Bedrooms are luxuriously comfortable, with CD players and mosaic bathrooms.

✉ Le Point du Jour, 35350 St-Méloir-des-Ondes ☎ 02 99 89 64 76 ⏲ Closed Jan ✋ €165–€310 (breakfast €21) ⓘ 13, including 2 apartments

VITRÉ

LE PETIT BILLOT

www.hotel-vitre.com

You get a warm welcome from the cheerful *patronne* at this neat, clean place (part of the independent Citotel group) on the edge of the old town. It's a cream-painted building with blue shutters, on a main street within easy reach of the station and tourist office. Bedrooms are modern, but surprisingly varied in size and style. All have excellent little showers and are light and pleasing. Breakfast is served in a green-panelled room to the rear. The hotel shares premises with a recommendable restaurant called Le Potager. Though under separate management, good-value half-board terms can be arranged with this and another local restaurant.

✉ 5 bis place du Général Leclerc, 35500 Vitré ☎ 02 99 75 02 10 ⏲ Closed Christmas and New Year ✋ €48 (breakfast €7) ⓘ 21

PRACTICALITIES

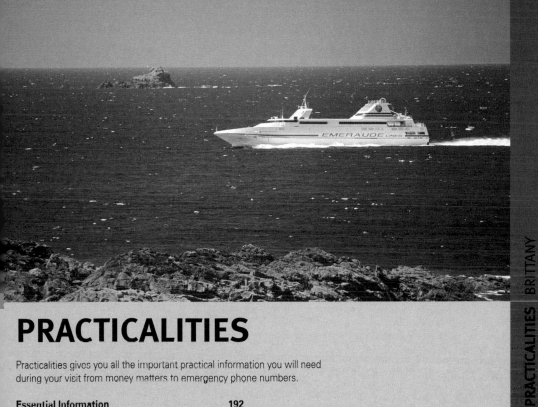

Practicalities gives you all the important practical information you will need during your visit from money matters to emergency phone numbers.

ESSENTIAL INFORMATION

WEATHER

» Brittany has a generally mild, dampish climate tempered by sea breezes. Some sheltered areas bathed by the Gulf Stream, such as the Golfe du Morbihan or the islands of Batz and Bréhat, enjoy a microclimate benign enough for vines and subtropical plants to flourish.

» Extremes of temperature are rare, but the weather is always unpredictable, and can change very quickly. Rain may occur at any time of year, but is most prevalent in autumn and winter. Short-lived bursts of frost and snow occasionally shock the flowering mimosa in winter, and gales assail the ocean coastline from time to time.

» Summer temperatures average just over 20°C (70°F), and are at their highest in August. Southern Brittany is warmest of all, with some 2,200 hours of sunshine a year, compared with just around 1,700 on the Channel coast.

» The interior, whose gentle hills are high enough to puncture Atlantic rain-clouds, is generally wetter than low-lying coastal zones, and has wider temperature variations.

» For up-to-date weather information on Brittany, visit the website www.meteo.fr

BREST

TEMPERATURE

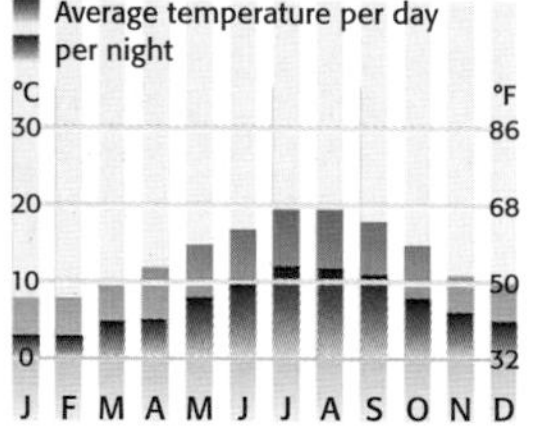

RAINFALL

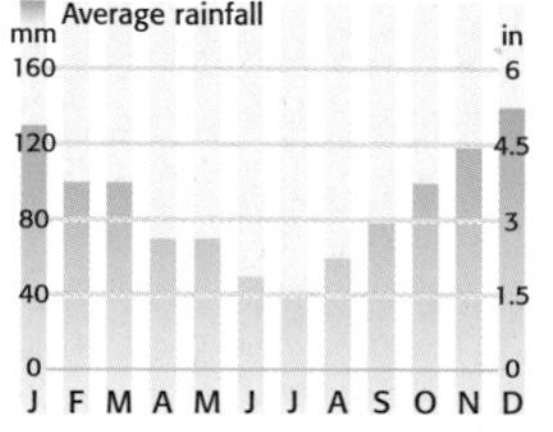

RENNES

TEMPERATURE

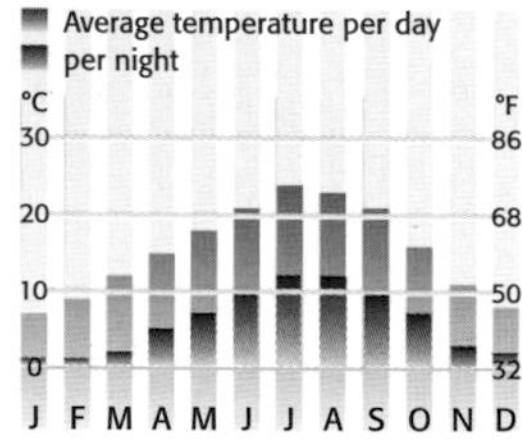

RAINFALL

WHEN TO GO

» In July and August, the beaches and campsites of the popular coastal resorts overflow with French families taking their traditional summer break. Prices soar, and traffic clogs the roads. It can be difficult to find a bed for the night, or a restaurant table. But the resorts are at their liveliest, providing a seamless round of happenings—regattas and boat-trips, open-air concerts, fireworks and son-et-lumière shows. The biggest festivals attract huge gatherings.

» To miss the crowds, try to avoid visiting Brittany in school holidays (British or French), and check whether your destination plans any festivals or events during your visit.

» Spring is always lovely in Brittany, when the cider orchards froth into blossom, hillsides are ablaze with gorse, and local markets display cornucopias of top-quality early vegetables. Autumn is a season of mellow fruitfulness, of apple-picking and mushroom-hunting. Late hydrangeas and geraniums still glow in gardens and window-boxes. Huge equinoctial tides continually reshape coastal views, and migrant birds stream through the skies.

» In the remote coastal locations of Brittany, or on offshore islands, many holiday establishments don't open until well after Easter, and pull down the shutters by the end of September.

» The enticing tropical appearance of Breton beaches can be deceptive. The shallow seas of Morbihan warm up a little by September, but in general sea temperatures stay cool all year.

» Many monuments and museums in France close on key national

TIME ZONES

CITY	TIME DIFFERENCE	TIME AT 12 NOON FRANCE
Amsterdam	0	12 noon
Berlin	0	12 noon
Brussels	0	12 noon
Chicago	-7	5am
Dublin	-1	11am
Johannesburg	+1*	1pm
London	-1	11am
Madrid	0	12 noon
Montréal	-6	6am
New York	-6	6am
Perth, Australia	+7*	7pm
Rome	0	12 noon
San Francisco	-9	3am
Sydney	+9*	9pm
Tokyo	+8*	8pm

Clocks in France go forward one hour on the last Sunday in March, until the last Sunday in October.

* One hour less during Summer Time.

CUSTOMS

From another EU country

Below are the guidelines for the quantity of goods you can bring to France from another EU country, for personal use:

- » 800 cigarettes
- » 400 cigarillos
- » 200 cigars
- » 1 kg of smoking tobacco
- » 110 litres of beer
- » 10 litres of spirits
- » 90 litres of wine (of which only 60 litres can be sparkling wine)
- » 20 litres of fortified wine

From a country outside the EU

You are entitled to the allowances shown below only if you travel with the goods and do not plan to sell them. If you come from outside the EU, check with your local customs and excise office what you can take home.

- » 200 cigarettes or 100 cigarillos or 50 cigars or 250gms of tobacco
- » 50cc/ml of perfume
- » 250cc/ml of eau de toilette
- » 2 litres of still table wine
- » 1 litre of spirits or strong liqueurs over 22% volume; or 2 litres of fortified wine, sparkling wine or other liqueurs
- » Up to €175 of all other goods

holidays (1 January, 1 May, 1 November, 11 November, 25 December), and bus and train services are much reduced.

WHAT TO TAKE

» The key things to remember are travel and health insurance documents, money, credit cards and any medication you'll need. If you plan to drive in France, take your driving licence and, if using your own car, the vehicle registration and insurance certificates.

» Take the details of emergency contacts, including the numbers to call if your credit cards are stolen. Make photocopies of your passport, insurance documents and tickets, in case of loss. Keep a note of your credit card numbers in case you need to report a theft to the police.

» Visitors from the UK and US will need adaptors for electrical equipment (▷ 194).

» There is a language guide, ▷ 216–221 of this book, but if you are keen to communicate in French a separate phrasebook may be helpful.

» A first aid kit is a useful precaution.

» Take wet-weather gear, some warm, windproof clothing, and comfortable, robust footwear.

» When visiting churches or cathedrals, wear suitably modest clothing—beachwear and shorts are not acceptable.

» A lightweight pair of binoculars is worth stowing away, and possibly a bird or flower identification guide.

DOCUMENTS AND CUSTOMS

» UK, US and Canadian visitors need a passport, but not a visa, for stays of up to three months. You should have at least six months' validity remaining on your passport. Citizens of EU countries that have National Identity cards need either a passport or National Identity card.

» For more information about visa and passport requirements, look up the French tourist office website (www.franceguide.com) or the French Embassy in the UK (www.frenchembassy.org.uk) or the General Consulate in the US (www.consulfrance-newyork.org).

» Before you travel, check visa and passport regulations since these are subject to change.

» Take a photocopy of the relevant pages of your passport to carry around with you, so you can leave your actual passport in your hotel safe. Always keep a separate note of your passport number and a photocopy of the information page.

LONGER STAYS

» UK and other EU citizens who want to stay longer than three months no longer need a *carte de séjour*. US and Canadian visitors should apply for a *carte de séjour* and a visa. For information call the Immigration Department of the French Consulate (see chart below).

TRAVEL INSURANCE

» Make sure you have full health and travel insurance before you set off.

» EU citizens (plus nationals of Iceland, Liechtenstein, Norway and Switzerland) are entitled to receive reduced-cost emergency health care within any member state if they have the relevant documentation. For Britons, this is the European Health Insurance Card (EHIC). However, comprehensive travel insurance is still advised for all visitors.

FRENCH EMBASSIES AND CONSULATES ABROAD

COUNTRY	ADDRESS	WEBSITE
Australia	31 Market Street, St. Martin Tower, Level 26, Sydney, NSW 2000 Tel (02) 92 61 57 79	www.ambafrance-au.org
Canada	1501 McGill College, Bureau 1000, Montréal, Quebec H3A 3M8 Tel 514 878-4385	www.consulfrance-montreal.org
Republic of Ireland	36 Ailesbury Road, Ballsbridge, Dublin 4. Tel 01 277 5000	www.ambafrance.ie
New Zealand	34–42 Manners Street, Wellington, 12th floor, PO Box 11-343 Tel 64 4384 2555	www.ambafrance-nz.org
UK	58 Knightsbridge, London, SW1X 7JT, Tel 020 7073 1000	www.ambafrance-uk.org
US (Los Angeles)	10390 Santa Monica Boulevard, Suite 4–10, Los Angeles CA 90025 Tel 310/235-3200	www.consulfrance-losangeles.org
US (New York)	934 Fifth Avenue, New York, NY 10021. Tel 212/606-3600	www.consulfrance-newyork.org

MONEY MATTERS

THE EURO

» France is one of 15 European countries that have adopted the euro as the official currency. Euro notes and coins were introduced in January 2002, replacing the former currency, the French franc.

BEFORE YOU GO

» It is advisable to use a combination of cash, traveller's cheques and credit cards rather than relying on only one means of payment during your trip. Bear in mind that the number of banks and other outlets offering exchange facilities has plummeted since the introduction of the euro, so organize some euros in advance and take a credit card with you.

» Check with your credit and/or debit card company that your card can be used to withdraw cash from Automated Teller Machines (ATMs) in France. It is also worth checking what fee will be charged for this and what number you should ring if your card is stolen.

» Traveller's cheques are a safer way of bringing in money as you can claim a refund if they are stolen—but commission can be high when you cash them.

ATMS

» ATMs are common in France, often with on-screen instructions in a choice of languages. Among the cards accepted are Visa, MasterCard and Diners Club. You'll need a four-digit numerical PIN.

» Your card issuer will probably charge you for withdrawing cash.

» Some British credit cards are still not accepted in certain automatic machines in France because the 'smart' technology doesn't match. Recent chip and pin cards should be more compatible.

BANKS

» Hours vary, but usual opening hours are Monday to Friday 8.30 or 9–12 and 2–5, although banks in cities may not close for lunch.

» In smaller towns and villages banks often close on Mondays but open on Saturday mornings instead.

» Banks close at noon on the day before a national holiday, as well as on the holiday itself. Only banks with *change* signs change traveller's cheques or foreign currency and you'll need your passport to do this.

BUREAUX DE CHANGE

» Bureaux de Change have longer opening hours than banks, but the exchange rates may not be as good. You'll find them at airports, ferry terminals, large railway stations and in major cities.

» Avoid changing large amounts of traveller's cheques at hotels as the rates may not be competitive.

CREDIT CARDS

» Most restaurants, shops and hotels accept credit cards, although some have a minimum spending limit.

TAXES

» Non-EU residents can claim a sales tax refund *(détaxe)* of 12 per cent on certain purchases, although you must have spent more than €175 in one shop, at one time. Ask the store for the relevant forms, which the trader should complete and stamp. Give these forms to customs when you leave the country, along with the receipts, and they will be stamped. Post the forms back to the shop and they will either refund your credit card account or send you a cheque.

» Remember that you may have to show the goods to Customs when you leave France, so keep them within easy reach.

» Exempt products include food and drink, medicine, tobacco, unset gems, works of art and antiques.

» The company Global Refund offers a reimbursement service (01 41 61 51 51; www.globalrefund.com).

Above *Most ATMs have instructions in a choice of languages*

WIRING MONEY

» In an emergency, you can have money wired to you from your home country, but this can be expensive (as agents charge a fee for the service) and time-consuming.

» You can send and receive money via agents such as Western Union (www.westernunion.com) and Travelex (www.travelex.com).

PRICES OF EVERYDAY ITEMS		
Takeout sandwich		€3–€5
Bottle of mineral water	(from a shop, 0.5 litres)	€0.30–€0.60
Cup of coffee	(from a café, *espresso)*	€1.50–€2.50
	(Crème, larger cup with milk)	€2–€3
Beer	*(Un demi,* half a litre)	€2.50–€3.50
Glass of house wine		€2.50–€3.50
French national newspaper		€1–€1.50
International newspaper		€2–€3
Litre of fuel	(98 unleaded)	€1.50
	(diesel)	€1.20

» Money can be wired from bank to bank, which takes up to two working days, or through Travelex and Western Union, which is normally faster.

CONCESSIONS

» If you are a student or teacher, apply to the International Student Travel Confederation (www.isic.org) in your own country for an International Student Identity Card (ISIC). This entitles you to various reductions during your visit.
» Seniors often get reduced-rate tickets on public transport and on admission to museums and sights by showing a valid identity card or passport.
» Small children often have free entry to sights.

POST OFFICES

» Some post offices have ATMs.
» Cards accepted are listed on each dispenser and instructions are available in English.
» Money can be wired, through Western Union, via most post offices, and generally takes only a few minutes to receive.
» International Money Orders can be sent from all post offices (for a fee).
» Some larger post offices offer exchange services in the following currencies: American, Australian and Canadian dollars, yen, British pounds sterling, Swiss francs, Swedish kronor, and Danish and Norwegian kroner.

TIPS

» Try to avoid using higher denomination notes when paying taxi drivers and when buying low-cost items in smaller shops.
» Never carry money or credit cards in back pockets, or other places that are easy targets for thieves.
» Keep your spare money and traveller's cheques in your hotel safe *(coffre-fort)* until you need them.
» Check the exchange rates for traveller's cheques and cash offered in post offices as well as in banks, as banks do not always offer the best rate.
» In France, Mastercard is sometimes known as Eurocard and Visa is known as Carte Bleue.
» Some smaller hotels and inns don't accept credit cards, so find out before you check in.

TIPPING GUIDE	
Restaurants (service included)	Change *
Hotels (service included)	Change *
Cafés (service included)	Change *
Taxis	10 per cent
Tour guides	€1–€2
Porters	€1–€2
Hairdressers	€1–€2
Cloakroom attendants	50c
Toilets	Change
Usherettes	50c

* Or more if you are impressed with the level of service

HEALTH

BEFORE YOU GO

» EU citizens receive reduced-cost healthcare in France with the relevant documentation. For UK citizens, this is the European Health Insurance Card (EHIC). An application form is available in post offices. A leaflet on health advice for travellers is also available, explaining in full the usage of EHIC, and including the appropriate form should you need to make a claim. Full health insurance is still strongly advised. For all other countries full insurance is a must.

» Make sure you are up to date with anti-tetanus boosters. Bring any medication you need with you and pack a first aid kit. In summer, always bring sun-protection cream.

IF YOU NEED TREATMENT

» The French national health system is complex. Any salaried French citizen who receives treatment by a doctor or public hospital can be reimbursed by up to 70 per cent. The same is true if you are an EU citizen and have a valid EHIC.

» If you are relying only on EHIC, rather than travel insurance, make sure the doctor you see is part of the French national health service (a *conventionné)*, rather than the private system, otherwise you may face extra charges. In any case, you will have to pay up front for the consultation and treatment. To reclaim part of these costs, send the *feuille de soins* (a statement from the doctor) and your EHIC claim form to the Caisse Primaire d'Assurance-Maladie (state health insurance office) before you leave the country. Call 0820 904 175 to find the nearest office. You should also attach the labels of any medicine you have to buy.

» If you have to stay overnight in a public hospital, you will have to pay 25 per cent of the treatment costs, as well as a daily charge *(forfait journalier)*. These are not refundable. It is better to have full health insurance than to rely on the EHIC.

» Citizens of non-EU countries must have full health insurance.

» If you are hospitalized and have insurance, ask to see the *assistante sociale* to arrange reimbursement of the costs directly through your insurers.

» In an emergency, dial 15 for Service d'Aide Médicale d'Urgence (SAMU) unit (ambulance). They work closely with hospital emergency units and are accompanied by trained medical personnel.

» If you are able to get yourself to a hospital, make sure it has a casualty or emergency department *(urgences)*.

Opposite *Make sure any seafood you buy is fresh, particularly in the summer*
Below *The sun can be strong in Brittany; remember to pack high-factor sun block*

FINDING A DOCTOR

» In a medical emergency, your hotel should be able to help find a hospital or an English-speaking doctor. The number of the regional *SOS Médecins* (a duty-rota of doctors on call) is in the phonebook, also listed in local newspapers; otherwise call 15 for an ambulance. Main hospitals with casualty (emergency) units are located in all major cities—ask for the nearest *centre hospitalier* or *services des urgences*.

» Any pharmacy should be able to direct you to a doctor (look for the green cross sign—if it is closed, a card in the window will tell you where the nearest one is). Pharmacists are trained to deal with minor medical problems and can provide first aid as well as over-the-counter medication.

FINDING A HOSPITAL

» Hospitals are listed in the phone book under *Hôpitaux*, and round-the-clock emergency services are called *urgences*.

» Private hospitals are a lot more expensive than public ones and treatment is not necessarily better. If you choose a private hospital, check that you are covered for the costs before receiving treatment.

DENTAL TREATMENT

» EU citizens can receive reduced-cost emergency dental treatment with their EHIC, although insurance

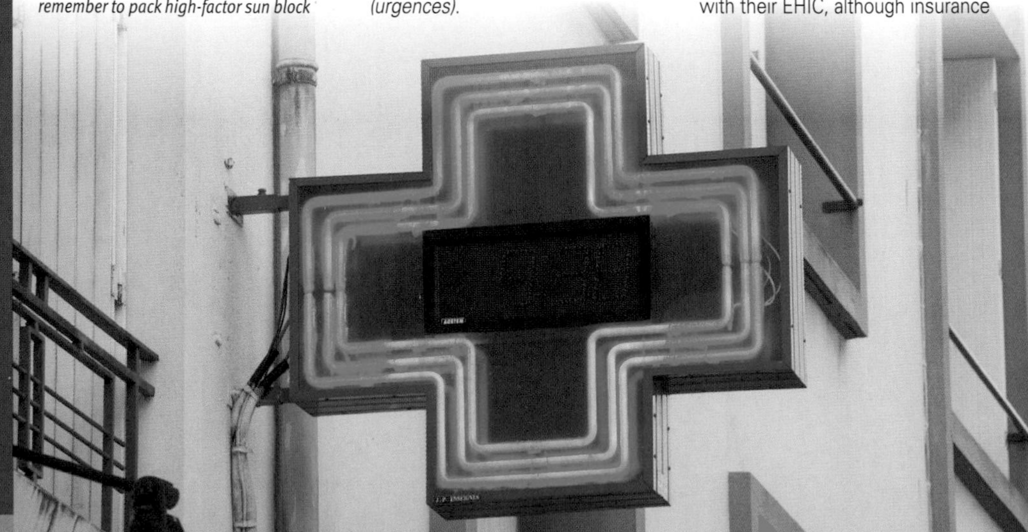

is still advised. The reclaim procedure is the same as for general medical treatment.

» Other visitors should check that their insurance covers dental treatment. It's a good idea to have a dental check-up before your trip.

PHARMACIES

» A pharmacy *(pharmacie)* will have an illuminated green cross outside (above). Most are open Mon–Sat 9–7 or 8, but when closed they usually post details on the door of another pharmacy that is open later (called the *pharmacie de garde)*.

» Pharmacists are highly qualified and provide first aid, as well as supplying medication (some drugs are by prescription, or *ordonnance*, only). But they cannot dispense prescriptions written by doctors outside the French health system, so bring sufficient supplies of any prescribed drugs you need.

» Some pharmacists speak English and can direct you to local doctors or specialists.

» They also sell a range of health-related items, although it is less expensive to go to the supermarket for items such as soap, toothbrushes and razors.

» Some commonly used medicines sold in supermarkets at home (such as aspirins and cold remedies) can be bought only in pharmacies in France.

TAP WATER

» Tap water is safe to drink and restaurants will often bring a carafe of water to the table, although most French people opt instead for bottled water.

» In public places look for the sign *eau potable* (drinking water). Don't drink from anything marked *eau non potable*.

SUMMER HAZARDS

» The sun can be strong in Brittany between May and September, so pack a high-factor sun block. An effective insect repellent is useful, although insect bites are more likely to be irritating than dangerous.

HEALTHY FLYING

» If you are visiting France from the US, Australia or New Zealand, you may be concerned about the effect of long-haul flights on your health. The most widely publicized concern is Deep Vein Thrombosis, or DVT. DVT occurs when a blood clot forms in the body's deep veins, particularly in the legs. The clot can move around the bloodstream and could be fatal.

» Those most at risk include the elderly, pregnant women and those using the contraceptive pill, smokers and the overweight. If you are at increased risk of DVT see your doctor before departing. Flying increases the likelihood of DVT because passengers are often seated in a cramped position for long periods of time and may become dehydrated.

Drink water (not alcohol).
Don't stay immobile for hours at a time.
Stretch and exercise your legs periodically.
Do wear elastic flight socks, which support veins and reduce the chances of a clot forming.

Exercises

1 ankle rotations	2 calf stretches	3 knee lifts
Lift feet off the floor. Draw a circle with the toes, moving one foot clockwise and the other counterclockwise	Start with heel on the floor and point foot upward as high as you can. Then lift heels high, keeping balls of feet on the floor	Lift leg with knee bent while contracting your thigh muscle. Then straighten leg, pressing foot flat to the floor

Other health hazards for flyers are airborne diseases and bugs spread by the plane's air-conditioning system. These are largely unavoidable, but if you have a serious medical condition seek advice from a doctor before setting off.

» The likelihood of contracting food poisoning from shellfish is greater in the summer when ambient temperatures are higher. Toxic algal blooms (sudden proliferations of microscopic sea organisms) can sometimes affect fish—look out for local warnings.

ALTERNATIVE MEDICAL TREATMENT

» Alternative medicine, such as homeopathy, is generally available from most pharmacies.

» Alternative treatment is available and is on the increase, although chiropractics and reflexology are not widespread. Useful websites include www.chiropratique.org (the Association Française de Chiropratique), www.efcam.eu (European Forum for Complementary and Alternative Medicine) and www. naturosante.com (a site about alternative medical treatments).

BASICS

CAR RENTAL

» The absence of satisfactory public transport makes driving the only practical way to explore the rural villages and remote countryside of Brittany in depth, though it affords little pleasure in the larger cities. Congestion and parking can be a real headache in popular coastal areas in high season.

» It is often best to reserve a car in advance, making sure that full insurance is included in the package. You can also arrange car rental through some travel agents when you make your travel arrangements.

» For information on driving, ▷ 32–35.

CHILDREN

» Look for service stations (selling food and fuel, with play areas) or *aires* (scenic pull-ins with lavatories and space to run around) on *autoroutes* and expressways, where children can stretch their legs.

» Most restaurants welcome children, although not many have highchairs and children's menus are not common outside family-friendly tourist resorts, so it's probably best to aim for family-style bistros where facilities are better and staff are more helpful.

» If you need special facilities in your hotel, such as a cot, or a child seat in your rented car, reserve them in advance.

» For baby-changing facilities while out and about, try the restrooms in department stores and the larger museums.

» Supermarkets and pharmacies sell nappies (diapers) and baby food, although they are often closed on a Sunday so make sure you stock up.

» Entrance to museums is often free to young children.

ELECTRICITY

» Voltage in France is 220 volts. Sockets take plugs with two round pins. UK electrical equipment will need an adaptor plug, which you can buy at airport and Eurostar terminals. American appliances using 110–120 volts will need an adaptor and a transformer. Equipment that is dual voltage should need only an adaptor.

LAUNDRY

» There are two options if you need a laundry service—a *laverie automatique* (laundrette) and a *pressing/nettoyage à sec* (dry-cleaners). Dry-cleaners are easier to find, but are more expensive. Some have an economy service, but this is not recommended for your best silk jacket.

Below *The local churches and parish closes are great attractions*

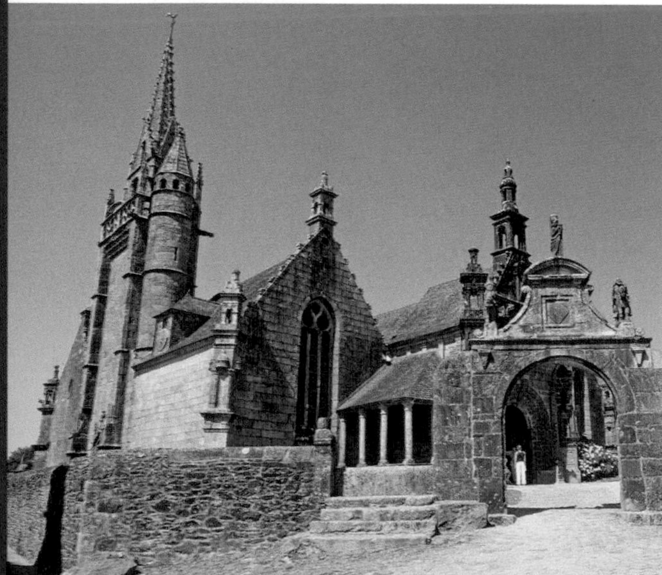

LOCAL WAYS

» Greetings are often quite formal in France. Offer to shake hands when you are introduced to someone, and use *vous* rather than *tu*. It is polite to use *Monsieur, Madame* or *Mademoiselle* when speaking to people you don't know. For very young women and teenage girls use *Mademoiselle*, otherwise use *Madame*.

» The continental kiss is a common form of greeting between friends, and the number of times friends kiss each other on the cheek varies from region to region.

» Address waiters and waitresses as *Monsieur, Madame* or *Mademoiselle* when you are trying to attract their attention.

» Communicating in French is always the best option, even if you can manage only *bonjour, s'il vous plaît* and *merci* (hello, please and thank you). The French are protective of their language and your efforts to speak it will be appreciated. If your knowledge of French is limited, ask the fail-safe *Parlez-vous anglais?* and hope the answer is *oui*.

» Remember that it is traditional to say hello as you enter a shop, bar or café, particularly in small towns and villages, and that you are greeting your fellow customers as well as the proprietor. For a mixed audience, a *Bonjour Messieurs Dames* is the appropriate phrase. When it is your turn to be served, greet the server with *Bonjour Madame* or *Bonjour Monsieur*, then don't forget to say *merci* and *au revoir* or *bonne-journée* as you leave.

MEASUREMENTS

» France uses the metric system. Road distances are measured in kilometres, fuel is sold by the litre and food is weighed in grams and kilograms.

CONVERSION CHART		
From	**To**	**Multiply by**
Inches	Centimetres	2.54
Centimetres	Inches	0.3937
Feet	Metres	0.3048
Metres	Feet	3.2810
Yards	Metres	0.9144
Metres	Yards	1.0940
Miles	Kilometres	1.6090
Kilometres	Miles	0.6214
Acres	Hectares	0.4047
Hectares	Acres	2.4710
Gallons	Litres	4.5460
Litres	Gallons	0.2200
Ounces	Grams	28.35
Grams	Ounces	0.0353
Pounds	Grams	453.6
Grams	Pounds	0.0022
Pounds	Kilograms	0.4536
Kilograms	Pounds	2.205
Tons	Tonnes	1.0160
Tonnes	Tons	0.9842

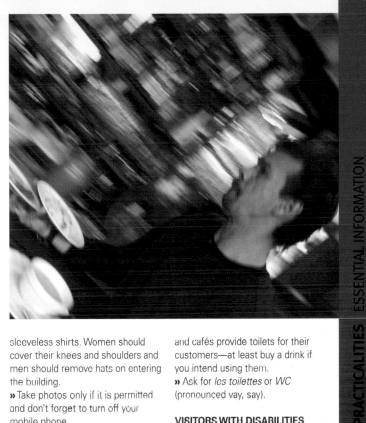

PLACES OF WORSHIP

» Some of France's greatest architectural treasures are the idiosyncratic parish churches and closes of western Brittany.

» They have become so popular as visitor attractions that it's easy to forget that they are still active places of worship (western Brittany, in particular, is devoutly Catholic). It's important to respect these churches and worshippers by dressing appropriately. Men should wear long trousers and should avoid sleeveless shirts. Women should cover their knees and shoulders and men should remove hats on entering the building.

» Take photos only if it is permitted and don't forget to turn off your mobile phone.

SMOKING

» Smoking is now officially banned in all public places in France, including cafés, bars and restaurants. Despite the €75 fine imposed for infringements, the rule is still ignored in some places. But polls suggest that most people in France, even smokers, are in favour of the ban.

TOILETS

» Today's modern unisex public toilets are a vast improvement on previous facilities. Coin-operated and self-cleaning, you can find them in most large cities.

» In smaller towns and villages, free public toilets can normally be found by the market square or near tourist offices, although cleanliness varies.

» Facilities in museums and other visitor attractions generally reach a good standard, so take advantage of them while you can. Restaurants and cafés provide toilets for their customers—at least buy a drink if you intend using them.

» Ask for *les toilettes* or *WC* (pronounced vay, say).

VISITORS WITH DISABILITIES

» France has made some headway in recent years in providing access and facilities for visitors with disabilities. All new buildings must take the needs of people with special requirements into account, and, where possible, existing buildings such as town halls, airports and train stations must be adapted with ramps and automatic doors. But the cobbled, hilly streets of many picturesque historic towns and villages in Brittany and Normandy can be a trial for wheelchair-users.

» Some visitor offices, museums and restaurants that are in historic, protected buildings are still not fully accessible. A telephone call before going to a restaurant is a good idea to organize a more easily accessible table.

» For organizations that give advice to people with disabilities, ▷ 40.

COMMUNICATION

TELEPHONING

French numbers All numbers in France have ten digits. The country is divided into five regional zones, indicated by the first two digits of the phone number (see chart below). You must dial these two digits even if you are calling from within the zone. Numbers in Brittany begin with 02.

International calls To call France from the UK dial 00 33, then drop the first zero from the 10-digit number. To call the UK from France, dial 00 44, then drop the first zero from the area code. To call France from the US, dial 011 33, then drop the first zero from the 10-digit number. To call the US from France, dial 00 1, followed by the number.

Call charges For calls within France, peak period is from 8am to 7pm, Monday to Friday. Numbers beginning with 08 have special rates. 0800 or 0805 numbers are free. 0810 and 0811 numbers are charged at local rate. Other 08 numbers cost more than national calls—sometimes considerably more.

PAYPHONES

» Nearly all public payphones in France use a phone card *(télécarte)* rather than coins. You can purchase these at post offices, *tabacs*, newsagents and France Telecom shops. Cards are rated at 50 or 120 units. You do not need to pay for the call if you are telephoning an emergency number.

» If the telephone displays the blue bell sign, this means that you can receive incoming calls.

MOBILE PHONES

You can usually use your own mobile, but there are a few points to check before leaving:

» Check the call charges, which can rise dramatically when you use your phone abroad for both incoming and outgoing calls.

» Make sure the numbers memorized in your directory are in the international format.

GUIDE PRICES

TYPE OF CALL	INITIAL CHARGE	EACH FURTHER MINUTE
Local, peak	€0.091 (1 min)	€0.033
Local, off-peak	€0.091 (1 min)	€0.018
National, peak	€0.112 (39 sec)	€0.091
National, off-peak	€0.112 (39sec)	€0.061
Calling the UK, off-peak	€0.11 (15 sec)	€0.12
Calling the US, off-peak	€0.11 (27 sec)	€0.15

SENDING A LETTER

» You can buy stamps *(timbres)* for a letter *(lettre)* or a postcard *(carte postale)* at post offices and *tabacs*. Write *par avion* (by air) on the envelope or postcard.

» If you want registered post, ask at the post office for the letter to be sent *recommandé*. For a parcel *(colis)*, you can choose either *prioritaire* (priority) or the less expensive, but slower, *économique*.

» Mailboxes are yellow. In larger cities, some have two sections, one for the local *département*, and another for national and international mail *(autres départements/étranger)*. Mail sent from France should take up to five days to arrive.

POST OFFICES

» Post offices *(bureaux de poste)* are well signposted. The postal service is known as La Poste.

» Opening hours are generally Monday to Friday 8–5 or 6, Saturday 8–12. Some branches close for lunch.

» Facilities usually include phone booths, photocopiers, fax *(télécopieur)* and access to the Minitel directory service.

» Money can be wired through Western Union via most post offices, and international money orders can be sent from post offices (a charge is payable). Many also have exchange services in the following currencies: American, Australian and Canadian dollars, yen, British pounds sterling, Swiss francs, Swedish kronor, and Danish and Norwegian kroner.

INTERNET ACCESS

» Many towns have internet cafés. Look for the *Cyberposte* sign in larger post offices, or check www.cyberposte.com. You buy a card at the counter, which can be recharged. Certain hotels, libraries, supermarkets, bars and tourist offices also have internet terminals, many operated by France Telecom using a *télécarte* (look for the word *Borne)*.

COUNTRY CODES FROM FRANCE

Australia	00 61
Belgium	00 32
Canada	00 1
Germany	00 49
Republic of Ireland	00 353
Italy	00 39
Monaco	00 377
Netherlands	00 31
New Zealand	00 64
Spain	00 34
Sweden	00 46
UK	00 44
US	00 1

PREFIXES

00	International
01	Île-de-France (including Paris)
02	Northwest France
03	Northeast France
04	Southeast France
05	Southwest France
06	Mobile telephone numbers
0800/0805	Toll-free
08	Special-rate numbers

POSTAGE RATES FOR LETTERS

Within France	€0.55
To Western Europe	€0.65
To Eastern Europe	€0.85
To America	€0.85
To Africa	€0.85
To Asia	€0.85
To Australia	€0.85

FINDING HELP

Most visits to northwestern France are trouble-free, but make sure you have adequate insurance to cover any health emergencies, thefts or legal costs that may arise. If you do become a victim of crime, it is most likely to be at the hands of a pickpocket, so always keep your money and mobile phones safely tucked away.

PERSONAL SECURITY

» Take a note of your traveller's cheque numbers and keep it separate from the cheques themselves, as you will need it to make a claim in case of loss.

» Don't keep wallets, purses or mobile phones in the back pockets of trousers, or anywhere else that is easily accessible to thieves. Money belts and bags worn around the waist are targets, as thieves know you are likely to have valuables in them. Always keep an eye on your bags and cameras in restaurants, bars and on the Métro, and hold cameras and bags, fastener inwards, close to you when you are walking in the streets.

» Thieves and pickpockets are especially fond of crowded places, such as rush-hour buses and trains, busy markets or popular festivals. Beware if someone bumps into you—it may be a ploy to distract you while someone else snatches your money.

» If you are the victim of theft, you must report it at the local police station *(commissariat)* if you want to claim on your insurance. Keep hold of the statement the police give you. You must also contact your credit card company as soon as possible to cancel any stolen cards.

» Keep valuable items in your hotel safe *(coffre-fort)*.

» When you park your car, don't leave anything of value inside. It's even risky leaving anything at all in view that may attract the interest of a thief. Carry your belongings with you or leave them behind.

» On trains, try to keep your luggage where you can see it.

LOSS OF PASSPORT

» Always keep a separate note of your passport number and a photocopy of the page that carries your details, in case of loss or theft. You can also scan the relevant pages of your passport and then email them to yourself at an email account that you can access anywhere (such as www.hotmail.com).

» If you do lose your passport or it is stolen, report it to the police and then contact your nearest embassy or consulate.

POLICE

» There are various types of police officer in France. The two main forces are the Police Nationale, who are under the control of the local mayor, and the Gendarmerie Nationale, who you often see at airports.

» You are likely to encounter the armed CRS riot police only at a demonstration.

» In France, the police have wide powers of stop and search. It is wise to carry your passport in case a police officer stops you and requests your ID.

FIRE

» The French fire brigade deals with a number of emergencies in addition to actual fires. These range from stranded cats to road accidents and gas leaks. They are trained to give first aid.

EMBASSIES AND CONSULATES IN PARIS

» Most national embassies are in the capital (see chart below). There is no UK consular assistance anywhere in Brittany, but the US has an American Presence Post at 30 quai Duguay Trouin, 35000 Rennes, tel 02 23 44 09 60.

EMERGENCY NUMBERS	
112	General emergency number
15	Ambulance
17	Police
18	Fire

EMBASSIES AND CONSULATES IN PARIS		
COUNTRY	**ADDRESS**	**WEBSITE**
Australia	4 rue Jean-Rey, 75015. Tel 01 40 59 33 00	www.france.embassy.gov.au
Canada	35 avenue Montaigne, 75008 Tel 01 44 43 29 00	www.dfait-maeci.gc.ca
Germany	13–15 avenue Franklin Roosevelt, 75008 Tel 01 53 83 45 00	www.paris-diplo.de
Ireland	12 avenue Foch, 75116. Tel 01 44 17 67 00	www.embassyofirelandparis.com
Italy	51 rue de Varenne, 75007 Tel 01 49 54 03 00	www.ambparigi.esteri.it
Spain	22 avenue Marceau, 75008 Tel 01 44 43 18 00	www.amb-espagne.fr
UK	35 rue du Faubourg-St-Honoré, 75008 Tel 01 44 51 31 00	www.amb-grandebretagne.fr
US	2 avenue Gabriel, 75008 Tel 01 43 12 22 22	www.amb-usa.fr

OPENING TIMES AND TOURIST OFFICES

TICKETS

» Many popular tourist towns, for example, Vitré or Fougères in Brittany, provide a reduced-rate card or pass for entry to the main sights and museums. Some schemes include other benefits, such as low-cost transport, a free guided tour, a boat-trip or a *petit-train* ride. Ask the tourist office for details of any inclusive deals.

» For information on transport tickets, ▷ 36–39.

» Students with an International Student Identity Card (ISIC) and seniors get reduced-price entry at some museums.

» For information on show and concert tickets, ▷ 210.

TOURIST OFFICES

» France has a complex but generally efficient tourist information system. At the top end of the scale is the centralized regional office known as Comité Régional de Tourisme. In Brittany, the head office is in Rennes. This and their subordinate Comités Départementaux (one in each *département*) mostly handle postal, fax or telephone enquiries, some from overseas, rather than face-to-face encounters.

» Visitors are much more likely to have direct contact with the *offices de tourisme* or *syndicats d'initiative* in individual towns and villages, where you can collect all sorts of maps, leaflets and brochures on the attractions of the local area. Just about everywhere you may want to visit in France has some kind of tourist office (often well-signed or highly visible on the main square by the church).

» A useful document is a *Guide Pratique*, an informative listing of more or less everything a town has to offer from dentists to DIY shops, rather than glossy pictures. Accommodation brochures and public transport timetables are generally published separately, however.

» Most promotional information can be obtained free of charge, but you may have to pay for guidebooks, detailed touring maps or walks guides. Some brochures are available in English (though occasionally the translation can appear more baffling than the *version originale)*.

» Tourist offices can book accommodation for you, and sometimes sell tickets for excursions or events. Some have internet points, or provide exchange facilities.

» A sign with a letter 'i' ('information' logo) on it may simply denote a display board with a local map and other information such as hotel listings, rather than an office.

» If you arrive when a tourist office is closed (perhaps on a Sunday), a local hotel may be able to provide a guide or map of the town, or information leaflets. These are sometimes available at museums or tourist attractions, and of course, passers-by may be only too happy to tell you about their home town.

» Other kinds of tourist office include small seasonal *Points d'Information*, commercially operated *Maisons du Tourisme* and *Pays d'Acceuil Touristiques*, which provide excellent regional information by post or email but are not generally open to the public.

» The French government tourist offices overseas are generally called Maisons de la France.

OPENING TIMES		
Banks	Usual opening hours are Monday to Friday 9–12, 2–5, but these can vary	Banks close at noon on the day before a national holiday, as well as on the holiday itself.
Shops	Food shops are open Tuesday to Friday 7 or 8am–6.30 or 7.30pm.	Some close all day Monday while others will open in the afternoon only. On Saturday and Sunday they may open mornings only. Smaller shops tend to close at lunchtime from 12–2. Bakers *(boulangerie)* open on Sunday mornings and supermarkets and hypermarkets are open six days a week and have long business hours, opening at about 9am and staying open until 9 or 10pm, but closing on Sundays. Some also remain closed on Monday mornings.
Museums	Off-season, most municipal museums are closed on Monday, and some national museums close on Tuesday, but in high season they are generally open every day.	If you are planning to travel any distance for a special museum, ring in advance to check it is open. Sometimes public holidays, local festivals or renovation works may cause unexpected closures.
Restaurants	Lunch is generally served from 12–2 or 2.30 and dinner from 7.30–10 or 11.	Restaurants generally take at least one day off a week (often Sunday or Monday) except in high season (July and August), when they stay open longer hours. Except in larger business towns, many restaurants close completely from November to Easter.
Post offices	These generally open Monday to Friday 8–5, 6 or 7 weekdays and 8–noon on Saturday.	Small branches may close for lunch.
Pharmacies	Most are open Monday to Saturday 9–7 or 8.	They all display a list of local pharmacies that open later and on a Sunday.

Above *There are tourist offices in many towns throughout Brittany where you will find useful local information*

USEFUL WEBSITES

www.aeroport.fr
Information on all of France's airports. (French)

www.fodors.com
A comprehensive travel-planning site that lets you research prices, reserve air tickets and put questions to fellow visitors. (English)

www.franceguide.com
Practical advice from the French Tourist Office on everything from arriving in France to buying a property. The site also has features on holidays and attractions. (French, English, German, Spanish, Italian, Dutch, Portuguese)

www.francetourism.com
The official US website of the French Government Tourist Office. (English)

www.lemonde.fr
Catch up on current events on the site of *Le Monde* newspaper. (French)

www.meteo.fr/meteonet
Weather forecasts for France. (French, English and Spanish)

www.monum.fr
Find out more about some of France's most historic monuments, on the site of the Centre des Monuments Nationaux. (French and English)

www.pagesjaunes.fr
France's Yellow Pages online. (French and English)

www.radio-france.fr
News, music and sport. (French)

www.theAA.com
The AA website contains a route planner, helpful if you are driving in France. You can also order maps of the country. (English)

www.tourist-office.org
Lists details of every tourist information office in France. (French)

Other websites are listed alongside the relevant sights and towns in the Sights section, and in the On the Move section.

Important ones include:
www.brittanytourism.com
www.fncrt.com
www.tourisme.fr
www.discoverbrittany.com
www.fco.gov.uk
www.cotesdarmor.com
www.finisteretourisme.com
www.bretagne35.com
www.morbihan.com
www.bretagne.com

MEDIA

TELEVISION

» France has seven terrestrial television stations, including the nationally owned and operated channels 2 and 3, the privately owned 1 and 6, and the Franco-German ARTE (channel 5). Almost all the shows are in French. There are commercials on all terrestrial channels except ARTE.

» TF1 has news, recent American and French films, soaps and shows.

» France 2 has news, recent French and foreign films, soaps, shows and documentaries.

» France 3, a regional and national channel, has regional and national news, regional shows, documentaries, mostly French films and, once a week, a film in its original language.

» ARTE is a Franco-German channel operating with shows in French and German. International films are shown in their original language and there are also cultural documentaries.

» M6 shows a lot of low-budget films and past American sitcoms and soaps. There are also some interesting documentaries.

» Digital television has now taken off in France. More than 100 channels are on offer either through satellite or cable.

» If the TV listings mention VO *(version originale)*, the show or film will be in the language in which it was made, with French subtitles (Channel 3 usually screens a good VO film every Sunday at around midnight).

» Note that French television channels do not always keep exactly to schedule.

» Many hotels now provide a basic cable service; this may include Sky or Eurosport, BBC World and CNN. Cable channels now offer multilingual versions of some shows. Ask at your hotel how to use this option as the mechanics vary.

» The commercial-free ARTE usually offers a choice between French and German as the main language for its cultural shows.

CABLE TV

Depending on what cable option your hotel has, you may have some of the following channels:

BBC World	News and magazine reports of international interest
Canal+	Shows recent films (some in the original language)
MTV	Contemporary music channel
MCM	The French version of MTV
Eurosport or Infosport	For major sporting events
Planète	Nature and science documentaries
RAI Uno	Italian
TVE 1	Spanish
Euronews	A European all-news channel
LCI	All news in French
Canal Jimmy	Popular British and American shows in English or multilingual versions
Paris Première	A cultural channel with some films in English
Canal J	Children's shows until 8pm
Téva	A women's channel that runs some English-language shows

RADIO

» French radio stations are available mainly on FM wave lengths, with a few international stations on LW. All FM stations are in French.

Stations include:

» Chérie FM: 91.3 FM; French mainstream pop, news, reports.

» France Info: 105.5 FM; news bulletins every 15 minutes.

» France Musique: 91.7 FM; classical and jazz music, concerts, news.

» NRJ: 100.3 FM; French and international pop, techno, rap, R'n'B.

» Radio Classique: 101.1 FM; classical music.

» Skyrock: 96 FM; rap, hip-hop, R'n'B.

» BBC Radio 4 198 kHz MW; news, current affairs, drama, (reception is patchy in northwestern France).

» BBC Five Live 909 kHz MW; news and sport, (reception is patchy in northwestern France).

» BBC World Service 648 kHz LW.

NEWSPAPERS

» In tourist areas and the major cities you can buy the main English dailies, sometimes a day old, at a price premium.

» *The Economist, USA Today* and *The Wall Street Journal* can be found at news-stands in cities, along with the *International Herald Tribune,* which reports international news from a US standpoint.

» You may be disappointed to find an international edition of your preferred paper rather than the one you would get at home.

» Most French cities and regions have their own newspapers. In Brittany, you'll find the popular daily *Ouest France* and the Morlaix-based *Le Télégramme,* plus regional periodicals like *Ar Men* and *Bretagne Magazine.*

» Leading local newspapers play an active part in pressure politics, though the issues of some may seem parochial to the outsider.

» If you want to find out what's happening in a French city during your stay, consult the 'what's on' supplements that are issued with some newspapers.

» Listings magazines in Brittany include Côtes d'Armor's *Le Cri de l'Ormeau.* You'll often see these distributed free of charge in tourist offices, cafés and hotels.

» Weekly news magazines include *Le Nouvel Observateur, Le Point* and *L'Express.*

» When you want celebrity gossip and lots of pictures, buy *Paris Match, Voici* or *Gala.*

NEWSPAPERS

French daily newspapers have clear political leanings.

Le Monde
Until recently this stately paper, left-of-centre, refused to run photos and used illustrations.

Libération
This lively youth-focused paper is more clearly leftist.

L'Humanité
Left wing.

Le Figaro
Mainstream conservative daily.

Ouest France
A popular daily paper covering Brittany, Lower Normandy and Pays de la Loire

Journal du Dimanche
Sunday newspaper.

FILMS AND BOOKS

FILMS

» Watching a French film is a good way to get the feel of the place before you visit.

» For a classic, try *Les Enfants du Paradis* (1945) directed by Marcel Carné. For *nouvelle vague* (new wave) cinema—often filmed with a hand-held camera—try *Jules et Jim* (1962), directed by François Truffaut and starring Jeanne Moreau, or *À Bout de Souffle* (1959), directed by Jean-Luc Godard. The surreal *Belle de Jour* (1967), starring Catherine Deneuve, caused a scandal at the time due to its erotic subject matter. The 1987 weepie *Au Revoir les Enfants* tells the story of a Jewish boy in occupied France in World War II.

» No reference to French movies would be complete without mentioning Gérard Depardieu, the actor who conquered France and then Hollywood. His best-known works include *Cyrano de Bergerac* (1990) and *Jean de Florette* (1986).

» Jean-Pierre Jeunet's *Delicatessen* (1991) turns the controversial subject of cannibalism into a black comedy.

» Roman Polanski's *Tess* was filmed on location in Brittany.

» Brittany's most famous cinematic coup was perhaps Alfred Hitchcock's spooky thriller *The Birds*, filmed in Dinard.

» The historical drama *The Vikings* put the romantic Emerald Coast setting of Fort La Latte to good effect.

» Now in Pays de la Loire, though it was still in Brittany when the film was made, the little village of St-Marc is where Jacques Tati's wonderful creation Monsieur Hulot had that hilarious holiday way back in 1953.

BOOKS

» Brittany can lay claim to associations with the Romantic writer René de Chateaubriand (*Mémoires*), Honoré de Balzac (*Les Chouans*—the royalist rebellion based in Fougères), Alexandre Dumas (*The Three Musketeers*—partly set on Belle-Île) and Pierre Loti (*Pêcheur d'Islande*—about the cod-fishing community of Paimpol). Madame de Sevigné wrote her letters about the French court from Vitré.

SHOPPING

MARKET FORCES

Only major business cities such as Rennes or Brest have large department stores or multinational branded chains. City-centre stores like Monoprix and Prisunic usually have a supermarket section. Chain mini-markets include 8 à Huit, Shopi and Marché Plus. In smaller neighbourhoods, the specialist family-run businesses which have disappeared from many places in Britain remind us how well the French balance their way of life despite commercial pressures. Every town and village has its selection of *boulangeries-pâtisseries* (bakery/cake shops), *boucheries* (butchers), and probably one or two *charcuteries-traiteurs* (delicatessens) or *poissonneries* (fishmongers) as well. Small grocery stores selling general food supplies are called *épiceries* or *alimentations*.

These are the backbone of the food-shopping experience in Brittany, underpinned by the weekly markets that spill so vividly on to the streets and squares of larger towns, and the covered produce markets or *halles*, which display enticing wares most weekdays in regional centres. Farmers' markets are a growing phenomenon, selling items like goats' cheese, buttermilk, or home-cured *charcuterie* from independent producers once or twice a month in summer. In the countryside, farm shops and roadside stalls offer surplus produce to passers-by, especially at harvest time. Pick your own soft fruit at St-Meloir-des-Ondes, or stock up on early vegetables *(primeurs)* and artichokes in the fertile Golden Belt near St-Pol-de-Léon.

CATCH OF THE DAY

Some of Brittany's larger fishing ports, including Roscoff, Concarneau, Douarnenez, Quiberon and Le Guilvinec, hold a *criée* or fish auction, generally very early on weekday mornings. These are aimed primarily at professional wholesale buyers who distribute the catch to shops and restaurants throughout northern France in refrigerated containers, but it is often possible to buy superb fresh fish and seafood at quayside stalls.

Look too, for shoreside *viviers* (fish farms), where live shellfish await in large tanks. Just point out which lobster or langoustine takes your fancy, and it's yours. Le Forêt-Fouesnant, Primel-Trégastel (near Morlaix), Camaret and Aber-Benoît have viviers offering direct sales to the general public. At Cancale and along the River Bélon you can buy oysters inexpensively from producers' stalls, while the commercial mussel-rearing ports of Le Vivier-sur-Mer and St-Jacut-de-la-Mer are the places to look for fresh *moules*.

Processed seafood is an important Breton export. The days of the great sardine fleets are long

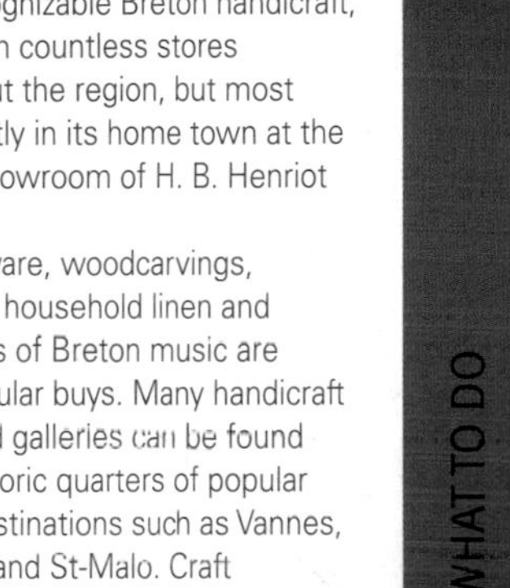

Left *A Brittany boutique*
Far left *Freshly caught crab for sale*
Opposite *France is famous for its excellent markets*

gone, but firms like La Belle-Iloise (with outlets all over Brittany) and Gonidec (based in Concarneau) still produce a superb range of gourmet fish products (mackerel rillettes, marinaded tuna, smoked salmon, cured sprats), all enticingly packaged in tins and jars.

Seaweed is an important marine industry. Finistère's north coast supports some 800 different varieties, some of which are used in pharmaceutical, cosmetic and culinary products. The Roscoff firms of Thalado and Algoplus make an interesting range of seaweed soaps, skincare lotions and nutritional supplements, on sale locally.

HEADY BREWS

Since the *département* of Loire-Atlantique was transferred to the Pays de la Loire region in 1973, Brittany no longer produces significant quantities of wine. The crisp, dry Muscadet wines from Nantes are widely available, but the more typical local drink is cider, produced from the lush orchards of the Rance and Odet valleys and sold directly by many producers. Beer is another traditional Breton tipple. A resurgence of independent microbreweries has resulted in an interesting range of real ales such as Coreff, Dremmwell and Telenn Du. Chouchen is a kind of mead, made with honey and strongly alcoholic, while Pommeau is an aperitif made with apple juice and Calvados. Lambig is a powerful cider brandy, good for flambéed dishes. Brittany even distills its own whisky (Warenghem) near Lannion. You'll see all sorts of fruit-flavoured liqueurs and digestifs on sale too.

SAILOR GEAR

The signs Coopérative Maritime or Comptoir de la Mer in any Breton harbour town indicate a hybrid chandlery store for visiting holidaymakers as well as amateur and professional seafarers. Among the anti-fouling paints and outboard motors you'll find a selection of fashionably rugged weatherproof clothes (brightly coloured sailing jackets, sou'westers and *kabigs*—a heavy outdoor cape with scallop fastenings), along with classy Breton knitwear in jaunty red or navy stripes, just as wearable ashore as on board. Reputable designer labels include Armor Lux, Guy Cotten and Saint-James. Maritime souvenirs (barometers, sextants, knot pictures, ship models) are also on sale, but if you're looking for a genuine nautical antique, visit a specialist dealer, or look for marine markets held occasionally, for instance at Douarnenez or La Trinité-sur-Mer.

ARTS AND CRAFTS

Quimper *faïence* (tin-glazed earthenware) with its classic designs of flowers, birds and costumed figures is perhaps the most recognizable Breton handicraft, available in countless stores throughout the region, but most prominently in its home town at the factory showroom of H. B. Henriot (▷ 118).

Glassware, woodcarvings, paintings, household linen and recordings of Breton music are other popular buys. Many handicraft shops and galleries can be found in the historic quarters of popular tourist destinations such as Vannes, Quimper and St-Malo. Craft workshops and artists' studios are concentrated in villages such as Locronan, Brasparts, St-Meloir-des-Ondes, Camaret-sur-Mer, Rochefort-en-Terre, La Gacilly and Pont-Scorff. Antique and bric-à-brac shops are places to look for traditional Breton furniture or smaller keepsakes like wooden spoons, butter-moulds and decorated biscuit tins.

MODERN STORES

Supermarkets and hypermarkets have sprung up in and around most Breton towns, undeniably convenient for car-borne travellers wanting a one-stop shopping fix. Branches of Champion, Intermarché or Casino supermarkets are easily spotted along many urban highways. Best of the big hypermarkets is the Breton-based chain Leclerc, which originated in Edouard Leclerc's home town of Landerneau. At these large undercover malls you can buy everything from wet fish to dishwashers. Besides a classy selection of fresh and processed food, you'll find a wide choice of books, magazines, stationery, clothing, electronics and housewares. Leclerc can also oblige with well-maintained, free toilets, a coffee shop and a cheaper-than-average fuel top-up.

SPORTS AND ACTIVITIES

BICYCLING

Brittany isn't the most challenging terrain for serious bikers, but perfectly suits recreational cyclists who don't want too many gradients. Several bicycling routes are recommended by the bicycling federation, including VTT (mountain bike) ones. Accommodation and luggage transportation can be arranged. The UK operator Cycling for Softies organizes undemanding holidays staying in small family hotels (tel 0161 248 8282; www.cycling-for-softies.co.uk). Breton Bikes is another British-owned operator, based in Plelauff, Côtes d'Armor (tel 02 96 24 86 72; www.bretonbikes.com).

BIRD-WATCHING

Brittany is one of the best places in Europe to spot birds. It lies on transatlantic migration routes, and has a huge diversity of habitats. More than 20 areas are designated as bird sanctuaries, including several islands.

BOATING

Cruising Brittany's estuary rivers and inland waterways is immensely popular. Rent a canal cruiser from one of the many boating centres (such as Dinan, Redon, Pontivy, Carhaix) on the Ille-et-Rance or Nantes–Brest canals, and take life in the slow lane for a while.

CANOEING AND KAYAKING

The calm bays and estuaries around the Breton coast make ideal playgrounds for these popular sports, which can be easily mastered.

DIVING

The clear waters off the Breton coast are ideal for scuba diving. Sub-aqua activities are especially popular on the Crozon peninsula (wreck diving off Finistère), St-Malo and Concarneau. Look for PADI-accredited clubs.

FISHING

Sea-fishing has been a way of life for centuries in Brittany. Many local boat-owners will take visitors out for a day or two in search of mackerel and sea-bass. More than 20,000km (12,500 miles) of rivers and inland waterways make an angling paradise too, mainly for trout and salmon. *Pêche à pied*, or low-tide shell-fishing with nets, hoes and rakes, is another favourite pastime for Breton families. Strict regulations apply to all types of fishing for environmental and conservation reasons, and the fines levied for transgressions can be hefty.

GOLF

Brittany has more than 30 golf courses. There are many choices available, ranging from a single round to a full week's play on several courses. Golf is a more sociable, family-oriented game in France than in other countries, and course etiquette is generally unstuffy, though fees can be high. Tailor-made golfing packages are available from a number of specialist operators.

HORSE-RIDING

Lots of horsy activities can be pursued in Brittany, where most resorts lie within easy reach of riding stables. Riding along the quieter beaches, or across the Baie de St-Brieuc, is particularly popular. Equibreizh is a 2,000km (1,250-mile) network of signposted bridleways traversing Brittany (ask for the Topo-Guide describing the routes). The two national stud farms at Lamballe and Hennebont organize many equine events in summer. Horse-racing is very popular in France, and Brittany has numerous race-courses *(hippodromes)*, of which Loudéac is one of the most renowned.

SAILING

Brittany's glorious coastline and long-established seafaring traditions give it a head start in the water sports world. Breton yachtsmen like Eric Tarberly have become legends in their own lifetime. Numerous sailing schools and marinas offer splendid facilities, and many have strong links with British yacht clubs (hundreds of yachts cross the Channel in both directions each year).

SAND-YACHTING

This sport, also called sand-karting or land-sailing *(char à voile)*, is almost as exhilarating for spectators as for

Below left *A golf course overlooking the sea in St-Cast-le-Guildo*

Below *Walkers following one of the many hiking trails in Brittany*

participants. The Baie du Mont-St-Michel and the Baie de Quiberon are two of the best venues, but there are more than a dozen schools.

SURFING

The wilder shores of Brittany, such as Plage de la Torche near Audierne, attract adventurous, experienced surfers, but there are also less challenging places to have a go, such as Dinard and Larmor-Plage.

THALASSOTHERAPY

Seawater health cures are big news in Brittany, and thalassotherapy centres specializing in this form of treatment have sprung up in a dozen or so resorts all around the coastline, including St-Malo, Dinard, Roscoff, Bénodet, Quiberon and Carnac. In these luxurious spas, you can be bombarded with high-pressure jets, massaged with seaweed creams and assailed with aerosol vapours in the pricey pursuit of health and beauty—or just relax in the Jacuzzi.

WALKING

Brittany has one of the longest coastal footpaths anywhere in France. The GR34 (waymarked in red-and-white) runs all the way from Mont-St-Michel on the Normandy border to the Golfe du Morbihan. Much of it follows the old watchpaths *(sentiers des douaniers)* used by armed coastguards against smugglers in the 18th century. There are also many beautiful walks to be discovered in inland Brittany, particularly the trails striking through the scenic Monts d'Arrée. You can also follow canal towpaths and ancient pilgrim routes, or circuit offshore islands.

FOR CHILDREN

BEACHES AND WATER SPORTS

Brittany's beaches are the greatest attraction for young families. Here children can build sandcastles and explore rock pools to their heart's content. Remember, though, that the Breton coast can be dangerous, and observe warning signs. Virtually all the seaside resorts make special efforts in the holiday season with beach clubs, festivals and activities designed with children in mind. Some hold a *Fête aux Mômes*, which includes lots of clowns, bands, acrobats, rides and parades. Water sports clubs involve children from an early age, and it is not uncommon to see tiny tots barely past the nappy stage setting fearlessly off into the Big Blue in some sailing craft or other, albeit carefully supervised.

Above *There are many places to rent bicycles throughout Brittany*
Below *Children playing on trampolines on the beach at Bénodet*

ENTERTAINMENT AND NIGHTLIFE

INFORMATION AND BOOKING

Strong oral and musical traditions encourage live performance art throughout the year. The mainstream cultural venues, predictably enough, are in the larger cities, especially those with a sizeable student population, such as Rennes and Brest. To find out what's going on, call in at any tourist office, or look for listings in local papers and magazines. Tickets for shows and events can sometimes be purchased at tourist offices too.

MUSIC

Music is one of the strongest social bonds in Brittany, and the clearest expression of the region's cultural distinctiveness. Some of the biggest folk festivals in Europe are staged here, including Lorient's Festival Interceltique. Some half million visitors are drawn here annually to hear traditional instruments like the Celtic harp, the *bombarde* (a kind of oboe) and the *biniou* (Breton bagpipes), played by Breton bands known as *bagadou*. Other styles of music are also celebrated, including jazz, classical and rock. Concerts are held in major arts venues, particularly Ubu in Rennes, or the Quartz in Brest. Musical events also take place at summer festivals.

CINEMA

The overwhelming majority of films shown in Brittany are dubbed into French, but a few places show some foreign films in the original version *(version originale)* with French subtitles. Several successful film festivals have raised Brittany's cinematic profile in the past decade, notably at Dinard, Rennes, Brest and Douarnenez.

NIGHTLIFE

University towns and the more glamorous seaside resorts are the places to find most going on after dark, though in winter most places are very quiet indeed. In summer, however, you'll find clubs and pubs, piano bars, café-theatre and casinos humming until the small hours. There isn't a particularly overt gay scene in Brittany, though you will obviously find gay bars and clubs in the larger cities such as Rennes and Brest.

Below *Bagpipe players can be seen at the Celtic Festival in Roscoff*

FESTIVALS AND EVENTS

Events take place all year round throughout Brittany, although the vast majority are held during the main holiday season between Easter and October. Any tourist office should be able to provide a full list of local events, and most publish their social calendar on official websites. Some are internationally famous and attract huge gatherings.

PARDONS AND PILGRIMAGES

Many Breton communities celebrate the feast day of their patron saint with a ceremony called a *pardon*, beginning with a solemn mass and followed by a procession behind the saint's relics. The day then proceeds more merrily with music, dancing and feasting. On these occasions you can see traditional costumes worn by men, women and children, and hear Breton spoken or sung. Other religious events are annual pilgrimages to a religious site, such as Locronan or Ste-Anne-d'Auray.

FESTOU-NOZ

The *fest-noz*, or night festival, is a more secular Breton tradition involving Celtic music and dancing in much the same style as an Irish or Scottish *ceilidh*. The original purpose of the *fest-noz* was to inject a little impetus into the important business of stamping down the earthen floors of the villagers' houses.

FOOD, MARITIME AND FOLK FESTIVALS

Many coastal ports celebrate the source of their livelihood, the sea, with an annual festival. This may have its roots in a service of thanksgiving, or be a purely secular jamboree, as at Côtes d'Armor's Fête de la Coquille St-Jacques (scallop festival), or Binic's Fête de la Morue (cod festival). Some commemorate former fishing communities, such as Concarneau's Fête des Filets Bleus (Blue Nets) or Paimpol's Fête des Terres-Neuvas (Newfoundland Fishermen). Many include parades, fireworks and regattas down by the port. Events involving traditional working boats are especially popular.

Above *The Creperie du Salle in Quimper*

In recent years, a move to lighter dishes and simpler techniques has acknowledged changing dietary habits. These days, many restaurants provide at least one completely vegetarian option, although notions of vegetarianism can be a little hazy. Meat stocks are often used in innocent-sounding vegetable soups, and *lardons* sprinkled on salads or omelettes. If you eat neither fish nor flesh, your choice will be rather restricted in northwestern France. Ethnic restaurants are not nearly as widespread as in other regions, but you will find the odd North African or Asian restaurant in large towns like Rennes or Brest.

RESTAURANTS

Every town has its hallowed restaurants, quite different from the bistros and brasseries for everyday eating. In these, you'll find a more refined setting, with starched linen, polished glass and silverware and a sense of hushed reverence for the gastronomic offerings to come. Here, families celebrate birthdays and communions, promises are whispered and business deals settled over something even more important than a handshake. Dress smartly and reserve in advance. Northwestern France has its fair share of leading chefs, such as Olivier Roellinger in Cancale (▷ 184), Jacques Thorel in La Roche-Bernard (▷ 74), and Georges Paineau in Questembert (▷ 73). But you can find excellent regional food in many less grand dining rooms, especially in members of the Logis de France hotel group (▷ 215).

CRÊPERIES

No Breton town or village seems to be without a *crêperie* or two, an inexpensive way to stave off hunger pangs. Imaginative, sometimes bizarre combinations of ingredients are used, both sweet and savoury, but exotic seafood fillings will cost much more than something simple like egg, cheese or mushrooms. *Crêpes* are useful fast-food options for children or vegetarians. An accompanying salad makes a meal.

BRASSERIES AND BISTROS

Brasseries were once brewery bars that served meals. Today, they are mostly informal restaurants that open long hours. Here you can enjoy local dishes, as well as familiar meals such as *steak-frites* (steak and chips/fries) and *assiettes de fruits de mer* (seafood platter). Bistros may be small, independent, family-run restaurants serving traditional cooking, with a modest wine list. Some also have a delicatessen.

CAFÉS AND BARS

Cafés and bars serve hot, soft and alcoholic drinks, snacks and sometimes light meals. Catering more for holidaymakers or leisure visitors than hard-pressed businessfolk, *salons de thé* or *glaciers* serve cakes and ice creams as well as drinks. They open from breakfast until late in the evening. As in all eating places, the smartness of the surroundings greatly affects the price you pay. Expect to pay a little more for your drink if you sit down rather than stand at the bar; and a coveted sea-view terrace table may be priciest of all.

CUTTING COSTS

If you are on a budget, have your main meal at lunchtime, when most restaurants serve an inexpensive *formule* or *menu du jour* (daily menu), of two or three courses with a glass of wine *(vin compris)* for around 50 per cent of the cost in the evening. Sometimes you can simply order a *plat du jour* (daily dish) and a drink for very low prices. On weekdays, lunch menus at even the most stellar establishments are often reasonably priced. Sticking to fixed-price or *table d'hôte* menus is almost always a much better deal than dining à la carte.

MENUS

A menu in a French restaurant is a set-price, multi-course meal, served at lunchtime and in the evening. If you want to see the menu, ask for *la carte*. A wine-list is a *carte à vins*. Take care you are presented with the bottle you ordered (it should be shown to you before it is opened). A *menu dégustation* or *menu gastronomique*, found in the finest restaurants, offers a sample of speciality dishes sometimes accompanied by a selection of appropriate wines, and is expensive.

OPENING TIMES

With few exceptions, restaurants and bistros tend to keep fairly strict serving times, though in popular holiday resorts all-day diners cater for the less disciplined habits of foreign visitors. Restaurants generally open at 12, close by 2.30, then reopen for dinner at 7.30. Except in large towns and resorts, restaurants mostly stop taking orders between 9pm and 9.30pm. In high season, however, you will find many places accept orders until at least 10pm. Many restaurants are closed at Saturday lunchtime, on Sunday evening and Monday, but may stay open every day or longer hours in July and August . Many establishments in remoter parts of Brittany's coast, or on islands, often close completely between November and Easter.

ETIQUETTE

Service is always included in the price of your meal, indicated by the words *service compris* or *s.c.*, but it is still customary to leave some change behind also if the service has been exceptionally good. Only very exclusive restaurants in Brittany insist on a dress code, but it is courteous to dress up a little when dining in a smarter venue. Address staff as *Monsieur*, *Madame* or *Mademoiselle*. Smoking is now banned in all bars, cafés and restaurants in France, and fines are imposed for breaking the rules.

MENU READER

Agneau de pré-salé: lamb raised on the coastal saltmarshes, for example around Ouessant.
Andouille: a smoked pork-tripe sausage consisting mainly of offal. Also called *chitterlings*.
Andouillette: similar to Andouille, but usually eaten hot.
Assiette (or plateau) de fruits de mer: seafood platter, typically containing oysters, langoustines, clams *(palourdes)*, cockles *(coques)*, mussels *(moules)*, winkles *(bigourneaux)*, whelks *(bulots)*, spider crab *(araignée)*.
Bar de ligne au sel: line-caught sea-bass baked in a salt crust (a speciality of southern Brittany).
Beurre blanc: butter whipped with white wine vinegar and shallots.
Boudin noir: black pudding.
Cervoise: Breton beer, as drunk by the Gauls (including Asterix!).
Chateaubriand: a thick cut of tenderloin steak with shallot, herb and white-wine sauce.
Cidre: cider, the local hooch of Brittany. *Doux* is sweet, *brut* is dry and *bouché* means fermented in the bottle.
Cocos de Paimpol: high-quality haricot beans produced around Paimpol and regarded as a delicacy.
Coquilles St-Jacques: scallops (fished in winter around the Baie de St-Brieuc); *petoncles* are baby or queen scallops.
Cotriade: a fish stew, also called the *bouillabaisse* of the north.
Chouchen: mead, a strong, sweet drink made with fermented honey.
Crêpes and galettes: pancakes are the staple diet of Brittany. A *crêpe* is made with a wheat-flour batter and has a sweet filling, while a *galette* is traditionally made from heavier buckwheat or sarassin flour and has a savoury one. *Crêpes-dentelles* are wafer-thin pancakes.
Far breton: a thick, sweet tart with prunes or raisins, similar to a flan.
Galettes de Pont-Aven: not to be confused with pancakes, these are buttery biscuits.
Gigot à la Bretonne: roast leg of lamb with haricot beans.
Homard à l'armoricaine: lobster served flambéed in a cream and wine sauce.
Huîtres plates: flat or native oysters (as opposed to *huîtres creuses,* or hollow oysters).
Kig-ha-farz: a hearty stew containing ham or bacon.
Kouign amann: a traditional Breton cake made with sugar, butter and almonds, best eaten warm.
Lambig: a rare kind of Breton calvados (apple brandy).
Niniches: sugar-cane lollipops, especially popular in Morbihan.
Primeurs: early, high-quality vegetables, grown on the Ceinture d'Orée (Golden Belt) near Roscoff.

Above *The canopied entrance to the Hotel de la paix, Dinard*

CLASSIFICATION

Registered hotels are inspected regularly and classified into six categories: no star, 1*, 2*, 3*, 4* and 4*L (Luxury). Don't attach too much importance to star-ratings. They give some idea of the level of facilities you can expect (such as a lift, or 24-hour reception), but are no guide whatever to how pleasant or interesting your stay will be. Some two-star hotels are much more appealing than four-stars, if less luxuriously equipped. For perfectly legitimate reasons, some excellent hotels choose not to register with the local tourist office, and may not be included in official listings.

TARIFFS

Hotel tariffs are generally quoted per room and not per person, though this doesn't apply if meals are included. Breakfast is nearly always quoted as an optional extra, except of course in *chambres d'hôtes* (bed-and-breakfast) accommodation. Young children can sometimes stay free of charge in parents' rooms, but extra beds for adults will attract a supplement, as will pets brought into hotels. Lone visitors nearly always have to pay the full price for a double room; single rooms are not plentiful and generally are of an inferior standard.

Hotels must display their rates (including tax) both outside the hotel and in each bedroom. In Brittany, prices vary enormously according to season, and rise sharply in July and August *(haute saison)*. Some hotels give reduced rates for stays of more than one night. Many local authorities impose a small tourist tax, known as a *taxe de séjour*, on visitors staying overnight. This is nearly always quoted separately, and on average may add an extra euro or so to your daily room bill.

Most hotels accept major credit cards belonging to the Carte Bancaire scheme (Visa/Barclaycard, MasterCard/Eurocard), but American Express and Diners Club are less widely favoured. Service is always included in hotel bills; you are under no obligation to leave anything extra as a tip, though many guests leave the spare change if paying by cash.

RESERVATIONS

During busy holiday periods or major festivals, accommodation can be very difficult to find, especially in popular coastal areas. It is advisable to reserve ahead rather than taking pot luck. Advance bookings require some kind of deposit, generally in the form of a credit card number; you may be charged a penalty if you have to cancel or amend your reservation, and should always check the hotel's policy on refunds. The internet has made booking accommodation much easier, especially from overseas, but has its pitfalls. Most places will only guarantee to hold a room for you until a specified time (usually 6pm), so be sure to telephone if you are running late. Many tourist offices will help find local accommodation, but only if you arrive in person, not by phone. A small fee may be charged (deductable from your final bill). Tourist office staff are not allowed to

make personal recommendations, and can only book officially registered establishments.

PACKAGES
Many agencies and holiday companies, including Brittany Ferries, organize inclusive package deals. Low-cost flights to small regional airports from the UK have widened the choice of short-break packages available. Many discounted deals are available by reserving online over the internet.

LUXURY STAYS
Brittany has many fine château hotels. Some belong to well-known groups such as Relais & Châteaux or Châteaux & Hôtels de France. Also at the top end of the range are hedonistic spa resorts, the swanky casino hotels of the Lucien Barrière group, and a few glamorously designed boutique hotels. But these luxurious places are the exception rather than the rule.

ON A BUDGET
Most hotels in this part of France cater for simple family holidays on the beach or in the countryside, or offer traditional auberge hospitality in small towns and villages. Most familiar of these are the Logis de France hotels—pick up a regional list at any tourist office. These small, family-run inns and hotels are individually owned, but subscribe to a charter of agreed standards and are regularly inspected. They pledge to offer a friendly welcome (especially to families and foreign visitors), regional authenticity, value-for-money and good cooking (www.logis-de-france.fr). Low-cost *(économique)* chain hotels are a convenient if far less interesting accommodation option.

DEALS ON MEALS
Half-board *(demi-pension)* or full-board *(pension)* terms are sometimes obligatory in high season and can often be excellent value, but may be irksomely restrictive over longer stays. Hotel breakfasts are optional extras and often seriously overpriced; local cafés or bars serve coffee and croissants or pastries at a fraction of the cost.

BED-AND-BREAKFAST
Chambres d'hôtes are France's answer to the traditional concept of bed-and-breakfast. You'll get croissants and jam for breakfast, and these may well be home-made. Some places offer *table d'hôte* evening meals by prior arrangement. Dining *en famille* is a sociable way to meet the locals, though a little stressful if you speak no French (many hosts near the Channel coast speak some English). Tourist offices all have lists of families who offer rooms to visitors, but some of the best *chambres d'hôtes* are affiliated to the Gîtes de France organization (see below), and graded from one to four ears of corn *(épis)*, depending on the level of comfort and facilities. You may even find yourself mixing with the nobility at the upper echelons of the *chambres d'hôtes* market. A consortium called Bienvenue au Château offers classy stays in grand private homes in western France (www.bienvenue-au-chateau.com), while Bienvenue a la Ferme lists more modest *chambres d'hôtes* accommodation on farms (www.bretagnealaferme.com).

SELF-CATERING
Self-catering accommodation includes holiday parks with lots of entertainment and organized activities, and low-key *gîtes*. These self-contained cottages, villas and apartments are found mainly in rural areas, and range from basic to luxurious. *Gîtes* are generally rented on a weekly basis, and are advertised in national newspapers or listed by tourist offices. For a large selection of accredited *gîtes* see www.gites-de-france.fr

CAMPING
Brittany has some of France's best campsites, especially along its popular holiday coasts. Campsites are graded up to 4*. Some have mobile homes and pre-pitched tents, and cater for visitors bringing their own caravans or campervans. Most sites are open from Easter to September. In high season (July and August) it is essential to reserve ahead; you may not park a motorhome or put up a tent except on a designated site. Consult the National Federation of Campsites (www.campingfrance.com) for a list. Camping Plus is a superior group of about 30 high-quality sites in Brittany (www.campingplus.com).

USING A LAPTOP
Most hotels of two stars and above provide modem points. You can connect to the internet providing this service is supported by your ISP (Internet Service Provider). Local telephone charges will apply. You may need a modem plug adaptor. Laptops should be compatible with the 220V current in France; otherwise you will need both a converter and an adaptor, or a French modem lead. A global modem should work in France.

WORDS AND PHRASES

BRETON LANGUAGE

Only about 250,000 people are thought to speak the Breton language well these days, though recent efforts to teach it in schools have revived interest. You don't need to speak any Brezhoneg, as it's known, to make yourself understood in Brittany, but the odd word here and there will be much appreciated in certain parts of the region.

EVERYDAY WORDS AND PHRASES

Good day	**Demat**
Goodbye	**Kenavo**
Thank you	**Trugarez**
Good health/Cheers	**Yermat**
festival	**fest-noz**
Brittany	**Breizh**

PLACE-NAME WORDS

coast, beach	**aod**
river	**aven**
headland	**beg**
wood	**coat**
island	**enez**
church	**iliz**
castle	**kastell**
village	**ker**
monastery	**lan**
mountain, hill	**menez**
sea	**mor**
parish	**plou**
port, cove	**pors**
pond	**poul**
rock	**roc'h**
mound	**roz**
lake	**stang**
stream	**ster**
house	**ti**

NUMBERS

one	**unan**
two	**daou**
three	**tri**
four	**pevar**
five	**pemp**
six	**c'hwec'h**
seven	**seizh**
eight	**eizh**
nine	**nav**
ten	**dek**

Even if you're far from fluent, it is always a good idea to try to speak a few words of French while in France. The words and phrases on the following pages should help you with the basics.

CONVERSATION

What is the time?
Quelle heure est il?
When do you open/close?
À quelle heure ouvrez/fermez-vous?
I don't speak French.
Je ne parle pas français.
Do you speak English?
Parlez-vous anglais?
I don't understand.
Je ne comprends pas.
Please repeat that.
Pouvez-vous répéter (s'il vous plaît)?
Please speak more slowly.
Pouvez-vous parler plus lentement?
What does this mean?
Qu'est-ce que ça veut dire?
Write that down for me please.
Pouvez-vous me l'écrire, s'il vous plaît?
Please spell that.
Pouvez-vous me l'épeler, s'il vous plaît?
I'll look that up (in the dictionary).
Je vais le chercher (dans le dictionnaire).

My name is...
Je m'appelle ...

What's your name?
Comment vous appelez-vous?
This is my wife/husband.
Voici ma femme/mon mari.
This is my daughter/son.
Voici ma fille/mon fils.
This is my friend.
Voici mon ami(e).
Hello, pleased to meet you.
Bonjour, enchanté(e).
I'm from ...
Je viens de ...
I'm on holiday.
Je suis en vacances.
I live in ...
J'habite à ...
Where do you live?
Où habitez-vous?
Good morning.
Bonjour.
Good evening.
Bonsoir.
Goodnight.
Bonne nuit.
Goodbye.
Au revoir.
See you later.
À plus tard.
How much is that?
C'est combien?
May I/Can I...?
Est-ce que je peux ... ?
I don't know.
Je ne sais pas.
You're welcome.
Je vous en prie.
How are you?
Comment allez-vous?
I'm sorry.
Je suis désolé(e).
Excuse me.
Excusez-moi.
That's all right.
De rien.

USEFUL WORDS

Yes .... Oui
No .... Non
There .... Là-bas
Here Ici

Where .... Où
Who .... Qui
When .... Quand
Why .... Pourquoi
How .... Comment
Later .... Plus tard
Now .... Maintenant
Open .... Ouvert
Closed .... Fermé
Please .... S'il vous plaît
Thank you .... Merci

SHOPPING

Could you help me, please?
(Est-ce que) vous pouvez m'aider, s'il vous plaît?
How much is this?
C'est combien?/Ça coûte combien?
I'm looking for ...
Je cherche ...
When does the shop open/close?
À quelle heure ouvre/ferme le magasin?
I'm just looking, thank you.
Je regarde, merci.
This isn't what I want.
Ce n'est pas ce que je veux.
This is the right size.
C'est la bonne taille.
Do you have anything less expensive/smaller/larger?
(Est-ce que) vous avez quelque chose de moins cher/plus petit/plus grand?
I'll take this.
Je prends ça.
Do you have a bag for this, please?
(Est-ce que) je peux avoir un sac, s'il vous plaît?
Do you accept credit cards?
(Est-ce que) vous acceptez les cartes de crédit?
I'd like ... grams please.
Je voudrais ... grammes, s'il vous plaît.
I'd like a kilo of ...
Je voudrais un kilo de ...
What does this contain?
Quels sont les ingrédients?/ Qu'est-ce qu'il y a dedans?
I'd like ... slices of that.
J'en voudrais ... tranches.
Bakery .... Boulangerie
Bookshop .... Librairie
Chemist .... Pharmacie
Supermarket .... Supermarché
Market .... Marché
Sale .... Soldes

NUMBERS

1 .... un
2 .... deux
3 .... trois
4 .... quatre
5 .... cinq
6 .... six
7 .... sept
8 .... huit
9 .... neuf
10 .... dix
11 .... onze
12 .... douze
13 .... treize
14 .... quatorze
15 .... quinze
16 .... seize
17 .... dix-sept
18 .... dix-huit
19 .... dix-neuf
20 .... vingt
21 .... vingt et un
30 .... trente
40 .... quarante
50 .... cinquante
60 .... soixante
70 .... soixante-dix
80 .... quatre-vingts
90 .... quatre-vingt dix
100 .... cent
1000 .... mille

POST AND TELEPHONES

Where is the nearest post office/ mail box?
Où se trouve la poste/la boîte aux lettres la plus proche?
How much is the postage to...?
À combien faut-il affranchir pour ...?
I'd like to send this by air mail/ registered mail.
Je voudrais envoyer ceci par avion/ en recommandé.
Can you direct me to a public phone?
Pouvez-vous m'indiquer la cabine téléphonique la plus proche?
What is the number for directory enquiries?
Quel est le numéro pour les renseignements?
Where can I find a telephone directory?
Où est-ce que je peux trouver un annuaire?
Where can I buy a phone card?
Où est-ce que je peux acheter une télécarte?
Please put me through to...
Pouvez-vous me passer ..., s'il vous **plaît?**
Can I dial direct to ...?
Est-ce que je peux appeler directement en ...?
Do I need to dial 0 first?
Est-ce qu'il faut composer le zéro (d'abord)?
What is the charge per minute?
Quel est le tarif à la minute?
Have there been any calls for me?
Est-ce que j'ai eu des appels téléphoniques?
Hello, this is ...
Allô, c'est ... (à l'appareil)?
Who is speaking please ...?
Qui est à l'appareil, s'il vous plaît?
I would like to speak to ...
Je voudrais parler à ...

DAYS/MONTHS/HOLIDAYS/TIMES

Monday .... lundi
Tuesday .... mardi
Wednesday .... mercredi
Thursday .... jeudi
Friday .... vendredi
Saturday .... samedi
Sunday .... dimanche

January .... janvier
February .... février
March .... mars
April .... avril
May .... mai
June .... juin
July .... juillet
August .... août
September .... septembre
October .... octobre
November .... novembre
December .... décembre

spring .... printemps
summer .... été
autumn .... automne
winter .... hiver

holiday .... vacances

Easter .... Pâques
Christmas .... Noël

morning .... matin
afternoon .... après-midi
evening .... soir
night .... nuit
today .... aujourd'hui
yesterday .... hier
tomorrow .... demain
day .... le jour
month .... le mois
year .... l'année

HOTELS

Do you have a room?
(Est-ce que) vous avez une chambre?
I have a reservation for ... nights.
J'ai réservé pour ... nuits.
How much each night?
C'est combien par nuit?
Double room.
Une chambre pour deux personnes/ double.
Twin room.
Une chambre à deux lits/ avec lits jumeaux.
Single room.
Une chambre à un lit/pour une personne.
With bath/shower/toilet.
Avec salle de bain/ douche/WC.
Is the room air-conditioned/ heated?
(Est-ce que) la chambre est climatisée/chauffée?
Is breakfast/lunch/dinner included in the cost?
(Est-ce que) le petit déjeuner/le déjeuner/le dîner est compris dans le prix?
Is there an elevator in the hotel?
(Est-ce qu')il y a un ascenseur à l'hôtel?
Is room service available?
(Est-ce qu')il y a le service en chambre?
When do you serve breakfast?
À quelle heure servez-vous le petit déjeuner?
May I have breakfast in my room?
(Est-ce que) je peux prendre le petit déjeuner dans ma chambre?
Do you serve evening meals?
(Est-ce que) vous servez le repas du soir/le dîner?
I need an alarm call at...
Je voudrais être réveillé(e) à ... heures.
I'd like an extra blanket/pillow.
Je voudrais une couverture/ un oreiller supplémentaire, s'il vous plaît.
May I have my room key?
(Est-ce que) je peux avoir la clé de ma chambre?
Will you look after my luggage until I leave?
Pouvez-vous garder mes bagages jusqu'à mon départ?
Is there parking?
(Est-ce qu')il y a un parking?
Where can I park my car?
Où est-ce que je peux garer ma voiture?
Do you have babysitters?
(Est-ce que) vous avez un service de babysitting/garde d'enfants?
When are the sheets changed?
Quand changez-vous les draps?
The room is too hot/cold.
Il fait trop chaud/froid dans la chambre.
Could I have another room?
(Est-ce que) je pourrais avoir une autre chambre?
I am leaving this morning.
Je pars ce matin.
What time should we leave our room?
À quelle heure devons-nous libérer la chambre?
Can I pay my bill?
(Est-ce que) je peux régler ma note, s'il vous plaît?
May I see the room?
(Est-ce que) je peux voir la chambre?
Swimming pool.
Piscine.
No smoking.
Non fumeur.
Sea view.
Vue sur la mer.

GETTING AROUND

Where is the information desk?
Où est le bureau des renseignements?
Where is the timetable?
Où sont les horaires?
Does this train/bus go to...?
Ce train/bus va à ...?
Do you have a Métro/bus map?
Avez-vous un plan du Métro/des lignes de bus?
Please can I have a single/ return ticket to...?
Je voudrais un aller simple/ un aller-retour pour ..., s'il vous plaît.
I'd like to rent a car.
Je voudrais louer une voiture.
Where are we?
Où sommes-nous?
I'm lost.
Je me suis perdu(e).
Is this the way to...?
C'est bien par ici pour aller à ...?
I am in a hurry.
Je suis pressé(e).
Where can I find a taxi?
Où est-ce que je peux trouver un taxi?
How much is the journey?
Combien coûte le trajet?
Go straight on.
Allez tout droit.
Turn left.
Tournez à gauche.
Turn right.
Tournez à droite.
Cross over.
Traversez.
Traffic lights.
Les feux.
Intersection.
Carrefour.
Corner.
Coin.
No parking.
Interdiction de stationner.
Train/bus/Métro station.
La gare SNCF/routière/la station de Métro.
Do you sell travel cards?
Avez-vous des cartes d'abonnement?
Do I need to get off here?
(Est-ce qu')il faut que je descende ici?
Where can I buy a ticket?
Où est-ce que je peux acheter un billet/ticket?
Where can I reserve a seat?
Où est-ce que je peux réserver une place?
Is this seat free?
(Est-ce que) cette place est libre?

MONEY

Is there a bank/currency exchange office nearby?
(Est-ce qu')il y a une banque/un bureau de change près d'ici?

Can I cash this here?
(Est-ce que) je peux encaisser ça ici?
I'd like to change sterling/dollars into euros.
Je voudrais changer des livres sterling/dollars en euros.
Can I use my credit card to withdraw cash?
(Est-ce que) je peux utiliser ma carte de crédit pour retirer de l'argent?
What is the exchange rate today?
Quel est le taux de change aujourd'hui?

RESTAURANTS

I'd like to reserve a table for ... people at ...
Je voudrais réserver une table pour ... personnes à ... heures, s'il vous plaît.
A table for ..., please.
Une table pour ..., s'il vous plaît.
We have/haven't booked.
Nous avons/n'avons pas réservé.
What time does the restaurant open?
À quelle heure ouvre le restaurant?
We'd like to wait for a table.
Nous aimerions attendre qu'une table se libère.
Could we sit there?
(Est-ce que) nous pouvons nous asseoir ici?
Is this table taken?
(Est-ce que) cette table est libre?
Are there tables outside?
(Est-ce qu')il y a des tables dehors/à la terrasse?
Where are the toilets?
Où sont les toilettes?
Could you warm this up for me?
(Est-ce que) vous pouvez me faire réchauffer ceci/ça, s'il vous plaît?
Do you have nappy-changing facilities?
(Est-ce qu')il y a une pièce pour changer les bébés?
We'd like something to drink.
Nous voudrions quelque chose à boire.
Could we see the menu/ wine list?
(Est-ce que) nous pouvons voir le menu/la carte des vins, s'il vous plaît?
Is there a dish of the day?
(Est-ce qu')il y a un plat du jour?
What do you recommend?
Qu'est-ce que vous nous conseillez?
This is not what I ordered.
Ce n'est pas ce que j'ai commandé.
I can't eat wheat/sugar/salt/ pork/beef/dairy.
Je ne peux pas manger de blé/sucre/ sel/porc/bœuf/ produits laitiers.
I am a vegetarian.
Je suis végétarien(ne).
I'd like...
Je voudrais ...
Could we have some more bread?
(Est-ce que) vous pouvez nous apporter un peu plus de pain, s'il vous plaît?
How much is this dish?
Combien coûte ce plat?
Is service included?
(Est-ce que) le service est compris?
Could we have some salt and pepper?
(Est-ce que) vous pouvez nous apporter du sel et du poivre, s'il vous plaît?
May I have an ashtray?
(Est-ce que) je peux avoir un cendrier, s'il vous plaît?
Could I have bottled still/ sparkling water?
(Est-ce que) je peux avoir une bouteille d'eau minérale non-gazeuse/gazeuse, s'il vous plaît?
We didn't order this.
Nous n'avons pas commandé ça.
The meat is too rare/overcooked.
La viande est trop saignante/trop cuite.
The food is cold.
Le repas/Le plat est froid.
Can I have the bill, please?
(Est-ce que) je peux avoir l'addition, s'il vous plaît?
The bill is not right.
Il y a une erreur sur l'addition.
I'd like to speak to the manager, please.
Je voudrais parler au directeur, s'il vous plaît.
The food was excellent.
Le repas/Le plat était excellent.

FOOD AND DRINK

Breakfast .... Petit déjeuner
Lunch .... Déjeuner
Dinner .... Dîner
Coffee .... Café
Tea .... Thé
Orange juice .... Jus d'orange
Apple juice .... Jus de pomme
Milk .... Lait
Beer .... Bière
Red wine .... Vin rouge
White wine .... Vin blanc
Bread roll .... Petit pain
Bread .... Pain
Sugar .... Sucre
Wine list .... Carte/liste des vins
Main course .... Le plat principal
Salt/pepper .... Sel/poivre
Cheese .... Fromage
Knife/fork/ spoon .... Couteau/ Fourchette/Cuillère
Soups .... Soupes/potages
Vegetable soup .... Soupe de légumes
Chicken soup .... Soupe au poulet
Lentil soup .... Soupe aux lentilles
Mushroom soup .... Soupe aux champignons
Sandwiches .... Sandwichs
Ham sandwich .... Sandwich au jambon
Dish of the day .... Plat du jour
Fish dishes .... Les poissons
Prawns ..... Crevettes roses/bouquet
Oysters .... Huîtres
Salmon .... Saumon
Haddock .... Églefin
Squid .... Calmar
Meat dishes .... Viandes
Roast chicken .... Poulet rôti
Casserole .... Plat en cocotte
Roast lamb .... Gigot
Mixed cold meat .... L'assiette de charcuterie
Potatoes .... Pommes de terre
Cauliflower .... Chou-fleur
Green beans .... Haricots verts
Peas .... Petits pois
Carrots .... Carottes
Spinach .... Épinards
Onions .... Oignons
Lettuce .... Laitue
Cucumber .... Concombre
Tomatoes .... Tomates
Fruit .... Les fruits
Apples .... Pommes
Strawberries .... Fraises
Peaches .... Pêches
Pears .... Poires
Fruit tart .... Tarte aux fruits
Pastry .... Pâtisserie
Chocolate cake . Gâteau au chocolat

Cream .... Crème
Ice cream .... Glace
Chocolate mousse .... Mousse au chocolat

TOURIST INFORMATION

Where is the tourist information office, please?
Où se trouve l'office du tourisme, s'il vous plaît?
Do you have a city map?
Avez-vous un plan de la ville?
Where is the museum?
Où est le musée?
Can you give me some information about...?
Pouvez-vous me donner des renseignements sur ...?
What are the main places of interest here?
Quels sont les principaux sites touristiques ici?
Please could you point them out on the map?
Pouvez-vous me les indiquer sur la carte, s'il vous plaît?
What sights/hotels/restaurants can you recommend?
Quels sites/hôtels/restaurants nous recommandez-vous?
We are staying here for a day.
Nous sommes ici pour une journée.
I am interested in...
Je suis intéressé(e) par ...
Does the guide speak English?
Est ce qu'il y a un guide qui parle anglais?
Do you have any suggested walks?
Avez-vous des suggestions de promenades?
Are there guided tours?
Est-ce qu'il y a des visites guidées?
Are there organized excursions?
Est-ce qu'il y a des excursions organisées?
Can we make reservations here?
Est-ce que nous pouvons réserver ici?
What time does it open/close?
Ça ouvre/ferme à quelle heure?
What is the admission price?
Quel est le tarif d'entrée?
Is there a discount for seniors/students?
Est-ce qu'il y a des réductions pour les personnes âgées/les étudiants?
Do you have a brochure in English?
Avez-vous un dépliant en anglais?
What's on at the cinema?
Qu'est-ce qu'il y a au cinéma?
Where can I find a good nightclub?
Où est-ce que je peux trouver une bonne boîte de nuit?
Do you have a schedule for the theatre/opera?
Est-ce que vous avez un programme de théâtre/ d'opéra?
Should we dress smartly?
Est-ce qu'il faut mettre une tenue de soirée?
What time does the show start?
À quelle heure commence le spectacle?
How do I reserve a seat?
Comment fait-on pour réserver une place?
Could you reserve tickets for me?
Pouvez-vous me réserver des places?

ILLNESS

I don't feel well.
Je ne me sens pas bien.
Could you call a doctor?
(Est-ce que) vous pouvez appeler un médecin/un docteur, s'il vous plaît?
Is there a doctor/pharmacist on duty?
(Est-ce qu')il y a un médecin/docteur/une pharmacie de garde?
I feel sick.
J'ai envie de vomir.
I need to see a doctor.
Il faut que je voie un médecin/docteur.
Please direct me to the hospital.
(Est-ce que) vous pouvez m'indiquer le chemin pour aller à l'hôpital, s'il vous plaît?
I have a headache.
J'ai mal à la tête.
I've been stung by a wasp/bee/jellyfish.
J'ai été piqué(e) par une guêpe/abeille/méduse.
I have a heart condition.
J'ai un problème cardiaque.
I am diabetic.
Je suis diabétique.
I'm asthmatic.
Je suis asmathique.
I'm on a special diet.
Je suis un régime spécial.
I am on medication.
Je prends des médicaments.
I have left my medicine at home.
J'ai laissé mes médicaments chez moi.
My blood pressure is too high.
Ma tension est trop élevée.

AT THE DENTIST

I need to see a dentist.
Il faut que je voie un dentiste.
I have bad toothache.
J'ai mal aux dents.
How much do I owe you?
Combien vous dois-je?

ACCIDENTS AND EMERGENCIES

Help!
Au secours!
I have lost my passport/wallet/purse/handbag.
J'ai perdu mon passeport/portefeuille/porte-monnaie/sac à main.
I have had an accident.
J'ai eu un accident.
My car has been stolen.
On m'a volé ma voiture.
I have been robbed.
J'ai été volé(e).
My child has had a fall.
Mon enfant a fait une chute.
He/she is unconscious.
Il/Elle s'est évanoui(e).
He/She is bleeding badly.
Il/Elle perd du sang.
I have a pain in my chest.
Je ressens une douleur dans la poitrine.
I think his/her arm is broken.
Je crois qu'il/elle s'est cassé le bras.
Where is the police station?
Où est la gendarmerie?
Call the police.
Appelez la police.
I want a copy of the police report.
Je voudrais une copie du constat.
Emergency exit
Sortie de secours
Push
Poussez
Pull
Tirez
Information
Renseignements

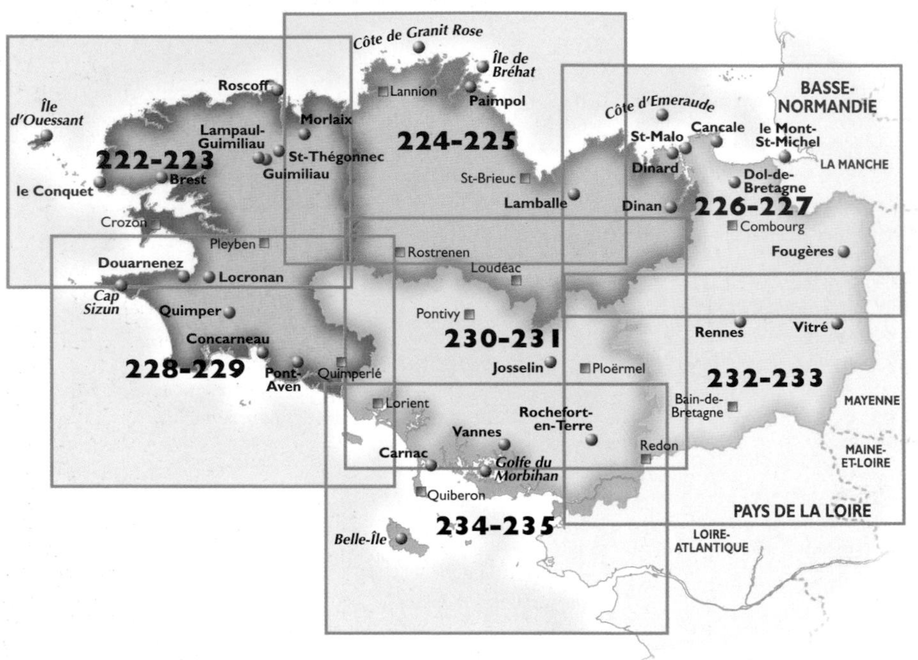

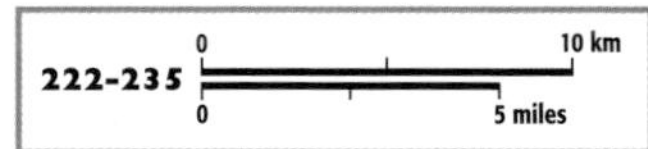

Toll motorway (Turnpike)

Motorway (Expressway)

Motorway junction with and without number

National road

Regional road

Other road

Railway

Administrative region boundary

Département boundary

City

Town / Village

National Park

Featured place of interest

Airport

621 Height in metres

Ferry route

MAPS

Map references for the sights refer to the atlas pages within this section or to the individual town plans within the regions. For example, Rennes has the reference 233 M11, indicating the page on which the map is found (233) and the grid square in which Rennes sits (M11).

A
B
C
6
7
8
9
10
Côte des Légendes
les Abers
Île Vierge
Île Stagadon
St-Michel
Lilia
Île Tariec
D10
Île Guenioc
Vourch
Plouguerneau
Île du Bec
Île Garo
Aber Vrac'h
Landéda
le Grouannec
Aber
Pointe de Landunvez
St-Pabu
Benoît
Lannilis
D28
Tréglonou
D28
Île Yoc'h
D27
Landunvez
Ploudalmézeau
Porspoder
Plouguin
Plouvien
D28
D26
Coat-Méal
D13
Île d'Ouessant
Plourin
D35
Pointe de Pern
Lampaul
Île Melon
Melon
D68
D168
Bourg-Blanc
Pointe de Porz Doun
Passage du Fromveur
Chenal de la Helle
Brélès
Lanrivoaré
Plabennec
Lampaul-Plouarzel
Aber Ildut
Pays
Milizac
D13
Île de Bannec
Île Ségal
D3
D26
D788
Plouarzel
St-Renan
D67
Gouesnou
Île de Balanec
Trézien
D5
Île de Molène
Lamber
Guilers
Bohars
Kerhornou
Ploumoguer
Île de Trielen
D28
D67
Pointe de Kermorvan
Île de Quéménès
Trébabu
Locmaria-Plouzané
Plouzané
BREST
Parc Naturel Régional d'Armorique
Chenal du Four
le Conquet
D789
Île de Beniguet
Porsmilin
Ste-Anne-du-Portzic
Plougonvelin
Pointe de St-Mathieu
Goulet de Brest
Pointe de Creac'h-Meur
Pointe des Espagnols
Rade de Brest
Roscanvel
Pointe de l'Armorique
Pointe de Toulinguet
le Fret
Camaret-sur-Mer
Lanvéoc
Anse de Poulmic
D355
Pointe de Pen-Hir
D8
Presqu'île de Crozon
Crozon
Tal-ar-Groas
Pointe de Dinan
Morgat
Kerglintin
D255
Cap de la Chèvre
Baie de Douarnenez
Chaussée de Sein
Pointe de Brézellec
Pointe de Millier
228
Lescogan
Pointe du Van
Beuzec-Cap-Sizun
D7
Poullan-sur-Mer
Baie des Trépassés
Cap Sizun
Cléden-Cap-Sizun
Île de Sein
Moulin-Castel
Pouldavid
Pointe du Raz
Lescoff
D784
D765
Confort
Plogoff

D
E
F
Cork, Rosslare Harbour, Plymouth
6
Île de Batz
Baie de Lannion
Pointe de Beg Pol
Theven-Kerbrat
Île de Siec
Roscoff
Pointe du Diben
Pointe de Primel
Point
Brignogan-Plage
Croazou
Plounéour-Trez
Kerlouan
Guissény
Ker-Emma
D10
Plouescat
D10
Sibiril
Santec
St-Pol-de-Léon
D58
Cléder
Plougoulm
Carantec
Plougasnou
D46
St-Jean-du-Doigt
Donant
7
D78
D64
Guimaëc
Quélimadec
D770
Goulven
Tréflez
Lochrist
D110
Plouider
Plounévez-Lochrist
D125
Pont-du-Chatel
D788
D30
D788
D769
D10
Ste-Catherine
Henvic
Plouénan
Baie de Morlaix
D46
Plouézoch
Lanmeur
D786
Berven
Léon
St-Vougay
Plouzévédé
D58
Taulé
Brévalaire
Lesneven
Lanhouarneau
Château de Kerjean
Plouvorn
Penzé
224
Ste-Genev
Douron
le Folgoët
St-Méen
D35
D19
D31
Coatoulsach
Morlaix
D64
le Drennec
Ploudaniel
D32
Flèche
D30
Plougourvest
D69
Guiclan
Penzé
Plouigneau
D770
Trémaouézan
Plounéventer
E50
N12
St-Thégonnec
Plourin-lès-Mortaix
Kersaint-Plabennec
E50
N12
Landivisiau
D769
Plougonven
Plouédern
D712
Lampaul-Guimiliau
Guimiliau
Pleyber-Christ
Guerlesquin
Landerneau
la-Roche-Maurice
D764
D11
D19
Cloitre-St-Thégonnec
D9
Lannéan
8
Gulpavas
la Forest-Landerneau
la Martyre
Ploudiry
D30
Loc-Eguiner-St-Thégonnac
D785
Kervian
D769
Kermeur
Elorn
e Relecq-Kerhoun
D770
St-Sauveur
Plounéour-Menez
Tréflévénez
Elorn
D18
Penze
Mendy
Squiriou
D42
D54
Bolazec
St-Urbain
Sizun
Commana
Scrignac
E60
N165
Daoulas
le Tréhou
D764
Moulins de Kérouat
384
Roc'h Trévezel
Plougastel-Daoulas
Loperhet
Irvillac
Monts d'Arrée
Daoulas
Barrage du Drennec
St-Cadou
Botmeur
la Feuillée
Berrien
D769
Tinduff
Goasven
D770
St-Eloy
Domaine de Menez-Meur
D18
217
Pen-ar-Hoat
St-Rivoal
380
St-Michel
Réservoir de St Michel
Brennilis
Fao
D14
Aulne
Logonna-Daoulas
Hôpital-Camfrout
Hanvec
Elez
Huelgoat
le Gu
Landévennec
le Faou
Faou
Parc Naturel Régional d'Armorique
D785
Loqueffret
D36
274
Roc'h Begheor
D14
St-Herbot
Poullaouen
D769
Brasparts
Plouyé
D764
D791
Rosnoën
Quimerch
Lopérec
D14
Lannédern
Argol
Aulne
Châteaulin
Collorec
9
Telgruc-sur-Mer
D887
Bassin de
Pont-de-Buis
le Cloitre-Pleyben
Goanes
D36
Penquer Lois
Kergloff
330
Ménez-Hom
Dinéhault
Pleyben
Plonévez-du-Faou
N164
230
Cléden-Poher
Pentrez-Plage
Châteaulin
Landeleau
Ancien
Plomodiern
D769
Lothey
D785
Aulne
Lennon
Châteauneuf-du-Faou
D7
Gouézec
Spézet
Motref
Cast
D72
D38
Ste-Anne-la-Palud
D63
Plonévez-Porzay
D770
E60 N165
326
Roc de Toullaëron
St-Goazes
D107
FINISTÈRE
229
D36
290
Coat
Montagnes Noires
10
Douarnenez
D7
Kergoat
Quéménéven
D72
D41
Laz
D1
Locronan
Briec
D51
les Montagnes
D6
Roudouallec
Gourin
Ploaré
Plogonnec
D770
D785
Edern
Trégourez

E
F
G
6
7
8
9
Côte de Granit Rose
les Sept Îles
Île Renote
Pointe du Squéouel
Île Tomé
Île St-Gildas
Pointe du Château
Îles d'Er
Côte des Ajoncs
Ploumanac'h
Pointe du Château
Plougrescant
Pleubian
Île Grande
Port-Blanc
Île à Canton
Trégastel
Perros-Guirec
Trévou-Treguignec
Penvern
St-Quay-Perros
Trélévern
Penvénan
Plouguiel
Pleumeur-Gautier
Louannec
le Jaudy
Baie de Lannion
Trébeurden
Pointe de Bihit
Pleumeur-Bodou
Kermaria-Sulard
Tréguier
Trédarzec
Pointe du Diben
Pointe de Primel
Pointe de Séhar
la Ville-Blanche
Pleudaniel
Pouldouran
Lannion
la Roche-Derrien
Boloí
-le-Léon
Plougasnou
St-Jean-du-Doigt
Ploulec'h
Rospez
Guindy
Jaudy
Pommerit-Jaudy
Locquirec
Trédrez
Buhulien
Baie de Morlaix
Ploubezre
Trégor
Ploëzal
St-Michel-en-Grève
Confort
Guimaëc
Ploumilliau
Plouézoch
Lanmeur
Tonquédec
Cavan
Prat
Pontrieux
Plestin-les-Grèves
Brélidy
Plouëc-du-Trieux
Yar
Trieux
Dourdull
Pluzunet
Lanvellec
Plufur
Plouaret
Begard
Ste-Geneviève
Douron
Morlaix
Plouégat-Moysan
le Vieux-Marché
Plouigneau
Pédernec
Plourin-lès-Mortaix
Louargat
302
Ménez Bré
Plouisy
Pabu
Plounevez-Moëdec
Guingamp
Plougonven
Guic
Belle-Isle-Benac'h
Pleyber-Christ
Loguivy-Plougras
Guerlesquin
Grâces
St-Agathon
Ploumagor
Cloitre-St-Thégonnec
Léguer
le Dresnay
Lannéanou
Gurunhuel
Moustéru
Kervian
Coadut
Kermeur
Plougonver
Mendy
223
Lohuec
Scrignac
Bolazec
la Chapelle-Neuve
St-Péver
Bourbriac
Calanhel
Plésidy
la Feuillée
Berrien
Bulat-Pestivien
St-Norgant
Réservoir de St Michel
Fao
Callac
Aulne
Brennilis
le Guilly
St-Servais
Elez
Huelgoat
Kerien
la Clarté
274
Roc'h Begheor
St-Herbot
Loc'h
Kerpert
Poullaouen
Etang de Kerne Unel
Plouyé
Hyère
Collorec
Locarn
Kergrist-Moëlou
le-Haut-Corlay
St-Nicolas-du-Pélem
Kergloff
Carhaix-Plouguer
Penquer Lois
Maël-Carhaix
Plounévez-Quintin
St-Lubin
230
la Pie
Blavet
Plussulien
Ancien
Cléden-Poher
Landeleau
Ste-Tréphine
Canal
Nantes
Plouguernével
Châteauneuf-du-Faou
Glomel
Rostrenen
Gouarec
Laniscat
Motreff
Etang du Coronc
Brest
St-Gelven
326
E50
N12
N164
D786
D767
D30
D33
D11
D6
D8
D15
D787
D788
D65
D46
D64
D78
D58
D42
D9
D769
D28
D31
D54
D14
D36
D764
D790
D3
D44

H
J
K
6
7
8
9
5
Sillon de Talbert
Armor
Île Modez
Phare du Paon
Île de Bréhat
Lanmodez
D70
Loguivy de-la-Mer
Pointe de l'Arcouest
Ploubazlanec
Lézardrieux
Paimpol
Kerity
Pointe de Plouézec
Côte de Goëlo
Plouézec
Pointe de Minard
Plourivo
D7
D15
D786
Pointe Berjule
Quemper-Guézennec
Lanloup
Pléhédel
Pointe de Plouha
D6
Plouha
Trévérec
Lannebert
D7
St-Quay-Portrieux
D9
Pléguien
Pommerit-le-Vicomte
Lanvollon
Plourhan
Etables-sur-Mer
Goudelin
Tréguidel
Binic
la Corderie
Leff
la Ville-Louais
D786
Pordic
les Rosaires
Plélo
D6
E50
N12
Plouagat
Châtelaudren
Lanrodec
Plerin
Tremuson
St-Brieuc
Senven
Boqueho
D7
D36
Ploufragan
St-Donan
Trégueux
Cohiniac
St-Julien
D700
D10
Urne
Plaine Haute
Pledran
St-Gildas
le Fœil
Gouet
D7
Quintin
Plaintel
le Vieux-Bourg
Carestremble
St-Brandan
St-Carreuc
D700
D7
D790
Corlay
la Bodéo
D44
D44
l'Hermitage-Lorge
Côte de Penthievre
Cap d'Erquy
Sables-d'Or-les-Pins
Cap Fréhel
Erquy
Plurien
Frèhel
D786
Pléboulle
Montbran
D14
D13
Pointe de Pléneuf
le Val-André
Pléneuf-Val-André
D786
Baie de Saint-Brieuc
Pointe du Roselier
Pointe des Guettes
St-Alban
le Poirier
St-Jacques
la Bouillie
Frémur
226
Hénanbihen
D786
Planguenoual
Hénansal
D13
St-Denoual
D768
Hillion
Langueux
Ponts-Neufs
Coëtmieux
St-Aaron
D791
D768
Yffiniac
St-René
Gouessant
St-Symphorien
E50
E401
N12
Pommeret
Lamballe
Evron
l'Hôpital
Meslin
Trégomar
Gast
D1
Quessoy
Noyal
Plédéliac
D768
Landéhen
D14
CÔTES D'ARMOR
Plestan
Bréhand
D765
Hénon
la Malhourne
Jugo
D1
Moncontour
Trédaniel
Penguily
D44
D6
D14
D792
Plémy
Ploeuc-sur-Lié
Plény-Jugon
Gouessant
le Rieule
Lié
la Porte-aux-Moines
Cust
Gausson
D768
231
le Gouray
Landes du Ménez
Collinée
Daoulas
D767
Uzel
St-Hervé
Plouguenast
Broon
St-Jacut-du-Mené
Langourla
Plessala
Rance
le Quillio
D35
D7
D700
D768
Eréac
St-Gilles-

K
L
M
Plymouth, Jersey
Grand Île
7
8
9
10
Côte d'Emeraude
Cap Fréhel
Anse des Sevignes
Forte la Latte
Penthieve
Cap d'Erquy
Sables-d'Or-les-Pins
Île de Cézembre
Pointe du Grouin
Île des Landes
Rothéneuf
le Verger
D201
D355
St-Jouan
Cancale
St-Coulomb
le Beuglais
St-Malo
Dinard
Pointe de St-Cast
St-Cast-le-Guildo
Baie de la Frênaye
Erquy
Plurien
Frèhel
D786
Pléboulle
Montbran
D14
Matignon
D13
St-Lunaire
Île des Hébihens
St-Briac-sur-Mer
Lancieux
la Richardais
D168
D266
Rance
St-Meloir-des-Ondes
D76
D155
St-Benoit-des-Ondes
St-Jouan-des-Guérets
la Gouesnière
Hirel
la Fresnais
St-George
D4
N137
le Grand Biez de Cardéquin
Pléneuf-Val-André
la Bouillie
Frémur
D17
St-Jacques
Hénanbihen
D794
St-Jacut-de-la-Mer
N D du Guido
Ploubalay
Pleurtuit
Hénansal
D13
St-Pôtan
Tregon
D768
Créhen
Tréméreuc
Trébéfour
D2
Planguenoual
St-Denoual
D768
Pluduno
Pleslin-Trigavou
Châteauneuf-d'Ille-et-Vilaine
St-Aaron
D791
225
Plancoët
St-Symphorien
Arguenon
Languénan
D766
Plouër-Langrolay-sur-Rance
Miniac-Morvan
Plerguer
D676
Baguer-Morvan
Lamballe
Bourseul
D794
D2
Corseul
Trégomar
Gast
D792
St-Michel-de-Plélan
St-Samson-sur-Rance
Pleudihen-sur-Rance
D676
Noyal
Plédéliac
Quévert
St-Helen
Landéhen
D14
Plestan
Plélan-le-Petit
Dinan
Lanvallay
Molene
D73
Bonnemain
St-Solent
Lanhélin
Léhon
St-Pierre-de-Plesguen
la Malhourne
Trélivan
E401
N176
D794
Etang de Tremigon
Jugon-les-Lacs
les Champs-Géraux
Grand Etang de Jugon
le Hinglé
D2
Meillac
Penguily
D14
D792
Pléné-Jugon
D793
Brusvily
Rosette
Megrit
Guinefort
Evran
Pleugueneuc
D13
la Chapelle-aux-Filtzméens
le Rieule
D39
St-Domineuc
Yvignac
D766
le Quiou
D13
le Gouray
Broons
D39
Tréfumel
Collinée
D795
St-Jacut-du-Mené
Langourla
D793
Etang de Neal
Tinténiac
D20
la Baussaine
du Ménéz
Caulnes
Plouasne
Rance
Eréac
Bécherel
St-Symphorien
D27
les Iffs
Hédé
Gilles-Mené
Lanrelas
Plumaugat
D220
Médréac
St-Vran
St-Launeuc
Rance
Quédillac
E50
N12
Landujan
Irodouër
Hivet
D6
D71
Langan
N137
N164
Merdrignac
D166
la Chapelle-du-Lou
Vaunoise
Flume
D72
Trémorel
Romillé
Gévezé
St-Méen-le-Grand
N164
N164
Moutauban-de-Bretagne
la Mezière
D27
D793
Yvel
Meu
D125
D61
Garun
Bédée
Pleumeleuc
Méneac
Illifaut
Boisgervilly
232
la Nouaye
la Chapelle-des-Fougereiz
E50
N12
D304
D166
Gaël
Muel
D30
St-Maugan
Montfort
Breteil
St-Gilles
D125
D29
St-Brieuc-de-Mauron
Meu
l'Hermitage
la Chapelle-Thouarault
Vezin-

N
P
Q
St-Martin-de-Bréhal
Bréhal
Coudeville
Gavray
Percy
Mont Robin
Montaigu-les-Bois
le Mesnil-Hue
Margueray
St-Vigor des-Monts
Drôme
Granville
le Loreur
le Mesnil-Garnier
Sienne
Airou
A84 E03
Villedieu-les Poêles
Sept-Frères
le Mesnil-Caussois
St-Aubin-des-Bois
St-Sever-Calvados
7
D924
le Repas
St-Planchers
Beauchamps
Champrepus
Fleury
St-Pair-sur-Mer
St-Jean-des-Champs
Folligny
Kairon-Plage
le Pont-Bleue
Jullouville
La Haye-Pesnel
la Chapelle-Cécelin
Chérence-le-Héron
Sterne
Braise
Carolles
Falaise de Champeaux
Angey
Sartilly
Ste-Pience
St-Nicolas-des-Bois
St-Lauren-de-Cuves
Ronthon
Dragey-Ronthon
St-Pois
Tirepied
Brécey
Cuves
le Mesnil-Gilbert
Chérences le-Roussel
Marcey-les-Grèves
Genêts
St-Senier-sous-Avranches
Avranches
LA MANCHE
Bellefontaine
Baie du Mont Saint Michel
le Val-St-Pierre
St-Martin-des-Champs
Reffuveille
Juvigny-le-Tertre
St-Quentin-sur-le-Homme
le Mont-St-Michel
Montigny
Bas-Courtil
Courtils
la Rive
Vivier-sur-Mer
Cherrueix
la Poultière
Beauvoir
Couesnon
Précey
Ducey
Isigny-le-Buat
Fontenay
8
St-Broladre
Roz-sur-Couesnon
Parigny
Vezins
Mont-Dol
E401 N176
St-Hilaire
Dol-de-Bretagne
Pontorson
Pleine-Fougères
la Croix-Avranchin
Beauvron
Hamelin
St-Martin-de-Landelles
Epiniac
la Boussac
St-Symphorien-des-monts
St-Léonard
Trans
St James
St-Georges-de-Reintembault
Buais
Montanel
Argouges
le Ferré
Broualan
Mellé
Louvigné
Tronçon
Landivy
Cuguen
Antrain
Poilley
Fugerolles-du-Plessis
Tréméheuc
la-Selle-en-Coglés
Montours
Combourg
Tremblay
Bazouges-la-Pérouse
Parigne
9
St-Léger-des-Prés
St-Brice-en-Coglès
St-Etienne-en-Coglès
Landéan
St-Mars-sur-la-Futaie
Marcillé-Raoul
St-Germain-en-Coglès
St-Ellier-du-Maine
St-Rémy-du-Plain
Dingé
Romazy
St-Marc-le-Blanc
Lécousse
Montaudin
Ille
Etang de Boulet
Minette
Baillé
Laignelet
Larchamp
Sens-de-Bretagne
Fougères
Feins
St-Ouen-des-Alleux
St-Sauveur-des-Landes
Romagné
Beaucé
Fleurtigné
Montreuil-sur-Ille
St-Marc-sur-Couesnon
Rollon
Neuville
Gahard
Javené
Guipel
Mézières-sur-Coueson
Vendel
St-Médard-sur-Ille
Etang d'Ouée
Billé
Chandon
Luitré
Monguerre
Ernée
St-Aubin-d'Aubigne
St-Aubin-du-Cormier
Dompierre-du-Chemin
Montreuil-le-Gast
Ercé-près-Liffre
St-Pierre-des-Landes
Gosné
Etang de Châtillon
Chasné-sur-Illet
Melesse
St-Christophe-des-Bois
Epronnières
10
Chévaigné
Liffré
Livré-sur-Changeon
Châtillon-en-Vendelais
Juvigné
la Meule
St-Hilaire-du-Maine
Bassin de
Betton
Dourdain
233
la Croixille
Montgermont
la Bouëxière
Taillis
Montautour
St-Grégoire
Thorigné-Fouillard
Val-d'Izé
St-M'Hervé
Etang de Pain Tourteau
ILLE-ET-VILAINE
Balazé
Champeaux
Cesson-
Acigné
Vilaine

A
B
C
9
10
11
12
13
222
Cap de la Chèvre
Baie de Douarnenez
Pentrez-Plage
Plomodiern
Ste-Anne-la-Palud
Plonéve Porzay
Chaussée de Sein
Île de Sein
Pointe du Van
Pointe de Brézellec
Baie des Trépassés
Pointe du Raz
Lescoff
Cap Sizun
Cléden-Cap-Sizun
Plogoff
D784
Primelin
Beuzec-Cap-Sizun
Moulin-Castel
Esquibien
Audierne
Pointe de Lervity
Pointe de Millier
Lescogan
D7
Douarnenez
Poullan-sur-Mer
Pouldavic
Ploaré
Locronan
Plogonnec
D107
D765
Confort
Pont-Croix
D143
Nevet
D56
Pouldergat
D43
Goyen
Guengat
Plouhinec
Ty-Pic
Landudec
D784
Ploneis
Plozévet
D2
D143
Plogastel-StGermain
Pluguffan
Pouldreuzic
Penhors
Pont l'Abbé
D156
Tréogat
Plovan
D785
Baie d'Audierne
Plonéour-Lanvern
Combrit
D57
St-Jean-Trolimon
Pont-l'Abbé
Pointe de la Porche
Plomeur
D2
St-Guénolé
D785
D53
Plobannalec
Loctudy
Penmarc'h
Treffiagat
Pointe de Penmarc'h
Guilvinec
Lodonnec
Présqu'Île de Penmarc'h

Châteaulin
Châteauneuf-du-Faou
Landeleau
Cléden-Poher
Lothey
Lennon
Gouézec
Cast
Spézet
Motreff
Glomel
Etang du Coronc
223
224
FINISTÈRE
St-Goazes
Roc de Toullaëron
Groas-Brenn
Laz
Coat
les Montagnes Noires
Tregornan
St-Nicolas
Quéménéven
Kergoat
Briec
Edern
Trégourez
Roudouallec
Gourin
Langonnet
Quilinep
Croëzou
Steir
Landudal
Langolen
Coray
Coadry
Odet
Quelennec
Lestonan
Guiscriff
Scaër
Priziac
Ellé
Quimper
Ergué-Gabéric
Kerdévot
Tourc'h
Elliant
le Faouët
St-Fiacre
Lanvénégen
230
Meslan
Baie de Kerogan
Bourdonnel
Rosporden
St-Yvy
Anse de Toulven
St-Jacques
Kernével
Plomelin
St-Evarzec
Cadol
St-Thurien
Querrien
Ty-Glaz
Menez-St-Jean
Pleuven
la Forêt-Fouesnant
Bannalec
Roches du Diable
Clohars-Fouesnant
Fouesnant
Poteau-Vert
Melgven
Concarneau
Bénodet
Baie de la Forêt
Mellac
Tréméven
Arzano
le Trévoux
Anse de Bénodet
Beg-Meil
Pointe de Mousterlin
Tregunc
Pont-Aven
Kéraël
Baye
Quimperlé
Pendrus
Pointe de la Jument
Baie de Concarneau
Riec-sur-Belon
Rédené
Cléguer
Névez
Moëlan-sur-Mer
Pont-Scorff
Trévignon
Pointe de Trevignon
Port Manec'h
Belon
Clohars-Carnoet
Coat-erMalo
Gestel
Île aux Moutons
Langlazic
Guidel
Queven
le Pouldu
Îles de Glénan
Anse du Pouldu
Plomemeur
le Fort-Bloque
Lorient
Larmor-Plage
Pointe du Talut
Port-Louis
234
Pointe de Bileric
Groix
Île de Groix
Locmaria
D
E
F
9
10
11
12
13

F
G
H
9
10
11
12
13
224
229
234
Carhaix-Plouguer
Locarn
Kergrist-Moëlou
Maël-Carhaix
Plounévez-Quintin
St-Nicolas-du-Pélem
le-Haut-Corlay
Corlay
la Bodéo
Kergloff
Hyère
D8
D790
D44
D31
St-Lubin
la Pie
N164
Canal
Nantes à Brest
Ancien
D769
Motreff
Glomel
Etang du Coronc
Rostrenen
Plouguernével
Gouarec
Ste-Tréphine
Blavet
Plussulien
Laniscat
Daoulas
D767
la Porte-aux-Moines
le Quillio
D3
D790
Bonen
D23
Doré
D764
St-Gelven
Caurel
D35
St-Guen
Rigole d'Hilvern
Noires
Trégornan
Ellé
Mellionnec
Etang des Salles
Lac de Guerlédan
D5
Mur-de-Bretagne
N164
St-Nicolas
D1
Plouray
le Corboulo
Silfiac
St-Caradec
D27
Kerguzul
Langonnet
Langoëlan
D18
Neuilliac
D32
D780
Poul-Grellec
Séglien
Cléguérec
le Moustoir
D769
Stêr Laer
Scorff
Sarre
D764
Blavet
Priziac
Ploërdut
le Croisty
Guéméné-s-Scorff
Locmalo
D782
Malguénac
Stival
D767
D768
le Faouët
Lignol
Niziao-d'en-Bas
Pontivy
St-Fiacre
D3
le Sourn
Noyal-Pontivy
Lanvénégen
D782
Kernascléden
Guern
D2
Meslan
Berné
Pays de Pontivy
Naïc
Querrien
St-Thurien
Inguiniel
St-Fiacre
St-Thuriau
St-Armel
Melrand
Naizin
Isole
D790
Roches du Diable
D18
D2
Bubry
Brandifrout
St-Nicolas-des-Eaux
Pluméliau
Mellac
Evel
D17
Tréméven
D23
St-Yves
St-Barthélemy
Remungol
Arzano
D2
Plouay
Quimperlé
Quistinic
D768
Guernic
Moréac
Guénin
Baye
D62
Calan
St-Symphorien
N24
Rédené
Cléguer
Penquesten
Blavet
Baud
Locminé
Pont-Scorff
D26
D769
Inzinzac-Lochrist
Evel
la Chapelle-Neuve
Plumelin
D16
Laita
Clohars-Carnoët
Gestel
Lambel
Camros
D16
Coat-erMalo
Hennebont
N24
Languidic
Moustoir-Ac
Kerhéro
Lanvaux
D24
Guidel
Queven
D24
D779
Locoal-Camors
Le Pouldu
D265
Malachappe
Kerglois
Bienzy-Lanvaux
Colpo
Lanester
Brandérion
D16
Anse du Pouldu
E60
N165
D17
Plomemeur
D781
D194
Pluvigner
Brandivy
D767
le Fort-Bloque
Lorient
Kervignac
Landévant
Grand-Champ
D152
Merlevenez
Nostang
Landaul
Loc'h
D768
Larmor-Plage
Locmiquelic
D33
Ste-Hélène
Plumergat
Locmaria-Grand-Champ
Riantec
D9
D19
Pointe du Talut
Port-Louis
Plouhinec
D781
Locoal-Mendon
Brech
Ste-Anne-d'Auray
D779
Sal
Pointe de Gavres
Mériadec
Pointe de Bileric
Belz
Auray
Plescop
D22
D19
Groix
Pluneret
Île de Groix
Étel
Vincin
Locmaria
Erdeven
Ploemel
Plougoumelen
Ploeren
Pointe d'Erdeven
D768
Bono
D781
D29
D101
Crac'h
Arradon
Baden
Plouharnel
Crac'h
Auray
D781
la Trinité-sur-Mer
Ile-aux-Moines
Ile d'Arz

Grand Etang
de Jugon
Ploeuc-
sur-Lié
Plémy
Trédaniel
Penguily
Pléné-Jugon
Rosette
Megrit
Brusvily
l'Hermitage-
Lorge
225
le Gouray
Yvignac
Gausson
Collinée
Landes du Ménéz
Broons
Uzel
St-Hervé
Plouguenast
Plessala
St-Jacut-
du-Mené
Langourla
Caulnes
La Motte
St-Gilles-
du-Mené
Eréac
Lanrelas
Plumaugat
Rance
Quédillac
Trévé
St-Vran
St-Launeuc
Hivet
Laurenan
Loudéac
Plémet
Merdrignac
Trémorel
St-Méen-
le-Grand
de-Breta
St-Gonnery
St-Barnabé
la Ferrière
la Chèze
Ménéac
Illifaut
Boisgervilly
St-Maudan
St-Etienne
du-Gué-de-l'Isle
Plumieux
Gaël
Muel
St-Maugan
Meu
Iffendi
la Trinite-
Porhoët
St-Brieuc-
de-Mauron
Rohan
Bréhan
Evriguet
Mauron
St-Lery
Mohon
Crédin
Canal de Nantes à Brest
Guilliers
Forêt de Paimpont
St-Péran
Lanouée
St-Malo-des-
3-Fontaines
Paimpont
Pleugriffet
les Croix
Néant-
sur-Yvel
Plélan-
le-Grand
Réguiny
Loyat
232
les Forges-
de-Paimpont
Etang Duc
Taupont
Beignon
Maxent
Josselin
Campénéac
St-Malo-
de-Beignon
Guégon
Gourhel
Bellevue-
Coëtquidan
St-Allouestre
Ploërmel
Loutehel
Bigan
Kerguéhennec
Guéhenno
Guillac
Augan
MORBIHAN
Porcaro
Guer
Oyon
St-Jean-
Brévelay
Lizio
le Roc-
St-André
la Chapelle-
Caro
Monteneuf
Réminiac
Caro
Comblessac
Plumelec
la Telhaie
Sérent
Landes de Lanvaux
St-Marcel
Malestroit
Ruffiac
Carentoir
Quelneuc
Plaudren
Trédion
St-Laurent
Claire
Locqueltas
Morbouleau
St-Guyomard
la Chapelle-
Gaceline
St-Congard
Monterblanc
la Gacilly
Sixt-
sur-Aff
Pleucadeuc
Meucon
Elven
le Cours
235
Molac
Mont
Hersé
St-Martin
les Fougerêts
St-Nolff
St-Ave
Larré
Rochefort-
en-Terre
St-Gravé
Glénac
Menimur
Trefiléan
la Vraie-Croix
Bel-Air
Pluherlin
Peillac
Bains-
sur-Oust
St-Vincent-
sur-Oust
Sulniac
Malansac
Vannes
Questembert
le Gorvello
Séné
Thiex
Berric
Limerzel
Allaire
Noyalo
Lauzach
Caden
N164
N24
N166
D793
D766
D776
D775
E60 N165
E50 N12

N164
Merdrignac
K
Trémorel
St-Méen-le-Grand
L
la Chapelle-du-Lou
Romillé
M
Gévezé
la Mezière
N164
226
Moutauban-de-Bretagne
D72
Flume
D27
10
D793
Yvel
Meu
Garun
Bédée
Pleumeleuc
la Chapelle-des-Fougereiz
Ménéac
Illifaut
D61
Boisgervilly
la Nouaye
E50
N12
Gaël
Muel
D30
St-Maugan
Breteil
St-Gilles
D166
Montfort
Pacé
Meu
Iffendic
D125
l'Hermitage
D2
D304
St-Brieuc-de-Mauron
la Chapelle-Thouarault
Vezin-le-Coquet
D2
Evriguet
St-Lery
Talensac
Cintré
D287
Mauron
D62
Meu
le Rheu
D288
D16
D773
D35
Monterfil
Mordelles
Guilliers
St-Jacques-de-la-Lande
D16
Forêt de Paimpont
St-Péran
Chavagne
St-Malo-des-3-Fontaines
D13
D766
Treffendel
N24
D8
Levernin
Néant-sur-Yve
Paimpont
D61
Bréal-sous-Montfort
D36
D40
D177
Plélan-le-Grand
D21
11
Loyat
231
les Forges-de-Paimpont
Goven
Bruz
Etangu Duc
Canut
D39
Pont-Réan
Taupont
Beignon
Maxent
Baulon
D724
St-Malo-de-Beignon
D65
Celar
Campéneac
Lassy
D776
Guichen
Gourhel
Bellevue-Coëtquirdan
Ploërmel
N24
Loutehel
Augan
Campel
D84
D48
Guillac
D772
la Chapelle-Bouëxic
D42
Vilaine
Porcaro
D773
Guer
Combs
N166
Oyon
Guignen
Bourg-des-Comptes
Maure-de-Bretagne
Roc-André
la Chapelle-Caro
D8
D776
St-Senoux
Semnon
Monteneuf
D772
D177
Chaumeray
Pléchâtel
Caro
Réminiac
Comblessac
la Telhaie
u
x
D114
Lodéac
Oust
St-Séglin
Combs
Lieuron
St-Marcel
Malestroit
Ruffiac
D65
Quelneuc
Carentoir
Bruc-sur-Aff
Guipry
D776
D777
St-Laurent
12
Noyal
Gravot
Messac
la Chapelle-Gaceline
Pipriac
D8
D777
D53
St-Congard
D112
D14
la Noë-Blanche
la Gacilly
Sixt-sur-Aff
D5
Pleucadeuc
80
Mont Hersé
D177
D59
St-Martin
St-Just
D774
D777
Molac
D764
Vaux-Bourg
les Fougerêts
D773
St-Ganton
St-Gravé
la Dominelais
Rochefort-en-Terre
D777
Glénac
Port-de-Roche
D69
D764
D56
Peillac
Oust
Renac
Bel-Air
D777
Bains-sur-Oust
Pluherlin
St-Vincent-sur-Oust
Grand Fougeray
Malansac
235
D873
D177
la Chapelle-St-Melaine
Vilaine
Beslé
Chère
Questembert
Lac de Murin
D775
D3
Pierric
D14
Redon
Massérac
Limerzel
Allaire
Avessac
la Bertinerie
E03
D1
D15
D775
Derval
D774
Caden
la Ville-en-Pierre
Guémene-Penfao
D775
Trévélo
D164
N137
D20
D20
Conquereuil
13
Bocquéreux
Rieux
D124
D20
Péaule
Vilaine
Fégréac
D3
D35
Dastres
Marsac-sur-Don
D139
Ste-Cry
D131
D774
D164
D114
Isac
D15
Marzan
Dreny
le Coudray
D42
D44
Nivillac
D34
Sévérac
Trelan
St-Dolay
D2
D2
Arzal
la Bonne-Façaon
Plessé
le Plessis
Vay
D128
la Roche-Bernard
E60
N165
D773
D3
D2
D34
St-Gildas-des-Bois
Guenrouet
la Grigonnais
le Gâvre
Pirudel
Camoël
Férel
D2
D4
D315
Missillac
D15
Brivé
14
Drefféac
l'Epaud
D17
D82
Herbignac
la Chapelle-des-Marais
K
L
Ste-Reine-de-Bretagne
St-Anne-sur-Brivet
Quilly
le Pessuais
Blain
D33
M
Canal de Nantes
Assérac
Mayun
D33
St-Lomer
D81
la Chevallerais

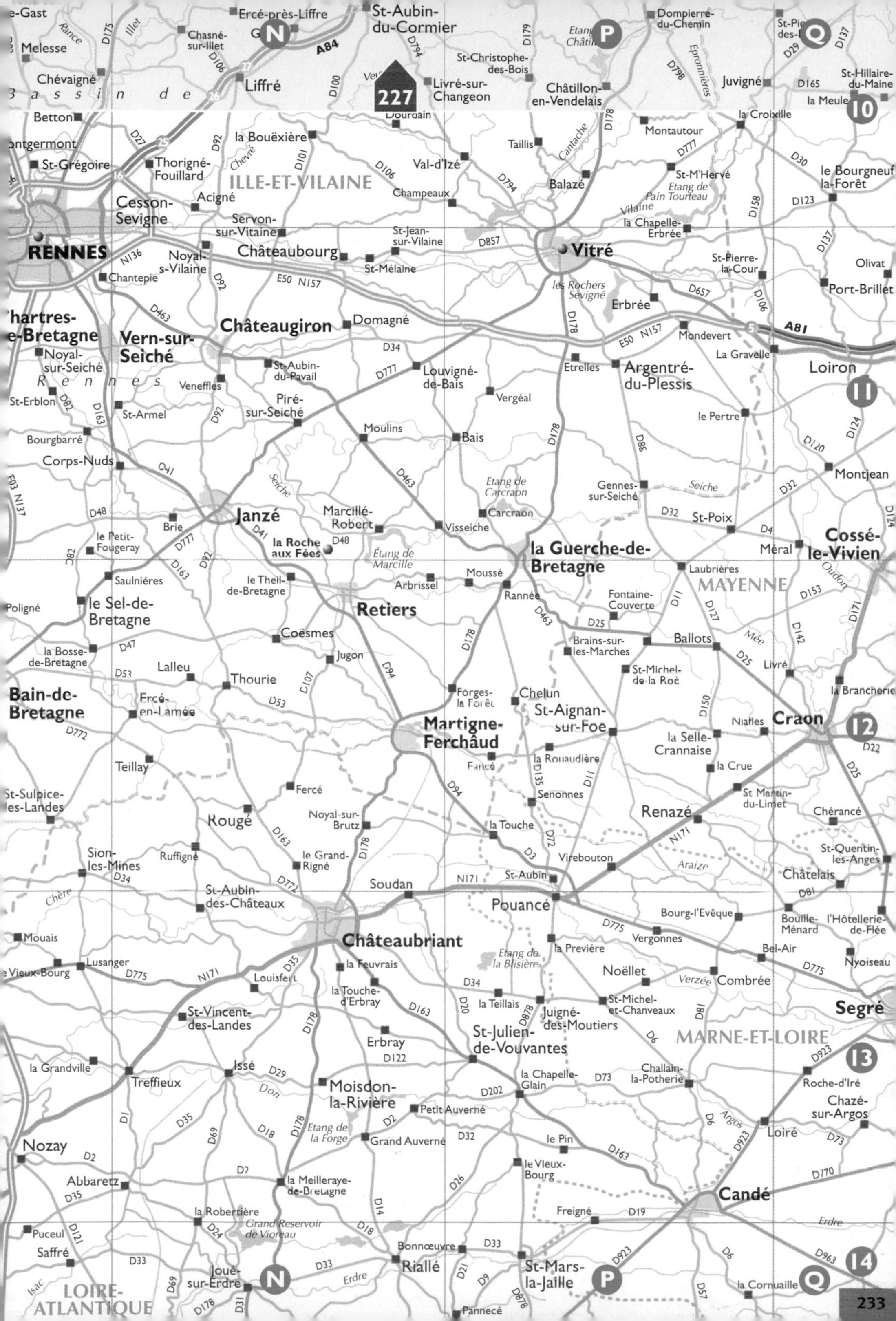

Ercé-près-Liffré
St-Aubin-du-Cormier
Dompierre-du-Chemin
Melesse
Chasné-sur-Illet
A84
St-Christophe-des-Bois
Chévaigné
Liffré
227
Livré-sur-Changeon
Châtillon-en-Vendelais
Juvigné
St-Hillaire-du-Maine
Bassin de Rennes
la Meule
10
Betton
Dourdain
la Croixille
Montautour
Montgermont
la Bouëxière
Taillis
St-Grégoire
Thorigné-Fouillard
Val-d'Izé
ILLE-ET-VILAINE
St-M'Hervé
Etang de Pain Tourteau
Balazé
le Bourgneuf-la-Forêt
Cesson-Sevigné
Acigné
Champeaux
Vilaine
la Chapelle-Erbrée
Servon-sur-Vilaine
St-Jean-sur-Vilaine
RENNES
Châteaubourg
Vitré
Noyal-s-Vilaine
St-Mélaine
St-Pierre-la-Cour
Olivat
Chantepie
les Rochers Sevigné
Port-Brillet
Erbrée
Chartres-de-Bretagne
Châteaugiron
Domagné
Mondevert
A81
Vern-sur-Seiché
Noyal-sur-Seiché
St-Aubin-du-Pavail
Louvigné-de-Bais
Etrelles
Argentré-du-Plessis
La Gravelle
Loiron
Veneffles
11
St-Erblon
St-Armel
Piré-sur-Seiché
Vergéal
le Pertre
Bourgbarré
Moulins
Bais
Corps-Nuds
Montjean
Seiche
Etang de Carcraon
Gennes-sur-Seiché
Janzé
Brie
Marcillé-Robert
Carcraon
St-Poix
le Petit-Fougeray
la Roche aux Fées
Visseiche
Cossé-le-Vivien
Méral
la Guerche-de-Bretagne
Etang de Marcillé
Laubrières
Oudon
Saulniéres
le Theil-de-Bretagne
Mousse
Arbrissel
MAYENNE
Poligné
le Sel-de-Bretagne
Retiers
Rannée
Fontaine-Couverte
la Bosse-de-Bretagne
Coësmes
Brains-sur-les-Marches
Ballots
Jugon
St-Michel-de-la Roë
Livré
Lalleu
Thourie
la Brancherie
Bain-de-Bretagne
Ercé-en-Lamée
Forges-la Forêt
Chelun
St-Aignan-sur-Roe
Craon
Martigné-Ferchâud
Niafles
12
la Selle-Craonnaise
la Rouaudière
Teillay
Fercé
la Crue
Senonnes
St Martin-du-Limet
St-Sulpice-des-Landes
Rougé
Noyal-sur-Brutz
Renazé
Chérancé
la Touche
Ruffigné
Sion-les-Mines
le Grand-Rigné
Virebouton
St-Quentin-les-Anges
Araize
St-Aubin
Châtelais
Chère
St-Aubin-des-Châteaux
Soudan
Pouancé
Bourg-l'Evêque
Bouille-Ménard
l'Hôtellerie-de-Flée
Mouais
Châteaubriant
Vergonnes
la Previère
Bel-Air
Etang de la Blisière
Vieux-Bourg
Lusanger
la Feuvrais
Nyoiseau
Louisfert
Noëllet
Combrée
Verzée
la Touche-d'Erbray
la Teillais
St-Michel-et-Chanveaux
St-Vincent-des-Landes
Juigné-des-Moutiers
Segré
St-Julien-de-Vouvantes
MARNE-ET-LOIRE
Erbray
13
la Grandville
Issé
la Chapelle-Glain
Challain-la-Potherie
Treffieux
Moisdon-la-Rivière
Don
Roche-d'Iré
Chazé-sur-Argos
Petit Auverné
Etang de la Forge
Grand Auverné
le Pin
Argos
Loiré
Nozay
le Vieux-Bourg
Abbaretz
la Meilleraye-de-Bretagne
Candé
la Robertière
Grand Reservoir de Vioreau
Freigné
Erdre
Puceul
Saffré
Bonnœuvre
14
Joué-sur-Erdre
Riallé
St-Mars-la-Jaille
la Cornuaille
Isac
LOIRE-ATLANTIQUE
Pannecé
N
P
Q

Hennebont
Languidic
Queven
Guidel
Pouldu
Kerhéro
Locoal-Camors
Malachappe
Kerglois
Bienzy-Lanvaux
Colpo
Brandérion
Lanester
Plomemeur
Lorient
Kervignac
Landévant
Pluvigner
Brandivy
Anse du Pouldu
le Fort-Bloque
Merlevenez
Nostang
Landaul
Grand-Champ
Larmor-Plage
Locmiquelic
Riantec
Ste-Hélène
Plumergat
Brech
Port-Louis
Plouhinec
Locoal-Mendon
Ste-Anne-d'Auray
Pointe du Talut
Pointe de Gavres
Belz
Mériadec
Auray
Plescop
Pointe de Bileric
Groix
Île de Groix
Locmaria
Étel
Erdeven
Ploemel
Pluneret
Plougoumelen
Bono
Ploeren
Pointe d'Erdeven
Crac'h
Baden
Arradon
Plouharnel
Carnac
la Trinité-sur-Mer
Locmariaquer
Île de Gavrinis
Île-aux-Moines
Golfe du Morbihan
Penthièvre
Sables Blancs
Portivy
Pointe du Percho
St-Pierre-Quiberon
Port-Navalo
Arzon
Côte Sauvage
Presqu'île de Quiberon
Île Méaban
Brillac
Sarzeau
Baie de Quiberon
Beg er Houlannec
Quiberon
St-Gildas-de-Rhuys
Kerignard
Pointe du Conguel
Pointe de St-Jacques
Passage de la Teignouse
Pointe des Poulains
Pointe du Cardinal
Grotte de l'Apothicairerie
Sauzon
Pointe de Taillefer
Île d'Houat
le Palais
Passage des Sœurs
Port de Donnant
Belle-Île
Pointe de Vieux Château
Île d'Hœdic
Kervilahouen
Bangor
Aiguilles de Port-Coton
Pointe de Kerdonis
Côte Sauvage
Locmaria
Pointe de Pouldon
Pointe de l'Échelle
229
230
F
G
H
12
13
14
15

Brévelay
Lizio
le Roc-St-André
la Chapelle-Caro
Monteneuf
Comblessac
J
K
L
Plumelec
D1
D10
D8
Réminiac
la Telhaie
Landes de Lanvaux
Sérent
D10
D114
Oust
St-Séglin
D778
D126
Loc'h
St-Marcel
Malestroit
Ruffiac
Quelneuc
Carentoir
Trédion
D776
Plaudren
Claire
St-Laurent
Morbouleau
Locqueltas
St Guyomard
la Chapelle-Gaceline
12
St-Congard
D8
Monterblanc
D112
231
D14
D777
Sixt-sur-Aff
la Gacilly
D177
le Cours
Pleucadeuc
80
Mont Hersé
St-Martin
Elven
D5
D126
Molac
D774
D764
D777
les Fougerêts
D773
Meucon
Arz
St-Nolff
St-Gravé
St-Ave
D1
Larré
Rochefort-en-Terre
D777
Glénac
D775
D775
D764
Oust
Peillac
Bains-sur-Oust
Menimur
N166
Tréffléan
la Vraie-Croix
Bel-Air
D777
Pluherlin
St-Vincent-sur-Oust
Sulniac
Malansac
Vannes
E60 N165
Questembert
D873
D177
D7
le Gorvello
D7
D775
Séné
Thiex
Berric
Limerzel
Allaire
D14
Redon
Avessac
Noyalo
Lauzach
D1
Caden
D775
Noyal-Muziliac
D153
D774
Trévélo
232
D164
D780
D20
D20
Surzur
Bocquéreux
D20
D140
13
Rieux
Fégréac
St-Colombier
D20
Péaule
Vilaine
D195
Ambon
Muzillac
D139
D164
le Tour-du-Parc
Pehert
D774
Ste-Cry
D114
Isac
D153
Marzan
Sévérac
Kermoizan
D140
Damgan
Nivillac
D34
St-Dolay
Penerf
Arzal
la Bonne-Façaon
D128
Pointe de Penvins
la Roche-Bernard
E60 N165
D773
D2
Pénestin
D34
St-Gildas-des-Bois
D34
Camoël
Férel
D315
D2
D4
Missillac
Brivé
Drefféac
D83
D82
Herbignac
la Chapelle-des-Marais
Ste-Reine-de-Bretagne
St-Anne-sur-Brivet
Assérac
Mayun
D33
St-Lomer
Île Dumet
D774
D47
D51
Pontchâteau
Balasson
Pont-d'Armes
l'Ebaupin
Mesquer
Pompas
D50
Crossac
Campbon
Piriac-sur-Mer
D52
St-Molf
St-Lyphard
D773
14
D33
D51
Parc Naturel
St-Joachim
Lerat
Revin
la Turballe
Fourbihan
la Madeleine
Régional
la Chapelle-Launay
Trescalan
Ile-d'Aignac
Prinquiau
Clis
D99
D47
de Brière
Montoir-de-Bretagne
N171
Guérande
D100
Marais Salants
D92
St-André-des-Eaux
Donges
la Calebasse
le Croisic
Saillé
N171
Trignac
D3
Brais
Lavau-sur-Loire
Batz-sur-Mer
ST NAZAIRE
Loire
Grotte des Korrigans
Pornichet
D92
la-Baule-Escoublac
D723
D277
St-Brevin-les-Pins
St Vraud
Frossay
St-Brevin-l'Ocean
D213
D86
D5
St-Père
Pays
15
St-Michel-Chef-Chef
D78
la Sicaudais
D5
D58
Tharon-Plage
le Feuillardais
D97
D86
de Rietz
D6
Chauve
Préfailles
D213
D13
Pornic
Haute Perche
J
K
L
la Croix
Ste-Marie

A

B

C

D

Q

R

S

T

U

V

W

Y

Z

PICTURES

The Automobile Association would like to thank the following photographers, companies and picture libraries for their assistance in the preparation of this book.

Abbreviations for the picture credits are as follows: (t) top; (b) bottom; (l) left; (r) right; (AA) AA World Travel Library.

2 © Christophe Boisvieux/Corbis;
3t AA/R Strange;
3c AA/A Kouprianoff;
3b AA/S Day;
4 AA/A Kouprianoff;
5 AA/C Sawyer;
6 AA/J Tims;
7bl AA/A Kouprianoff;
7br AA/J Tims;
8 AA/A Kouprianoff;
9 AA/J Tims;
10 AA/A Kouprianoff;
11 AA/A Kouprianoff;
12 AA/A Kouprianoff;
13 AA/A Kouprianoff;
14 AA/A Kouprianoff;
15bl Adrian Sherratt/Rex Features;
15tr AA/A Kouprianoff;
15br AA/A Kouprianoff;
16 AA/R Strange;
17bl AA/P Bennett;
17br AA/R Strange;
18 AA/A Kouprianoff;
19t © FRED TANNEAU/AFP/Getty Images;
19b AA/A Kouprianoff;
20 AA/J Tims;
21 AA/R Moore;
22 Ms Lat 1141 fol.2v The Coronation of Charles II (823-877) with the Archbishops of Reims and Treves, from the 'Sacrementaire de Metz' (vellum) (see also 159999), French School, (9th century)/Bibliotheque Nationale, Paris, France,/The Bridgeman Art Library;
23tl AA/R Strange;
23bl Battle between Romans and Gauls, from 'Le Vite di Dodici Cesari' by Gaius Suetonius Tranquillus (c.75-150) (vellum), Italian School, (14th century)/Biblioteca Marciana, Venice, Italy, Giraudon/The Bridgeman Art Library;
23br Mary Evans Picture Library;
24 AA/R Strange;
25l AA/S Day;
25r AA;
26tl © Pascal Le Segretain/Getty Images;
26tr © F1online digitale Bildagentur GmbH / Alamy
27 Digitalvision;
28 Digitalvision;
29 Digitalvision;
30 AA/W Voysey;
32 AA/S Day;
33 AA/P Kenward;
34t AA/S Day;
34b AA/J Tims
35tl K Glendenning
35tc AA/J Wyand;
35tr AA/R Strange;
35cl AA/R Strange;
35cc AA/N Setchfield;
35cr AA/R Moore;
35bl AA/C Sawyer;
35bc K Glendenning;
35br AA/R Victor;
36 AA/A Kouprianoff;
38 AA/J Tims;
41 AA/A Kouprianoff;
42 AA/R Strange;
44 © Tristan Deschamps/Alamy;
45 AA/A Kouprianoff;
46 AA/J Tims;
47l AA/R Victor;
47r AA/J Tims;
48 AA/A Baker;
49 AA/R Strange;
50 AA/A Baker;
51l AA/A Baker;
51r AA/J Tims;
52l AA/A Kouprianoff;
52r © Christophe Boisvieux/Corbis;
53 © Terence Waeland/Alamy;
54l AA/R Victor;
54r AA/A Kouprianoff;
55 AA/P Bennett;
56 AA/R Strange;
57 AA/A Baker;
58 AA/R Strange;
59l Photolibrary;
59r Photolibrary;
60 AA/A Baker;
61l AA/R Strange;
61r AA/A Kouprianoff;
62 AA/R Strange;
63t AA/R Strange;
63b AA/A Baker;
64 AA/R Victor;
65 AA/R Strange;
66 AA/R Strange;
69 AA/A Kouprianoff;
71 AA/P Kenward;
72 AA/J Tims;
74 AA/J Tims;
75 AA/J Tims;
76 AA/C Sawyer;
78 AA/A Kouprianoff;
80 AA/A Baker;
81 AA/R Strange;
82 AA/J Tims;
83 AA/A Kouprianoff;
84l AA/A Kouprianoff;
84r © 4Corners Images/ SIME/ Giovanni Simeone;
85t AA/J Tims;
85b AA/B Smith;
86l AA/R Strange;
86r AA/R Strange;
87 AA/A Baker;
88 AA/A Kouprianoff;
89 AA/A Kouprianoff;
90 AA/R Strange;
91 AA/R Strange;
92 AA/A Kouprianoff;
93 © CuboImages srl/Alamy;
94 AA/A Kouprianoff;
95 AA/J Tims;
96 AA/R Victor;
97 © Cro Magnon/Alamy;
98l © 4Corners Images/SIME/Fantuz Olimpio;
98r AA/C Coe;
99 AA/A Kouprianoff;
100l AA/R Strange;
100r AA/R Strange;
101 AA/A Kouprianoff;
102 AA/R Strange;
103 AA/R Strange;
104 AA/A Kouprianoff;
105l AA/A Kouprianoff;
105r AA/B Smith;
106 AA/A Kouprianoff;
107 AA/R Victor;
108 AA/R Strange;
109 AA/A Kouprianoff;
110 AA/R Strange;
111t AA/P Bennett;
111b AA/R Strange;
113t AA/A Kouprianoff;
113br AA/R Strange;
114 AA/A Baker;
115 AA/P Bennett;
116 AA/R Victor;
118 Digitalvision;
119 Photodisc;
120 AA/C Sawyer;

122 AA/J Tims;
123 AA/C Sawyer;
124 AA/C Sawyer;
126 AA/A Kouprianoff;
128 AA/S Day;
129 AA/A Kouprianoff;
130 AA/R Strange;
131 AA/P Bennett;
132 AA/A Kouprianoff;
133l AA/A Kouprianoff;
133r AA/A Kouprianoff;
134 AA/S Day;
135t AA/S Day;
135b AA/R Victor;
136 AA/A Kouprianoff;
137 AA/A Kouprianoff;
138 AA/A Kouprianoff;
139t AA/R Strange;
139b AA/P Bennett;
140 AA/P Bennett;
141 AA/S Day;
142l AA/A Kouprianoff;
142r AA/R Victor;
143 AA/A Kouprianoff;
144l AA/R Strange;
144r AA/A Kouprianoff;
145 AA/A Kouprianoff;
146 AA/A Kouprianoff;
147l AA/S Day;
147r AA/A Kouprianoff;
148 AA/P Bennett;
149 AA/R Strange;
150 AA/A Kouprianoff;
152 Corbis;
154 AA/J Tims;
156 AA/J Tims;
158 AA/S Day;
160 AA/J Tims;
161 AA/S Day;
162 AA/R Victor;
163 AA/S Day;
164 AA/S Day;
165 AA/S Day;
166 AA/A Baker
167 AA/R Victor;
168 AA/I Dawson;
169bl AA/I Dawson;
169br AA/C Sawyer;
170 AA/S Day;
171 AA/S Day;
172l AA/B Smith;
172r AA/S Day;
173t AA/S Day;
173b AA/A Kouprianoff;
174 AA/S Day;
175 AA/S Day;
176l AA/S Day;
176r AA/S Day;
177 AA/S Day;
178t AA/R Moore;
178b AA/S Day;
179 AA/S Day;
180 AA/C Sawyer;
182 Stockbyte Royalty Free;
184 AA/J Tims;
186 AA/J Tims;
187 AA/J Tims;
189 AA/J Tims;
190 AA/P Bennett;
191 AA/S Day;
194 AA/A Kouprianoff;
195 AA/C Sawyer;
196 AA/C Sawyer;
197 AA/J Tims;
198 AA/J Tims;
199 Bananastock;
201 AA/C Sawyer;
205 AA/J Tims;
206 AA/C Sawyer;
207l AA/A Kouprianoff;
207r AA/J Tims;
208l AA/A Kouprianoff;
208r AA/P Bennett;
209t AA/A Kouprianoff;
209b AA/R Strange;
210 AA/A Kouprianoff;
211 AA/J Tims;
213 AA/R Victor;
214 AA/J Tims;
221 AA/S Day.

Every effort has been made to trace the copyright holders, and we apologise in advance for any accidental errors. We would be happy to apply the corrections in the following edition of this publication.

CREDITS

Managing editor
Sheila Hawkins

Project editor
Lodestone Publishing Ltd

Design
Drew Jones, pentacorbig, Nick Otway

Picture research
Liz Stacey

Image retouching and repro
Sarah Montgomery

Mapping
Maps produced by the Mapping Services Department of AA Publishing

Main contributors
David Halford, Lyndsay Hunt, Laurence Phillips, The Content Works

Updater
Lyndsay Hunt

Indexer
Marie Lorimer

Production
Lyn Kirby, Karen Gibson

Published by AA Publishing, a trading name of Automobile Association Developments Limited, whose registered office is Fanum House, Basing View, Basingstoke, RG21 4EA. Registered number 1878835.
A CIP catalogue record for this book is available from the British Library.

ISBN 978-07495-5957-1

KeyGuide is a registered trademark in Australia and is used under license.
Colour separation by Keenes, Andover, UK
Printed and bound by Leo Paper Products, China

We believe the contents of this book are correct at the time of printing. However, some details, particularly prices, opening times and telephone numbers do change. We do not accept responsibility for any consequences arising from the use of this book.
This does not affect your statutory rights. We would be grateful if readers would advise us of any inaccuracies they may encounter, or any suggestions they might like to make to improve the book. There is a form provided at the back of the book for this purpose, or you can email us at Keyguides@theaa.com

A03307
Maps in this title produced from mapping © MAIRDUMONT / Falk Verlag 2009
Weather chart statistics © Copyright 2004 Canty and Associates, LLC.

Find out more about AA Publishing and the wide range of travel publications and services the AA provides by visiting our website at **www.theAA.com/bookshop**

READER RESPONSE

Thank you for buying this KeyGuide. Your comments and opinions are very important to us, so please help us to improve our travel guides by taking a few minutes to complete this questionnaire.

You do not need a stamp (unless posted outside the UK). If you do not want to cut this page from your guide, then photocopy it or write your answers on a plain sheet of paper.

Send to: **KeyGuide Editor, AA World Travel Guides**
FREEPOST SCE 4598, Basingstoke RG21 4GY

Find out more about AA Publishing and the wide range of travel publications the AA provides by visiting our website at www.theAA.com/bookshop

ABOUT THIS GUIDE

Which KeyGuide did you buy? ....

Where did you buy it?...

When? ....month .... year

Why did you choose this AA KeyGuide?
☐ Price ☐ AA Publication
☐ Used this series before; title
☐ Cover ☐ Other (please state)

Please let us know how helpful the following features of the guide were to you by circling the appropriate category: very helpful (VH), helpful (H) or little help (LH)

Size	VH	H	LH
Layout	VH	H	LH
Photos	VH	H	LH
Excursions	VH	H	LH
Entertainment	VH	H	LH
Hotels	VH	H	LH
Maps	VH	H	LH
Practical info	VH	H	LH
Restaurants	VH	H	LH
Shopping	VH	H	LH
Walks	VH	H	LH
Sights	VH	H	LH
Transport info	VH	H	LH

What was your favourite sight, attraction or feature listed in the guide?

Page.................. Please give your reason ....

....

Which features in the guide could be changed or improved? Or are there any other comments you would like to make?

....

ABOUT YOU

Name (Mr/Mrs/Ms)...

Address ....
....
....
....
Postcode.. Daytime tel nos..

Email..
Please only give us your mobile phone number/email if you wish to hear from us about other products and services from the AA and partners by text or mms.

Which age group are you in?
Under 25 ☐ 25–34 ☐ 35–44 ☐ 45–54 ☐ 55+ ☐

How many trips do you make a year?
Less than1 ☐ 1 ☐ 2 ☐ 3 or more ☐

ABOUT YOUR TRIP

Are you an AA member? Yes ☐ No ☐

When did you book?............. month................. year

When did you travel?.............month................. year

Reason for your trip? Business ☐ Leisure ☐

How many nights did you stay? ....

How did you travel? Individual ☐ Couple ☐ Family ☐ Group ☐

Did you buy any other travel guides for your trip? ....

If yes, which ones?..

Thank you for taking the time to complete this questionnaire. Please send it to us as soon as possible, and remember, you do not need a stamp (unless posted outside the UK).
AA Travel Insurance call 0800 072 4168 or visit www.theaa.com

Titles in the KeyGuide series:
Australia, Barcelona, Britain, Brittany, Canada, China, Costa Rica, Croatia, Florence and Tuscany, France, Germany, Ireland, Italy, London, Mallorca, Mexico, New York, New Zealand, Normandy, Paris, Portugal, Prague, Provence and the Côte d'Azur, Rome, Scotland, South Africa, Spain, Thailand, Venice, Vietnam, Western European Cities.
Published in July 2009: Berlin

The information we hold about you will be used to provide the products and services requested and for identification, account administration, analysis, and fraud/loss prevention purposes. More details about how that information is used is in our privacy statement, which you'll find under the heading "Personal Information" in our terms and conditions and on our website: www.theAA.com. Copies are also available from us by post, by contacting the Data Protection Manager at AA, Fanum House, Basing View, Basingstoke, Hampshire RG21 4EA.

We may want to contact you about other products and services provided by us, or our partners (by mail, telephone, email) but please tick the box if you DO NOT wish to hear about such products and services from us. ☐

AA Travel Insurance call 0800 072 4168 or visit www.theaa.com